The Phonology of English

THE PHONOLOGY OF THE WORLD'S LANGUAGES

Series Editor: Jacques Durand, Université de Toulouse-le-Mirail

———

The phonology of most languages has until now been available only in a fragmented way, through unpublished theses, or articles scattered in more or less accessible journals. Each volume in this series will offer an extensive treatment of the phonology of one language within a modern theoretical perspective, and will provide comprehensive references to recent and more classical studies of the language. The following will normally be included: an introduction situating the language geographically and typologically, an overview of the theoretical assumptions made by the author, a description of the segmental system and of the rules or parameters characterizing the language, an outline of syllable structure and domains above the syllable, a discussion of lexical and postlexical phonology, an account of stress and prominence, and, if space allows, some overview of the intonational structure of the language.

While it is assumed that every volume will be cast in a modern non-linear framework, there will be scope for a diversity of approach which reflects variations between languages and in the methodologies and theoretical preoccupations of the individual authors.

Published in the series:

The Phonology of English
Michael Hammond

The Phonology of Armenian
Bert Vaux

The Phonology of Dutch
Geert Booij

The Phonology of German
Richard Wiese

The Phonology and Morphology of Kimatuumbi
David Odden

The Lexical Phonology of Slovak
Jerzy Rubach

The Phonology of
ENGLISH

A Prosodic Optimality-Theoretic Approach

———

Michael Hammond

OXFORD
UNIVERSITY PRESS

OXFORD
UNIVERSITY PRESS

Great Clarendon Street, Oxford OX2 6DP
Oxford University Press is a department of the University of Oxford.
It furthers the University's objective of excellence in research, scholarship,
and education by publishing worldwide in

Oxford New York

Athens Auckland Bangkok Bogotá Buenos Aires Calcutta
Cape Town Chennai Dar es Salaam Delhi Florence Hong Kong Istanbul
Karachi Kuala Lumpur Madrid Melbourne Mexico City Mumbai
Nairobi Paris São Paulo Singapore Taipei Tokyo Toronto Warsaw
and associated companies in Berlin Ibadan

Oxford is a registered trade mark of Oxford University Press
in the UK and in certain other countries

Published in the United States
by Oxford University Press Inc., New York

British Library Cataloguing in Publication Data
Data available

Library of Congress Cataloging in Publication Data
Hammond, Michael
The phonology of English: a prosodic optimality-theoretic approach
(The phonology of the world's languages)
Includes bibliographical references
Includes index
1. English language—Phonology
I. Title. II. Series.
PE1133.H25 1999 415—dc21 98–48472
ISBN 0–19–823797–9
ISBN 0–19–870029–6 (Pbk.)

1 3 5 7 9 10 8 6 4 2

Typeset by Peter Kahrel, Lancaster
Printed in Great Britain
on acid-free paper by
Biddles Ltd., Guildford and King's Lynn

for Diane and Joe

PREFACE

The topic of this book is English phonology, from the perspective of what I will call Prosodic Optimality Theory (Prosodic OT). This work is distinct from other books on English phonology in a number of regards.

First, though the data and theory treated are complex and technically demanding, the perspective taken is introductory in two critical respects. I assume no prior knowledge of English phonology or of OT. My hope is that this will allow this book to be of use to readers who know relatively little about phonology, and to technical phonologists as well.

Second, the data treated here are drawn from several computer databases of English, occasionally augmented with the author's intuitions. This results both in a rather different view of what is or is not grammatical in English and in a more correct view (since it is based on a systematic and unbiased examination of the words of English).

Third, because of the nature of the theory of OT and the kind of data available, this work only treats distributional regularities in mono-morphemic English words. The theory lends itself to this because of its focus on surface regularities. The data lend themselves to this because while the corpus is clear, decisions about which forms alternate with each other or are even related morphologically to each other is far more subjective.

Fourth, this book focuses on the prosody of English—the allowable con-figurations of consonants, vowels, and phonetic prominence. This focus is dictated by a number of facts. First, OT has grown out of much work which leads to the conclusion that a surface-oriented constraint-based approach is appropriate for the theory of prosody. Other domains of phonology are not so readily treated or so obviously best treated in terms of such a theory. Another reason to treat prosody is that it is arguably the linchpin of English phonology. The seminal work on English prosody, *The Sound Pattern of English* (Chomsky and Halle 1968) took the position that the vowel shift was the central organizing point of English phonology. This book challenges that view.

Fifth, this book takes an OT perspective on English phonology. This is the first full treatment of English prosody from an OT perspective and the first analysis of a prosodic system of this complexity from the perspective of that theory. This offers a unique pedagogical opportunity for students to understand Optimality Theory (since the data are familiar) and a unique opportunity to test this theory (since the data are so complex).

Sixth, this book makes a number of novel theoretical proposals within Optimality Theory. For example, it is argued that the ranking of certain 'derived' constraints is a function of the ranking of other constraints. I call this proposal 'derived ranking of syntactically combined constraints'. In addition, it is argued that quantitative effects in English stress are best captured with distinct principles requiring that heavy syllables of various sorts bear stress, rather than in terms of the binarity of feet. These and the other proposals made are argued for on empirical and theoretical grounds.

This book is thus intended for two audiences. On the one hand, it is intended for people interested in phonology or in English phonology, but who know relatively little about the subject. Such readers should pay particular attention to introductory material in Chapters 1, 2, and 5. The book is also intended for technical OT phonologists, who may wish to skim those chapters. Examples cited are all transcribed in my own dialect of American English, but most of the generalizations treated appear to be true in most dialects of English. It would be impossible to treat the range of material offered here with proper attention to all varieties of English.

ACKNOWLEDGEMENTS

This work has benefited from discussion with a number of people. I would particularly like to thank the following: Diana Archangeli, Allyson Carter, Stuart Davis, Dick Demers, Emmanuel Dupoux, Jacques Durand, Colleen Fitzgerald, Amy Fountain, Kumi Kogure, Chantal Lyche, Mizuki Miyashita, Diane Ohala, Curt Rice, and Tania Zamuner. All errors are my own. The first draft of this book was completed with the help of a Research Professorship from the Social and Behavioral Sciences Research Institute from the University of Arizona.

CONTENTS

TRANSCRIPTION

Since this is a book about phonology, a transcription system is required. Symbols are defined where introduced, and the first appearance and definition can be found in the index. In most cases the symbols are drawn from the International Phonetic Alphabet, but in keeping with the custom of the American linguistic community, some non-IPA characters are used. These are listed below, with their IPA equivalents.

Symbol used here	Description	IPA
[š]	voiceless palato-alveolar fricative	[ʃ]
[ž]	voiced palato-alveolar fricative	[ʒ]
[č]	voiceless palato-alveolar affricate	[tʃ]
[ǰ]	voiced palato-alveolar affricate	[dʒ]

NOTATION

SMALL CAPITALS	constraint names
italics	words cited in orthography
[ ]	outputs or phonetic representations or prosodic boundaries (foot or syllable)
//	inputs
{ }	an unpronounced morpheme or a prosodic word
$\begin{Bmatrix} x \\ y \end{Bmatrix}$	x and y are constraints that are unranked or whose ranking is irrelevant
x >> y	x outranks y
☞	marks the correct output in tableaux
?	multiple outputs in tableaux; or marginal categories in charts (those having very few examples)
#	categories instantiated in another place in a different chart
%	categories instantiated only in certain dialects
✘	the incorrect output in a tableau
full stop or period	syllable edge
✔	an attested pattern
Ø	an absent pattern
!	a telling violation in a tableau
|	edge of an aligned element
||	adjacent edges of aligned elements
shading in tableaux	irrelevant cells (because of ranking)
shading in charts	contrasting cells
°	lexical accent
σ	syllable
μ	mora or morpheme
Σ	foot
H	heavy syllable
L	light syllable

1

Some Basic Ideas

Every spoken language has a unique system whereby sounds are organized. This unique pattern of organization can be termed 'phonology'. This book treats the phonology of English, within the framework of Optimality Theory. In this chapter, I outline the inventory of sounds in English and the general structure of the framework I adopt.

1.1. THE SOUNDS OF ENGLISH

In this section, the sounds of English are treated in a systematic fashion. First, I will show what the sounds of English are at a convenient level of description. Second, I will provide a notation, exemplification, and a set of descriptors for crossclassifying sounds. Finally, I will give some arguments for that system of description.

It is a rather difficult matter to define the sounds of a language, and doing so for English poses a special challenge. First, English is probably the most widely spoken language in the world, and the phonology varies widely with geographic and social differences. (See e.g. Wells 1992.) A detailed phonological analysis of all of these variants in a single volume is quite impossible.

A second problem is that English exhibits a great deal of allophonic variation, though probably no more than any other language. (The general phenomenon of allophonic variation is discussed below.) It is difficult to state the sounds of a language without first considering the allophonic variation.

The chart below gives the basic consonants of English, along with examples. The position of the relevant sound in each example word is indicated with underlining.

Consonants of English

[p]	pan			[t]	tan		[k]	can
[b]	bun			[d]	done		[g]	gun
[f]	fin	[θ]	thin	[s]	sin	[š] shin		
[v]	vie	[ð]	thy	[z]	zoo	[ž] beige		
						[č] chin		
						[ĵ] gin		
[m]	ram			[n]	ran		[ŋ]	rang
				[l]	low			
				[r]	row			
[w]	watt					[y] yacht	[h]	hot

In some cases, some oppositions are exemplified with minimal pairs. For example, *bun–done–gun* is a three-way minimal pair for the consonants [b,d,g]. One can find additional minimal pairs for almost any pair of sounds chosen above, e.g. *hot–lot* for [h,l] and *tact–tax* for [t,s]. As will be seen below, because of the limited distribution of some sounds, it is not always possible to find minimal pairs for all pairs.

This chart is an oversimplification in several respects. First, as noted above, English is spoken all over the world and there are many different dialects. Not all of these sounds appear in every dialect of English, and other sounds appear only in some dialects. The consonants that appear above are intended to be representative of the most standard dialect of American English.

In general, dialect variation with respect to the consonant inventory revolves around the following cases. First, the pronunciation of [r] varies widely. In this dialect, it is a retroflex approximant, but there are many other variants. In addition, as also noted below with respect to vowels, there are a number of dialects where postvocalic [r] vocalizes. A second area of variation concerns the glides [w] and [y]. In some dialects, there are voiceless versions of these, e.g. *which* [w̥ɪč] and *hue* [y̥u]. Finally, the relatively marked dental fricatives [θ,ð] are also marginal or missing in some dialects. These are just the most common; there are a number of other possibilities.

A second, much more interesting oversimplification is allophonic variation. I will have much more to say on this below, but a familiar example will suffice here. Consider the pronunciation of [p,t,k] in the two columns below.

Allophonic variation of [p,t,k]

	Word-initial	After [s]
/p/	pin	spin
/t/	tin	stin(t)
/k/	kin	skin

The pronunciation of these three sounds is different in these two different contexts. When these sounds occur at the beginning of words, they are produced with aspiration, usually transcribed as follows: $[p^h,t^h,k^h]$. However, when these sounds occur after an [s] there is no aspiration, and they are transcribed as in the chart above. For now, distinctions of this sort are not indicated in the chart of consonants above.

Let us now turn to the vowels of English. There is far more dialectal variation where vowels are concerned, but the basic set is as below.

Vowels of English

[i]	heed	[u]	who'd
[ɪ]	hid	[ʊ]	hood
[e]	hayed	[o]	hoed
[ɛ]	head	[ʌ]	Hud
[æ]	had	[ɔ]	hawed
		[u]	hod

Dialect variation with respect to the vowel inventory is extreme, but the most common differences follow several general patterns. First, the most dramatic point of variation is (as also noted above) postvocalic [r]. In a number of dialects postvocalic [r] is lost, resulting in a number of interesting vocalic changes. Second, dialects vary widely in the degree and extent of diphthongization. Third, the low vowels exhibit an extensive amount of variation.

The vowels above are all monophthongs. This means that these vowels are basically produced with a single unvarying quality throughout the duration of the vowel. (This is actually a matter of debate, especially for the vowels [e,o].) There are also vowels that can be characterized uncontroversially as diphthongs, or as composed of several qualities in sequence.

Diphthongs

[aw]	bout
[ay]	bite
[yu]	butte
[ɔy]	Boyd

There are no triphthongs in English (though this is not necessarily the case in dialects where postvocalic [r] is lost).

There is one additional vowel not in the charts above. This is the stressless vowel schwa [ə] that occurs in the first and last syllables of *banana* [bənænə]. Schwa includes a number of different vowel qualities that are rather difficult to pin down.

In addition to schwa, there are a number of consonants that can sometimes behave as vowels. An example of this is the [r] in the middle of a word like *bird*. Another example is the [l] at the end of *boggle*. Such consonants can be termed syllabic and are transcribed as follows: [br̩d], [bɑgl̩]. I will return to syllabic consonants in Chapter 2 below.

1.2. CHARACTERIZING THE SOUNDS OF ENGLISH

The sounds of a language are a product of at least three intersecting concerns. First, the sounds must be within the range of what can be heard and distinguished by the human auditory system. Second, the sounds must be within the range of what can be produced by the human articulatory apparatus.

In addition, the sounds of a language must satisfy whatever cognitive limits may apply. For example, there is surely an upper and lower bound on the number of sounds a language can employ such that a sound system with too many sounds would tax the speaker beyond his or her limit, while a sound system with too few sounds would be inadequate to make up a sufficient vocabulary of words (within some length limit).

In this section I will propose a system of description that will allow us to characterize the sounds of English. The description of speech sounds that I will make use of is articulatory in nature (rather than perceptual or acoustic), and draws heavily on traditional Articulator Theory (Sagey 1990). In articulator theory, place of articulation is denoted by reference to the active articulator. Thus labial sounds are still called labials (LABIAL or LAB) by virtue of the lower lip as active articulator instead of the upper lip (or teeth) as passive articulator. Dental and alveolar sounds are grouped together as coronal sounds (CORONAL or COR), because the front of the tongue, the tongue corona, is the active articulator. Finally, velar sounds involve the body or tongue dorsum as active articulator and are thus called dorsal sounds (DORSAL or DOR). Coronal sounds are distinguished in terms of the length of the constriction. Long constrictions, the alveolar ones in English, are characterized as 'distributed' and short constrictions, the dental ones in English, are characterized as 'not distributed'.

This system of description still leaves the palatals and labiovelars untreated. Both of these classes are treated as multiply articulated. The labiovelar, naturally enough, is treated as LAB-DOR, while the palatals are treated as COR-DOR.

This distinction in terms of passive versus active articulators may seem inconsequential, but there are a number of implications (some of which we will see in the following chapters).

With articulator theory and traditional manners of articulation (voiced and voiceless stop, fricative, affricate, nasal, and approximant), we can label the rows and columns of the chart of consonants above.

Consonants of English crossclassified in terms of articulator theory

	LAB	COR not dist.	COR dist.	COR-DOR	DOR	LAB-DOR	Ø
Stop							
voiceless	[p]		[t]		[k]		
voiced	[b]		[d]		[g]		
Fricative							
voiceless	[f]	[θ]	[s]	[š]			
voiced	[v]	[ð]	[z]	[ž]			
Affricate							
voiceless				[č]			
voiced				[j]			
Nasal							
voiced	[m]		[n]		[ŋ]		
Approximant							
voiced			[l]				
voiced			[r]	[y]		[w]	
voiceless							[h]

Within the approximant class, [l] is distinguished as the only lateral segment.

Let us now turn to the vowels. Vowels are described using a traditional system that is notionally articulatory, but really much more perceptually grounded. I will use the usual four basic descriptors for vowels: height, backness, rounding, and tenseness or vowel length.

It has also been argued that tense vowels are similar to the 'advanced tongue root' vowels that are exhibited in various other languages. The discussion of the vowel phonology of English below will show that there is good reason to characterize the difference between tense and lax vowels of English as basically that between long and short vowels.

Summarizing, the vowels of English can be represented for backness, height, and tenseness as follows.

Vowels of English

	Front	Back
High	[i]	[u]
	[ɪ] [ʊ]	
Mid	[e]	[o]
	[ɛ] [ʌ]/[ə]	
Low	[æ]	[ɔ]
		[ɑ]

'Tense' vowels appear in the periphery of the diagram and 'lax' vowels in the central regions. Notice that the vowels [ʌ] and [ə] really differ only in whether they are stressed. Hence there is really no need for different symbols when stress is marked. Nonetheless, this distinction is typically marked in discussions of English vowels, and I will follow this practice.

There is a huge literature on the proper characterization of speech sounds in terms of features and feature geometry. Much of this literature seems to have been left behind as constraint-based Optimality Theory has taken hold. At this point, it is unclear how many issues formerly treated in terms of featural and geometric contrasts are to be treated in OT. Since the body of this book does not deal with such questions, the distinctions above are left as they are. A specific proposal in terms of binary phonetic features or feature geometry awaits other data.

1.3. PHONOLOGICAL GENERALIZATIONS

In this section, several instances of phonological generalizations in English are presented. These lay the groundwork for the remainder of this chapter, where I will show how best to treat such generalizations.

1.3.1. Aspiration

In §1.2 I presented the fact that the sounds [p,t,k] are pronounced in two different ways. Word-initially they are aspirated, while after a word-initial [s] they are unaspirated. (The relevant figure is repeated below.)

Allophonic variation of [p,t,k]

	Word-initial	After [s]
/p/	pin	spin
/t/	tin	stin(t)
/k/	kin	skin

As indicated above, aspiration will be notated as e.g. [pʰ,tʰ,kʰ], lack of aspiration as e.g. [p,t,k].

Let us consider the problem in a little more detail. First, only certain consonants exhibit aspiration word-initially. Examples of all singleton consonants are given below, and the reader should extract the generalization that only voiceless stops and affricates exhibit aspiration word-initially. (The consonants [ž,ŋ] do not appear in this chart because they cannot occur word-initially in English. More on this below.)

Aspiration with word-initial singleton consonants

[pʰ]	pan			[tʰ]	tan			[kʰ]	can
[b]	bun			[d]	done			[g]	gun
[f]	fin	[0]	thin	[s]	sin	[š]	shin		
[v]	vie	[ð]	thy	[z]	zoo	[ž]	–		
						[čʰ]	chin		
						[ǰ]	gin		
[m]	mat			[n]	gnat			[ŋ]	–
				[l]	low				
				[r]	row				
[w]	watt					[y]	yacht	[h]	hot

The following chart shows all consonants that can occur after an [s] at the beginning of a word. Notice that not all of the consonants above can occur in this context; but of those that do, none exhibit aspiration.

No aspiration with word-initial s+C clusters

[p]	span			[t]	Stan			[k]	scan
[b]	–			[d]	–			[g]	–
[f]	Sphinx	[θ]	–	[s]	–	[š]	–		
[v]	–	[ð]	–	[z]	–	[ž]	–		
						[č]	–		

[j̊] –

[m] smack	[n] snack	[ŋ] –
	[l] slow	
	[r] –	
[w] swell	[y] –	[h] –

Several things should be made clear at this point. First, this is not some accidental fact about English words. When English speakers are presented with nonsense words where aspiration is distributed in some other fashion, they reject them as foreign- or strange-sounding, e.g. *[pæn], *[mʰæt].

A second and extremely important observation here is that the distribution of aspiration is systematic in another way as well. The only sounds that exhibit aspiration are [p,t,k,č], the voiceless stops and affricates. If we recall that affricates are composed of a stop portion followed by a fricative portion, then we can say that only voiceless stops, and elements composed from stops, exhibit aspiration. This generalization is thus in conformity with a system of phonological description that distinguishes stops from other segment types.

There will be much more to say about aspiration in subsequent chapters.

1.3.2. Nasalization

Another phonetic property we have not yet considered is nasalization. I have already presented the class of nasal consonants, but nasal airflow is also possible with other segments in English, e.g. vowels.

Vowel nasalization is contrastive in some languages. For example, in French there are minimal pairs for vowel nasalization. (Nasalized vowels in French are occasionally qualitatively different from their oral counterparts, e.g. [la] vs. [lɑ̃].)

Minimal pairs for some nasal
vowels in French

[lɛ] laid 'ugly'	[lɛ̃] lin 'flax'
[la] là 'there'	[lɑ̃] lent 'show'
[lo] lot 'prize'	[lõ] long 'long'

In English, however, there are no minimal pairs for nasal vowels. Instead, what we find is complementary distribution of oral and nasal vowels depending on the following consonant. The following chart shows the free distribution of oral and nasal vowels with respect to the preceding consonant for the representative vowels [ɪ,ɪ̃]. Both vowels can occur after virtually any consonant. Double lines separate different oral–nasal vowel pairs. (In this and following charts, there are other interesting distributional patterns that will be treated over the remainder of the book.)

Oral and nasal vowels by preceding consonant

[pĩn]	pin			[tĩn]	tin			[kĩn]	kin
[pɪk]	pick			[tɪk]	tick			[kɪk]	kick
[bɪl]	bill			[dɪl]	dill			[gɪl]	gill
[bĩn]	bin			[dĩn]	din			[g]	–
[fɪt]	fit	[θɪk]	thick	[sɪk]	sick	[šɪp]	ship		
[fĩn]	fin	[θĩn]	thin	[sĩn]	sin	[šĩn]	shin		
[v]	–	[ðɪs]	this	[zɪp]	zip	[ž]	–		
[vĩm]	vim	[ð]	–	[zĩŋ]	zing	[ž]	–		
						[čɪp]	chip		
						[čĩn]	chin		
						[ǰɪl]	Jill		
						[ǰĩn]	gin		
[mɪt]	mitt			[nɪt]	knit	[ŋ]	–		
[mĩnt]	mint			[nĩm]	Nim	[ŋ]	–		
				[lɪk]	lick				
				[lĩŋk]	link				
				[rɪp]	rip				
				[rĩŋk]	rink				
[wɪt]	wit					[y]	–	[hɪt]	hit
[wĩn]	win					[y]	–	[hĩnt]	hint

The following chart shows that this distribution is not free with respect to the following consonant. Nasal vowels can occur only before the consonants [m,n,ŋ], while oral vowels occur everywhere else.

Oral and nasal vowels by following consonant

[lɪp]	lip			[lɪt]	lit			[lɪk]	lick
[rɪb]	rib			[rɪd]	rid			[rɪg]	rig
[mɪf]	miff	[mɪθ]	myth	[mɪs]	miss	[fɪš]	fish		
[lɪv]	live	[ð]	–	[lɪz]	Liz	[ž]	–		
						[ɪč]	itch		
						[rɪǰ]	ridge		
[kĩm]	Kim			[kĩn]	kin			[kĩŋ]	king
				[kɪl]	kill				
				[r]	–				
[w]	–					[y]	–	[h]	–

This distribution occurs with other vowels as well. The following chart shows the distribution of [æ, æ̃] with respect to following consonants.

Oral and nasal [æ] by following consonant

[ræp]	rap			[ræt]	rat			[ræk]	rack
[læb]	lab			[læd]	lad			[læg]	lag
[læf]	laugh	[læθ]	lath	[læs]	lass	[læš]	lash		
[kæv]	calve	[ð]	–	[ǰæz]	jazz	[ž]	–		
						[læč]	latch		
						[bæǰ]	badge		
[ræ̃m]	ram			[ræ̃n]	ran			[ræ̃ŋ]	rang
				[pæl]	pal				
				[r]	–				
[w]	–					[y]	–	[h]	–

A similar chart could be constructed for all oral-nasal vowel pairs in English. The fact that all vowels exhibit the same complementary distribution in the same environment obviously supports a system of phonological distinctions that makes these oppositions (as ours does).

1.3.3. Word-final vowels

Let us now consider the distribution of another property of vowels. Recall that there are eleven full vowels in most dialects of American English (repeated below).

Vowels of English

[i]	heed	[u]	who'd
[ɪ]	hid	[ʊ]	hood
[e]	heyed	[o]	hoed
[ɛ]	head	[ʌ]	Hud
[æ]	had	[ɔ]	hawcd
		[a]	hod

A striking fact about English is that if a word has only one vowel and no final consonant, only the tense vowels are possible.

Word-final tense vowels

[mi]	me	[mu]	moo
[me]	may	[mo]	Moe
		[mɔ]	maw
		[ma]	ma

Both classes of vowels can occur before a single consonant at the end of a word (as shown above), but only lax vowels can occur before certain sequences of consonants. (I will return to a careful characterization of these consonants in Chapters 3 and 4 below.)

Lax vowels before certain
two-consonant sequences

[mɪlk]	milk	[wʊlf]	wolf
[hɛlp]	help	[hʌlk]	hulk
[θæŋk]	thank		

This case is unlike the two preceding ones, in that tense and lax vowels are not in complementary distribution. This is shown by the fact that both sets of vowels occur (and contrast) when followed by a single consonant. Despite the fact that the two sets of vowels contrast in this environment, there is, of course, still a phonological generalization at stake.

1.3.4. Some word-initial restrictions

As a final example of a phonological generalization, consider some of the restrictions on sequences of word-initial consonants. We have already seen that certain consonants do not occur in word-initial position, e.g. [ž,ŋ]. (I will return to these in Chapter 3.) Let us now consider the set of possible word-initial two-consonant clusters.

Many consonants can cooccur with a following approximant [l,r,w]. (There are interesting limits concerning the palatal approximant [y] which I deal with in depth in Chapter 4.)

Word-initial C+[approximant] clusters

[plæn]	plan	[pray]	pry	[pwɛblo]	pueblo(?)
[blu]	blue	[bru]	brew	[bwɑnə]	bwana(?)
[t]	–	[tru]	true	[twɪg]	twig
[d]	–	[dru]	drew	[dwɛl]	dwell
[flæt]	flat	[fre]	fray	[f]	–
[θ]	–	[θrɛt]	threat	[θwɔrt]	thwart
[slæp]	slap	[s]	–	[swɪm]	swim
[š]	–	[šrɛd]	shred	[š]	–

There are three important patterns to be extracted from these data. First, there is a pattern of complementary distribution between [s] and [š], even though these sounds contrast as singletons both word-initially (*sew* [so] vs. *show* [šo]) and word-finally (*mass* [mæs] vs. *mash* [mæš]). The fricative [š] can occur before [r], but not before other consonants; [s] can occur before other consonants, but not [r].

Second, there appears to be a general proscription against any coronal consonant but [s] cooccurring with [l]. (In general, [s] has a much wider range of occurrence than other consonants. For example, only [s] among the fricatives, stops, and affricates can be followed by another stop or fricative, *spy*, *sty*, *sky*, *sphinx*, *sthenic*, etc.)

Third, there is a general proscription against any of the labial consonants being followed by [w]. There do appear to be a few very foreign-sounding borrowings like *Pueblo* or *bwana*, but these are clearly exceptional.

The restrictions on [l] and [w] are quite naturally stated in terms of natural classes: coronal segments are not allowed before the coronal lateral [l], while labial segments are not allowed before the labiovelar [w].

1.4. TREATING PHONOLOGICAL GENERALIZATIONS

In the preceding section I presented four examples of phonological generalizations. Each offers insights into the character of phonological generalizations as a general phenomenon.

Aspiration occurs only on voiceless stops and affricates in English and is distributed word-initially, but not after an [s]. The set of elements that exhibit this aspiration difference are defined as a natural class. Aspirated and nonaspirated voiceless stops and affricates are in complementary distribution.

Nasalized vowels only occur before nasal consonants. Here, both the set of elements exhibiting the nasality property and the context in which the property is distributed are defined as natural classes. Likewise, oral and nasal vowels are in complementary distribution.

The third example involved tense and lax vowels. Tense vowels can occur before a single consonant or word-finally. Lax vowels can occur before a single consonant or before (certain) two-consonant sequences. The set of elements, tense and lax vowels, exhibiting this pattern are defined as natural classes, but they are not in complementary distribution. Rather, they exhibit a kind of restricted distribution.

The fourth example concerned the distribution of consonants in obstruent-approximant sequences word-initially. This example was rather complex in that it involved the intersection of several generalizations. First,

[s] and [š] exhibited complementary distribution in the relevant environments, with [s] occurring before [l,w] and [š] occurring before [r]. Second, coronals are precluded before [l], except for [s] (which exhibits a surprisingly broad distribution). Third, labials are precluded before [w], except for a few borrowings. Any treatment of these generalizations will also have to account for their relationships to each other.

1.5. OPTIMALITY THEORY

In this section I introduce the model that will be used in the remainder of the book. The model is called Optimality Theory (Prince and Smolensky 1993; McCarthy and Prince 1993a; Archangeli and Langendoen 1997). Optimality Theory developed out of earlier work in Parallel Distributed Processing, but represents a sharp break from that work in many fundamental ways.

Optimality Theory (OT) holds that there is some set of possible pronunciations for any particular form. I will call the form 'the input' and I will term the possible pronunciations 'candidates'. The specific generalizations of some language are expressed in the selection of the best candidate pronunciation for some input.

1.5.1. **Aspiration**

The selection of the optimal candidate is accomplished by constraints on the mapping from input to output. Consider, for example, the distribution of aspiration in English. If we assume that aspiration is absent in the input, and that candidate pronunciations bearing aspiration can occur freely, then the presence of aspiration on word-initial voiceless stops can be expressed as follows.

> *ASPIRATION constraint*
> Word-initial voiceless stops (and affricates) must be aspirated.

Let us see how this works for a word like *pie* [pʰay]. If aspiration is absent from the input, then the input is /pay/. (Slashes, //, are used for inputs.) If only aspiration is manipulated in the candidate set, candidate pronunciations are [pay] and [pʰay]. The ASPIRATION constraint above will select the second candidate.

Analyses of this sort are typically represented in a constraint table, or tableau. The tableau corresponding to the case above is given below. The input is given in the upper left corner. Relevant constraints are given in columns to the right. Relevant candidates are given in rows below. Constraint violations are marked with asterisks and the winning candidate is indicated with the pointing hand, ☞.

Analysis of [pʰay]

	/pay/	ASPIRATION
☞	[pʰay]	
	[pay]	*

The system as presented so far is incomplete in a number of respects. First, consider what happens with a word like *spy* [spay]. Nothing as given prevents this form from surfacing with aspiration on the [p]: *[spʰay]. This is shown in the following tableau, where, since the ASPIRATION constraint is unviolated, a choice between the candidates given is impossible.

Analysis of [spay]

/spay/	ASPIRATION
[spʰay]	
[spay]	

Let us contrast two solutions to this problem. One possibility would be to include a second constraint limiting the distribution of aspiration.

ANTIASPIRATION constraint
Consonants after [s] are not aspirated.

If we add this constraint to the tableau above, the right results are obtained for [spay].

Analysis of [spay]

	/spay/	ASPIRATION	ANTIASP
	[spʰay]		*
☞	[spay]		

There are two clear problems with this approach. First, the ANTI-ASPIRATION constraint seems to recapitulate, in the negative, much of the ASPIRATION constraint. A second problem is that the ANTIASPIRATION constraint misses a general fact about phonological derivations. In general, forms are what they appear to be unless there is some reason to believe otherwise. In the present context, this means that there should be some general consideration that says outputs do not differ from inputs unless they are forced to.

A simple way to implement this idea and do away with the ANTI-ASPIRATION constraint is to posit a general constraint FAITH:

FAITH constraint
The output is identical to the input.

To account for the fact that this constraint can be violated in forms like *pie* [pʰay], let us assume that constraints differ in their importance. Specifically, in English, ASPIRATION is more important than FAITH.

This difference in importance is expressed as constraint ranking, where ASPIRATION outranks FAITH. The formal instantiation of ranking is that a violation of a higher-ranked constraint has a greater effect than a lower-ranked constraint. This is exemplified in the following tableau for [pʰay]. Here, constraint ranking is encoded with the left-to-right ordering of constraints. Both candidates get a violation, but the higher violation is the telling one. This is indicated with an exclamation point, !.

Analysis of [pay]

/pay/	ASPIRATION	FAITH
☞ [pʰay]		*
[pay]	*!	

Notice how the violation of FAITH is irrelevant because of the violation of higher-ranked ASPIRATION. This is indicated with shading of the lower-ranked constraint. Contrast this with the tableau for [spay].

Analysis of [spay]

/spay/	ASPIRATION	FAITH
[spʰay]		*!
☞ [spay]		

Here FAITH carries the day, because there is no violation of ASPIRATION.

This latter approach is superior to the ANTIASPIRATION approach above. First, the FAITH constraint does not recapitulate any part of the ASPIRATION constraint. Second, the FAITH constraint is a direct reflection of the inertia of inputs.

We can conclude, then, that constraints can interact via this relationship of 'importance' which is formalized as ranking.

At this point, however, there are several interpretations that can be made of the ranking relationship. Both interpretations are exemplified in the following two tableaux.

Two interpretations of ranking

/x/	A	B
[y]	*!	
☞ [z]		**

☞

/x/	A	B
[y]	*	
[z]		**!

Both tableaux have two candidate pronunciations and in both cases the first candidate gets a single violation of the higher-ranked constraint A and two violations of the lower-ranked constraint B. In the first tableau, candidate [z] wins because constraint A strictly outranks constraint B. No number of violations of B is sufficient to overpower the higher-ranked constraint. This ranking relationship can be termed 'strict ranking'. In the second tableau, candidate [y] wins because two violations of the lower-ranked constraint B are sufficient to overpower the single violation of constraint A. On this view, there can be apparent ranking reversals when more violations of lower-ranked constraints occur.

Strict ranking is adopted in orthodox OT, and I will adopt it here as well.

Strict ranking
One violation of a higher-ranked constraint is infinitely worse than any number of violations of a lower-ranked constraint.

Strict ranking constitutes a strong claim about the kinds of interactions that can occur between phonological generalizations (expressed as constraints). To give this limit the broadest effect possible, I assume that all constraints are strictly ranked.

Ranking Principle
All constraints are strictly ranked.

Let us consider the analysis of aspiration above in a little more detail. First, notice that I have not been explicit about what constitutes a proper mapping from input to output. (This mapping is usually called GEN, for 'generate'.) There is a simpler issue confronting us now, however. So far, only the addition of aspiration has been allowed in the mapping from inputs to outputs (in phonetic transcription, the addition of [ʰ]). Since phonological generalizations govern other properties of sounds, other things must be allowed to happen in the mapping.

Three broad positions could be taken here. One possibility would be to stipulate that languages differ in terms of what properties GEN can manipulate. This would effectively say that while GEN in English can manipulate aspiration, GEN in, for example, French could not. The advantage of this approach is that it would allow us to maintain a simple and universal set of constraints. The disadvantage is that it would expand the domains in which OT could treat phonological generalizations. So far, generalizations can be described only with constraints and with the ranking of constraints.

A second possibility would be to maintain the universality of GEN, but still limit it in some way. There are two types of limit: substantive and formal. A substantive limit on GEN would prevent GEN from manipulating any phonetic property that never figured in some phonological generalization. For example, imagine (falsely) that there were no generalizations in any language that affected the nasality of vowels. This could be treated by disallowing GEN from altering the nasality of a vowel in the mapping from input to output.

Substantive limits of this sort may very well be the best way to treat putative universals of this type. However, this is a huge issue that we cannot even begin to resolve here. I will therefore leave aside the question of whether there are any substantive limits on GEN.

Another possibility would be formal limits on GEN. For example, we have characterized all phonetic representations as a string of letters. Representations of the following sort are simply incoherent.

Incoherent phonetic representations

---
a

p   ɘbɘ   ɒqɒ

a

It is generally assumed that GEN cannot produce such monstrosities.

To return to the issue at hand, how then do we guarantee that the correct output for some input /pay/ will be selected? For example, we need to rule out the last three candidates in the following tableau.

Other candidates to rule out

	/pay/	ASPIRATION	FAITH
?	[pʰay]		*
	[pay]	*!	
?	[bay]		*
?	[may]		*
?	[apay]		*

The simplest solution to this problem is to enrich our understanding of FAITH. Basically, what we need is that in order to satisfy the requirement that a word-initial voiceless stop be aspirated, nothing but the aspiration value of such a stop may be affected. If FAITH is decomposed into separate constraints requiring faithfulness to the input for different phonetic properties, then we must merely specify the different rankings of those constraints with respect to ASPIRATION.

Let us assume that FAITH is decomposed into separate constraints for each of the phonetic properties of consonants. In addition, we need to add faithfulness constraints for vowels. Presumably, vowel faithfulness should also be decomposed, but the present example does not require this, so simple faithfulness with respect to vowels will be adopted as a temporary convenience.

FAITH decomposed.

FAITH(ASPIRATION)
:   The output is identical to the input with respect to aspiration.

FAITH(VOICING)
:   The output is identical to the input with respect to voicing.

FAITH(POA)
:   The output is identical to the input with respect to place of articulation.

FAITH(MOA)
:   The output is identical to the input with respect to manner of articulation.

FAITH(VOWELS) [preliminary]
:   The output is identical to the input with respect to the number of vowels.

These different subconstraints will be abbreviated as F(X).

To get the result that the aspiration value of the relevant consonant may be manipulated to achieve aspiration, FAITH(ASPIRATION) must be outranked by ASPIRATION. To get the result that all these other values may not be manipulated to satisfy ASPIRATION, all these other faithfulness constraints must dominate FAITH(ASPIRATION). This is shown in the following tableau.

FAITH(x) exemplified

/pay/	F(VOI)	F(POA)	F(MOA)	F(VOW)	ASP	F(ASP)
☞ [pʰay]						*
[pay]					*!	
[bay]	*!					
[may]			*!			
[apay]				*!		

Here, alternative candidates involving the manipulation of phonetic values other than aspiration are ruled out by higher-ranked faithfulness constraints.

This is a rather simple case, where the presence of some property is required and the faithfulness constraint with respect to that property is immediately outranked by the relevant constraint. (We can schematize this common scenario as X >> F(X), where >> indicates ranking generally.) We will see below that there are also quite common cases that require more complexity than this.

Notice too that the story for aspiration that we have told would seem to require that inputs should not exhibit aspiration. Inputs like /pay/ and /spay/ surface correctly because aspiration is required in certain positions (word-initial) and FAITH(ASPIRATION) is ranked low enough to permit mismatches of aspiration between input–output pairs. However, what if the inputs were /pʰay/ and /spʰay/? (In the OT literature, this is referred to as the 'richness of the base' problem.) The following tableau shows how the constraints above in conjunction with inputs with aspirated segments produce the wrong output for /spʰay/. (In this tableau and all following ones, curly braces { } are used to indicate sets of constraints where ranking is unknown or irrelevant.)

Aspiration in inputs

/spʰay/	F({others})	ASP	F(ASP)
[spay]			*!
☞ [spʰay]			

Again, there are several ways of dealing with this. One possibility would be to simply adopt different constraints that limit the distribution of 'nonaspiration' as opposed to aspiration. Such an analysis would be minimally different from the one proposed above, but would miss the point.

This analysis would also depend on inputs being specified in a particular way for aspiration.

Another possibility would be to bite the bullet and restrict inputs in the way that seems to be required. Our analysis would then carry through unproblematically. The problem with this proposal, though, is that it requires a new theoretical device: constraints on the input. The theory would be more restrictive if all constraints were of the usual sort.

The third possibility is to limit the distribution of underlying aspiration on the surface. On this story, there is a general restriction against aspiration.

> *NoAspiration constraint*
> Nothing is aspirated.

This constraint must clearly be outranked by the ASPIRATION constraint to ensure that word-initial voiceless stops are aspirated. This constraint must outrank FAITH(ASPIRATION) to ensure that voiceless stops after [s] do not surface as aspirated because they are specified as such in the input. This is shown in the following tableaux. The first two tableaux show what happens to /pay/ and /spay/. The second two tableaux show what happens if the inputs are /pʰay/ and /spʰay/.

NoAspiration exemplified

/pay/	A	NoA	F(A)
[pay]	*!		
☞ [pʰay]		*	*

/spay/	A	NoA	F(A)
☞ [spay]			
[spʰay]		*!	*

/pʰay/	A	NoA	F(A)
[pay]	*!		*
☞ [pʰay]		*	

/spʰay/	A	NoA	F(A)
☞ [spay]			*
[spʰay]		*!	

When the stop is word-initial, ASPIRATION carries the day, demanding aspiration regardless of the general proscription against aspiration and the general faithfulness concerns. When the stop is not word-initial, NO-ASPIRATION carries the day, excluding aspiration whether in the input or added by GEN.

This third approach to the input problem thus successfully deals with inputs with aspiration, and does so with the same theoretical devices we have used all along: constraints and strict ranking.

1.5.2. Vowel nasalization

Let us now consider a second example to show how OT and strict ranking can treat phonological generalizations. The second case we will consider is vowel nasalization (§1.3.2). This example is similar structurally to the aspiration case just treated. Recall that vowels are nasalized if and only if they are followed by a nasal consonant. Thus the vowel of *ran* [ræ̃n] must be nasalized, but the vowel of *rat* [ræt] cannot be. The relevant phonetic property is nasality. This case is a little more complex than the aspiration case because, while the distribution of nasality is restricted with respect to vowels, it can also occur with consonants (while aspiration could not occur with vowels). Hence the distribution of nasality will be a little more difficult to describe.

The analysis requires a constraint that vowels before nasal consonants be nasalized.

NASAL constraint
A vowel before a nasal consonant must be nasalized.

This constraint guarantees that vowel nasalization will show up in the correct context.

NASAL exemplified

/ræn/	NASAL
☞ [ræ̃n]	
[ræn]	*!

As with aspiration, to prevent nasal from showing up in other contexts, NASAL must outrank a constraint that rules out nasal everywhere.

NONASAL constraint
Nothing is nasalized.

The following tableaux illustrate this interaction between NASAL and NONASAL.

NONASAL exemplified

/ræt/	NASAL	NONAS
☞ [ræt]		
[ræ̃t]		*!

/ræn/	NASAL	NONAS
[ræn]	*!	
☞ [ræ̃n]		*

This arrangement also guarantees that specifying inputs as nasal vowels produces the same results.

Nasal vowels in the input

/ræt/	NASAL	NoNAS
☞ [ræt]		
[rãet]		*!

/rãen/	NASAL	NoNAS
[ræn]	*!	
☞ [rãen]		*

To make sure that NASAL is satisfied by adding nasality via GEN as opposed to some other change, the relevant FAITH constraints must outrank NASAL. In the present context, this means that we need a faithfulness constraint that will prevent NASAL from being satisfied by changing a vowel into a consonant or by changing a nasal consonant into something else. The first constraint prevents /ræn/ from being paired with an output [rkt], while the second prevents the output [ræv].

To deal with the first problem, we need a constraint that forces faithfulness to vowelhood. The FAITH(VOWELS) constraint above will suffice here as well. The following tableau illustrates how this works.

Ruling out [rkt]

/ræn/	F(VOWEL)	NASAL	NoNAS
☞ [rãen]			*
[ræn]		*!	
[rkt]	*!		

The second constraint needed can also be taken from the first analysis: FAITH(MOA). This constraint prevents consonants from being paired with an output with a different manner of articulation. This constraint must also be ranked above NASAL.

Ruling out [ræv]

/ræn/	F(MOA)	NASAL	NoNAS
☞ [rãen]			*
[ræn]		*!	
[ræv]	*!		

There is no evidence so far for the ranking of FAITH(MOA) and FAITH (VOWELS).

The system proposed is quite similar to that proposed for aspiration.

However, there is the additional complication of accounting for how nasality can surface on consonants given the constraint NoNasal. Why doesn't a word like *not* [nɑt] surface as something like *[dɑt]? (The sequence [dɑt] is of course a word, *dot*; it is not an acceptable pronunciation of *not*, however.) In fact, the ranking we have argued for above already accounts for this directly.

Recall that we have argued that Nasal must outrank NoNasal so that nasality can be inserted in the appropriate contexts. In addition, we have argued that Faith(MOA) must outrank Nasal, so that nasal consonants do not surface as oral to avoid following oral vowels. It therefore follows that Faith(MOA) outranks NoNasal.

First, how does this follow? Second, how does this derived ranking solve the *dot* problem?

This ranking follows from the principle of transitivity. The relationship 'outranks' is parallel in this regard to the mathematical relationship 'greater than'. For example, if 6 is greater than 3, and 3 is greater than 1, it follows that 6 is greater than 1.

Transitivity of ranking
If constraint α outranks constraint β and constraint β outranks constraint γ, then α outranks γ.

How does having Faith(MOA) outrank NoNasal avoid the *dot* problem? While NoNasal might militate for a word like *not* to be pronounced [dɑt], the superordinate Faith(MOA) constraint precludes this mapping.

Avoiding the dot *problem*

	/nɑt/	Faith(MOA)	NoNasal
☞	[nɑt]		*
	[dɑt]	*!	

The ranking already proposed accounts for the *dot* problem. There is, of course, one other way a violation of NoNasal with respect to a consonant could be avoided that would not be ruled out by Faith(MOA). The consonant could simply be absent from the output: /nɑt/ would be paired with *[ɑt].

The ot *problem?*

	/nɑt/	Faith(MOA)	NoNasal
	[nɑt]		*!
✘	[ɑt]		

This too can be avoided if we can require that the number of consonants be constant in input–output pairings. This is easily done by generalizing the FAITH(VOWELS) constraint so that it applies to all segments.

> *FAITH(SEGMENTS)*
> The output is identical to the input with respect to the number of vowels or consonants.

Let us summarize the analysis of vowel nasalization given. There are two central constraints, NASAL and NONASAL. NASAL forces vowels to be nasalized before nasal consonants. NONASAL limits the distribution of nasality in outputs. The NASAL constraint is outranked by FAITH(MOA) so that nasality is satisfied by a difference in nasality for the vowel as opposed to the following consonant. FAITH(MOA) thus also outranks the NONASAL constraint by transitivity, which prevents the *dot* problem. Finally, the FAITH(VOWELS) constraint is generalized as FAITH(SEGMENTS) so that nasal consonants are not wantonly deleted. This analysis is offered as an additional and more complex instantiation of the OT paradigm.

1.5.3. Constraint schemata

The analyses presented necessitated the introduction of a number of constraints and thus beg the question of where the constraints come from. Let us consider this topic now.

In the earliest work on OT, it was assumed that the constraint set was finite and universal. This means that all languages have exactly the same constraints. This is a strong claim about the nature of language variation with respect to phonological generalizations. It requires that all differences between languages with respect to phonological generalizations emerge from constraint ranking.

This position is subject to two objections. First, other than the claim that the constraint set is finite, there was no theory of what a possible constraint could be. Thus membership in the constraint set could only be determined by empirical (and empiricist!) observation, hardly a satisfactory position. Moreover, one can wonder whether the claim that all constraint interactions are modelable with strict ranking is an empirical claim, given that any apparent violation could be treated by supposing some new constraint in the set.

A second problem is that some of the constraints that have been proposed in the literature and compellingly argued for seem very unlikely candidates for some universal constraint set. (Readers familiar with the OT literature can fill in their own favorites here; I will not take any specific constraint to task.) The alternative position that seems to be developing in the field is that the constraint set is not universally fixed, but the form of constraints is fixed according to certain universal constraint schemata. We have already seen one constraint schema: FAITH(X). This formalism allows us to require identity across input-output pairings with respect to some phonological property.

Two other general schemata have been extensively explored. The first is the Generalized Alignment schema (McCarthy and Prince 1993b) and the second is Correspondence Theory (McCarthy and Prince 1995).

The Generalized Alignment (GA) schema allows for constraints that align the edges of two elements, specifically a phonological element like a segment and a grammatical element like a word. The general schema is given formally below.

The Generalized Alignment schema
ALIGN(Cat1, Edge1, Cat2, Edge2) =$_{def}$
   $\forall$ Cat1 $\exists$ Cat2 such that Edge1 of Cat1
   and Edge2 of Cat2 coincide,

where
   Cat1, Cat2 $\in$ PCat $\cup$ GCat (Prosodic and
   Grammatical categories)
   Edge1, Edge2 $\in$ {Right, Left}

This can be stated informally as follows: the left or right edge of every instance of some category is aligned with the left or right edge of some instance of a second category. Both categories must be drawn from the set of prosodic and grammatical categories of the language. If all constraints are required to be stated in terms like this, this would constitute a welcome restriction on the set of possible constraints. (A number of examples of this schema will be presented in the following chapters.)

Consider how the ASPIRATION constraint can be stated with this formalism. The GA version of ASPIRATION says that aspiration is aligned with the left edge of a word.

The GA version of ASPIRATION
Align(word,left,aspiration,left)

There are too many arguments for this to be easily read, so I will adopt the following graphical formalism (which of course says the same thing). The vertical bar indicates the relevant edge of aligned elements.

Graphical restatement of the GA version of ASPIRATION

$$\left\| \begin{array}{l} \text{word} \\ \text{aspiration} \end{array} \right.$$

If this constraint is top-ranked, it would have the effect of making every word begin with aspiration. Therefore, the GA version of aspiration must be outranked by constraints that preclude aspirated voiced elements and aspirated fricatives.

Constraint against voiced aspirates

$$* \left[\begin{array}{l} \text{voiced} \\ \text{aspiration} \end{array} \right]$$

Constraint against aspirated fricatives

$$* \left[\begin{array}{l} \text{fricative} \\ \text{aspiration} \end{array} \right]$$

The NASAL constraint, which forces a vowel to be nasalized before a nasal consonant, can also be readily stated in GA terms: the right edge of nasality is aligned with the left edge of a nasal.

Graphical statement of the GA version of NASAL

$$\text{nasal} \left\| \begin{array}{l} \text{nasal} \\ \text{consonant} \end{array} \right]$$

Again, this constraint would have to be outranked by constraints prohibiting nasal from cooccurring with elements other than vowels.

So far, the only schemata I have introduced are FAITH(X) and GA. However, another schema is implied by the negative constraints employed to limit the GA constraints proposed above. These are 'negative GA' constraints: NGA. Both of the constraints on aspiration above can be recast as constraints against the alignment of two elements.

Constraint against voiced aspirates

$$* \left\| \begin{array}{l} \text{voiced} \\ \text{aspiration} \end{array} \right.$$

Constraint against aspirated fricatives

$$* \left\| \begin{array}{l} \text{fricative} \\ \text{aspiration} \end{array} \right.$$

Another general schema for constraints that has been widely adopted in the OT literature is Correspondence Theory. The general definition of correspondence is given below.

Correspondence
Given two strings S_1 and S_2, correspondence is a relation $\Re$ from the elements of S_1 to those of S_2. Segments $\alpha \in S_1$ and $\beta \in S_2$ are referred to as correspondents of one another when $\alpha \Re \beta$.

Researchers have interpreted this in a variety of ways, giving rise to various correspondence-based schemata. I will adopt a version here that can be termed Generalized Correspondence (GC), which requires that something in one representation (input or output) correspond to something in some other representation (input or output).

Generalized Correspondence
$\forall \alpha$, $\exists \beta$, α of representation x must correspond to β of representation y, where α, β are phonological elements and x,y are inputs or outputs.

This formalism subsumes the FAITH(X) schema. For example, FAITH (NASAL) can be restated as follows.

The GC statement of FAITH(NASAL)
All input nasals must correspond to output nasals.

Again, this can be cast in a graphical formalism. The relevant elements are given before the slash; the relevant representations are given after the slash. The arrow indicates the pairing.

Graphical version of GC statement of FAITH(NASAL)
nasal/input $\rightarrow$ nasal/output

The Generalized Correspondence schema is more powerful than FAITH(X) in two respects. First, the properties need not be identical. For example, one can imagine GC constraints stipulating that anything nasal in the input must correspond to something voiced in the output (which is incidentally true in English). In addition, the representations need not be input and output per se, but can include all sorts of other possibilities (that are not relevant to the facts to be treated here).

The three schemata I have presented, GA, NGA, and GC, provide a vocabulary to state constraints. They clearly allow for some growth in the set of possible constraints. However, they also impose limits on what can be a constraint. The strongest claim that might be maintained at this juncture is that all constraints in all languages must be instances of GA/NGA or GC. The analysis of English to be presented in the following chapters suggests that this may be true.

1.5.4. **The factorial typology**

Let us now turn to a slightly different topic. Imagine that there were only three constraints in the phonology of some language. Assume as well that the phonological and grammatical elements that can figure in the different schema are drawn from a universal set. This means that while the set of constraints may vary across languages, the set of possible constraints is fixed and constant. It is thus possible for languages to differ only in the ranking of their constraints. Given only three constraints, this would entail that there were six possible phonologies, since three constraints can only be ranked in six possible ways (3!).

Possible rankings for three constraints

{A,B,C}	1. A >> B >> C	2. A >> C >> B	3. B >> A >> C
	4. B >> C >> A	5. C >> A >> B	6. C >> B >> A

Of course, this number goes up massively for a larger number of constraints. With ten constraints, for example, there are 3,628,800 possible phonologies (10! = 3,628,800).

Possible rankings for n *constraints*

1! = 1	6! = 720
2! = 2	7! = 5,040
3! = 6	8! = 40,320
4! = 24	9! = 362,880
5! = 120	10! = 3,628,800

If the constraint set were open, there would be no upper bound on the number of phonologies. (∞! is a very large number.) The question of how to describe language variation in terms of a factorial typology received a lot of attention when researchers were convinced that the constraint set was finite and fixed. Two factors have led away from this. First, constraint schemata (and a variable constraint set) of the sort described in the previous section have become well entrenched in OT.

A second factor that has led away from simple factorial typology is fixed ranking. It has been proposed that some language universals may be best expressed in terms of fixed ranking relationships between two constraints. For example, if all languages exhibited vowel nasalization like English, this universal would require that all languages have the same constraints as English and that they be ranked in the same way.

This means that the number of phonologies possible with some number of fixed constraints may be far smaller than $n!$. For example, to return to our hypothetical example with three constraints (A, B, C), if the ordering of two of them (A,B) is fixed (A >> B), there are only half as many possible rankings.

Possible rankings for three
constraints with one fixed pair

{A,B,C}	1. A >> B >> C
A >> B	2. A >> C >> B
	3. C >> A >> B

While the ranking of C can change, the relative ranking of the other two constraints does not.

1.6. ORGANIZATION OF THE BOOK

I have not yet treated the last two examples of phonological generalizations introduced above: word-final vowels and word-initial consonants. In Chapter 2, we will see that these two examples involve syllable structure. In subsequent chapters I will argue that various other generalizations require reference to even higher-order structures than syllables: metrical feet. The general thrust of this book will be that alignment and correspondence (GA/NGA and GC) in conjunction with syllables and feet are the central organizing principles of English phonology, and presumably the phonology of any language.

1.7. FURTHER READING

This chapter has taken a very introductory tone. There are a number of books introducing linguistics to a general audience. One of the best is *The Language Lottery* by David Lightfoot (1982). There are classic works on language and linguistics. My favorite is *Language* by Edward Sapir (1921). Another classic by the same name was written by Leonard Bloomfield (1933).

There is much dialect variation in English, and there simply is not space to treat all of it in any satisfying detail here. For a very thorough overview of English dialects, see Wells (1992).

For a discussion of the physiology underlying the production of speech, Ladefoged (1975) offers a very nice overview.

Place Theory is introduced in a dissertation by Sagey (1990). There is an excellent discussion of the general properties of this model in a paper by Ladefoged and Halle (1988).

The Innateness Hypothesis is discussed by Chomsky in virtually everything he has written in linguistics. The classic reference is *Syntactic Structures* (1957), but the most readable is probably *Knowledge of Language* (1986).

Optimality Theory as a model of phonology was introduced in a 1993 manuscript by Alan Prince and Paul Smolensky. In the same year, Prince and John McCarthy wrote another extensive manuscript exploring OT with respect to issues in morphological theory.

The Generalized Alignment schema was introduced by McCarthy and Prince (1993b), and in another paper in 1995 the same authors introduced Correspondence Theory.

Archangeli and Langendoen (1997) is a collection of papers offering an overview of OT with respect to all sorts of domains in linguistics.

2

Syllables

In this chapter I will review what the syllable is, and the evidence from English that would lead one to believe such a thing exists. There are two broad categories of evidence for the syllable, intuitive and distributional, and each will be considered in turn.

First, what is a syllable? The most obvious evidence, and that most frequently overlooked by linguists, is that (for example) speakers of English seem to know with minimal or no instruction that *hat* has one syllable, *pony* has two syllables, and *potato* has three syllables. The simplest definition would be that the syllable is some grouping of sounds that recurs across words.

> *Simple definition of the syllable (preliminary)*
> The syllable is a recurring grouping of sounds across words.

In the following sections, we will see that this definition needs to be considerably revised and that there are a number of fascinating intricacies to it.

2.1. INTUITIVE EVIDENCE FOR THE SYLLABLE

There are a number of general arguments for the syllable. First, as noted above, speakers of English can readily count syllables. They can do this with minimal or no training and regardless of literacy. In contrast, speakers have a much harder time counting sounds or segments, and their ability to do so relies heavily on general notions of phonemic awareness. For example, speakers of English readily treat a word like *honesty* as having three syllables, but how many sounds does it have? The words below are quite similar, in that the number of syllables is far clearer than the number of segments.

How many segments do these words have?

Word	Syllables	IPA	Segments
honesty	3	[ɑnəsti]	6
thing	1	[θĩŋ]	3
box	1	[bɑks]	4
picnicking	3	[pɪknɪkĩŋ]	8

As we will see in Chapters 3 and 4, there are also cases where the number of syllables is less clear, but such examples are much rarer.

A second intuitive argument for the syllable comes from poetry. There are a number of metrical systems where the number of syllables is fixed. One example is iambic pentameter, where each canonical line has ten syllables.

Iambic pentameter (Shakespeare's 18th Sonnet)

Shall I compare thee to a summer's day?
Thou art more lovely and more temperate:
Rough winds do shake the darling buds of May,
And summer's lease hath all too short a date:
Sometime too hot the eye of heaven shines,
And often is his gold complexion dimm'd;
And every fair from fair sometime declines,
By chance or nature's changing course untrimm'd;
But thy eternal summer shall not fade
Nor lose possession of that fair thou owest;
Nor shall Death brag thou wander'st in his shade,
When in eternal lines to time thou growest:
   So long as men can breathe or eyes can see,
   So long lives this and this gives life to thee.

Another example is trochaic tetrameter, where each canonical line has eight syllables.

Trochaic tetrameter (from Longfellow's Hiawatha)

On the Mountains of the Prairie,
On the great Red Pipe-stone Quarry,
Gitche Manito, the mighty,
He the Master of Life, descending,
On the red crags of the quarry
Stood erect, and called the nations,
Called the tribes of men together.

Such systems are quite common, and lend support to the view that syllables are an integral part of the way we organize sounds.

Another argument for the syllable comes from language games. Consider the following sentence in the language game Geta. (The edges of words are marked with spaces for visual convenience.)

A sample sentence in a language game
[ðɪdɪgɪs lɪdɪgǽŋgwɪdɪgɪǰ gɪdɪgēm ɪdɪgɪz kʰɪdɪgɔld gɪdɪgetɪdɪgə]

The game is played by inserting the string [ɪdɪg] into each syllable. A similar game called Op does the same thing with the string [ɑp].

Almost the same sentence in Op
[ðɑpɪs lɑpǽŋgwɑpɪǰ gɑpēm ɑpɪz nɑpɑt kʰɑpɔld gɑpetɑpə]

Such games are quite common in English and in other languages, and support the idea that syllables are a part of our phonological system.

A third general argument for the syllable comes from writing systems. Many languages use an alphabetic writing system, but virtually all of these are historically descended from or inspired by the Phoenician alphabet. (The only exception here is Korean, which is unconnected to the Phoenician alphabet but is clearly alphabetic in nature.) The most common independently developed writing system is a syllabary.

2.2. DISTRIBUTIONAL EVIDENCE FOR THE SYLLABLE

The arguments above have really not been very linguistic. Let us then turn to a linguistic argument for the syllable. This argument comes from the distribution of consonants within and at the edges of words. Consider the set of one-consonant sequences that can occur at the beginnings of words.

Initial consonants of English

[pʰǽn]	pan			[tʰǽn]	tan			[kʰǽn]	can
[bʌ̃n]	bun			[dʌ̃n]	done			[gʌ̃n]	gun
[fɪ̃n]	fin	[θɪ̃n]	thin	[sɪ̃n]	sin	[šɪ̃n]	shin		
[vay]	vie	[ðay]	thy	[zu]	zoo	[ž]	–		
						[čɪ̃n]	chin		
						[ǰɪ̃n]	gin		
[mǽt]	mat			[nǽt]	gnat			[ŋ]	–
				[lo]	low				

                                    [ro]   row
[wɑt]   watt   [yɑt] yacht [hɑt] hot

The consonant [ŋ] cannot occur at all word-initially, and the consonant [ž] only sporadically in rather foreign-sounding pronunciations of borrowed words, e.g. *genre* [žɑnrə] (cf. French [žɑ̃ʁ]).

Contrast this with the final consonants that are possible.

Final consonants of English

[ræp]	rap			[ræt]	rat		[ræk]	rack
[læb]	lab			[læd]	lad		[læg]	lag
[læf]	laugh	[læθ]	lath	[læs]	lass	[læš]	lash	
[gɪv]	give	[beð]	bathe	[fez]	phase	[bež]	beige	
						[bæč]	batch	
						[bæǰ]	badge	
[ræ̃m]	ram			[ræ̃n]	ran		[ræ̃ŋ]	rang
				[mɔl]	mall			
				[mɑr]	mar			
[kʰaw]	cow?			[may]	my?		[h]	–

Final consonants are also restricted. The consonant [h] cannot occur word-finally, while the consonants [w,y] can only occur word-finally as part of the diphthongs [aw,ay,ɔy].

Consider now sequences of two consonants in a row between vowels (in polysyllabic words), e.g. the [sp] in a word like *aspen* [æspn̩]. Strikingly, the first member of such a cluster is restricted just like final consonants: [h] cannot occur in this position, while [w,y] can occur here only as part of a diphthong. In a complementary fashion, [ŋ] cannot occur as the second member of such a sequence. (The consonant [ž] can apparently occur as the second member of a medial cluster in rare examples like *luxury* [lʌgžr̩i].) Following is first a chart of all the consonants of English that can occur as the first member of a medial cluster and then a chart of all the consonants of English that can occur as the second member of a medial cluster. The relevant cells are double-outlined.

Medial preconsonantal consonants

[p]	tipsy [tʰɪpsi]		[t]	chutney [čʰʌtni]		[k]	acme [ækmi]
[b]	object [abǰɛkt]		[d]	cadmium [kʰædmiə̃m]		[g]	stigma [stɪgmə]

[f]	afghan [æfgǽn]	[θ]	athlete [ǽθlɪt]	[s]	aspen [ǽspn̩]	[š]	mishmash [mɪšmǽš]		
[v]	bivouac [bɪvwǽk]	[ð]	rhythmic [rɪðmɪk]	[z]	miasma [miǽzmə]	[ž]	cashmere [kʰǽžmir]		
						[č]	–		
						[ǰ]	hodgepodge [haǰpʰaǰ]		
[m]	bamboo [bǽmbu]			[n]	bandy [bǽndi]			[ŋ]	finger [fĩŋgr̩]
				[l]	halter [haltr̩]				
				[r]	harbor [harbr̩]				
[w]	drowsy [drawzi]					[y]	icon [aykʰãn]	[h]	–

Medial postconsonantal consonants

[p]	pulpit [pʰʌlpət]			[t]	alto [ǽlto]			[k]	alcove [ǽlkʰov]
[b]	akimbo [əkʰĩmbo]			[d]	mildew [mɪldu]			[g]	argon [argãn]
[f]	alfalfa [ǽlfælfə]	[θ]	anthem [ǽnθə̃m]	[s]	axiom [ǽksiə̃m]	[š]	worship [wɔršəp]		
[v]	envy [ẽnvi]	[ð]	swarthy [swɔrði]	[z]	clumsy [klʌ̃mzi]	[ž]	luxury [lʌgžr̩i]		
						[č]	anchovy [ǽnčovi]		
						[ǰ]	banjo [bǽnǰo]		
[m]	army [armi]			[n]	chimney [čʰĩmni]			[ŋ]	–
				[l]	garlic [garlək]				
				[r]	kohlrabi [kʰolrabi]				
[w]	wigwag [wɪgwæg]					[y]	–	[h]	adhere [ædhir]

The critical observation is that there is a similarity between the first member of a medial cluster and a final consonant and a similarity between the second member of a medial cluster and a word-initial consonant. This relationship can be captured if we make one assumption: words are exhaustively parsed into syllables. This is termed 'syllabic licensing' (Itô 1989).

Syllabic licensing
Words are exhaustively parsed into syllables.

The way this works is as follows. Imagine syllables in English are all of the form consonant-vowel-consonant (CVC), and that words all satisfy syllabic licensing. It would then follow that all word-final consonants are syllable-final as well. (The consonants on the right edge of a syllable are referred to as the 'coda'.) In addition, all word-initial consonants are syllable-initial. (Consonants on the left edge of the syllable are referred to as the 'onset'.) In addition, it follows that all medial consonants are parsed into syllables as well. For example, a string of consonants and vowels might be divided as follows. (A period, or full stop, is used to mark syllable edges. All syllabified representations used in the text will be enclosed in braces of some sort to avoid confusions about punctuation.)

Schematic syllable parsing
.CVC.CVC.CVC.CVC.CVC.

Two interesting facts follow from syllabic licensing. First, words are not composed of a random array of consonants and vowels. Rather, they are composed of repeating instances of one general syllable template. If this is true, it constitutes a strong claim about the form of words in languages. Notice another fact as well. Any restriction on what can constitute a syllable edge thus extends to medial consonants. If certain consonants are precluded word-finally and that exclusion is a function of syllable structure, then it follows that such consonants will be excluded in all underlined positions below.

Syllable-final positions
.CVC.CVC.CVC.CVC.CVC.

To return to the example above, if [h] is excluded word-finally because it is excluded syllable-finally, it follows that it will not occur in any syllable-final position, even word-medially. Likewise, if [ŋ] is excluded word-initially because it is excluded syllable-initially, it follows that it will be excluded in any syllable-initial position even word-medially.

The relationships exemplified above are thus accounted for on the assumption that the restrictions demonstrated at word edge are actually restrictions on syllable edges, and on the assumption that all segments are parsed into syllables.

If this kind of restriction is general, it constitutes a distributional (linguistic) argument for the syllable. Syllables are a necessary part of linguistic theory because without them the generalization that word-internal restrictions are related to word-edge restrictions could not be captured.

The careful reader will have noted a gap in the argument above. The argument relies on the assumption that all syllables are CVC. This clearly cannot be true. Consider the following monosyllabic words. The columns vary the number of onset consonants; the rows vary the number of coda consonants. A question mark indicates that no examples of the relevant type are found.

Some other syllable shapes

V	CV	CCV	CCCV
'A'	ray	tray	stray
[e]	[re]	[tʰre]	[stre]
VC	CVC	CCVC	CCCVC
oat	boat	bloat	stroke
[ot]	[bot]	[blot]	[strok]
VCC	CVCC	CCVCC	CCCVCC
apt	range	trains	strange
[æpt]	[rẽnǰ]	[tʰrẽnz]	[strẽnǰ]
VCCC	CVCCC	CCVCCC	CCCVCCC
angst	text	sphinx	strengths
[ãŋst]	[tʰɛkst]	[sfĩŋks]	[strẽŋθs]
VCCCC	CVCCCC		
angsts	texts	?	?
[ãŋsts]	[tʰɛksts]		

On the assumption that these words are all monosyllabic and from the assumption that all words must be exhaustively parsed into syllables, it follows that we have many more syllable types than CVC. When we factor in more syllable shapes, the distributional arguments above need to be reconsidered.

Consider first the recurring-pattern argument. The argument was that the shape of words would be understood as a function of recurring syllables.

When we factor in these additional shapes, we see that there must be many more word types as well.

Consider first two-syllable words. If syllables were only of the type CVC, it would follow that all monosyllabic words were CVC and all disyllabic words were CVCCVC. If we admit the eighteen types above, then it follows that there can be at most 324 word types. This number is derived by combining each of the eighteen types above as a first syllable, with the same eighteen as a second syllable (18^2). This may seem like a large number, but it constitutes a strong limit on the set of possible disyllabic words. For example, if there are no monosyllabic words that begin with four consonants, it follows that there can be no two-syllable words that begin with four consonants. More strikingly, if words can begin with no more than three consonants and can end with no more than four consonants, it follows that there can be no more than seven consonants in a row in the middle of a word (. . .VCCCC.CCCV. . .). (In point of fact, possible medial sequences are much shorter, as we will see below, but the general argument still holds.)

The second argument above was based on restrictions on word-initial and word-final clusters. These force us to consider the precise affiliation of medial consonants in submaximal strings. Consider a word like *happy* [hæpi]. Based on the list of syllable types given above, there is no question about the syllabic affiliation of all the segments except the [p]. The problem is that this word can be syllabified in either of the following two ways: [hæp.i] or [hæ.pi]. Since either parse is composed of two well-formed syllables, there is no reason to choose one or the other. However, this is not the case with a word like *dinghy* [dĭŋi]. Here, we know that [ŋ] is precluded syllable-initially. Hence the parse *[dĭ.ŋi] is excluded, and we must assume [dĭŋ.i]. Considering restrictions on word-final position, a name like *Ahab* [ehæb] must be syllabified [e.hæb], rather than *[eh.æb], and a word like *peewee* [piwi] as [pi.wi] rather than *[piw.i].

What now of medial consonant clusters? These too are potentially ambiguous, and force us to a consistent but somewhat more complex story about the restrictions above. What we said above, for example, was that sequences of *VhCV were excluded because [h] is excluded word-finally. Hence [h] is excluded syllable-finally. Hence *VhCV is excluded medially. The problem with this reasoning is that it only holds if some hypothetical VhCV string were necessarily syllabified as [Vh.CV]. However, nothing a priori prevents it from being syllabified as [V.hCV] or [VhC.V]. If either of those latter syllabifications is possible, then VhCV is not ruled out by the simple exclusion of [h] syllable-finally.

It turns out that the alternative syllabifications for [h] are also ruled out. The syllabification [V.hCV] should only be possible if it is generally possible to have syllables beginning with [h] followed by some consonant. We would expect to find such things word-initially. Since we do not, we can conclude that [h] followed by a consonant is ruled out syllable-initially. Likewise, the syllabification [VhC.V] should only be possible if [h] can be followed by a consonant syllable-finally. If this were possible, we would expect to find VhC sequences word-finally. Since we do not, we can conclude that VhC is ruled out syllable-finally.

Thus *VhCV sequences are ruled out because all possible syllabifications are ruled out.

*VhCV ruled out

V.hCV	hCV ruled out syllable-initially
Vh.CV	Vh ruled out syllable-finally
VhC.V	VhC ruled out syllable-finally

Of the two other cases described above, consider first [ŋ]. This consonant is ruled out syllable-initially, and this was used as an account of why this consonant does not occur word-initially or in the sequence *VCŋV. We now know that the latter is excluded only if all alternative syllabifications are excluded. There are three such syllabifications: [V.CŋV], [VC.ŋV], and [VCŋ.V]. It turns out here too that the other syllabifications are also excluded. Thus CŋV is ruled out syllable-initially and VCŋ is ruled out syllable-finally. Hence our general result with respect to [ŋ] can be maintained.

*VCŋV ruled out

V.CŋV	ŋCV ruled out syllable-initially
VC.ŋV	ŋV ruled out syllable-initially
VCŋ.V	VCŋ ruled out syllable-finally

The last case to consider is the diphthongs. The general observation was that [w,y] could only occur word-finally when part of a diphthong [aw,ay,ɔy]. We concluded that this restriction held syllable-finally, and that it followed that such sequences should be excluded medially (using M to denote a monophthong and G to denote a glide: *MGCV). This only follows if all syllabifications are excluded, and this is the case. There are no words ending in MGC and there are no words beginning with GCV.

MGCV ruled out

M.GCV	GCV ruled out syllable-initially
MG.CV	MG ruled out syllable-finally
MGC.V	MGC ruled out syllable-finally

Notice that while a consideration of consonant clusters at the ends of words renders this argument somewhat more complex, it also admits new arguments. Consider the sequence VntlV in the word *antler* [ǽntlr̩]. The absence of word-final Vntl sequences and the absence of word-initial ntlV or tlV sequences tells us this must be syllabified as [.ǽnt.lr̩.]. Imagine now a hypothetical and ungrammatical word *[æbtlr̩]. Such a word is impossible, because there is no syllabification of the relevant consonants that satisfies syllabic licensing.

[æbtlr̩] ruled out

[.æ.btlr̩.]	btlV ruled out syllable-initially
[.æb.tlr̩.]	tlV ruled out syllable-initially
[.æbt.lr̩.]	Vbt ruled out syllable-finally
[.æbtl.r̩.]	Vbtl ruled out syllable-finally
[.æb.t.lr̩.]	t not a legal syllable

This argument, of course, hinges on the assumption that syllable well-formedness is not generally a function of the position of the syllable in the word. (I return to this assumption specifically in Chapter 6.)

The range of possible clusters syllable-initially and syllable-finally is quite complex and interesting, and Chapter 3 is devoted to working these out. For now, I hope only to have established the general utility of the syllable in accounting for the shape of English words.

We have not yet established a single syllabification for most strings. For example, we still do not know if there is a single most appropriate parse of a word like *happy*, e.g. [hæ.pi] or [hæp.i]. In fact, no definitive syllabification will be provided for most sequences in this chapter, and their resolution will have to wait until Chapter 6.

2.3. A GENERAL THEORY OF THE SYLLABLE

In this section I introduce the moraic theory of the syllable. (This approach to syllable structure comes from the work of Larry Hyman 1985, and Bruce Hayes 1989.) Moras are traditionally defined as a unit of quantity for syllables. Syllables, then, vary in terms of how many moras they have. Most linguists recognize monomoraic and bimoraic syllables; some also recognize zero-moraic and trimoraic syllables. Over the course of this chapter and the next two, we will see that English has all four types.

One bit of evidence for moraic theory of an intuitive sort comes from languages like Japanese, where poetic meter is built on moras. For example, most people are familiar with the verse form known as 'haiku', where there are three lines each composed of a strict number of moras: 5, 7, 5. Each syllable has at least one mora, and can contain a second mora if the syllable contains a long vowel or a coda consonant.

Haiku by Issa Kobayashi
(translation courtesy of Kumi Kogure)

Yo.ru no yu.ki
 1 1 1   1 1
night of snow

Da.mat.te too.ru
 1   2 1 2 1
silently pass

Hi.to mo a.ri
 1 1   1 1 1
person also there

Snow at night. There is also a person who passes silently.

Notice that the presence, absence, or size of an onset has no effect on mora count.

Evidence for moras in English comes from restrictions on the distribution of syllables. English content words must apparently satisfy a bimoraic minimum. Polysyllabic words satisfy this easily if each syllable must contain a mora. Monosyllabic words must make up this two-mora limit on their own. Hence syllables containing a single mora are impossible as words on their own. A monosyllabic word ending in a lax vowel is impossible; hence lax vowels have only one mora. A monosyllabic word ending in a tense vowel is possible; hence tense vowels have two moras. This is in accord with the observation in Chapter 1 that tense vowels are longer than lax vowels. Monosyllables ending in diphthongs are also legal; hence diphthongs are also at least bimoraic. Finally, monosyllables closed by a consonant are also legal; hence coda consonants can contribute a mora.

Possible minimal words

$C\begin{bmatrix} V \\ \text{tense} \end{bmatrix}$ pay [pʰe], clay [kʰle], spray [spre]

$*C\begin{bmatrix} V \\ \text{lax} \end{bmatrix}$ *[pʰɛ], *[pʰlæ], *[sprʌ], *[skrɪ]

$C\begin{bmatrix} V \\ \text{diphthong} \end{bmatrix}$ tie [tʰay], try [tʰray], spry [spray]

$C\begin{bmatrix} V \\ \text{tense} \end{bmatrix}C$ seat [sit], treat [tʰrit], street [strit]

$C\begin{bmatrix} V \\ \text{lax} \end{bmatrix}C$ tip [tʰɪp], trip [tʰrɪp], strip [strɪp]

$C\begin{bmatrix} V \\ \text{diphthong} \end{bmatrix}C$ type [tʰayp], tripe [tʰrayp], stripe [strayp]

Notice how, as in Japanese, the number of onset consonants is irrelevant.

This connection between mora count and vowel length and the presence of a coda is captured in the notation for syllables adopted in moraic theory. Each syllable is denoted with a lower-case Greek sigma, σ. The relationship between syllables and segments is shown either by placing segments and sigmas on parallel lines (one above the other) and drawing a line between each segment and the appropriate sigma, or by using square brackets with subscripted sigmas. For example, the different syllabification possibilities of *silly* are indicated as follows.

Syllable membership

σ σ
ΛΛ   ≈[sɪ]σ [li]σ
sɪli

σ σ
ΛΙ   ≈[sɪl]σ [i]σ
sɪli

Mora count is indicated by the Greek letter mu (μ). For example, the relevant examples from above are notated as follows.

Mora count indicated graphically

σ σ
ΛΛ
sɪli
Ι Λ
μ μμ

σ σ
ΛΙ
sɪli
ΙΙΙΛ
μμμμ

When syllabified as [sɪ.li], the first syllable has a single mora and the second syllable two moras. This difference in mora count corresponds to the fact that the first syllable cannot be an autonomous word, while the second can (and is: *lee* [li]). When syllabified as [sɪl.i], the first syllable has two moras as well as the second, corresponding to the fact that both syllables can be independent autonomous words.

The fact that the size of the onset has no bearing on mora count is captured by a general proscription against moraic onset material. This means that no language can exhibit the following kind of representation.

Onsets cannot
bear moras

Since no language exhibits this kind of structure, I will assume that GEN does not produce such representations in the candidate set.

In addition, languages appear to vary as to whether coda consonants are moraic. In fact, as we will see in Chapter 4 below, English exhibits this kind of variation as well (and more . . .).

Codas vary in moraicity

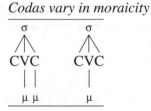

In the notation above, moras and syllables have been drawn independently, although, as we have just seen, there is clearly a connection between mora count and syllabic membership. This is simply a matter of convenience. In any particular case, I will make use of the flattest notation possible to conserve space.

Let us consider now how to encode these assumptions about syllable structure and mora count into OT. Certain of these assumptions reflect universals of human language, while others reflect generalizations about English. I will distinguish each of these and formalize them in a way that allows for a natural treatment of languages that differ from English and that allows for no alternative analysis in the case of universal properties of language.

The goal of the analysis is to account for (i) the fact that strings of segments are syllabified in certain ways, and (ii) the fact that they must be syllabified at all. To capture the fact that they can be syllabified at all, we must stipulate that GEN can add syllables. To force syllabic structure to be added, we must add a constraint requiring it. The relevant constraint has been called PARSE (for obvious reasons).

PARSE
Segments must be syllabified.

The simplest statement of what can go where in a syllable requires a distinction between syllable peaks and syllable margins. All syllables must have one and only one syllable peak. The syllable margins include all the material that surrounds the peak. These assumptions are part of GEN.

The basic story for English is that vowels must be syllable peaks and consonants must be syllable margins. (This will be revised when more complex data are considered in following sections.) Following much earlier work, let us assume that there is a constraint schema that assigns violations when some segment is a syllable peak. Call this *PEAK/X.

*PEAK/X
X must not be a syllable peak.

As a preliminary statement, this schema is instantiated in English with a constraint: *PEAK/C. In addition, we will assume that there are similar schemata for onset and coda: *ONSET/X and *CODA/X.

*ONSET/X
X must not be an onset.

*CODA/X
X must not be a coda.

Again, as a preliminary statement, these schemata are instantiated in English as: *ONSET/V and *CODA/V.

Let us now consider how these four constraints capture some basic facts about English syllable structure. Consider first a word like *hat* [hæt]. This word can only be syllabified as a single syllable. Any other syllabification would entail more than one syllable and, since there is only one vowel in this word, that would mean an otherwise unnecessary violation of

*PEAK/C. Another possibility would be to strand segments and leave them unsyllabified, but that would result in violations of PARSE. Still another possibility would be to leave segments unpronounced, but that would violate FAITH (§1.5.1). (In this and following tableaux, unlabeled square brackets indicate syllable membership.)

Simple tableau for hat

/hæt/	FAITH	*PEAK/C	PARSE
☞ [hæt]			
[hæ][t]		*!	
[hæ]t			*!
[hæ]	*!		

There are no apparent ranking relationships between these constraints yet.

The following tableau for *boa* [boə] shows the need for *ONSET/V and *CODA/V. (The subscript indicates a vowel in onset or coda position.)

Simple tableau for boa

/boə/	PARSE	*ONSET/V	*CODA/V
☞ [bo][ə]			
[boə̯]			*!
[bo̯ə]		*!	
boə	*!		

There are no apparent ranking relationships between these constraints either.

The system presented thus allows for a straightforward treatment of most of the specific restrictions on margin consonants exemplified above. The proscription against syllable-initial [ŋ] can be formalized as *ONSET/ŋ. The restriction against syllable-final [h] is *CODA/h.

The restrictions against [w,y] in coda position except when part of a diphthong would be easily treated if the glide portion of the diphthongs [ay,aw,ɔy] were not really in coda position. If this can be maintained, constraints like *CODA/w and *CODA/y would do the trick. (I return to the structure of diphthongs in Chapter 4.)

Let us now investigate the treatment of polysyllabic words. Consider first a word like *puppy* [pʰʌpi]. So far, nothing tells us whether the medial [p] is to be syllabified as an onset or as a coda.

Ambiguous syllabification of puppy

/pʌpi/	FAITH	*CODA/h	PARSE
☞ [pʌ][pi]			
☞ [pʌp][i]			
[pʌ]p[i]			*!

On the other hand, *Ahab* [ehæb] is unambiguous in its syllabification because of *CODA/h.

Unambiguous syllabification of Ahab

/ehæb/	FAITH	*CODA/h	PARSE
☞ [e][hæb]			
[eh][æb]		*!	
[e]h[æb]			*!

Let us now briefly turn to moraic theory. I outline the basic aspects of this theory here; full details will be presented when data are at stake. First, as noted above, onsets are never moraic. Since no language ever exhibits such structures, I assume that such candidates are never allowed by GEN.

A limit on GEN
Onsets are never moraic.

To account for the variable assignment of moras to different elements, I assume a constraint schema of (essentially) the following form. This forces elements of different sorts to be moraic.

Mora assignment schema (preliminary)
μ/segment: Moras are assigned to 'segment' when it occurs as a syllable peak or coda.

To get the result that words of English must be minimally bimoraic, this constraint interacts with a constraint that forces bimoraicity (motivated in Chapter 6). I defer exemplification of this until Chapters 4 and 6.

This simple theory of syllabification can treat the facts presented so far, but will have to be extensively revised to treat the facts to be presented in the following chapters.

2.4. FURTHER READING

The syllable has been written about extensively in linguistic theory, and the material covered in this chapter only touches the tip of the iceberg.

For a general introduction and arguments for the syllable in linguistic theory, the reader should read Joan Hooper's 1972 paper and Daniel Kahn's influential 1976 dissertation.

The analysis presented in this chapter builds on moraic theory. Readers should look to Larry Hyman's important 1985 book or Bruce Hayes's 1989 paper.

Finally, for a discussion of syllable theory in Optimality Theory, Prince and Smolensky (1993) should be read. For the role of sonority in that theory, Diane Ohala's recent dissertation (1996) should be consulted.

3

English Syllables: Margins and Consonants

In the following two chapters, the facts of English syllabification are surveyed and treated. I begin with a discussion of what sequences of consonants are well-formed. While some of these restrictions are best treated in terms of simple constraints on adjacency, some require reference to syllables.

3.1. WORD ONSETS

Word onsets are restricted in English in a number of interesting ways. Some of these are readily treated in terms of syllable structure and some are best treated in terms of alignment (GA/NGA) constraints on simple linear order. The facts are presented in sequence below from smaller clusters through bigger clusters. The question of whether some generalization should be treated in terms of syllable structure or in terms of alignment will often be unresolvable until we have treated intervocalic clusters.

3.1.1. Single-consonant onsets

The structure of single-consonant onsets has already been reviewed above. Basically, all consonants can occur as single-consonant word onsets except [ŋ] and [ž]. As noted above, there are some exceptions in the latter case with borrowed words of French origin, e.g. *genre* [žãnrə] (cf. Fr. [žãʀ]). These typically sound quite foreign.

There are two logically possible treatments of these facts. One possibility would be to restrict these consonants from word-initial position. The other possibility would be to restrict these consonants from syllable-initial position. I already argued in Chapter 2 that the restriction should be in terms of syllable structure, since this generalizes these restrictions to word-medial position. Specifically, [ŋ,ž] must be ruled out syllable-initially because this will also account for the absence of these consonants medially after another consonant.

Treating these facts in terms of syllable structure is at once simple and complex. The absence of these consonants as onsets is readily treated by positing constraints *Onset/ŋ and *Onset/ž. The problem is dealing with potential inputs that might have these consonants in a position that could be syllabified as an onset.

There are three cases to consider. First, there are forms like *beige* [bež] and *sing* [sĩŋ] where the relevant consonant is only syllabifiable as a coda; these, of course, surface with no violations of *Onset/{ŋ,ž}. The second case is instantiated by words like *measure* [mɛž̩r̩] or *hanger* [hǣŋr̩], where the relevant consonants could in principle be syllabified as onsets or codas. Presumably, they are syllabified as codas in this position.

Intervocalic inputs

	/mɛž̩r̩/	*Onset/ž
☞	[mɛž][r̩]	
	[mɛ][ž̩r̩]	*!

The problem comes from potential inputs where the consonants that cannot be onsets could only be syllabified as onsets, e.g. a hypothetical word like /ŋɑ/ or /žɑ/. Since there is no preceding vowel, these consonants must either be syllabified as onsets or not be syllabified at all. Positing constraints like *Onset/ŋ or *Onset/ž is only half the work. The other half is ranking these constraints with respect to other relevant constraints.

The problem is that this ranking can only be achieved by considering the resolution of these inputs. In the case of /ŋɑ/ and /žɑ/, a number of possibilities can be entertained. One is that the relevant consonant is simply not pronounced; /ŋɑ/ and /žɑ/ would both be realized as [ɑ]. This result would be achieved by ranking *Onset/ŋ or *Onset/ž above Faith (Segments). Another possible resolution would be for the relevant consonant to be realized as some other consonant, e.g. /ŋɑ/ as [nɑ] or /žɑ/ as [jɑ]. In this case, the relevant *Onset/X constraint would be ranked above the relevant faithfulness constraint Faith(POA) or Faith(MOA). Yet a third possibility would be that segments might be inserted to avoid making these consonants onsets, e.g. [əŋɑ] or [əžɑ]. Again, this could be achieved by ranking the relevant *Onset/X constraint above Faith(Segments). Finally, the relevant consonant could simply surface unsyllabified. This could be ruled out by ranking Parse above *Onset/{ŋ,ž}.

Thus the appropriate ranking can be determined by considering how potentially violating inputs are realized. The problem is that such inputs do not occur in English. There are no input forms that we have any reason to believe should be characterized as beginning with the consonants [ŋ] or [ž].

There are three possible responses to this situation. The simplest would be to deny that this is a fact of any importance. It is simply an accident of the English lexicon that there are no inputs beginning with /ŋ/ or /ž/. This is clearly the least desirable option, since it would commit us to positing a resolution for such cases when we have neither empirical nor theoretical reasons to choose any particular one.

Another possibility would be to look outside the language for evidence. For example, one might consider how borrowings are treated. While there appear to be no borrowed words in English that begin with the sequence ŋV-, there are borrowings that begin with žV-, e.g. *genre*. If such a form is not produced with an initial [ž], then the usual realization is with [ǰ]. One might take this as evidence that the correct ranking of *ONSET/ž is above FAITH(MOA). The problem with this conclusion is that there is no evidence that speakers of English who produce [ǰãnrə] have anything other than /ǰ/ as input. Moreover, even if we assumed that speakers who pronounce such words as [ǰãnrə] were mapping [ž] onto [ǰ], the realization of onset [ž] as [ǰ] may have more to do with what sounds [ž] is acoustically similar to than with the ranking of OT constraints. A second analytical problem with this ranking solution is that it predicts that we should get alternations. Thus, alongside related forms like *generative* [ǰɛ̃nɹ̩atʰɪv] and *pregenerative* [pʰriǰɛ̃nɹ̩atʰɪv], we should get similar forms with [ž] alternating with [ǰ], i.e. hypothetical *jirf* [ǰɹ̩f] vs. *prejirf* [pʰriž̩ɹ̩f]. The absence of such alternations is a problem for this approach.

A second possibility would be simply to plead agnostic. We know the relevant *ONSET constraints figure in the grammar, but we simply do not know precisely where in the ranking they fall. The problem with this approach is metatheoretical. It does not answer the question and thus makes no predictions.

The final possibility is to acknowledge the absence of evidence for how sequences like /ža/ and /ŋa/ would be realized, and make that absence of evidence part of the analysis. That is, we should rank the *ONSET/X constraints in such a way that input strings like /ža/ and /ŋa/ simply could not arise.

The standard way to do this is to allow GEN to render entire words unpronounced and limit this option by making use of a constraint: M-PARSE.

M-PARSE
Words are pronounced.

If a morpheme is not pronounced, I will mark this in tableaux with curly braces, { }. Ranking *ONSET/ŋ above M-PARSE (and below PARSE and the faithfulness constraints) achieves the result that some hypothetical input /ŋɑ/ would be simply unsayable.

*Interaction of *ONSET/ŋ and M-PARSE*

/ŋɑ/	*ONSET/ŋ	M-PARSE
☞ {ŋɑ}		*
ŋɑ	*!	

This approach maintains that the grammar would not provide an audible output for a hypothetical input /ŋɑ/ or /žɑ/. The advantage of this approach is that it does not commit us to some particular strategy for pronouncing inputs like /ŋɑ/ or /žɑ/, and correctly accounts for the absence of such forms.

Summary of analysis of single-consonant onsets

$$\begin{Bmatrix} \text{PARSE} \\ \text{FAITH} \end{Bmatrix} >> \text{*ONSET/}\{ŋ,ž\} >> \text{M-PARSE}$$

3.1.2. Two-consonant onsets

In Chapter 1, twenty-four different consonants were presented. If these are freely combinable, then we would expect 576 possible two-consonant word onsets. The actual number is quite a bit smaller: there are three different groups, sC, Cy, and OA (obstruent-approximant) clusters.

The fricative [s] seems to have greater liberty than other consonants in clusters. The following chart shows all the possible word-initial sC clusters. Clusters that have very few examples are marked with question marks.

Word-initial sC clusters

[sp]	spot [spɑt], spy [spay], Spanish [spæ̃nɪš], etc.
[st]	step [stɛp], sting [stĩŋ], stolid [stɑlǝd], etc.
[sk]	skip [skɪp], scan [skæn], scholastic [skǝlæstɪk], etc.
[sf]?	sphere [sfɪr], sphinx [sfĩŋks], sphincter [sfĩŋktr̩]
[sθ]?	sthenic [sθĩnɪk]
[sm]	small [smɔl], smear [smɪr], smithereens [smɪðr̥ĩnz], etc.
[sn]	sneeze [sniz], snare [sner], snafu [snæfu], etc.
[sw]	swell [swɛl], swan [swɑ̃n], swagger [swægr̩], etc.
[sl]	slack [slæk], slow [slo], slovenly [slɑvn̩li], etc.

There may also be an [sv] cluster marginally in some dialects. (In my own dialect, however, the only potential exemplar of this cluster is the word *svelte*, and is pronounced [sfɛlt].)

The approximant [y] also clusters quite freely with preceding consonants. Strikingly, this freedom of distribution only happens when [y] is followed by [u] or [r̥]. (Clusters marked with % only occur in certain dialects.)

Cy clusters word-initially

[py]	pure [pyur]/[pyr̥], puce [pyus], pugilist [pyuǰl̩ɪst], etc.
[ty]%	tune [tyũn], tunic [tyũnɪk], tuba [tyubə], etc.
[ky]	cute [kyut], cube [kyub], curious [kyuriəs]/[kyr̥iəs], etc.
[by]	butte [byut], bugle [byugl̩], bureau [byuro]/[byr̥o], etc.
[dy]%	dune [dyũn], duel [dyul], durable [dyurəbl̩]/[dyr̥əbl̩], etc.
[gy]?	gules [gyulz], gubernatorial [gyubr̥nətoril̩]
[fy]	few [fyu], fuel [fyul], fumigate [fyuməget], etc.
[sy]%	suit [syut], Sue [syu], super [syupr̥], etc.
[vy]?	view [vyu]
[my]	muse [myuz], mural [myurl̩]/[myr̥l̩], mute [myut], etc.
[ny]%	news [nyuz], nuance [nyuãns], nude [nyud], etc.
[ly]%	lurid [lyurɪd], luminous [lyumɪnəs]

Since there is this clear correlation between the presence of the [y] and the following vowel, I will return to these cases in Chapters 4 and 6 and have nothing more to say about them here.

The remaining clusters are all composed of an obstruent followed by [l,r,w]. These are each presented in turn below. As above, a question mark denotes an underrepresented category.

Cl clusters word-initially

[pl]	play [pʰle], plan [pʰlæn], plasma [pʰlæzmə], etc.
[kl]	class [kʰlæs], Chloe [kʰloi], clinic [kʰlɪnɪk], etc.
[bl]	blue [blu], blandish [blændɪš], black [blæk], etc.
[gl]	glue [glu], glare [gler], glamour [glæmr̥], etc.
[fl]	flat [flæt], phlegm [flẽm], flavor [flevr̥], etc.
[sl]	*see above*
[šl]?	schlep [šlɛp], schlock [šlɑk]
[vl]?	Vladimir [vlædəmir]
[zl]?	zloty [zlɑri]

Cr clusters word-initially

[pr]	pry [pʰray], prop [pʰrɑp], profit [prɑfɪt], etc.
[tr]	try [tʰray], trash [tʰræš], trellis [tʰrɛlɪs], etc.
[kr]	cry [kʰray], krill [kʰrɪl], criminal [kʰrĩmə̃nl̩], etc.
[br]	bray [bre], brash [bræš], brother [brʌðr̩], etc.
[dr]	dray [dre], draw [drɔ], druid [druɪd], etc.
[gr]	gray [gre], grass [græs], gradual [græǰul̩], etc.
[fr]	fray [fre], frill [frɪl], fracas [frækəs], etc.
[θr]	three [θri], throw [θro], thrombosis [θrãmbosɪs], etc.
[šr]	shrill [šrɪl], shred [šrɛd], shrapnel [šræpnl̩], etc.

Cw clusters word-initially

[pw]?	pueblo [pʰwɛblo]
[tw]	twang [tʰwæ̃ŋ], tweed [tʰwid], twinkle [tʰwĩŋkl̩], etc.
[kw]	quick [kʰwɪk], choir [kʰwayr], cuisine [kʰwəzĩn], etc.
[bw]?	bwana [bwãnə]
[dw]?	dwell [dwɛl], dwarf [dwɔrf], dwindle [dwĩndl̩]
[gw]?	Gwen [gwɛ̃n], guano [gwãno]
[θw]?	thwack [θwæk], thwart [θwɔrt]
[sw]	*see above*

The occurring two-consonant word onsets are summarized in the following chart. Columns indicate the first consonant and rows indicate the second consonant. An x indicates that a cluster is robustly attested and a ? indicates that there are only a few examples. If a consonant does not appear in either first or second position, then that column or row (respectively) is missing from the chart completely. This is to render the chart a manageable size. In addition, the Cy clusters have been left out, since they are treated in Chapters 4 and 6.

Two-consonant onset clusters

	p	t	k	b	d	g	f	θ	s	š	v	z
p									x			
t									x			
k									x			
f									?			
θ									?			
m									x			

	p	t	k	b	d	g	f	θ	s	š	v	z
n									x			
w	?	x	x	?	?	?		?	x			
l	x		x	x		x	x		x	?	?	?
r	x	x	x	x	x	x	x	x		x		

A number of generalizations can be extracted from the chart above. Their precise formalization will have to wait, however, until I have presented additional facts concerning three-consonant onsets, final clusters, vowels, and syllable contact. There are two reasons why those facts are critical. First, the correct form of some generalizations will not be clear until larger clusters or the interaction of various clusters with vowels are considered. Second, a consideration of medial clusters will reveal that there are two broad categories of generalizations: generalizations about syllables versus generalizations about consonant sequencing.

The simplest and most striking observation about the initial clusters is that position matters. It is not the case that order is irrelevant to the makeup of these clusters. For example, while [sp] is well-formed, *[ps] is not. (There are, of course, instances of orthographic <ps>, but these do not correspond to *[ps], e.g. *psychology* [sayk^{h}aləǰi], *psalm* [sãm].) In fact, it is generally the case among initial clusters that if two segments can occur as a word onset in one order, then they cannot occur as an onset in the other order.

Position Generalization
If two segments, α and β, can occur as an onset in the order $\alpha\beta$, then they cannot occur as an onset in the order $\beta\alpha$.

A second, rather simple observation, due originally to Joseph Greenberg, is that, in the general case, all substrings of a well-formed cluster should be themselves well-formed. (I will refer to this as the Substring Generalization.) In the present context, we see that neither [ŋ] nor [ž] can be part of a two-consonant onset.

Substring Generalization
All substrings of a well-formed onset or coda should themselves be well-formed.

This regularity is a consequence of the fact that, for example, a constraint *ONSET/ŋ applies equally well to hypothetical *[ŋa], *[ŋwa], or *[tŋa].

Let us now turn to the substantive restrictions on the content of two-consonant clusters. The clearest observation is that [s] can cluster with just about any following consonant except voiced obstruents, affricates, and [r]. Another clear fact is that affricates do not participate in two-consonant onsets at all. While we might have expected clusters like [čr,čl,čw,ǰr,ǰl,ǰw] parallel to [tr,tw,dr,dw], these do not occur. Thus the restriction against clusters formed of [s] followed by an affricate is really a reflection of this broader fact.

Affricate proscription
Affricates do not appear in complex onsets.

This restriction against *[sr] is matched by the striking [šr] cluster. The only other clusters that [š] participates in are those of clearly German or Yiddish origin, e.g. *Schlemiel* [šlə̄mil], *Shtick* [štɪk], *Stuka* [štʊkə], etc.

[s]-[š] complementarity
[s] cannot precede an [r]; [š] can only precede an [r].

This still leaves the central generalizations untreated: (i) [s] clusters freely with a following voiceless stop or fricative, or with a following nasal; (ii) all the remaining clusters involve some obstruent (including [s]) clustering with [w,l,r]. This set of consonants comprises all the approximants except [lı,y].

Two-consonant word onsets
All two-consonant word onsets are composed of:
 (i) [s] followed by a voiceless stop, fricative, or nasal, or;
(ii) a stop or (voiceless) fricative followed by [w,l,r].

For the moment, let us assume that there are constraints that guarantee that all word onsets have the form stipulated above.

Within the class of obstruent-approximant clusters, there are several smaller limits. First, as noted above, voiced fricatives are not found in obstruent-approximant clusters.

Voiced fricative restriction
Voiced fricatives do not participate in obstruent-approximant onsets.

Second, the alveolar stops [t,d] do not cluster with [l].

Coronal dissimilation
Coronal stops do not cluster with the lateral [l] in onsets.

Third, the labial obstruents [p,b,f,v] do not cluster with a following [w].

Labial dissimilation
Labials cannot cluster with the labial approximant [w].

Finally, there appears to be some limit on voiced stops clustering with [w]. This is not absolute, however, as shown by rare but well-entrenched examples like *dwell* [dwɛl] or *Gwen* [gwɛ̃n].

To summarize this far, the following constraints on English syllable structure have been proposed.

Constraints for onsets so far
*ONSET/ŋ
*ONSET/ž

Some generalizations have been derived.

Derived generalizations
Substring generalization

Some generalizations have been left unformalized so far.

Generalizations so far unformalized	
if [αβ then *[βα	Position generalization
*$\left\{ \begin{matrix} č \\ ǰ \end{matrix} \right\}$C	Affricate proscription
[šC/[sr	[s]-[š] complementarity
sC,OL	General form of two-consonant onsets
*[VL	Voiced fricative restriction
*[$\left\{ \begin{matrix} p \\ b \\ m̌ \end{matrix} \right\}$m	Labial dissimilation

These will be formalized when the data on final and medial clusters have been presented. The fundamental question to be resolved is whether these generalizations are formalized in terms of syllable structure or simple linear order.

3.1.3. Three-consonant onsets

Let us now consider three-consonant onset sequences. There are far fewer of these. The most striking thing about them is that they all begin with the consonant [s]. A chart of these is given below.

Three-consonant onsets

[spr]	spring [sprĩŋ], spry [spray], spruce [sprus]
[str]	string [strĩŋ], strap [stræp], stride [strayd]
[skr]	scrape [skrep], skree [skri], scrunch [skrʌnč]
[spl]	splash [splæš], splint [splĩnt], splatter [splærɹ̩]
[skl]?	sklar [sklɑr], sclerosis [sklɹosɪs]
[skw]	squeeze [skwiz], squash [skwɑš], squalid [skwɑlɪd]
[sfr]?	sphragistic [sfræǰɪstɪk]

There are also a few sCy clusters, which I will again defer discussion of.

CCy onsets

[spy]	spew [spyu], sputum [spyuɜ̃m]
[sty]%	stew [styu], stupid [styupɪd]
[sky]	skewer [skyuɹ̩]

The principal generalization governing the three-consonant clusters is rather striking. Each three-consonant cluster is composed of two overlapping legal two-consonant clusters. Thus [spl] is composed of [sp] and [pl]; [sfr] is composed of [sf] and [fr]. This is yet another instance of the Substring Generalization.

While all occurring three-consonant clusters fall under the Substring Generalization, not all three-consonant clusters predicted by this generalization occur. If we combine all possible two-consonant clusters, the other three-consonant clusters that are predicted are: [spw], [stw], [sfl], [sθr], and [sθw]. In all these cases except [stw], one of the component clusters was marked as marginal (? in the charts above). It may then be that the absence of these clusters is less grammatical than statistical.

The account of the Substring Generalization offered above accounts for the facts concerning three-consonant clusters as well. The basic assumption was that a constraint like *ONSET/ŋ should apply to onsets of any length. The same interpretation applies to any constraint on two-consonant sequences: they should apply whether the two-consonant sequence constitutes the entire sequence or whether it is part of a larger sequence. If there are constraints that penalize adjacent consonants that cannot be analyzed as OL, OG, sO, sN, then those same constraints will apply to three-consonant sequences as well.

For example, the word onset [spr] of *spring* [sprĩŋ] is grammatical because each sequential pairing, [sp] and [pr], is legal. On the other hand, the hypothetical word onset *[zpr] is ruled out because the first pairing [zp] violates the relevant constraint that excludes simple [zp] as even a two-consonant onset.

3.2. WORD-FINAL CLUSTERS

Let us now consider the restrictions on word-final consonant sequences. We will see that very similar restrictions hold, plus some additional complications.

3.2.1. Single-consonant codas

The set of possible single-consonant syllable codas has already been established in §2.1.2. We saw that all consonants of English except [h] can appear as a single-consonant coda.

> *[h] proscription*
> [h] cannot occur in codas.

This is expressible as a *CODA constraint: *CODA/h. As argued in §2.2, to express this in terms of a constraint on the right word edge would miss the fact that [h] is also disallowed preconsonantally medially.

3.2.2. Two-consonant word-final clusters

Two-consonant clusters are far more numerous than two-consonant word onsets. One source of more complex final sequences comes from consonantal suffixes like *-ed*, *-th*, and *-s* in words like *teamed* [tʰīmd], *length* [lɛ̃ŋθ], and *songs* [sɔ̃ŋz]. The generalizations governing these clusters are somewhat looser than those governing unsuffixed words, so these latter suffixed cases will be presented separately.

Two-consonant clusters can be grouped into several large classes: (i) a nasal followed by an obstruent; (ii) [s] followed by a voiceless stop; (iii) a liquid [l,r] followed by a nasal, obstruent, or another liquid; and (iv) any consonant followed by a coronal obstruent. (In each case, the first group are clusters that can be found in unsuffixed words; the second group comprises clusters that can only be found in suffixed words.)

First, there are word-final clusters formed by a nasal followed by an obstruent. Some of these clusters could also be placed in one of the following groups; such clusters are marked with #. Clusters that we might expect but which do not occur are marked with *.

NC codas

[mp]	ramp [rãemp], limp [lĩmp], romp [rãmp]
[nt]#	lint [lĩnt], cant [kʰãent], font [fãnt]
[ŋk]	think [θĩŋk], bank [bãeŋk], sink [sĩŋk]
[nč]#	ranch [rãenč], bench [bẽnč], cinch [sĩnč]
[ɱf]	lymph [lĩɱf], nymph [nĩɱf], triumph [tʰrayʌ̃ɱf]
[nθ]#	absinthe [æbsĩnθ], labyrinth [læbrĩnθ], month [mʌ̃nθ]
[ns]#	fence [fẽns], trance [tʰrãens], mince [mĩns]
[mb]	*
[nd]#	mend [mẽnd], bond [bãnd], hand [hãend]
[ŋg]	*
[nǰ]#	lounge [lãwnǰ], arrange [ərẽnǰ], binge [bĩnǰ]
[ɱv]	*
[nð]	*
[nz]#	lens [lẽnz], bronze [brãnz], banns [bãenz]

NC codas only suffixed

[mt]?#	dreamt [drẽmt]
[ŋt]	*
[mθ]	*
[ŋθ]#	length [lẽŋθ], strength [strẽŋθ]
[mz]#	alms [ãmz], doldrums [doldrɔ̃mz], seems [sĩmz]
[ŋz]#	sings [sĩŋz], longs [lɔ̃ŋz], pangs [pʰãeŋz]
[md]#	teamed [tʰĩmd], blamed [blẽmd], famed [fẽmd]
[ŋd]#	hanged [hãeŋd], winged [wĩŋd], thronged [θrɔ̃ŋd]

(The charts above include the labiodental nasal [ɱ]. This sound occurs in English under only very specific circumstances and is discussed further below.) The unsuffixed NC clusters include sequences of nasals followed by various obstruents. All the nasals exhibit the same POA as the following consonant; they are homorganic. Certain combinations do not occur. These include: [mb,ŋg,ɱv,nž,nð]: all the voiced obstruents except [d,z].

Unsuffixed NC codas
Unsuffixed NC codas are all composed of a nasal followed by a homorganic voiceless obstruent or [d,z].

The suffixed NC codas also include the noncoronal nasals followed by coronals. It is quite striking that, in contrast to other voiced obstruents, the voiced coronals [d,z] can occur among unsuffixed clusters, e.g. *band* [bãend] and *lens* [lẽnz]. It is no doubt significant that they are identical to the voiced coronal affixes, e.g. in *banned* [bǽnd] and *hens* [hɛ̃nz]. Their distribution is, however, even wider when they occur as suffixes, e.g. *bombed* [bɑ̃md], *hams* [hǽmz].

Distribution of voiced obstruents in NC clusters
Voiced obstruents cannot occur in NC clusters except for [d,z]. These can occur in homorganic clusters when unsuffixed and after any nasal when suffixed.

Notice that the [ɱf] cluster would seem to refute the Substring Generalization. While [ɱf] is a possible word-final cluster, [ɱ] cannot occur word-finally. This violation is only apparent, however. The labiodental nasal [ɱ] in English occurs only optionally and only before [f], or [v] as in *anvil* [ǽɱvl̩]/[ǽnvl̩], *convict* [kʰɑ̃ɱvɪkt]/[kʰɑ̃nvɪkt], etc. All words containing [ɱ] can also be pronounced with [m] or [n]. The consonants [m,n] can, of course, occur word-finally, e.g. *team* [tʰĩm], *comb* [kʰõm], *tin* [tʰĩn]. Thus [m]/[n] and [ɱ] are in (optional) complementary distribution.

Complementary distribution of the labiodental nasal
[ɱ]occurs optionally only before the labiodentals [f,v].

The second group of two-consonant codas are sC codas.

Unsuffixed sC codas

[sp]	hasp [hæsp], clasp [kʰlæsp], crisp [kʰrɪsp]
[st]#	last [læst], most [most], best [bɛst]
[sk]	task [tʰæsk], Basque [bæsk], risk [rɪsk]

Suffixed sC codas
[st] passed [pʰæst], missed [mɪst], bossed [bɔst]

The sC clusters are composed of [s] followed by voiceless stops. Only [st] occurs as a suffixed sC cluster, since only coronals can occur as a single consonant suffix.

sC codas
An [s] can be followed by any voiceless stop to make a coda.

The third group consists of [l] or [r] followed by another consonant.

lC codas

[lp]	help [hɛlp], gulp [gʌlp], pulp [pʰʌlp]
[lt]#	felt [fɛlt], bolt [bolt], kilt [kʰɪlt]
[lk]	bilk [bɪlk], silk [sɪlk], ilk [ɪlk]
[lč]#	belch [bɛlč], squelch [skwɛlč], mulch [mʌlč]
[lb]?	bulb [bʌlb]
[ld]#	weld [wɛld], field [fild], cold [kʰold]
[lg]	*
[lǰ]#	bulge [bʌlǰ], bilge [bɪlǰ], divulge [dəvʌlǰ]
[lf]	wolf [wʊlf], self [sɛlf], elf [ɛlf]
[lθ]	*
[ls]#	false [fɑls], pulse [pʰʌls], else [ɛls]
[lš]?#	Welsh [wɛlš]
[lv]	solve [sɔlv], twelve [tʰwɛlv], valve [vælv]
[lz]	*
[lž]	*
[lm]	elm [ɛlm], helm [hɛlm], realm [rɛlm]
[ln]?%#	kiln [kʰɪln]/[kʰɪl]

lC codas only suffixed

[lθ]#	filth [fɪlθ], health [hɛlθ], wealth [wɛlθ]
[lz]#	falls [fɑlz], bells [bɛlz], tools [tʰulz]

The unsuffixed lC clusters include all the obstruents and nasals except a few of the voiced obstruents, [lg,lz,lž], [lθ], and [lŋ]. We will see below that [ŋ] cannot cooccur with any preceding consonant, and that the [lŋ] gap is thus part of a larger pattern. The other gaps reflect the general statistical limits on voiced obstruents, and the [lθ] gap is unexplained. Notice that the rarity of [lb] follows from the general rarity of voiced obstruents in clusters. The suffixed clusters add [lθ] and [lz].

lC clusters
[l] can occur freely with any following obstruent or nasal.

This generalization is thus limited by more general restrictions on voiced obstruents and [ŋ].

The rC clusters are rather similar, except that [rl] occurs where [lr] did not.

rC codas

[rp]	harp [hɑrp], gorp [gorp], sharp [šɑrp]
[rt]#	art [ɑrt], court [kʰort], part [pʰɑrt]
[rk]	bark [bɑrk], torque [tʰork], fork [fork]
[rč]#	march [mɑrč], torch [tʰorč], parch [pʰɑrč]
[rb]	orb [orb], Barb [bɑrb], absorb [əbzorb]
[rd]#	hard [hɑrd], cord [kʰord], beard [bird]
[rg]?	morgue [morg]
[rǰ]#	barge [bɑrǰ], large [lɑrǰ], gorge [gorǰ]
[rf]	barf [bɑrf], morph [morf], dwarf [dworf]
[rθ]#	hearth [hɑrθ], north [norθ], forth [forθ]
[rs]#	farce [fɑrs], parse [pʰɑrs], course [kʰors]
[rš]?#	harsh [hɑrš], marsh [mɑrš]
[rv]	carve [kʰɑrv], starve [stɑrv]
[rð]	*
[rz]	*
[rž]	*
[rl]	gnarl [nɑrl], Carl [kʰɑrl], marl [mɑrl]
[rm]	charm [čʰɑrm], harm [hɑrm], form [form]
[rn]	born [born], corn [kʰorn], tarn [tʰɑrn]
[rŋ]	*

rC codas only suffixed

[rz]?#	Mars[mɑrz], cars [kʰɑrz], chores [čʰorz]

Very similarly to the lC codas, the unsuffixed rC final clusters include all the obstruents, nasals, and [l], except for a few of the voiced fricatives [rð, rz, rž] and [rŋ]. The striking difference is the occurrence of [rl] but not [lr].

rC clusters
[r] can occur freely with any following obstruent or nasal or [l].

Finally, we have clusters composed of a consonant followed by a coronal obstruent [t,s,θ,d,z].

C+COR codas

[pt]	apt [æpt], adopt [ədapt], abrupt [əbrʌpt]
[kt]	act [ækt], pact [pʰækt], fact [fækt]
[ft]	lift [lɪft], aft [æft], oft [ɔft]
[ps]	lapse [læps], copse [kʰaps], traipse [tʰreps]

[ts]?	ersatz [erzɑts], Fritz [frɪts], klutz [kʰlʌts]
[ks]	box [bɑks], ax [æks], fix [fɪks]
[fs]	*
[bd]	*
[gd]	*
[vd]	*
[bz]	*
[dz]?	adz [ædz], woods [wʊdz], sheds [šɛdz]
[gz]	*

C + COR codas only suffixed

[θt]?	toothed [tʰuθt]
[št]	bashed [bæšt], wished [wɪšt], cashed [kʰæšt]
[čt]	matched [mæčt], latched [læčt], watched [wɔčt]
[fs]	laughs [læfs], giraffes [ǰr̩æfs], skiffs [skɪfs]
[pθ]?	depth [dɛpθ]
[tθ]	eighth [etθ]/[eθ]
[dθ]?%	width [wɪtθ]/[wɪdθ]
[fθ]?	fifth [fɪfθ]
[bd]	bribed [braybd], snubbed [snʌbd], grabbed [græbd]
[gd]	lagged [lægd], chugged [čʰʌgd], bogged [bɑgd]
[ǰd]	edged [ɛǰd], lodged [lɑǰd], waged [weǰd]
[vd]	moved [muvd], peeved [pʰivd], loved [lʌvd]
[ðd]	bathed [beðd], breathed [briðd], clothed [kʰloðd]
[zd]	bruised [bruzd], crazed [kʰrezd], dozed [dozd]
[bz]	tribes [tʰraybz], labs [læbz], knobs [nɑbz]
[gz]	bags [bægz], dogs [dɔgz], hugs [hʌgz]
[vz]	caves [kʰevz], chives [čʰayvz], eaves [ivz]
[ðz]	lathes [leðz], youths [yuðz], breathes [briðz]

(Keep in mind that many C+COR clusters were treated above as well.)
Except for the single example *adz* [ædz], the unsuffixed C+COR clusters
all involve a voiceless stop or fricative followed by a voiceless coronal stop
or fricative.

C+COR codas
Any voiceless stop or fricative followed by a voiceless coronal stop or
fricative constitutes a well-formed unsuffixed C+COR coda.

The suffixed C+COR clusters add clusters where the first member is an
affricate and clusters where both segments are voiced.

Suffixed C + COR codas
Any obstruent followed by a coronal stop or fricative constitutes a
well-formed suffixed C+COR coda.

Notice that the C+COR clusters show that the strongest form of the Position Generalization cannot be maintained. Clusters like [sp,st,sk] coexist
with [ps,ts,ks], e.g. *task* [tʰæsk] vs. *tax* [tʰæks].
The diacritics are plentiful enough that it would be useful to review them.

Diacritics used in cluster charts

#	Also an example of C+COR
%	Only in certain dialects
?	Very few examples
*	Nonoccurring and perhaps expected

A number of generalizations regarding word-final clusters have been
introduced above. The only one formalized is *CODA/h. The others have
not been formalized yet.

Generalizations from two-consonant clusters
Coda types allowed: NC, sC, lC, rC, C+COR
Voiced obstruents in NC clusters
Complementary distribution of the labiodental nasal
Suffixed vs. unsuffixed clusters

These will all be treated in §§3.4 and 3.5. As with the word onsets, the fundamental question is whether these are facts about linear position or syllable
structure.

3.2.3. Bigger word-final consonant clusters

Larger word-final consonant sequences are built on the same principles as
larger word-onset sequences; larger sequences are always built on well-
formed smaller sequences (the Substring Generalization). The following
examples are all grouped according to the type of two-consonant cluster
that makes up the first part of the sequence: NC, sC, lC, rC, C+COR.
The first examples below are built on NC clusters.

NC + final clusters

[mpt]	exempt [ɪgzẽmpt], tempt [tʰẽmpt], prompt [pʰrãmpt]
[mps]?	glimpse [glĩmps], mumps [mʌ̃mps], camps [kʰæ̃mps]
[nts]?	chintz [čʰĩnts], blintz [blĩnts], wants [wɔ̃nts]

[ŋks]	Manx [mæ̃ŋks], minx [mĩŋks], lynx [lĩŋks]
[ŋkt]	succinct [sʌksĩŋkt], distinct [dɪstĩŋkt], adjunct [æǰʌ̃ŋkt]
[ŋst]?	amongst [əmʌ̃ŋst]/[əmʌ̃ŋkst]

These are all composed of NC clusters that terminate with a voiceless stop or fricative followed by [s] or [t]. The latter two consonants thus constitute a well-formed unsuffixed C+COR cluster. We might have expected to get [nsp] or [nsk] clusters building on sC clusters, but these do not occur. (The latter only occur in foreign place names like *Minsk* [mĩnsk]; the cluster [nst] does occur, e.g. in *fenced* [fɛ̃nst], but this is not an unambiguous instance of sC, since it is also an instance of C+COR.)

NC+ final clusters
NC+ clusters are built of NC and C+COR substrings.

Following are the suffixed-only examples of NC+clusters.

NC+ clusters only suffixed

[nčt]	inched [ĩnčt], clinched [kʰlĩnčt], ranched [ræ̃nčt]
[mpst]?	glimpsed [glĩmpst]
[ɱft]?	triumphcd [tʰrəyʌ̃ɱft]
[ɱfs]?	nymphs [nĩɱfs]
[nθs]?	labyrinths [læbrĩnθs], months [mʌ̃nθs]
[nst]?	against [əgɛ̃nst], winced [wĩnst], fenced [fɛ̃nst]
[ndz]	lands [læ̃ndz], rinds [rãyndz], bounds [bãwndz]
[nǰd]	lounged [lãwnǰd], arranged [ərẽnǰd], binged [bĩnǰd]
[nzd]?	bronzed [brãnzd]

The suffixed NC+cases add additional examples of the same type, plus a few voiced cases.

Following are the clusters built on sC. The sC+ cases are also composed of sC clusters plus [s] or [t].

sC+ clusters only suffixed

[spt]	rasped [ræspt], clasped [kʰlæspt]
[sps]	hasps [hæsps], rasps [ræsps], clasps [kʰlæsps]
[sts]	toasts [tʰosts], pastes [pʰests], vests [vɛsts]
[skt]	whisked [wɪskt], basked [bæskt], asked [æskt]
[sks]	tasks [tʰæsks], Basques [bæsks], wisps [wɪsps]

sC + clusters

sC+clusters are built of sC and C+COR substrings.

The lC+ clusters are also built using C+COR substrings.

lC + codas

[lts]?	waltz [wɑlts], results [rəzʌlts], tilts [tʰɪlts]

lC+ final clusters only suffixed

[lpt]	helped [hɛlpt], gulped [gʌlpt], pulped [pʰʌlpt]
[lps]	helps [hɛlps], gulps [gʌlps], pulps [pʰʌlps]
[lts]	bolts [bolts], kilts [kʰɪlts], belts [bɛlts]
[lkt]?	bilked [bɪlkt], milked [mɪlkt], sulked [sʌlkt]
[lks]	bilks [bɪlks], ilks [ɪlks], silks [sɪlks]
[lčt]	belched [bɛlčt], squelched [skwɛlčt], mulched [mʌlčt]
[lbd]	*
[lbz]?	bulbs [bʌlbz]
[ldz]	folds [foldz], welds [wɛldz], emeralds [ɛ̃mrˌldz]
[lǰd]	bulged [bʌlǰd], divulged [dəvʌlǰd]
[lft]?	delft [dɛlft], engulfed [ĩŋgʌlft], golfed [gɑlft]
[lfθ]?	twelfth [tʰwɛlfθ]
[lfs]?	gulfs [gʌlfs]
[lst]?	pulsed [pʰʌlst], convulsed [kʰn̩vʌlst]
[lšt]	*
[lvd]	delved [dɛlvd], evolved [ivɑlvd], solved [sɑlvd]
[lvz]	delves [dɛlvz], wolves [wʊlvz], shelves [šɛlvz]
[lzd]	*
[lmd]?	filmed [fɪlmd]
[lmz]	elms [ɛlmz], films [fɪlmz], realms [rɛlmz]
[lnd]	*
[lnz]?%	kilns [kʰɪlnz]/[kʰɪlz]
[ltst]?	waltzed [wɑltst]

The lC+clusters are of a similar form. Unsuffixed cases include only the marginal [lts], as in *waltz*. Suffixed cases add additional clusters including voiced cases. However, also added are liquid+nasal cases. We might have expected clusters like [lnt] or [lmp], building on NC substrings, but these do not occur.

So far all the three-consonant word-final clusters are built using C+COR substrings; rC clusters confirm this general pattern that all three-consonant word-final clusters include a final C+COR substring.

rC + final clusters

[rps]?	corpse [kʰorps], warps [worps], tarps [tʰɑrps]
[rts]?	quartz [kʰworts], smarts [smɑrts], parts [pʰɑrts]
[ršt]?	borscht [boršt]

rC + clusters only suffixed

[rpt]	carped [kʰɑrpt], harped [hɑrpt], warped [worpt]
[rkt]	barked [bɑrkt], forked [forkt], sparked [spɑrkt]
[rks]	Marx [mɑrks], parks [pʰɑrks], forks [forks]
[rčt]	marched [mɑrčt], torched [tʰorčt], parched [pʰɑrčt]
[rbd]	absorbed [əbzorbd], barbed [bɑrbd], garbed [gɑrbd]
[rbz]	barbs [bɑrbz], orbs [orbz], absorbs [əbzorbz]
[rdz]	beards [birdz], lords [lordz], cards [kʰɑrdz]
[rgd]	*
[rgz]?	morgues [morgz]
[rǰd]	barged [bɑrǰd], gorged [gorǰd], forged [forǰd]
[rft]?	barfed [bɑrft]
[rfs]?	barfs [bɑrfs]
[rθt]	*
[rθs]?	hearths [hɑrθs]/[hɑrðz]
[rst]	parsed [pʰɑrst], forced [forst], divorced [dɔvorst]
[ršt]	*
[rvd]?	carved [kʰɑrvd]
[rvz]?	carves [kʰɑrvz], scarves [skɑrvz], varves [vɑrvz]
[rld]?	snarled [snɑrld], gnarled [nɑrld]
[rlz]?	gnarls [nɑrlz]
[rmd]	alarmed [əlɑrmd], formed [formd], swarmed [swɔrmd]
[rmz]	charms [čʰɑrmz], harms [hɑrmz], forms [formz]
[rmθ]?	warmth [wormθ]/[wormpθ]
[rnd]	darned [dɑrnd], mourned [mornd], warned [wɔrnd]
[rnz]	darns [dɑrnz], mourns [mornz], warns [wɔrnz]

The rC + clusters are exactly parallel to the lC + clusters except for the inclusion of rl + among the suffixed set. The unsuffixed clusters maintain the C + COR substring generalization.

C + COR Substring Generalization
All three-consonant word-final clusters and longer have final C + COR substrings.

Even C+COR clusters can be augmented with C+COR substrings.

C + COR + codas

[kst]?	text [tʰɛkst], next [nɛkst], boxed [bɑkst]

C + COR + clusters only suffixed

[pts]	adopts [ədɑpts], accepts [æksɛpts], sculpts [skʌlpts]
[kts]	acts [ækts], neglects [nəglɛkts], objects [ɑbǰəkts]
[fts]	lifts [lɪfts], crafts [kʰræfts], shifts [šɪfts]
[pst]	lapsed [læpst], traipsed [tʰrepst], eclipsed [ikʰlɪpst]
[tst]	*
[kst]	boxed [bɑkst], axed [ækst], fixed [fɪkst]
[dst]?	amidst [əmɪdst]/[əmɪtst]
[ksts]?	texts [tʰɛksts]

The C+COR+ cases all involve voiceless stops and fricatives. This, however, may be an artifact of the nonrecursiveness of inflectional suffixation
in English. If a verb can be made from *adz*, surely the past tense would be
adzed [ædzd].

What is missing in the three-consonant charts are any clusters built using
substring types other than C+COR. The missing possibilities are shown
below.

Missing coda types

rC+lC	*rlk
rC+NC	*rmp
rC+sC	*rsk
lC+NC	*lmp
lC+sC	*lsk
NC+sC	*nsk

Any account of English word-final clusters must account for the absence of
these cluster types.

3.3. MEDIAL CLUSTERS

If the generalizations reached above are based on syllabic licensing, then
they make clear predictions about possible medial clusters. Any medial
consonant cluster should be decomposable into a sequence composed of an
occurring word-final sequence and an occurring word-initial sequence. This

hypothesis follows from syllabic licensing and is given as a theorem below.

Decomposition theorem
All medial clusters should be decomposable into a sequence composed of an occurring word-final cluster and an occurring word-initial cluster.

If, on the other hand, the generalizations above are based on linear order, then they make rather different predictions. Specifically, a sequence ruled out at one edge of the word on linear grounds should be ruled out anywhere on the same grounds.

For example, recall the prohibition against word-initial labial-[w] sequences (with only borrowed exceptions like *Pueblo* and *bwana*). If these are ruled out as syllable onsets, then we might expect these sequences to be legal just in case (i.e. only if) they can be parsed in some other way. For example, we might expect [pw,bw,mw] sequences word-finally where they can be parsed as codas. We might also expect them word-medially where (at least) the first consonant can be parsed as a coda. On the other hand, if the restriction against labial [w] is linear in nature, then we would expect the sequence to be ruled out regardless of possible syllabic parses.

In this section I review the set of possible medial clusters and show that the decomposition theorem is correct for some generalizations but not for others. The generalizations to which the decomposition theorem applies will be formalized as *ONSET/X or *CODA/X constraints. Generalizations to which the decomposition theorem does not apply will be formalized as alignment constraints (GA or NGA).

However, we will also see that the set of medial clusters is far more restricted than syllabic licensing and alignment constraints predict. Some of these further limits can be ascribed to statistical skewing. Some, however, are due to higher-level prosodic considerations, and will be treated in Chapter 6.

3.3.1. **Morphology**

In the earlier discussion of codas, we saw that affixation clouds the set of possible clusters. Fortunately, there are no consonantal prefixes in English, so this complication does not affect the set of possible onsets. There are only a very few consonantal suffixes, so the effect on codas is minimal (though quite interesting, as we have seen).

In the case of medial clusters, the problem is greatly magnified. There are three broad reasons for this. First, virtually any two words can be combined

to form a new word with medial cluster. Consider the word *blackbird*
[blækbr̩d]. Here the words *black* and *bird* are combined, producing the
medial cluster [kb], which does not otherwise occur. Another example of
this type is *pickpocket* [pʰɪkpʰɑkət], formed from *pick* and *pocket*, and producing the cluster [kp]. Again, this cluster only occurs in combined words
of this sort.

Examples of [kp]

checkpoint [čʰɛkpʰɔ̃ynt]
crackpot [kʰrækpʰɑt]
pickpocket [pʰɪkpʰɑkət]
stockpile [stɑkpʰayl]

This process, compounding, happens quite freely in English to produce new
words and new consonant clusters. There is no restriction on the clusters
that result from compounding, as a word ending in any consonant can be
combined with a word beginning with any consonant.

Compounding is distinguished from other morphological processes in
that the elements combined can both occur as autonomous words. As we
saw with the final clusters above, however, there are other meaningful elements that are smaller than words, i.e. suffixes, e.g. *-s* in *books* [bʊks], *-ed*
in *sagged* [sægd], *-th* in *fourth* [forθ]. Medial clusters can also be produced
via suffixation. For example, the word *bleakness* [bliknəs] is made from
bleak and *-ness*. Likewise, *childhood* [čáyldhʊd] is made from *child* and
-hood. (The latter, of course, has no connection to the word referring to the
head covering.) Clusters can also be created by prefixation, as in *unhappy*
[ʌ̃nhæpi], from *un-* and *happy*, or *intolerable* [ĩntʰɑlr̩əbl̩], from *in-* and *tol-
erable*.

Some of the clusters produced by affixation also do not occur otherwise,
e.g. [dh].

Examples of [dh]

adhere [ædhir]
madhouse [mædhaws]
childhood [čʰayldhʊd]

The example *adhere* represents an especially difficult class of words,
those exhibiting Latinate morphology. These are words borrowed from
Latin or French that exhibit complex morphological structure from Latin.
The problem that these words pose is that while the morphological relations

are rather opaque, these words exhibit different phonological regularities from other words of English. For example, the prefix *ad-* does not mean a whole lot in English, but only by calling it a prefix would it be possible to maintain that the [dh] cluster only occurs heteromorphemically. Some additional examples of Latinate prefixes are given below.

Some Latinate prefixes

sub-	substantial [sʌbstǽnč̣], subterranean [sʌbtʰr̩ḛ́nɪṇ]
trans-	transgress [tʰrǽnzgrɛs], transfer [tʰrǽnsfr̩]
com-	comfort [kʰʌ́m̩fr̩t], colleague [kʰɑlig]
ad-	accept [æksɛpt], admonish [ædmɑ̃nɪš]
ab-	abstract [æbstrækt], abject [æbǰɛkt]
ob-	obtuse [ɑbtʰus], obfuscate [ɑbfʌsket]
ex-	exclaim [ɪksklḛm], excuse [ɪkskʰyuz]

While most speakers of English are incapable of assigning any sort of meaning to elements like *ob-*, they are aware that it forms some sort of building-block in the vocabulary of English. This is in contrast to an element like *un-*, which also occurs quite widely but which has a clear meaning of negation, e.g. in *unhappy* [ʌ̃nhæpi], *untrue* [ʌ̃ntʰru], *unable* [ʌ̃neb̩]. It is then an open question whether to treat Latinate elements as morphemes in English or not. The argument for doing so was exemplified in the discussion of [dh] above: the set of possible medial clusters changes. The argument against is that Latinate elements do not always have a clear meaning. I will therefore take a conservative position and not treat Latinate elements as separate morphemes in this discussion.

In the discussions of medial clusters that follow, I will consider only unaffixed and uncompounded words where the relevant clusters are not a consequence of any sort of clear morphology. Where some particular combination is only instantiated by Latinate examples, the relevant words will be marked with a superscript [L].

3.3.2. Two-consonant monomorphemic clusters

The following charts give all possible sequences of two consonants between vowels. Since there are lots of these, the charts are broken up based on the type of second consonant. The first chart has stops as a second member, the second fricatives and affricates, the third nasals and approximants. The relevant class of sounds (occurring in second position in the cluster) heads the different columns; rows give the consonants that can precede the consonants in question (thus occurring in first position in the cluster).

Intervocalic consonant-stop sequences

	p	t	k	b	d	g
p	–	Neptune [nɛptʰūn]	napkin [næpkn̩]	–	–	–
t	–	–	catkin [kʰætkn̩]	–	–	–
k	–	cactus [kʰæktəs]	–	–	–	–
b	–	–	–	–	abdomen [æbdə̄mn̩]	–
d	–	–	–	tidbit [tʰɪdbɪt]	–	–
g	magpie [mægpʰay]	–	–	rugby [rʌgbi]	magdalen [mægdələ̄n]	–
f	–	nifty [nɪfti]	–	–	–	–
s	aspen [æspn̩]	mustang [mʌstæ̃ŋ]	basket [bæskət]	asbestos [æsbɛstəs]	–	–
z	–	–	–	husband [hʌzbn̩d]	wisdom [wɪzdə̄m]	nosegay? [nozge]
ǰ	hodgepodge? [haǰpʰaǰ]	–	–	–	–	–
m	vampire [væ̃mpʰayr]	tomtit [tʰãmtʰɪt]	kumquat [kʰʌ̃mkʰwat]	mambo [mãmbo]	humdinger [hʌmdĩŋr̩]	–
n	nonpareil? [nãnpʰr̩ɛl]	fountain [fãwntn̩]	cancan? [kʰæ̃nkʰæ̃n]	bonbon? [bãnbãn]	candy [kʰæ̃ndi]	–
ŋ	–	–	donkey [dɔ̃ŋki]	–	–	finger [fĩŋgr̩]
l	alpaca [ælpʰækə]	filter [fɪltr̩]	alkali [ælkl̩ay]	albatross [ælbətʰrɔs]	boulder [boldr̩]	alga [ælgə]
r	carpet [kʰarpət]	tartan [tʰartn̩]	arcane [ãrkʰẽn]	harbor [harbr̩]	border [bordr̩]	target [tʰargət]
w	–	kowtow? [kʰawtʰaw]	–	baobab? [bawbab]	rowdy [rawɾi]	–
y	viper [vaypr̩]	mitre [mayɾr̩]	Michael [maykl̩]	libel [laybl̩]	idol [aydl̩]	gigantic [ǰaygæ̃ntɪk]

There are some clear generalizations to be made. First, there are no clusters formed from identical consonants (geminates). This is true regardless of syllabic constituency, so this can be stated as a (negative) GA constraint.

> *NOGEMINATES (prose version)*
> Identical consonants cannot cluster tautomorphemically.

NoGeminates (NGA version)
* α| |α

The NoGeminates constraint must of course outrank M-Parse.

Second, except for [s,z,f], fricatives and affricates cannot cluster with a following stop. In fact, [f] only occurs with a following [t].

Examples of [ft]

after [æftr̩]	caftan [kʰæftæn]
chieftain [čʰiftn̩]	crafty [kʰræfti]
hefty [hɛfti]	lofty [lɔfti]
mufti [mʊfti]	nifty [nɪfti]
rafter [ræftr̩]	safety [sefti]

What is ruled out are clusters consisting of [š,ž,v,θ,ð] and any following stop.

Comparison of this generalization with those established for word margins shows that there is substantial overlap across the three cases. Word-initially, a stop can only be preceded by [s]; word-finally, [p,k] can only be preceded by [s], but [t,d] can be preceded by precisely the voiceless fricatives that are permitted medially, [s,f]. The relevant data are repeated below.

Word-final fricative-stop sequences

[sp]	hasp [hæsp]
[sk]	husk [hʌsk]
[st]	mast [mæst]
[ft]	loft [lɔft]

The only clusters permitted word-medially and not permitted word-finally are those where the first element is [z]. An exhaustive list of these follows. Notice that there are strikingly few of these, and that most of them have a distinctly polymorphemic character.

Word-medial [z]-stop clusters

husband [hʌzbn̩d]
lesbian [lɛzbin̩]
nosegay [nozge]
presbyter [pʰrɛzbərr̩]
raspberry [ræzbr̩i]
wisdom [wɪzdə̃m]

Many of these cases are historically polymorphemic, but there is no definitive motivation for treating these as polymorphemic in modern English.
Therefore, I will assume that [z]-stop clusters are legal tautomorphemically.

To treat this array of facts, we need to posit linear constraints against all
fricative-stop sequences except those beginning with [s,f,z]. We then need
further constraints on syllable margins to rule out [f,z]-stop clusters as
onsets, and [z]-stop clusters as codas.

The relevant linear filters rule out any COR or DORS element before a
stop and a voiced LAB element before a stop.

Three linear constraints on fricative-stop sequences (preliminary)

$$* \left\{ \begin{array}{c} \text{COR} \\ \text{DORS} \\ \begin{bmatrix} \text{LAB} \\ \text{voiced} \end{bmatrix} \end{array} \right\} \Big| \text{ stop}$$

The necessary *ONSET/X and *CODA/X constraints are given below. (We
will see below that the *ONSET/X constraint is actually not necessary, but
I give it here for completeness.)

Two constraints on fricative-stop onsets (preliminary)

$$*\text{ONSET}/\left\{ \begin{array}{c} f \\ z \end{array} \right\} \text{stop}$$

A constraint against [z]-stop codas (preliminary)
*CODA/z-stop

Finally, clusters where consonants disagree in voicing are very rare. Most
of these are either quite foreign-sounding and/or appear more like com-
pounds.

Voicing differences

bodkin [bɑdkn̩]	jodhpur [ĭɑdpʰr̩]
madcap [mædkʰæp]	magpie [mægpʰay]
tadpole [tʰædpʰol]	vodka [vɑdkə]
afghan [æfgæ̃n]	anecdote [ænəkdot]
asbestos [æsbɛstəs]	jurisdiction [ĭr̩ɪsdɪkšn̩]
scapegoat [skepgot]	smorgasbord [šmorgəsbord]

Again, however, since there is no clear reason to reject these as
polymorphemic, I propose no constraint to rule them out.

The next chart gives clusters where the second element is a voiceless
fricative or affricate.

Intervocalic voiceless consonant-fricative/affricate sequences

	f	θ	s	š	č
p	–	naphtha [næpθə]	capsule [kʰæpsḷ]	option [apšṇ]	capture [kʰæpčṛ]
t		–	flotsam [flɑtsm̩]	–	chitchat? [čʰɪtčæt]
k	–	ichthyology [ɪkθiɑləǰi]	accent [æksẽnt]	auction [ɔkšṇ]	picture [pʰɪkčṛ]
b	obfuscate^L [abfʌsket]	–	absent^L [æbsṇt]	–	–
d	–	–	adsorb^L [ædsorb]	–	–
f	–	diphthong? [dɪfθɔ̃ŋ]	–	–	–
s	asphalt [æsfɔlt]	esthetic [ɛsθɛrɪk]	–	–	eschew [ɛsču]
m	camphor [kʰæ̃ɱfṛ]/ [kʰæ̃mfṛ]	–	circumcision^L [sṛkṃsɪžṇ]	–	–
n	confetti [kʰɱfɛri]/ [kʰn̩fɛri]	anthem [æ̃nθm̩]	answer [æ̃nsṛ]	banshee [bæ̃nši]	adventure [ædvɛ̃nčṛ]
l	alfalfa [ælfælfə]	–	also [ɔlso]	–	culture [kʰʌlčṛ]
r	orphan [orfṇ]	narthex [nɑrθɛks]	arson [ɑrsṇ]	partial [pʰɑršḷ]	orchard [orčṛd]
w	–	–	–	–	caoutchouc? [kʰawčuk]
y	cipher [sayfṛ]	python [pʰayθɑ̃n]	crisis [kʰraysɪs]	–	righteous [rayčəs]

Except for [s,f], fricatives and affricates can't be the first member of these clusters either. Therefore the three constraints above should be generalized to rule out these additional cases.

Three linear constraints on fricative-obstruent sequences (preliminary)

$$* \left\{ \begin{matrix} \text{COR} \\ \text{DORS} \\ \begin{bmatrix} \text{LAB} \\ \text{voiced} \end{bmatrix} \end{matrix} \right\} \Bigg| \text{obstruent}$$

Two constraints on fricative-obstruent onsets (preliminary)

$$*\textsc{Onset}/ \left\{ \begin{matrix} \text{f} \\ \text{z} \end{matrix} \right\} \text{obstruent}$$

A constraint against [z]-obstruent codas (preliminary)
$*\textsc{Coda}/\text{z-obstruent}$

These constraints will have to be revised still further below.

In addition, voicing disagreements involving obstruents are quite rare and largely limited to Latinate forms.

Voicing disagreements involving voiceless fricatives

abscess[L] [æbsɛs]	absence[L] [æbsn̩s]
absinthe [æbsɪ̃nθ]	absolute[L] [æbsl̩ut]
absorb[L] [əbsorb]/[əbzorb]	absurd[L] [əbsr̩d]
adsorb[L] [ædsorb]/[ədzorb]	obfuscate[L] [abfʌsket]
obscene[L] [əbsĩn]	obsequious[L] [ʌbsikwiəs]
observe[L] [ʌbsr̩v]/[əbzr̩v]	obsess[L] [əbsɛs]
obsidian [absɪdin̩]	obsolete[L] [absl̩it]
subsidy[L] [sʌbsəri]	

(Since we are treating Latinate forms as monomorphemic, this observation will have to go unformalized.)

The following chart shows clusters where the second element is a voiced fricative or affricate.

Intervocalic voiced consonant-fricative/affricate sequences

	v	ð	z	ž	ǰ
b	obvious[L] [abviəs]	–	absolve[L] [æbzalv]	–	object[L] [abǰəkt]
d	advantage[L] [ædvǽntəǰ]	–	–	–	–
g	–	–	eczema [ɛgzə̃mə]	luxury [lʌgžr̩i]	suggest[L] [sʌgǰɛst]

	v	ð	z	ž	ǰ
m	circumvent[L] [sr̩km̩vẽnt]/ [sr̩km̩vẽnt]	–	clumsy [kʰlʌ̃mzi]	–	–
n	envy [ɛm̩vi]/[ɛnvi]	–	benzene [bẽnzĩn]	–	banjo [bæ̃nǰo]
l	silver [sɪlvr̩]	–	palsy [pʰɔlzi]	–	algae [ælǰi]
r	larva [lɑrvə]	swarthy [swɔrði]	ersatz [erzɑts]	–	cordial [kʰorǰl̩]
w	–	–	trousers [tʰrawzr̩z]	–	–
y	rival [rayvl̩]	–	geyser [gayzr̩]	–	hygiene [hayǰĩn]

Here clusters are even more restricted. There are absolutely no clusters of voiceless obstruent followed by voiced fricative or affricate. The same restriction holds of peripheral clusters and so this can be expressed as a linear constraint.

Voicing with fricatives

$$* \ [\text{voiceless}] \left\| \left\| \begin{array}{c} \text{voiced} \\ \left(\begin{array}{c} \text{fricative} \\ \text{affricate} \end{array} \right) \end{array} \right\| \right\|$$

Forms like *anecdote* [æ̃nəkdot] show that this does not apply to stops.

In addition, sequences of two voiced obstruents are again quite restricted. There are actually two groups. First, there are the usual Latinate forms and a few morphologically complex words.

Obstruent + [voiced fricative] clusters

absolve[L] [æbzɑlv]	advance[L] [ædvæns]
advantage[L] [ædvæ̃rəǰ]	adventure[L] [ædvẽnčr̩]
adverb[L] [ædvr̩b]	adverse[L] [ædvr̩s]
advert[L] [ædvr̩t]	advice[L] [ædvays]
advocate[L] [ædvəkʰet]	observe[L] [ʌbzr̩v]
obverse[L] [ʌbvr̩s]	obviate[L] [ɑbviet]
obvious[L] [ɑbviəs]	subvention[L] [sʌbvẽnčn̩]
subvert[L] [sʌbvr̩t]	woodsy [wʊdzi]
zigzag [zɪgzæg]	

The second class is made up of words spelled with ⟨x⟩ (except for *eczema*). Here the first consonant is always [g], and there is no morpheme boundary between the relevant consonants, though these are almost all Latinate as well.

Voiced clusters with ⟨x⟩

auxiliary^L [ɔgzɪlyɾi]	eczema [ɛgzə̃mə]
exacerbate^L [ɪgzæsr̩bet]	exact^L [ɪgzækt]
exaggerate^L [ɪgzæǰɾet]	exalt^L [ɪgzɔlt]
exam^L [ɪgzæ̃m]	example^L [ɪgzæ̃mpl̩]
exasperate^L [ɪgzæspɾet]	executive^L [ɪgzɛkyərəv]
executor^L [ɪgzɛkyərr̩]	exempt^L [ɪgzẽmt]
exert^L [ɪgzr̩t]	exhaust^L [ɪgzɔst]
exhibit^L [ɪgzɪbət]	exhilarate^L [ɪgzɪlɾet]
exhort^L [ɪgzort]	exhume^L [ɪgzũm]
exiguous^L [ɛkzɪgyuəs]	exile^L [ɛgzayl]
exist^L [ɪgzɪst]	exit^L [ɛgzət]
exonerate^L [ɪgzãnɾet]	exorbitant^L [ɪgzorbərɔ̃nt]
exordium^L [ɪgzorrɪ̃m]	exotic^L [ɪgzɑrɪk]
exuberant^L [ɪgzubɾɔ̃nt]	exude^L [ɪgzud]
exult^L [ɪgzʌlt]	luxuriant^L [lʌgžɾɪ̃nt]

Since these cases cannot be ruled out on clear grounds of hetero-morphemicity, voiced obstruent clusters must be countenanced hetero-syllabically. Voiced obstruent clusters are ruled out in onsets, but only allowed in the single coda cluster *adz* [ædz]. I will propose a general mechanism below to rule out two elements in the same major class in a syllable margin.

The next class of clusters to be considered have a sonorant [m,n,l,r,w,y] as a second member.

Intervocalic obstruent + sonorant sequences

	m	n	l	r	w	y
p	chipmunk [čʰɪpmʌ̃ŋk]	grapnel [græpnl̩]	aplomb [əpʰlõm]	caprice [kʰəpʰris]	–	–
t	atmosphere [ætməsfir]	chutney [čʰʌtni]	atlas [ætləs]	citrus [sɪtrəs]	–	–
k	acme [ækmi]	acne [ækni]	cochlea [kʰokliə]	acrid [ækrɪd]	acquit [əkʰwɪt]	–

b	submerse[L]	obnoxious[L]	ablate[L]	abrade[L]	–	–
	[səbmr̩s]	[əbnɑkšəs]	[æblet]	[əbred]		
d	admire[L]	kidney	bedlam	adroit	–	–
	[ædmayr]	[kʰɪdni]	[bɛdlə̃m]	[ədrɔyt]		
g	enigma	magnet	igloo	egret	jaguar	–
	[ə̃nɪgmə]	[mægnət]	[ɪɡlu]	[igrət]	[ǰægwɑr]	
f	–	hafnium	soufflé	saffron	–	–
		[hæfnim̩]	[sufle]	[sæfrã̃n]		
θ	arithmetic	ethnic	athlete	–	–	–
	[ərɪθmətʰɪk]	[ɛθnɪk]	[æθlit]			
s	isthmus	–	legislate	–	assuage	–
	[ɪsməs]		[lɛǰəslet]		[əsweǰ]	
š	marshmallow	–	ashlar	–	–	–
	[mɑršmælo]		[æšl̩r]			
v	–	evening	–	chevron	bivouac	savior?
		[ivnĩŋ]		[šɛvrãn]	[bɪvwæk]	[sevyr̩]
ð	rhythmic	–	–	–	–	–
	[rɪðmɪk]					
z	asthma	business	grizzly	–	–	–
	[æzmə]	[bɪznəs]	[grɪzli]			
ž	cashmere	–	–	–	–	–
	[kʰæžmir]					
ǰ	–	–	fledgling?	–	–	–
			[flɛǰlĩŋ]			

Intervocalic sonorant+sonorant sequences

m	–	amnesia	hemlock	comrade	–	–
		[æ̃mnižə]	[hɛ̃mlɑk]	[kʰɑ̃mræd]		
n	enmity	–	only	–	–	bunion
	[ɛ̃nmɪ ̣ri]		[õnli]			[bʌ̃nyn̩]
l	dolmen	vulnerable	–	walrus	bulwark	valiant!
	[dolmn̩]	[vʌlnr̩əbl̩]		[wɔlrəs]	[bʊlwɔrk]	[vælyn̩t]
r	army	blarney	garlic	–	–	–
	[ɑrmi]	[blɑrni]	[gɑrlɪk]			
w	–	–	–	dowry	rauwolfia?	–
				[dawri]	[rawwʊlfiə]	
y	chimera	china	island	eyrie	–	–
	[kʰaymirə]	[čʰãynə]	[aylə̃nd]	[ayri]		

The most striking thing about these charts is the rarity of Cy clusters. This suggests that the absence of Cy onsets is a reflection of a nonsyllabic restriction against the sequence Cy. This can be formalized as a linear constraint.

Cy constraint (prose version)
The glide [y] is disallowed after a consonant.

Cy constraint (NGA version)
* [consonant]‖ [[y]

The only potential counterexamples involve [n,l] and perhaps the one example of [v], *savior*. (The former will be discussed in more depth in Chapter 6.)

3.3.3. **Three-consonant monomorphemic medial clusters**

There are very few examples of clear triconsonantal clusters in monomorphemic forms. Following are several lists where nativeness and monomorphemehood is construed generously.

The first three lists contain clusters that begin with an NC cluster. These are separated into cases where (i) both substrings are legal margins, (ii) only the first substring is a legal coda, or (iii) only the second substring is a legal onset. The interest of these distinctions is that the latter two show that two-consonant codas and onsets must be countenanced word-medially.

First, there are cases where both substrings are legal. These establish that either two-consonant onsets or codas are required medially, but they do not establish which, since either syllabification results in legal codas and onsets.

Both substrings are legal margins

[mpl]	accomplish [əkʰãmplɪš]	[mpr]	empress [ɛ̃mprəs]
[ɱfl]	pamphlct [pʰæ̃ɱflət]	[ndr]	androgen [æ̃ndrəǰɛ̃n]
[ndw]	sandwich [sæ̃ndwɪč]	[nst]	constable [kʰãnstəbl̩]
[nθr]	anthrax [æ̃nθræks]	[ntr]	antrum [æ̃ntrə̃m]
[ŋkl]	inkling [ĩŋklĩŋ]	[ŋkw]	banquet [bæ̃ŋkwət]
[ŋkr]	pancreas [pʰæ̃ŋkriəs]		

Following are examples of medial three-consonant clusters where the second substring is not a legal onset. These establish that two-consonant codas must be legal word-medially.

First substring is a legal coda

[mpč]	sumptuous [sãmpčuəs]	[ŋkč]	juncture [ǰʌ̃ŋkčr̩]
[mpt]	empty [ẽmpti]	[ntn]	vintner [vĩntnr̩]
[ntl]	antler [æ̃ntlr̩]	[ŋkf]	frankfurter [fræ̃ŋkfʊrr̩]
[mpk]	pumpkin [pʰʌ̃mpkɪn]	[mpš]	gumption [gʌ̃mpšn̩]
[ndl]	chandler [čʰæ̃ndlr̩]	[ŋkt]	plankton [pʰlæ̃ŋktn̩]
[mps]	palimpsest [pʰælĩmpsɛst]		

Following are three-consonant medial clusters where the first two consonants are not a licit coda. These establish that two-consonant onsets can occur medially.

Second substring is a legal onset

[mbr]	ambrosia [æ̃mbrožə]	[ŋgr]	angry [æ̃ŋgri]
[ŋgw]	anguish [æ̃ŋgwɪš]	[ŋgl]	anglicize [æ̃ŋgləsayz]
[mst]	hamster [hæ̃mstr̩]	[ŋst]	tungsten [tʰʌ̃ŋstn̩]
[mbl]	emblem [ẽmblə̃m]	[mkw]	kumquat [kʰʌ̃mkwɑt]

The next set of clusters are built on an initial liquid [l,r]. In the first group both substrings are legal codas and onsets respectively.

Both substrings are legal

[lbl]	chilblain [čʰɪlblẽn]	[lbr]	balbriggan [bælbrɪgn̩]
[ldr]	caldron [kʰaldrə̃n]	[lfr]	belfry [bɛlfri]
[lgr]	pilgrim [pʰɪlgrə̃m]	[lkr]	fulcrum [fʊlkrə̃m]
[lpl]	volplane [volplẽn]	[lpr]	culprit [kʰʌlprət]
[lsn]	pilsner [pʰɪlsnr̩]	[lst]	bolster [bolstr̩]
[ltr]	filtrate [fɪltret]	[rbl]	warbler [wɔrblr̩]
[rdr]	wardrobe [wɔrdrob]	[rgr]	margrave [mɑrgrev]
[rsl]	parsley [pʰɑrsli]	[rsn]	parsnip [pʰɑrsnɪp]
[rθr]	arthritis [arθrayrəs]	[rtr]	cartridge [kkɑrtrɪǰ]

The following list is also built on an initial liquid, but here only the first substring is legal.

First substring is legal

[lpč]	sculpture [skʌlpčr̩]	[lpt]	sculptor [skʌlptr̩]
[ltp]	saltpeter? [sɔltpʰirr̩]	[rdv]	aardvark [ardvark]
[rkt]	arctic [arktɪk]	[rps]	harpsichord [harpsəkʰord]
[rtf]	portfolio [pʰortfolio]	[rtk]	portcullis [pʰortkʰʌləs]
[rtn]	partner [pʰartnr̩]		

There are no examples of clusters built on an initial liquid where only the second string is legal. There is one recent borrowing where at least one pronunciation makes neither substring legal: *bourgeois* [buržwɑ]. This word is also pronounced [bužwɑ] or [bužwa] with only a two-consonant cluster.

Next, there are three-consonant clusters where the first consonant is an obstruent. In the first group below, both substrings are legal.

Both substrings are legal

[ksp]	expand [ɪkspǽnd]	[kst]	dexterity [dɛkstɛrəɾi]
[ktr]	electric [əlɛktrɪk]	[pst]	capstan [kʰǽpstæn]
[skr]	ascribe [əskrayb]	[skw]	esquire [ɛskwayr]
[spl]	display [dɪsple]	[spr]	espresso [ɛsprɛso]
[str]	apostrophe [əpʰastrəfi]		

The examples below are cases where only the first substring is legal. These are marginal examples, however, as *-ure* (*furniture*, *fracture*, *creature*) and *-ment* (*oddment*, *contentment*, *advertisement*) are both likely suffixes.

First substring is legal

[kst]	texture [tʰɛkscɾ̩]	[stm]	vestment [vɛstmn̩t]/[vɛsmn̩t]

Finally, there are a few examples where only the second substring is legal, but these are all built on words beginning with the Latinate prefix *ob-*.

Second substring is legal

[bsk]	obscure[L] [abskyɾ̩]	[bst]	obstacle[L] [abstəkl̩]
[btr]	obtrude[L] [abtʰrud]		

The absence of clear cases of the latter two types for obstruent-initial three-consonant clusters is surely significant. It suggests that the limiting factor on medial codas is in the obstruent-obstruent category. Thus of the following two-consonant coda types, only the first three can occur both finally and medially.

Coda types

Coda	Final	Medial
NC	✔	✔
r/lC	✔	✔
sC	✔	✔
C+COR	✔	—

Since, as noted above, all larger codas are built on the C+COR type, it follows that there cannot be three-consonant codas medially.

The C+COR class can be ruled out in several ways. One possibility is to posit a high-ranking constraint that excludes any sequence of two obstruents as a medial coda where the first consonant is not [s].

No Medial C+COR

$$*c \left/ \begin{bmatrix} \text{obstruent} \\ \neg s \end{bmatrix} \right. \text{[obstruent]} \; \sigma$$

This is undesirable as it requires negation in the *CODA/X constraint and requires reference to material outside the syllable (which has been unnecessary so far).

An alternative would be to allow word-final coronal sequences exceptionally, rather than rule them out medially. This is the approach that will be taken below.

3.3.4. Four-consonant monomorphemic medial clusters

Larger clusters are similarly restricted. There are very few clear examples of monomorphemic four-consonant clusters. Among the nasal-initial clusters, only words like *demonstrate* and *instrument* are vaguely convincing as monomorphemes. Both substrings are legal in these two examples.

Nasals

[mptr]	temptress [tʰɛ̃mptrəs]	[mskr]	circumscribe [sr̩km̩skrayb]
[mstr]	seamstress [sĩmstrəs]	[nzgr]	transgress [tʰrɛ̃nzgrɛs]
[nskr]	conscript [kʰãnskrɪpt]	[nspl]	transplant [tʰrɛ̃nsplɛ̃nt]
[mptr]	comptroller [kʰãmptʰrolr̩]	[nstr]	instrument [ĩnstrɔ̃mɔ̃nt]

The only convincing liquid-initial monomorphemic four-consonant cluster is *maelstrom*, but this word is clearly borrowed (from Danish). Again, both substrings are legal.

Liquids

[lstr]	maelstrom [melstrɔ̃m]

Among the obstruent-initial clusters, again there are very few clear monomorphemic cases. The best examples are words like *extra*. (*Blitzkrieg* is borrowed from German and quite foreign-sounding.)

Others

[bskr]	subscribe [sʌbskrayb]	[bstr]	abstract [æbstrækt]
[kskl]	exclaim [ɪksklẽm]	[kskr]	excrete [ɛkskrit]
[kskw]	exquisite [ɪkskwɪzət]	[kspl]	explain [ɪksplẽn]
[kspr]	express [ɪksprɛs]	[kstr]	extra [ɛkstrə]
[tskr]	blitzkrieg [blɪtskʰrig]		

The only example of a five-consonant cluster that I could find was *sempstress* [sẽmpstrəs]/[sẽmstrəs]. Such forms do not establish that three-consonant margins must be countenanced word-medially. As the transcription above indicates, the [p] is optional. In fact, this kind of optionality is typical of nonhomorganic NC clusters in certain stress configurations. For example, names like *Hampton*, *Compton*, and *Humpty Dumpty* all exhibit the same variability.

Nonhomorganic NC clusters

Hampton [hæ̃mptn̩]/[hæ̃mtn̩]
Compton [kʰɑ̃mptn̩]/[kʰɑ̃mtn̩]
Humpty Dumpty [hʌ̃mptidʌ̃mpti]/[hʌ̃mtidʌ̃mti]

Based on facts like these, I conclude that the [p] in *sempstress* is ephemeral, and that we can maintain a limit on medial syllable margins of two consonants.

3.3.5. Medial clusters

The crucial generalizations to be extracted from these charts are as follows. First, the general thrust of syllabic licensing is confirmed in that there are no medial clusters that cannot be analyzed as a sequence of a well-formed coda followed by a well-formed onset.

A second generalization is that many of the restrictions on onsets and codas can now be seen as sequential constraints. For example, while the consonant [y] can readily begin words, it cannot easily follow a consonant, whether it is in an onset or in a medial cluster. (It can only follow a consonant when the following vowel is [u], as in *puce* [pʰyus] or *accuse* [əkʰyuz].)

A third fact is that while larger codas are tolerated at word edge, only two-consonant codas are possible word-medially. Thus, while codas like [ksts] are tolerated word-finally (e.g. *texts*), they are disallowed word-medially.

A fourth fact is that voicing agreement seems to be a requirement on any two tautomorphemic consonants in sequence, and not a fact about onsets or codas specifically.

3.4. CLUSTERS VS. MARGINS AND THE SONORITY HIERARCHY

In this section, the general properties of medial clusters and syllable margins are considered. First I propose that margins are subject to the sonority hierarchy, and then I formalize the hierarchy. Remaining cluster generalizations are then treated.

There is a basic sequencing generalization governing word-final clusters that is parallel to the word onset sequences. Almost any cluster that is allowed word-initially is allowed word-finally when reversed. Thus [gr] is allowed word-initially in *grow* [gro], and [rg] is allowed word-finally in *morgue* [morg]. Likewise, [pl] is allowed word-initially in *plug* [pʰlʌg] and word-finally reversed in *gulp* [gʌlp].

This is not completely true, though. While clusters like [kw,tw,gw, dw,sw] occur, the reverse only occurs when [w] is part of the diphthong [aw], and only with coronals, e.g. *loud* [lawd], *pout* [pʰawt], *louse* [laws]. (See Chapter 4.) There are also a few rather mysterious gaps. While the following clusters can occur word-initially, their reversals cannot occur word-finally: [sm] as in *smart* [smart] and [gl] as in *glow* [glo].

This general property is reflective of the sonority hierarchy, which maintains that segments are intrinsically orderable such that segments further up the hierarchy cannot occur outside segments lower on the hierarchy within a syllable. Thus [l] is higher on the sonority hierarchy than [g]. This shows itself in the absence of onsets like *[lg . . .] and in the absence of codas like *[. . . gl].

Sonority hierarchy
Segments are intrinsically orderable such that segments higher on the hierarchy cannot occur outside segments lower on the hierarchy within a syllable.

The generalization that reversed onsets can largely all occur as codas is not remotely true for codas. That is, there are many coda sequences that cannot occur as onsets when reversed. For example, while liquid+nasal sequences are satisfactory codas, e.g. *barn* [barn], *alarm* [əlarm], *elm* [ɛlm], the reversed sequences do not constitute acceptable onsets. The NC clusters constitute a second example of this type; while NC clusters are well-formed finally, as in *bump* [bʌ̃mp], *bank* [bæ̃ŋk], *bent* [bɛ̃nt], and *band* [bæ̃nd], *CN never occurs word-initially, except in rare borrowings like *knish* [kʰnɪš], *tmesis* [tʰmɪsɪs], or *knesset* [kʰnɛsət]. (For most speakers, these clusters are not even pronounced as such but are pronounced instead with an epenthetic vowel breaking up the cluster, e.g. [kʰə̃nɪš] and [kʰə̃nɛsət].)

Thus, the version of the sonority hierarchy motivated word-initially is as follows.

> *Word-initial sonority*
> obstruent < approximant

This hierarchy captures the general fact that obstruents can cluster with [l,r,w] as onsets and other clusters are largely excluded. (There are, of course, additional restrictions, and sC clusters are not accommodated.)

Word-finally, a richer hierarchy is evidenced. (As with the word-initial hierarchy, this leaves aside sC clusters. In addition, C+COR clusters are not yet treated.)

> *Word-final sonority*
> obstruent < nasal < l < r

This hierarchy allows for the following sequences.

Word-final pairings allowed

N+O	camp [kʰæmp], tent [tʰɛ̃nt]
l+O	help [hɛlp], pulse [pʰʌls]
r+O	art [ɑrt], fork [fork]
l+N	elm [ɛlm], film [fɪlm]
r+N	barn [bɑrn], form [form]
r+l	gnarl [nɑrl], Carl [kʰɑrl]

This instantiation of the sonority hierarchy for codas also leaves aside coronals. Coronals can occur adjacently, e.g. *mast* [mæst], and can even reverse (violating the Position Generalization), e.g. *blitz* [blɪts].

Let us consider how the sonority hierarchy might be formalized in terms of OT. First, we can assume that there is an intrinsic ranking of consonants in terms of sonority. This ranking presumably includes every possible distinction among consonants and every possible consonant. Thus the sonority hierarchy of any particular language would be a subcase of this universal ranking.

The language-particular sonority hierarchy is more specific in several respects. First, clearly a language-specific sonority hierarchy only ranks the relevant consonants of the language in question. Second, while it may be possible to rank all consonants, a language clearly elects to collapse the full ranking in various ways. For example, there are, no doubt, differences in the sonority of the voiceless stops of English, but these are not made use of in the sonority hierarchy in English. A third sense in which the sonority hierarchy of a language is more specific is evident from the discussion above. English makes use of one sonority hierarchy for onsets and a different one for codas.

There are a number of possibilities for treating the sonority hierarchy in OT. Since OT is a theory of constraint interaction and ranking, we should start from the assumption that the sonority hierarchy is a ranking of constraints.

First, I assume, following the proposals above, that there is a schema *ONSET/X, and that this schema is instantiated for all relevant categories:

Simple onset restrictions
*ONSET/obstruent (*O/o)
*ONSET/nasal (*O/n)
*ONSET/approximant (*O/a)

Moreover, let us assume these are ranked by universal typological considerations such that it is better to have an obstruent onset than an approximant onset, etc. Since all categories of these segment types as simple onsets are tolerated in English, all must be ranked below the relevant faithfulness constraints and M-PARSE.

Typologically motivated ranking of simple onset restrictions

$$\begin{Bmatrix} \text{FAITH} \\ \text{PARSE} \end{Bmatrix} \gg \text{*O/a} \gg \text{*O/n} \gg \text{*O/o}$$

Among the complex onsets, there are six logically possible arrangements of these segment types, but only one is a legal onset in English: obstruent-approximant. Obstruent-nasal clusters are not generally acceptable, though there are a few exceptions, e.g. *knish* [kʰnɪš], *tmesis* [tʰmɪsɪs].

Logically possible onset types

approximant-nasal	(an)	[rn]	
approximant-obstruent	(ao)	[lp]	
nasal-obstruent	(no)	[ŋk]	
nasal-approximant	(na)	[nl]	
obstruent-approximant	(oa)	[pl]	(play [pʰle])
obstruent-nasal	(on)	[kn]	(knish [kʰnɪš]?)

The key observation is that the only complex cluster tolerated is where the difference in relative ranking of simplex *ONSET/X constraints is as extreme as possible: the first member of the cluster must be the best onset possible and the second member must be the worst. In other words, the rise in sonority must be as extreme as possible.

To formalize this, there must be some way to take the ranking of individual *ONSET/X constraints and combine them, preserving their ranking and capturing this slope restriction. Expressed diagrammatically, from the simple constraints and ranking in the first figure below, we must be able to derive the constraints and ranking in the second figure.

Reduced ranking of
simple constraints

*o/a >> *o/n >> *o/o

Ranking and constraints to be derived

$$\left\{\begin{matrix} *o/ao \\ *o/an \\ *o/no \end{matrix}\right\} >> {}^*o/na >> {}^*o/on >> {}^*o/oa$$

Clearly, the sonority reversals (approximant-obstruent, approximant-nasal, and nasal-obstruent) should be the worst cases. The other three cases should rank as given. M-PARSE should be ranked somewhere around *ONSET/ obstruent-nasal. If it is ranked above it, words like *tmesis* and *knish* are grammatical; if it is below it, such words are ungrammatical.

To get this result, we need a notion of syntactic combination of constraints (SCC). There are really two parts to this proposal. First, constraint schemata like *ONSET/X must be able to refer to strings. Second, the ranking of a constraint a/XY must be a function of the ranking of any basic constraint a/X and a/Y.

Syntactic combination of constraints (SCC)
Constraint schemata like *ONSET/X can refer to ordered strings or individual elements.

In its most general form, derived ranking of syntactically combined constraints means that the relative ranking of such constraints must be a projection of the ranking of the relevant simple constraints. There are several different ways this can be implemented for different syntactically combined constraint schemata.

Derived ranking
The ranking of syntactically combined constraints must reflect the relative ranking of the relevant simple constraints.

In the case of syntactically combined *ONSET constraints, their relative ranking is a function of the relative ranking of the leftmost element. If they tie, then their rankings are determined by considering the relative ranking of the rightmost elements. However, rankings determined by the rightmost elements are inverted.

*Derived ranking of *ONSET constraints (preliminary)*
The ranking of two syntactically combined *ONSET constraints, α and β, is determined by considering the relative ranking of the leftmost segment referred to by each. If they tie for that element, then the ranking of α and β is determined by considering the rightmost elements. The ranking of the constraints corresponding to the rightmost element is the inverse of the ranking of the complex constraints containing those elements.

For example, the relative ranking of *ONSET/obstruent-nasal and *ONSET/nasal-approximant is determined by comparing the relative rankings of the simplex constraints corresponding to their first members. Since *ONSET/nasal outranks *ONSET/obstruent, *ONSET/nasal-approximant outranks *ONSET/obstruent-nasal.

On the other hand, the relative ranking of *ONSET/obstruent-nasal and *ONSET/obstruent-approximant is determined by comparing the relative rankings of the simplex constraints corresponding to their second members; since both complex constraints refer to obstruents and thus to *ONSET/obstruent, they tie there and their relative ranking must be determined by considering the relative ranking of the simple constraints corresponding to nasals and approximants. Since *ONSET/approximant outranks *ONSET/nasal, it follows that *ONSET/obstruent-approximant is in turn outranked by *ONSET/obstruent-nasal.

There are, then, two observations to make here. First, the contribution of the two elements is not the same. The ranking of the leftmost element is mirrored by the combined constraints, but the ranking of the rightmost element is inverted by the combined constraints. A second observation is that the relative ranking of the second element is strictly outranked by the relative ranking of the first.

This can be expressed more formally as follows.

> *A more formal statement of derived ranking of *ONSET/X constraints (preliminary)*
>
> *o/xy >> *o/wz iff
> (a) *o/x >> *o/w or
> (b) x = w AND *o/z >> *o/y

Notice that the algorithm suggested actually makes a somewhat different claim from what we said above. This algorithm gives the following relative ranking of the six possible combined *ONSET/X constraints.

> *Predicted ranking of the complex *ONSET constraints*
> *o/ao >> *o/an >> *o/no >> *o/na >> *o/on >> *o/oa

The difference is that the algorithm presented actually ranks the reversal cases. Since these all outrank M-PARSE in English, the prediction is untestable.

> *Ranking of the complex *ONSET constraints with respect to PARSE*
>
> $$\text{*o/ao} >> \text{*o/an} >> \text{*o/no} >> \text{*o/na} >> \left\{ \begin{matrix} \text{M-PARSE} \\ \text{*o/on} \end{matrix} \right\} >> \text{*o/oa}$$

This approach captures the generalizations concerning onset clusters and sonority, and does so in a way that makes use of orthodox OT machinery: constraint ranking and constraint schemata. What is new in this approach is the proposal that the rankings of complex constraints are closely related to the rankings of related simple constraints. We will see confirmation of this idea when we consider the role of sonority with respect to coda sequences.

Notice that I have not yet treated sC clusters. This is because a proper treatment of these clusters requires a treatment of codas as well. Recall that sC occurred both as an onset and as a coda, e.g. *scat* [skæt] vs. *task* [tʰæsk]. Before treating sC, let us treat codas generally.

The sonority hierarchy for codas is repeated below.

Sonority hierarchy for codas
r > l > nasal > obstruent

This is readily treated in terms of the *CODA/X schema. First, I assume there is a series of *CODA/X constraints for each position on the hierarchy. In contrast to the *ONSET hierarchy, these are ranked such that the constraint corresponding to the least sonorous consonant is highest-ranked. This encodes the generalization that codas should be most sonorous.

*Intrinsic ranking of *CODA constraints*
*CODA/obstruent >> *CODA/nasal >> *CODA/l >> *CODA/r

The legal two-consonant codas include every pair of consonants that fall in sonority by this hierarchy. This reflects a general tendency on the part of syllable codas to exhibit the shallowest possible fall in sonority. Recall that onsets in English exhibit a sharp rise.

If all possible pairings are encoded by a *CODA constraint, this means we need to derive at least the following partial ranking.

Ranking of combined coda constraints needed

$$
\begin{pmatrix} *c/on \\ *c/ol \\ *c/or \\ *c/nl \\ *c/nr \\ *c/lr \end{pmatrix} >> \begin{Bmatrix} \text{FAITH} \\ \text{PARSE} \end{Bmatrix} >> \begin{pmatrix} *c/rl \\ *c/rn \\ *c/ro \\ *c/ln \\ *c/lo \\ *c/no \end{pmatrix}
$$

To obtain this ranking via derived ranking, the relative ranking of the syntactically combined constraints cannot be a function of the relative ranking of the corresponding simple constraints for the rightmost member of each pair of segments in the syntactically combined constraints. This results in the following incorrect partial ranking. (Occurring cases are underlined.)

Incorrect ranking for combined coda constraints
based on rank of second member

$$
\begin{Bmatrix} *c/or \\ *c/nr \\ *c/lr \end{Bmatrix} >> \begin{Bmatrix} *c/ol \\ *c/nl \\ *c/\underline{rl} \end{Bmatrix} >> \begin{Bmatrix} *c/on \\ *c/\underline{ln} \\ *c/\underline{rn} \end{Bmatrix} >> \begin{Bmatrix} *c/ro \\ *c/\underline{lo} \\ *c/\underline{no} \end{Bmatrix}
$$

The problem here is that the attested clusters are interspersed with the unattested clusters by this ranking.

Establishing a partial ranking based on the first member fares worse.

*Incorrect ranking for combined coda constraints
based on rank of first member*

$$\left\{\begin{matrix} *c/\underline{rl} \\ *c/\underline{rn} \\ *c/\underline{ro} \end{matrix}\right\} >> \left\{\begin{matrix} *c/lr \\ *c/\underline{ln} \\ *c/\underline{lo} \end{matrix}\right\} >> \left\{\begin{matrix} *c/nr \\ *c/nl \\ *c/\underline{no} \end{matrix}\right\} >> \left\{\begin{matrix} *c/or \\ *c/ol \\ *c/on \end{matrix}\right\}$$

Here again, well-formed coda sequences are interspersed with ill-formed ones. Moreover, the best clusters are at the wrong end of the hierarchy!

It must be the case, then, that the algorithm that maps simple rankings onto complex rankings is not strict. That is, the contribution of the rank of the first member of each pair can in the extreme case outweigh the contribution of the second member. This can be expressed as subtraction over rankings. Let us assume, then, that the rank of the second member is subtracted from the rank of the first member to provide a derived rank.

Numerical rank assignments

$$\underset{\text{*CODA/obstruent}}{1} >> \underset{\text{*CODA/nasal}}{2} >> \underset{\text{*CODA/l}}{3} >> \underset{\text{*CODA/r}}{4}$$

The relative rank of *CODA/obstruent-nasal would then be: 1 (1–2=–1). The relative rank of *CODA/nasal-obstruent would be: 1 (2–1=1). Doing this for all the complex constraints and ordering them correspondingly, we get the following ordering. Attested clusters are again underlined.

Calculation of relative derived rank for CODA/XY

obstruent-r	1–4	–3
obstruent-liquid	1–3	–2
nasal-r	2–4	–2
obstruent-nasal	1–2	–1
nasal-l	2–3	–1
l-r	3–4	–1
nasal-obstruent	2–1	1
l-nasal	3–2	1
r-l	4–3	1
l-obstruent	3–1	2
r-nasal	4–2	2
r-obstruent	4–1	3

The ranking produced is given below. The M-PARSE constraint has been placed at the appropriate point in the hierarchy.

Full ranking of complex coda constraints

$$*c/or \gg \begin{Bmatrix} *c/ol \\ *c/nr \end{Bmatrix} \gg \begin{Bmatrix} *c/on \\ *c/nl \\ *c/lr \end{Bmatrix} \gg \text{M-Parse} \gg \begin{Bmatrix} *c/no \\ *c/ln \\ *c/rl \end{Bmatrix} \gg \begin{Bmatrix} *c/lo \\ *c/rn \end{Bmatrix} \gg *c/ro$$

The algorithm for calculating the derived ranking for codas is given below in prose.

Derived ranking of complex codas
The relative ranking of complex coda constraints is calculated by subtracting the relative ranking of the second member from the relative ranking of the first member and ordering the results.

This can be expressed formally as follows, where $R(x)$ is defined as the rank of some constraint *c/x (or *o/x).

More formal expression of derived ranking of complex codas
*c/xy $\gg$ *c/wz iff $R(x)–R(y) < R(w)–R(z)$

The derived ranking of complex onsets can also be expressed arithmetically, where R_{max} is defined as the total number of constraints in the system.

Arithmetic expression of derived ranking for complex onsets
*o/xy $\gg$ *o/wz iff $[R(x) * R_{max}] – R(y) < [R(w) * R_{max}] – R(z)$

This arithmetic expression produces the same results as the previous algorithmic one. The ranking of simplex *ONSET/X constraints is given below. Since there are three, $R_{max}=3$.

*Values for R() for simplex *ONSET/X constraints*

*o/a		*o/n		*o/o
1	$\gg$	2	$\gg$	3

The results of applying the relevant math to the syntactically derived *ONSET/X constraints are given below.

*Results of arithmetic calculation of derived ranking of *ONSET/X constraints*

*o/ao		*o/an		*o/no		*o/na		*o/on		*o/oa
3–3=0	$\gg$	3–2=1	$\gg$	6–3=3	$\gg$	6–1=5	$\gg$	9–2=7	$\gg$	9–1=8

$(0 < 1 < 3 < 5 < 7 < 8)$

Thus the general theory of derived ranking of syntactically combined constraints is confirmed by the English coda facts, and rankings in both cases can be expressed as simple arithmetic operations over simple rankings.

Notice that this approach is not sufficient to describe the content of coda sequences. Aside from sC onsets, the onset sonority hierarchy predicts that onset clusters should be maximally two consonants in length: this is because any three-consonant sequence (aside from sCC) violates some superordinate constraint. However, the coda sonority hierarchy has four positions, predicting clusters of up to four consonants. While one can get clusters of that length by adding coronal consonants (e.g. *texts* [tʰɛksts]), one cannot get such clusters purely on the basis of the four categories given in the coda sonority hierarchy. For example, based on the following well-formed sequences, we would expect a coda sequence: *[rlmp].

Some well-formed coda sequences
making odd predictions

[rl] as in *gnarl* [nɑrl]
[lm] as in *helm* [hɛlm]
[mp] as in *bump* [bãmp]

This problem was already apparent above where I noted that, except for [rlz] and [rld], the final sequence in a larger coda was always an instance of C+COR.

Aside from C+COR sequences, the maximal coda sequence seems to be two consonants. This suggests that the two-consonant limit is independent of the sonority hierarchy.

Maximal coda
Aside from C+COR sequences, codas can have at most two consonants.

This is of course equally true of onsets, but does not need to be stated, since it already follows from the onset sonority hierarchy. This limit on the size of possible codas will be returned to below when the cooccurrence relations between vowels and codas are considered.

Notice that by virtue of the sonority hierarchy the occurring word-final sequences exhibit positionality restrictions. Thus the existence of r+N codas (e.g. in *barn* [bɑrn]) rules out N+r codas. This is not so in two classes of cases however. First, sC clusters can all be reversed as codas.

Reversible sC codas

[sp]	rasp [ræsp]	lapse [læps]
[st]	mast [mæst]	mats [mæts]
[sk]	mask [mæsk]	lax [læks]

The same is true of several C+COR clusters as well.

Reversible C+COR clusters

[dz]	adz [ædz]	buzzed [bʌzd]
[θt]	toothed [tʰuθt]	eighth [etθ]/[eθ]

This suggests that sC and C+COR clusters are not governed by the sonority hierarchy in the same way that other clusters are. sC clusters are also problematic for the sonority hierarchy of onsets.

Let us now turn to the problem of sC. There are several key generalizations about it that any account must deal with. First, sC occurs at both edges of the syllable: onset and coda, e.g. *scam* [skæm] and *mask* [mæsk]. Second, sC counts as two consonants for purposes of codas; one cannot get three-consonant codas like [nsk] or [nsp] except in very foreign-sounding words like *Minsk* [mĩnsk]. There is no clear evidence about whether sC counts as one or two consonants with respect to onsets. (This is because we have not had to propose any constraints governing the crude number of consonants in the onset.) Third, while [sm] and [sn] occur under the rubric of sC as possible onsets, there is no analog to these among codas; only [sp], [st], and [sk] can occur as sC codas.

What seems to be needed is some special licensing clause which says that sC can occur as a syllable margin. The relevant faithfulness constraints must be outranked by a constraint that says that if two obstruents are aligned next to each other in an onset, the first one must be [s] and the second must be a stop.

sC constraint
If two obstruents are aligned next to each other in an onset, the first one must be [s] and the second must be a stop.

This constraint must outrank M-PARSE.

Ranking of sC and M-PARSE
sC >> M-PARSE

This account assumes that any general restriction against two obstruents in onset position (*o/oo) is either absent or ranked below M-PARSE. Moreover, this account would require some new constraint schema, since it cannot be formalized using the schemata we have already considered.

This is therefore not a desirable treatment. A better treatment is suggested by the fact that the relevant *o/oo constraint would have to be absent (or ranked low in the hierarchy) for the CA schema to work. Why not build an account directly on that ranking of the relevant *o/oo constraint? The effect of this would be to transform the existing *ONSET/obstruent-obstruent constraint into a more articulated set of independent constraints that permit sC onsets.

The existing hierarchy is given below.

> *Ruling out all obstruent-obstruent onsets*
> *ONSET/obstruent-obstruent (*o/oo) >> M-PARSE

The necessary revision of the hierarchy is given below.

> *Ruling out all obstruent-obstruent onsets except sC*
>
> $$\left\{ \begin{array}{l} \text{*o/stop-o} \\ \text{*o/[f]-o} \\ \text{*o/[θ]-o} \\ \text{*o/[š]-o} \\ \text{*o/voiced-o} \end{array} \right\} \gg \text{M-PARSE} \gg \text{*o/[s]-o}$$

This analysis is simpler than the alternative above because only constraint ranking is at stake, not a new type of constraint.

It might be thought that the expression in curly braces is an unfortunate part of this analysis, but this is not the case. The expression in curly braces is a necessary consequence of constraint schemata, and the analysis proposed simply makes use of this independently required device. All the constraints in the curly braces are instantiations of a motivated constraint schema. In addition, all constraints must be ranked.

It is worth noting that the set of X-o clusters above M-PARSE is not a natural class, but the set of X-o clusters below M-PARSE is. This is, in fact, fully expected under a theory of constraint ranking incorporating constraint schemata; there is no requirement that the set of constraints instantiating some schema be ranked in any particular way. (The only exception to this is the notion of derived ranking explored above.)

A similar decomposition of *ONSET/obstruent-nasal will rule out obstruent-nasal onsets where the first consonant is not [s].

> *Licensing sN onsets*
>
> $$\left\{ \begin{array}{l} \text{*o/stop-N} \\ \text{*o/voiced-N} \\ \text{*o/[f]N} \\ \text{*o/[θ]N} \\ \text{*o/[š]N} \end{array} \right\} \gg \text{M-PARSE} \gg \text{*o/[s]N}$$

The same move will of course work for coda sC sequences.

Licensing sC codas

$$\left\{ \begin{array}{l} *c/\text{stop-o} \\ *c/[f]\text{-o} \\ *c/[\theta]\text{-o} \\ *c/[\check{s}]\text{-o} \\ *c/\left[\begin{array}{l}\text{voiced}\\\text{obst}\end{array}\right]\text{-o} \end{array} \right\} \; >> \; \text{M-Parse} \; >> \; *c/[s]\text{-o}$$

Let us consider some examples. A word like *spy* [spay] surfaces fine, because M-PARSE outranks sC.

An acceptable sC cluster

/spay/	M-PARSE	sC
☞ [spay]		
Ø	*!	

A hypothetical form like *[kpay] cannot surface because *ONSET/ stop-obstruent outranks M-PARSE.

An unacceptable stop-obstruent onset

/kpay/	*o/stop-o	M-PARSE
[kpay]	*!	
☞ Ø		*

Obstruent-nasal clusters are also treated correctly. The following two tableaux show how *snow* [sno] and *[bno] are distinguished.

Obstruent-nasal clusters

/sno/	M-PARSE	sN
☞ [sno]		*
Ø	*!	

/bno/	stop-N	M-PARSE
[bno]	*!	
☞ Ø		*

Clearly, all of these exceptions to the derived ranking principle involve [s]. Therefore there should be a general exception clause, or meta-constraint, for constraints involving [s]. There are a variety of ways this might be formalized, but choosing between these would take us far afield. The following is thus provided as a placeholder for a deeper understanding of why [s] specifically is exceptional.

Meta-constraint for [s]
Constraints involving [s] are not subject to derived ranking.

I have provided an account of sonority in terms of the *Onset/X and *Coda/X schemata and making use of syntactically combined constraints and derived ranking. I have treated sC onsets and codas and sN onsets making use of the same schemata and allowing for exceptions to derived ranking.

Let us now take care of C+COR codas. There are two key differences between C+COR cases and the sC cases just treated. First, C+COR allows for an unbounded number of coronal consonants, e.g. *texts* [tʰɛksts]. Second, C+COR clusters are disallowed word-medially (as seen in §3.3). (A third difference will be demonstrated in the following chapter.)

The fact that such clusters are disallowed medially suggests that the proper treatment of these cases is not in terms of *Onset/X or *Coda/X. So far, those constraints have not had to mention material outside the respective onset or coda and this limit on locality would be nice to preserve. Hence, it behooves us to consider a different treatment.

I propose that unparsed coronal obstruents are permitted exceptionally at the right edge of a word. This can be formalized in terms of decomposing Parse in conjunction with an align constraint. First, we need constraints that rule out unparsed noncoronals and unparsed sonorants.

Parse-Poa
A segment with a marked place of articulation must be syllabified.

Parse-Sonorant
A sonorant must be syllabified.

Second, we need a constraint against an unparsed segment before a parsed segment. This can be expressed as a negative alignment constraint (NGA).

Pre-Parse
$$*\begin{bmatrix} \text{unparsed} \\ \text{segment} \end{bmatrix} \| \| \begin{bmatrix} \text{parsed} \\ \text{segment} \end{bmatrix}$$

(Pre-Parse could also be expressed as Anchoring and Contiguity in Correspondence Theory.) These three constraints must outrank M-Parse.

Partial ranking

$$\left.\begin{array}{l}\text{Parse-Poa}\\\text{Parse-Son}\\\text{Pre-Parse}\end{array}\right\} \gg \text{M-Parse}$$

These constraints in this ranking insure that only coronal obstruents can surface unparsed and that this is only possible at the right edge of a word. This is demonstrated in the following tableaux. First, there is a well-formed word like *apt* [æpt]. (Unparsed segments are underlined in these tableaux.)

Tableau for apt

/æpt/	P-Poa	P-Son	P-P	M-P	Parse
☞ æp<u>t</u>					*
æpt	*!		*		*
Ø				*!	

Here is the tableau for hypothetical *[æpk].

Tableau for *[æpk]

/æpk/	P-Poa	P-Son	P-P	M-P	Parse
æp<u>k</u>	*!				*
æpk	*!		*		*
☞ Ø				*	

Here is the tableau for hypothetical *[æpn].

Tableau for *[æpn]

/æpn/	P-Poa	P-Son	P-P	M-P	Parse
æp<u>n</u>		*!			*
æp<u>n</u>	*!		*		*
☞ Ø				*	

Here is the tableau for hypothetical *[ætp].

Tableau for *[ætp]

/ætp/	P-Poa	P-Son	P-P	M-P	Parse
æt<u>p</u>	*!				*
æt<u>p</u>			*!		*
☞ Ø				*	

Finally, I present the tableau for hypothetical *[tpɑ].

*Tableau for *[tpɑ]*

/tpɑ/	P-Poa	P-Son	P-P	M-P	Parse
t̪pɑ			*!		*
tp̪ɑ	*!		*		*
☞ Ø				*	

This account will need to be revised considerably in the next chapter.

In this section, I have presented a syllable-based account of the kinds of consonants that can occur at the edges of words. First, we have seen that substrings of legal clusters are generally legal themselves (the substring generalization). Second, we have seen that clusters exhibit positional restrictions that are in a vaguely mirror-image relationship. I termed this ordering restriction 'the sonority hierarchy'. Third, I have argued that codas are restricted to two consonantal positions (independent of the effects of the sonority hierarchy and the role of coronals).

I have not yet formalized the restriction to two-consonant codas; this occupies much of the following chapter. So as not to leave a gaping hole (albeit temporary), I offer the following constraint as a temporary place-holder to describe this phenomenon.

Temporary constraint against three-consonant codas
*CODA/CCC

The sonority hierarchy has been formalized in terms of *ONSET/X, *CODA/X, syntactic combination of constraints, and derived ranking. The two other restrictions on margins, sC/sN and C+COR, have been formalized in terms of (i) a departure from derived ranking of syntactically combined constraints and (ii) nonparsing of coronal consonants on the right edge of the word.

3.5. LINEAR RESTRICTIONS

A number of generalizations that came up above were not treated there. Most of these are best treated in terms of alignment, rather than in terms of syllable structure generally or *ONSET/X or *CODA/X specifically.

The first generalization to be treated here is the absence of affricates in complex onsets.

Affricate proscription
Affricates do not appear in complex onsets.

Affricates can occur in complex codas of various sorts. (Affricates can occur first only in derived C+COR clusters.)

Affricates in complex codas

l+Aff	belch [bɛlč], bilge [bɪlǰ]
r+Aff	march [marč], barge [barǰ]
N+Aff	bench [bɛ̃nč], binge [bĩnǰ]
Aff+COR	reached [ričt], budged [bʌǰd]

Therefore the general restriction against affricates in complex onsets should not be treated in terms of a linear constraint. This can be captured with a generalization of the *ONSET/X schema as follows: *ONSET/[affricate]α. This constraint excludes an onset containing an affricate and any other segment. There is no need to posit a constraint against affricates following other segments, since the only possibility there is [sč] and this has already been ruled out above.

The second generalization to be treated is the fact that [s] cannot precede [r].

[s]-[š] complementarity
[s] cannot precede an [r]; [š] can only precede an [r].

The proscription against [sr] has nothing to do with syllable structure. This sequence only shows up in heteromorphemic clusters.

Examples of heteromorphemic [sr]

crossroad [kʰrasrod]	disregard [dɪsrəgard]
disrepair [dɪsrəpʰer]	disreputable [dɪsrɛpyurəbl̩]
disrepute [dɪsrəpʰyut]	disrobe [dɪsrob]
misrepresent [mɪsrɛprizẽnt]	misrule [mɪsrul]
viceregal [vaysrigl̩]	viceroy [vaysrɔy]

One possible treatment of this might be that [s] does cluster with [r] in inputs, but is paired with the output [šr]. Support for this story comes from dialects, such as my own, where /tr/ and /dr/ in onset position are pronounced [čr] and [ǰr] respectively, e.g. *draw* [ǰrɔ] and *truck* [črʌk], and even in sequences which are not necessarily onsets, e.g. *metro* [mɛčro] or *android* [æ̃nǰrɔyd]. In these dialects, then, there is a general restriction against alveolars with [r].

The simplest way to treat this would be to posit an alignment constraint against [sr] (or [{d,t,s}r] for the one dialect).

*Constraint against *[sr]*
*[sr]

This constraint would be outranked by various constraints that would allow only the realization [šr] to escape the constraint *[sr]. These higher-ranked constraints are given below.

*Constraints outranking *[sr]*
FAITH([r])
FAITH(SEGMENTS)
FAITH(MOA)

The following tableau shows how this works for *shrink* if the input is /srĩŋk/.

Tableau for shrink

/srĩŋk/	F([r])	F(SEG)	F(MOA)	*[sr]
☞ šrĩŋk				
sĩŋk	*!			
rĩŋk		*!		
khrĩŋk			*!	
srĩŋk				*!

Another possible output might be something like [zrĩŋk]. This could be ruled out by ranking FAITH(VOICING) above *[sr], but presumably the general proscription against clusters involving voiced fricatives would also rule this out. Notice that this same proposal rules out hypothetical (and ill-formed) *[mʌsrum] (cf. *mushroom* [mʌšrum]).

More problematic is how to exclude [frĩŋk] as the output for /srĩŋk/. The problem is that by ranking *[sr] above FAITH(POA), we allow any place of articulation change to resolve *[sr]. In fact, the general coronality of the segment is preserved, while shifting from an alveolar (coronal) place to a palatoalveolar (coronal) place. This result can be achieved by decomposing FAITH(POA) and positing a separate FAITH(CORONAL) which is ranked above *[sr]. The following tableau shows how these different rankings avoid *[frĩŋk] as the output for /srĩŋk/.

Faith(Coronal) exemplified

/srĩŋk/	F(COR)	*[sr]	F(POA)
☞ šrĩŋk			*
frĩŋk	*!		
srĩŋk		*!	

The third phenomenon to be treated is the proscription against coronal stops before laterals in onsets.

Coronal dissimilation
Coronal stops do not cluster with the lateral [l] in onsets.

We saw examples of tautomorphemic intervocalic sequences of this sort above, e.g. *atlas* [ætləs], *bedlam* [bɛdlɔ̃m]. This is easily formalized with the *ONSET/X schema.

Lateral constraint

$$*\text{ONSET}/\begin{bmatrix} \text{COR} \\ \text{stop} \end{bmatrix}[l]$$

There were several related generalizations about NC clusters. First, all unsuffixed NC codas are composed of a nasal followed by a homorganic voiceless obstruent or a coronal stop.

Unsuffixed NC codas
Unsuffixed NC codas are all composed of a nasal followed by a homorganic voiceless obstruent or [d,z].

That coronal stops are exceptional here can surely be traced to the fact that they are the only consonants that can be left unsyllabified at the right edge of a word. Confirmation of this comes from the observation that nonhomorganic NC clusters with coronals only occur word-finally. Therefore the proper treatment of these facts is in terms of a *CODA/X constraint against nonhomorganic codas.

Constraint against nonhomorganic NC codas

$$*\text{CODA}/\begin{bmatrix} \text{nasal} \\ \alpha\text{POA} \end{bmatrix}[-\alpha\text{POA}]$$

Another generalization about NC clusters was that voiced obstruents could not occur after the nasal, except for [d,z].

Distribution of voiced obstruents in NC clusters
Voiced obstruents cannot occur in NC clusters except for [d,z]. These
can occur in homorganic clusters when unsuffixed and after any nasal
when suffixed.

This would also seem to be treatable once we recognize that only coronal
obstruents can be unparsed at the right edges of words. What is required is
a constraint against NC sequences as codas where the second consonant is
voiced.

> *Constraint against NC codas with voiced obstruents*
> *CODA/[nasal][voiced]

3.6. SUMMARY

In the preceding sections I have presented an analysis of the content of English clusters. This analysis makes use of the following machinery. First, all
constraints are formalized in terms of Generalized Alignment and in terms
of the *ONSET/X and *CODA/X schemata. Second, we made extensive use
of the sonority hierarchy as formalized via syntactic combination of constraints and derived ranking.

Some facts, however, have not been treated. First, cooccurrence
restrictions involving vowels have been left out completely. Second, the
restriction on the number of coda segments has also not been treated. Both
of these are handled in Chapter 4.

In addition, no account has been offered of positional variation of
syllables. That is, the account presented here assumes that syllables are the
same all across a word. This simplifying assumption is actually false, and
will be treated in Chapter 6.

3.7. FURTHER READING

For works dealing with the syllable in English, readers should consult
Daniel Kahn's influential 1976 dissertation or the subsequent extremely
important but never published paper by Morris Halle and Jean-Roger
Vergnaud (1977). Selkirk (1982) and Clements and Keyser (1983) offer
very nice discussions of the structure of the syllable in English. There are
also dissertations by Toni Borowsky (1986) and Greg Lamontagne (1993),
and various works by myself (Hammond 1990; 1997*a*; 1997*b*; to appear).

The sonority hierarchy has been treated extensively in syllable theory.
Steriade (1982) is a nice rule-based treatment; Prince and Smolensky
(1993) and Ohala (1996) offer OT-style treatments.

4

English Syllables: Peaks and Moras

In this chapter, the facts of English syllabification with respect to vowels are surveyed and treated. We will see that there are restrictions on the distribution of vowels with respect to consonants and that many of these are best treated in terms of moras (introduced in Chapter 2).

First, I review the inventory of vowels and consider the dependencies that hold between the vowel and adjacent consonants at the edges of words. The restrictions that hold at word edge are then compared with the restrictions that hold medially. Restrictions that hold medially should, as in the previous chapter, be treated in terms of alignment constraints. Once such linear constraints have been isolated and factored out, we will see that there is a basic distinction between tense and lax vowels, and that the best way to treat this distinction is in terms of mora count. Specifically, lax vowels have one mora and tense vowels have two.

I will also survey the diphthongs of English and show that their behavior requires an amplification of this basic system. Specifically, there are three classes of diphthong. Some behave like lax vowels and are best treated as monomoraic. Some diphthongs behave like tense vowels and are best treated as bimoraic. There is yet a third class of diphthongs, however, and they are best treated as trimoraic.

Finally, we will see that it is also necessary to distinguish among coda consonants in terms of the number of moras they are assigned. Some codas always contribute a mora; some never contribute a mora; some only sometimes contribute a mora; while others contribute two moras.

4.1. VOWELS AND DIPHTHONGS

The vowels of English are repeated below. The first chart gives the monophthongs while the second gives the diphthongs.

Vowels of English

[i]	heed	[u]	who'd
[ɪ]	hid	[ʊ]	hood
[e]	heyed	[o]	hoed
[ɛ]	head	[ʌ]	hud
[æ]	had	[ɔ]	hawed
		[ɑ]	hod

Diphthongs of English

[ay]	bye
[aw]	bow
[ɔy]	boy
[yu]	pew

(Syllabic consonants are treated in §4.4.)

These vowels are not distributed freely at all. The crudest measure of this is a numerical comparison. The following gives the number for each of these (rows) in a database of 20,000 words according to the number of syllables in each word (columns).

Number of each vowel in words of different lengths

Vowel	1	2	3	4
[i]	295	1100	1041	1013
[ɪ]	438	1798	1610	1372
[e]	322	700	626	694
[ɛ]	306	905	977	775
[æ]	411	1212	1075	705
[u]	183	352	240	196
[ʊ]	44	124	100	47
[o]	314	802	574	330
[ʌ]	299	607	373	148
[ɔ]	220	451	315	140
[ɑ]	273	853	676	577
[ay]	254	603	522	287
[aw]	108	237	71	12
[ɔy]	36	87	35	8
[yu]	34	102	127	123

While this chart shows that there are sharp differences in the number of occurrences of each vowel, it gives little insight into the factors governing the distribution of each vowel.

4.2. COOCCURRENCE RESTRICTIONS

The following sections treat the distribution of these different vowels in terms of what consonants the different vowels can occur next to. Once any restrictions on adjacent consonants have been identified, the goal will be to determine whether those restrictions are based on syllable structure or simple linear adjacency. To this end, I will first consider possible restrictions on word-initial consonants. Second, I turn to restrictions on vowels in terms of possible word-final consonants. Third, to establish whether the word-edge restrictions are linear or syllabic, we consider vowel-consonant and consonant-vowel restrictions in VCV contexts.

4.2.1. Restrictions on CV strings in word-initial position

In this section, we consider whether there are any cooccurrence restrictions involving a word-initial consonant and a following vowel. We have already identified one factor above in the distribution of the diphthong [yu]: we saw that this vowel generally does not occur after coronal consonants. The other stressed vowels are not similarly restricted. The following chart shows all the vowels and diphthongs above occur after all the voiceless stops, and [yu] is blocked only after a coronal.

Distribution of vowels relative to initial coronals

Vowel	/p/	/t/	/k/
[i]	peel [pʰil]	teal [tʰil]	keel [kʰil]
[ɪ]	pick [pʰɪk]	tick [tʰɪk]	kick [kʰɪk]
[e]	pale [pʰel]	tail [tʰel]	kale [kʰel]
[ɛ]	pen [pʰɛ̃n]	ten [tʰɛ̃n]	Ken [kʰɛ̃n]
[æ]	pan [pʰæ̃n]	tan [tʰæ̃n]	can [kʰæ̃n]
[u]	pool [pʰul]	tool [tʰul]	cool [kʰul]
[ʊ]	put [pʰʊt]	took [tʰʊk]	cook [kʰʊk]
[o]	pore [pʰor]	tore [tʰor]	core [kʰor]
[ʌ]	puff [pʰʌf]	tough [tʰʌf]	cuff [kʰʌf]
[ɔ]	Paul [pʰɔl]	tall [tʰɔl]	call [kʰɔl]
[ɑ]	pot [pʰɑt]	tot [tʰɑt]	cot [kʰɑt]
[ay]	pine [pʰãyn]	tine [tʰãyn]	kine [kʰãyn]

Vowel	/p/	/t/	/k/
[aw]	pout [pʰawt]	tout [tʰawt]	cow [kʰaw]
[ɔy]	poise [pʰɔyz]	toys [tʰɔyz]	coin [kʰɔ̃yn]
[yu]	puke [pʰyuk]	–	cute [kʰyut]

There are, however, no other restrictions on the distribution of vowels with respect to word onsets. Except for [yu] and coronals, any vowel can cooccur with any word onset.

Coronal-[yu] generalization
[yu] cannot occur with a preceding coronal.

This will be formalized when we have determined whether it is linear or syllabic in origin.

4.2.2. Restrictions on VC strings in word-final position

Let us now consider the restrictions on vowels in terms of word-final consonants. (These restrictions can be fully exemplified with rather short words, as will be seen below.) There are a number of restrictions of this sort. We already identified a simple one in Chapter 1, where it was pointed out that only tense vowels can occur word-finally.

Word-final tense vowels

[mi]	me	[mu]	moo
[me]	may	[mo]	Moe
		[mɔ]	maw
		[mɑ]	ma

Diphthongs can also occur word-finally.

Word-final diphthongs

[kʰɔy]	coy
[kʰyu]	queue
[kʰaw]	cow
[skay]	sky

The generalization is given below.

Word-final lax vowels
Lax vowels cannot occur word-finally.

When we consider word-final closed syllables, the vowels and consonants partition themselves further. It turns out that coronals are again an outlying class of segments. The following chart gives examples of all vowels before [p,t,k].

Distribution of vowels relative to final voiceless stops

Vowel	/p/	/t/	/k/
[i]	leap [lip]	elite [əlit]	leek [lik]
[ɪ]	lip [lɪp]	lit [lɪt]	lick [lɪk]
[e]	rape [rep]	rate [ret]	rake [rek]
[ɛ]	pep [pʰɛp]	pet [pʰɛt]	peck [pʰɛk]
[æ]	rap [ræp]	rat [ræt]	rack [ræk]
[u]	coop [kʰup]	coot [kʰut]	kook [kʰuk]
[ʊ]	–	put [pʰʊt]	hook [hʊk]
[o]	soap [sop]	float [flot]	soak [sok]
[ʌ]	cup [kʰʌp]	cut [kʰʌt]	luck [lʌk]
[ɔ]	–	ought [ɔt]	chalk [čʰɔk]
[ɑ]	top [tʰɑp]	tot [tʰɑt]	lock [lɑk]
[ay]	ripe [rayp]	right [rayt]	like [layk]
[aw]	–	bout [bawt]	–
[ɔy]	–	adroit [ədrɔyt]	–
[yu]	–	butte [byut]	puke [pʰyuk]

There are several generalizations of note above. First, certain round vowels are limited before the labial [p], e.g. [ʊ,ɔ,yu]. (The latter two do not occur before [p], but do occur before the voiced bilabial stop [b] in *cube* [kʰyub] and *lob* [lɔb].) A second restriction is that the diphthongs [aw,ɔy] do not occur before the noncoronals. These specific limits will be treated below when the full array of such distinctions is clear.

In addition, notice that lax vowels can occur in monosyllabic words as long as they are closed by a consonant. Notice also that word onsets contribute nothing to the well-formedness of words ending in lax vowels. The following hypothetical words are all ruled out regardless of the number of preceding (word-initial) consonants: *[æ], *[bæ], *[gwæ], *[blæ], *[spræ].

Continuing with the specific restrictions on vowel-consonant sequences, the following chart shows how vowels can cooccur with a following voiced stop.

Distribution of vowels relative to final voiced stops

Vowel	/b/	/d/	/g/
[i]	grebe [grib]	lead [lid]	league [lig]
[ɪ]	bib [bɪb]	bid [bɪd]	big [bɪg]
[e]	babe [beb]	fade [fed]	plague [pʰleg]
[ɛ]	ebb [ɛb]	bed [bɛd]	beg [bɛg]
[æ]	tab [tʰæb]	tad [tʰæd]	tag [tʰæg]
[u]	tube [tʰub]	food [fud]	–
[ʊ]	–	hood [hʊd]	–
[o]	robe [rob]	road [rod]	rogue [rog]
[ʌ]	rub [rʌb]	bud [bʌd]	bug [bʌg]
[ɔ]	daub [dɔb]	laud [lɔd]	log [lɔg]
[ɑ]	cob [kʰɑb]	cod [kʰɑd]	cog [kʰɑg]
[ay]	bribe [brayb]	ride [rayd]	–
[aw]	–	loud [lawd]	–
[ɔy]	–	avoid [əvɔyd]	–
[yu]	cube [kʰyub]	feud [fyud]	fugue [fyug]

Similar generalizations are of note here. First, [ʊ] is limited before the labial [b] and velar [g]. A second restriction is that the diphthongs [aw,ɔy] do not occur before the noncoronals and [ay] does not occur before [g].

The general pattern seems to be that the diphthongs [aw,ɔy] are limited before noncoronals and [g] and [ʊ] are in general limited. The general limits on [ʊ] can be seen from the statistical observations above, and the limits on [g] can be seen from its similarly limited distribution in onsets (discussed in the previous chapter).

Let us continue with the fricatives to see if this pattern recurs.

Distribution of vowels relative to final voiceless fricatives

Vowel	/f/	/θ/	/s/	/š/
[i]	leaf [lif]	wreath [riθ]	lease [lis]	leash [liš]
[ɪ]	miff [mɪf]	myth [mɪθ]	miss [mɪs]	fish [fɪš]
[e]	safe [sef]	faith [feθ]	mace [mes]	–
[ɛ]	deaf [dɛf]	death [dɛθ]	mess [mɛs]	fresh [frɛš]

Vowel	/f/	/θ/	/s/	/š/
[æ]	laugh [læf]	lath [læθ]	lass [læs]	lash [læš]
[u]	roof [ruf]	couth [kʰuθ]	moose [mus]	douche [duš]
[ʊ]	hoof [hʊf]	–	puss [pʰʊs]	push [pʰʊš]
[o]	loaf [lof]	loath [loθ]	dose [dos]	–
[ʌ]	tough [tʰʌf]	–	plus [pʰlʌs]	plush [pʰlʌš]
[ɔ]	cough [kʰɔf]	moth [mɔθ]	moss [mɔs]	wash [wɔš]
[ɑ]	doff [dɑf]	swath [swɑθ]	dross [drɑs]	quash [kʰwɑš]
[ay]	rife [rayf]	blithe [blayθ]	rice [rays]	–
[aw]	–	mouth [mawθ]	mouse [maws]	–
[ɔy]	coif [kʰɔyf]	–	choice [čʰɔys]	–
[yu]	–	–	use [yus]	–

Here, the diphthong [aw] again fails to occur before the noncoronal [f] and palatoalveolar [š]. Surprisingly, [ɔy] occurs before the labiodental in *coif*, but this is the only example of this combination and is clearly borrowed from French *coiffe*. (Note that the pronunciation in French would be quite different however: [kwɑf].) The other restrictions are less sensical and may not reflect any particular combinatorial restriction. The diphthong [yu] is rather limited and the fricatives [θ,š] are restricted. The same pattern does seem to continue with the voiceless fricatives.

The following chart shows the distribution of vowels before voiced fricatives.

Distribution of vowels relative to final voiced fricatives

Vowel	/v/	/ð/	/z/	/ž/
[i]	leave [liv]	wreathe [rið]	freeze [friz]	liege [liž]
[ɪ]	live [lɪv]	–	fizz [fɪz]	–
[e]	rave [rev]	bathe [beð]	faze [fez]	beige [bež]
[ɛ]	rev [rɛv]	–	fez [fɛz]	–
[æ]	calve [kʰæv]	–	has [hæz]	–
[u]	prove [pʰruv]	soothe [suð]	lose [luz]	rouge [ruž]
[ʊ]	–	–	–	–
[o]	rove [rov]	loathe [loð]	rose [roz]	loge [lož]
[ʌ]	love [lʌv]	–	buzz [bʌz]	–
[ɔ]	–	–	cause [kʰɔz]	–
[ɑ]	suave [swɑv]	swathe [swɑð]	–	garage [gərɑž]
[ay]	live [layv]	lithe [layð]	realize [riḷayz]	–
[aw]	–	mouthe [mawð]	rouse [rawz]	–
[ɔy]	–	–	poise [pʰɔyz]	–
[yu]	–	–	fuse [fyuz]	–

The voiced fricatives are extremely circumscribed in their postvocalic distribution. As with their voiceless counterparts, [ð,ž] are the most restricted and diphthongs [ɔy,aw] are generally limited.

The pattern with [ž] is particularly interesting, as it seems to occur after roughly half the monophthongs and after no diphthongs; the tense–lax distinction is neutralized before it. This can be contrasted with [ð]. The tense–lax distinction is also neutralized before this consonant, but unlike the case with [ž], [ɔy,aw] can occur here.

A similar sort of restriction is evident with the nasals.

Distribution of vowels relative to final nasals

Vowel	/m/	/n/	/ŋ/
[i]	team [tʰĩm]	lean [lĩn]	–
[ɪ]	limb [lĩm]	tin [tʰĩn]	sing [sĩŋ]
[e]	lame [lẽm]	rain [rẽn]	–
[ɛ]	hem [hẽm]	hen [hẽn]	–
[æ]	ham [hæ̃m]	ban [bæ̃n]	fang [fæ̃ŋ]
[u]	tomb [tʰũm]	boon [būn]	–
[ʊ]	–	–	–
[o]	tome [tʰõm]	bone [bõn]	–
[ʌ]	hum [hʌ̃m]	bun [bʌ̃n]	tongue [tʰʌ̃ŋ]
[ɔ]	–	lawn [lɔ̃n]	long [lɔ̃ŋ]
[ɑ]	psalm [sɑ̃m]	argon [ɑrgɑ̃n]	–
[ay]	time [tʰãym]	rine [rãyn]	–
[aw]	–	town [tʰãwn]	–
[ɔy]	–	coin [kʰɔ̃yn]	–
[yu]	fume [fyũm]	impugn [ĩmpyũn]	–

First, [ʊ] is precluded with any of the nasals. Second, as expected, the diphthongs [ɔy,aw] are precluded with the noncoronal nasals. Third, [ŋ] is extremely limited in terms of the vowels it can follow; like [ž], the tense–lax distinction is neutralized before it and diphthongs are precluded. Unlike [ž], the vowels that surface before it show up as lax.

Finally, the following chart shows the distribution of coda liquids and affricates.

Distribution of vowels relative to final liquids and affricates

Vowel	/l/	/r/	/č/	/ǰ/
[i]	feel [fil]	fear [fɪr]	each [ič]	–
[ɪ]	fill [fɪl]	–	itch [ɪč]	bridge [brɪǰ]
[e]	fail [fel]	fair [fer]	"h" [eč]	rage [reǰ]
[ɛ]	fell [fɛl]	–	ketch [kʰɛč]	edge [ɛǰ]
[æ]	pal [pʰæl]	–	catch [kʰæč]	badge [bæǰ]

Vowel	/l/	/r/	/č/	/ǰ/
[u]	pool [pʰul]	poor [pʰur]	mooch [muč]	stooge [stuǰ]
[ʊ]	pull [pʰʊl]	–	–	–
[o]	pole [pʰol]	pore [pʰor]	roach [roč]	–
[ʌ]	hull [hʌl]	–	much [mʌč]	budge [bʌǰ]
[ɔ]	haul [hɔl]	–	watch [wɔč]	–
[ɑ]	hall [hɑl]	par [pʰɑr]	notch [nɑč]	lodge [lɑǰ]
[ay]	rile [rayl]	pyre [pʰayr]	–	oblige [əblayǰ]
[aw]	cowl [kʰawl]	hour [awr]	couch [kʰawč]	gouge [gawǰ]
[ɔy]	boil [bɔyl]	–	–	–
[yu]	fuel [fyul]	pure [pʰyur]	–	–

The lateral [l] is extremely freely distributed, while the tense–lax distinction is again eliminated before [r].

The general pattern that emerges with word-final singleton consonants is complex, but there are several clear recurring regularities. First, certain consonants do not tolerate a preceding tense–lax distinction: [ž,r,ŋ,ð].

A second generalization is that coronals and noncoronals are partially partitioned with respect to the diphthongs. Basically, except for [ay,yu], the diphthongs cannot occur before noncoronals.

The third overarching generalization is that the voiced obstruents are more restricted than the voiceless obstruents. This is presumably a consequence of general statistical limits on the number of voiced obstruents. This is confirmed by the following chart, which shows the raw number of voiced and voiceless stops, fricatives, and affricates from a sample of 20,000 words.

Numerical comparison of voiced and voiceless obstruents

Voiceless	No.	Voiced	No.	Ratio
[p]	338	[b]	126	2.68
[t]	2774	[d]	1122	2.47
[k]	1071	[g]	123	8.7
[f]	159	[v]	322	.49
[s]	1514	[z]	507	2.98
[θ]	113	[ð]	19	5.94
[š]	185	[ž]	22	8.4
[č]	157	[ǰ]	239	.65

Except for [f]/[v] and [č]/[ǰ], voiceless obstruents greatly outnumber their voiced counterparts.

Let us now consider the distribution of vowels with respect to more complex two-consonant clusters. There are basically five types to consider. First, there are clusters composed of [s] followed by a voiceless obstruent. Second and third, there are clusters composed of the liquids [l] or [r] followed by another consonant. The broadest array of preceding vowels occurs with the lateral, e.g. [lp,lt,lk]; very few vowels cooccur with [r] in complex clusters, e.g. [rp,rt,rk]. The fourth case to consider is NC cases: [mp,nt,ŋk]. The last case is obstruent-coronal clusters: [ps,ts,ks]. Let us consider sC clusters first.

Distribution of vowels relative to final sC clusters

Vowel	/sp/	/st/	/sk/
[i]	–	least [list]	–
[ɪ]	lisp [lɪsp]	list [lɪst]	risk [rɪsk]
[e]	–	baste [best]	–
[ɛ]	–	best [bɛst]	desk [dɛsk]
[æ]	hasp [hæsp]	last [læst]	mask [mæsk]
[u]	–	boost [bust]	–
[ʊ]	–	–	–
[o]	–	boast [bost]	–
[ʌ]	cusp [kʰʌsp]	bust [bʌst]	musk [mʌsk]
[ɔ]	–	lost [lɔst]	–
[ɑ]	wasp [wɑsp]	–	mosque [mɑsk]
[ay]	–	heist [hayst]	–
[aw]	–	joust [ǰawst]	–
[ɔy]	–	foist [fɔyst]	–
[yu]	–	–	–

The tense–lax distinction is neutralized in favor of lax vowels before [sp] and [sk] clusters, showing the coronal–noncoronal asymmetry. The only tense vowel that occurs in this position is [ɑ]. The vowels [yu,ʊ] are curiously missing before [st].

The following chart shows final clusters involving [l].

Distribution of vowels relative to final lC clusters

Vowel	/lp/	/lt/	/lk/
[i]	–	–	–
[ɪ]	–	silt [sɪlt]	milk [mɪlk]
[e]	–	–	–
[ɛ]	help [hɛlp]	felt [fɛlt]	elk [ɛlk]
[æ]	scalp [skælp]	–	talc [tʰælk]
[u]	–	–	–
[ʊ]	–	–	–
[o]	–	bolt [bolt]	–
[ʌ]	pulp [pʰʌlp]	adult [ədʌlt]	bulk [bʌlk]
[ɔ]	–	salt [sɔlt]	–
[ɑ]	–	malt [mɑlt]	–
[ay]	–	–	–
[aw]	–	–	–
[ɔy]	–	–	–
[yu]	–	–	–

The lC clusters are more restricted, but show the same general pattern, with [lp,lk] precluding the tense–lax contrast, but [lt] allowing it (to a limited degree).

The rC clusters exhibit a rather different pattern from what might be expected. The chart is given below for completeness at this point, but [r] will be treated in §4.4.

Distribution of vowels relative to final rC clusters

Vowel	/rp/	/rt/	/rk/
[i]	–	–	–
[ɪ]	–	–	–
[e]	–	–	–
[ɛ]	–	–	–
[æ]	–	–	–
[u]	–	–	–

Vowel	/rp/	/rt/	/rk/
[ʊ]	–	–	–
[o]	warp [wɔrp]	port [pʰɔrt]	pork [pʰɔrk]
[ʌ]	–	–	–
[ɔ]	–	–	–
[ɑ]	harp [hɑrp]	heart [hɑrt]	hark [hɑrk]
[ay]	–	–	–
[aw]	–	–	–
[ɔy]	–	–	–
[yu]	–	–	–

The following chart shows the distribution of NC clusters.

Distribution of vowels relative to final NC clusters

Vowel	/mp/	/nt/	/ŋk/
[i]	–	–	–
[ɪ]	limp [lĩmp]	lint [lĩnt]	link [lĩŋk]
[e]	–	feint [fẽnt]	–
[ɛ]	hemp [hẽmp]	tent [tʰẽnt]	–
[æ]	camp [kʰæ̃mp]	pant [pʰæ̃nt]	sank [sæ̃ŋk]
[u]	–	–	–
[ʊ]	–	–	–
[o]	–	–	–
[ʌ]	pump [pʰʌ̃mp]	punt [pʰʌ̃nt]	hunk [hʌ̃ŋk]
[ɔ]	stomp [stɔ̃mp]	taunt [tʰɔ̃nt]	honk [hɔ̃ŋk]
[ɑ]	pomp [pʰɑ̃mp]	font [fɑ̃nt]	conk [kʰɑ̃ŋk]
[ay]	–	pint [pʰãynt]	–
[aw]	–	fount [fãwnt]	–
[ɔy]	–	point [pʰɔ̃ynt]	–
[yu]	–	–	–

The NC clusters are not quite as expected. The tense–lax contrast is eliminated before [mp], but preserved before [nt] as expected. The problem is that we would expect [ŋk] to be impossible. We already saw that word-final [ŋ] and word-final [k] exhibit quite limited distribution. Together, they should exclude virtually any preceding vowel.

The following chart shows the distribution of vowels before Cs clusters, which are surprisingly sparse.

Distribution of vowels relative to final Cs clusters

Vowel	/ps/	/ts/	/ks/
[i]	–	–	–
[ɪ]	ellipse [əlɪps]	blitz [blɪts]	fix [fɪks]
[e]	–	–	–
[ɛ]	biceps [baysɛps]	castanets [kʰastənɛts]	hex [hɛks]
[æ]	lapse [læps]	–	tax [tʰæks]
[u]	–	–	–
[ʊ]	–	kibbutz [kʰɪbʊts]	–
[o]	–	–	hoax [hoks]
[ʌ]	–	–	crux [kʰrʌks]
[ɔ]	–	–	–
[ɑ]	copse [kʰɑps]	–	ox [ɑks]
[ay]	–	–	–
[aw]	–	–	–
[ɔy]	–	–	–
[yu]	–	–	–

Except for *hoax* [hoks], tense vowels cannot occur before tautomorphemic [ps,ks]. It is perhaps meaningful that [ɔ], which can generally occur in lax-only contexts, seems to be precluded before [ks] consonants. The other oddity about C+COR clusters is that [ts] seems to be confined to borrowings.

Because the facts here are so murky, additional [pt] and [kt] clusters are considered below.

Distribution of vowels relative to final Ct clusters

Vowel	/pt/	IMPOSSIBLE	/kt/
[i]	–	*	–
[ɪ]	script [skrɪpt]	*	edict [irɪkt]
[e]	–	*	–
[ɛ]	adept [ədɛpt]	*	correct [kʰərɛkt]
[æ]	rapt [ræpt]	*	act [ækt]
[u]	–	*	–
[ʊ]	–	*	–
[o]	–	*	–
[ʌ]	abrupt [əbrʌpt]	*	duct [dʌkt]
[ɔ]	–	*	–
[ɑ]	opt [ɑpt]	*	concoct [kʰŋkʰɑkt]

Vowel	/pt/	IMPOSSIBLE	/kt/
[ay]	–	*	–
[aw]	–	*	–
[ɔy]	–	*	–
[yu]	–	*	–

The same pattern is confirmed. These clusters are curiously limited. We might have expected them to exhibit a fairly broad distribution because of the generally freer distribution of coronals, but such is not the case.

The general pattern that emerges from the restrictions on vowels with respect to word-final consonants is as follows. With respect to consonants there appear to be three classes. First, there are the coronals, which freely allow virtually any preceding vowel. Second, there is the set [ž,ŋ,ð,r], which are quite restricted. Finally, all other consonants fall somewhere in between. The number of consonants that follow the vowel also makes a difference. In general, the more consonants that follow, the fewer vowels are permitted. The vowels are also ranked. The diphthongs [ɔy,aw] are the most restrictive, followed by tense vowels and bimoraic diphthongs, and then lax vowels. (The lax vowel [ʊ] is the most limited, but this may be less a function of syllabic or linear restrictions than of the relative rarity of this vowel.)

4.2.3. VCV restrictions

Let us now consider the distribution of vowels with respect to medial consonants and clusters. This will allow us to separate out sequential restrictions from syllabic restrictions. There are two crucial cases to consider. First, any restriction on vowels with respect to word-initial consonants could be either syllabic or linear. If a restriction on CV sequences observed word-initially is also observed in VCV sequences, this would show that the restriction is linear. The restriction would have to be linear because VCV sequences can be syllabified in two different ways: the medial consonant can be an onset to the following syllable or a coda to the preceding syllable. (This is, of course, not the case in a language which disallows medial codas.)

The same logic applies to restrictions on VC sequences. If a restriction on VC sequences proposed on the basis of word-final sequences is also observed in VCV sequences, then this restriction must be linear in nature. Again, this is because the syllabification of VCV sequences is ambiguous.

The only word-initial CV restriction noted above was that the diphthong [yu] could not cooccur with coronals. This generalization also holds with medial obstruent coronals, but does not hold with medial sonorant coronals.

[yu] with medial coronals

t	–
d	–
s	–
z	–
θ	–
ð	–
š	–
ž	–
n	menu [mẽnyu]
l	value [vǽlyu]
r	erudite [ɛryudayt]/[ɛrədayt]

This would seem to imply that the restriction against coronal obstruents followed by [yu] is linear, but that the restriction against coronal sonorants followed by [yu] is syllabic. There is some evidence that [θ] can also occur with [yu] from the name *Matthew* [mæθyu]. Again, I leave aside the treatment of [yu] for now; it is taken up again in Chapter 6.

Let us now turn to VC restrictions. First consider the case of vowels before vowels.

Distribution of vowels relative to a following vowel

Vowel	V
[i]	neon [niã̃n]
[ɪ]	–
[e]	chaos [kʰeɑs]
[ɛ]	–
[æ]	–
[u]	duo [duo]
[ʊ]	–
[o]	boa [boə]
[ʌ]	–
[ɔ]	–
[ɑ]	–
[ay]	diet [dayət]
[aw]	prowess [pʰrawes]
[ɔy]	voyage [vɔyəǰ]
[yu]	minuet [mĩnyuɛt]

Here, we see only tense vowels and diphthongs. However, unlike word-final position, we see only nonlow tense vowels. There are no tautomorphemic examples of prevocalic [ɔ,ɑ].

NoLo: No prevocalic low vowels
Low vowels cannot occur prevocalically.

Notice that these facts show that there is something more going on than a constraint on minimal word size. Such a constraint requires that words be at least two moras. The requirement that prevocalic syllables be bimoraic clearly cannot be a consequence of a constraint on word size. This issue is taken up again in Chapter 6.

This still leaves the restriction against prevocalic low vowels to be treated. The most reasonable formalization of this is as an alignment constraint against prevocalic low vowels.

No-Low

$$*\begin{bmatrix} V \\ low \end{bmatrix} \| | V$$

Turning to medial preconsonantal position, I will consider the same environments as with final position. Consider first the case of voiceless stops.

Distribution of vowels relative to medial obstruents

Vowel	/p/	/t/	/k/
[i]	teepee [tʰipi]	detour [ditʰur]	decal [dikʰæl]
[ɪ]	chipper [čʰɪpɽ]	bitter [bɪɾɽ]	bicker [bɪkɽ]
[e]	tapir [tʰepɽ]	latex [letʰɛks]	acorn [ekʰorn]
[ɛ]	weapon [wɛpṇ]	petty [pʰɛɾi]	pepper [pʰɛpɽ]
[æ]	dapper [dæpɽ]	attic [ærɪk]	khaki [kʰæki]
[u]	blooper [blupɽ]	duty [duɾi]	cuckoo [kʰuku]
[ʊ]	–	–	rookie [rʊki]
[o]	opine [opʰāyn]	proton [pʰrotʰãn]	trochee [tʰroki]
[ʌ]	guppy [gʌpi]	butter [bʌɾɽ]	stucco [stʌko]
[ɔ]	pauper [pʰɔpɽ]	haughty [hɔɾi]	gawky [gɔki]
[ɑ]	topic [tʰɑpɪk]	cottage [kʰɑɾəǰ]	hockey [hɑki]
[ay]	stipend [staypṇd]	mitre [mayɾɽ]	icon [aykʰãn]
[aw]	–	doughty [dawɾi]	–
[ɔy]	coypu [kʰɔypu]	loiter [lɔyɾɽ]	boycott [bɔykʰɑt]
[yu]	pupa [pʰyupə]	beauty [byuɾi]	euchre [yukɽ]

The pattern here differs from the final case in that [ɔy] is not restricted. The diphthong [aw] exhibits analogous restrictions here suggesting that the constraint on [aw] before noncoronals is sequential rather than syllable-based.

This is confirmed with the voiced stops.

Distribution of vowels relative to medial voiced stops

Vowel	/b/	/d/	/g/
[i]	rebus [ribəs]	cedar [sir̩]	meager [migr̩]
[ɪ]	ribald [rɪbɔld]	widow [wɪro]	spigot [spɪgət]
[e]	saber [sebr̩]	radon [redãn]	sago [sego]
[ɛ]	debit [dɛbət]	cheddar [čʰɛrr̩]	legate [lɛget]
[æ]	abbot [æbət]	shadow [šæro]	laggard [lægr̩d]
[u]	ruby [rubi]	hoodoo [huru]	cougar [kʰugr̩]
[ʊ]	–	pudding [pʰʊrĩŋ]	sugar [šʊgr̩]
[o]	oboe [obo]	soda [sorə]	ogre [ogr̩]
[ʌ]	blubber [blʌbr̩]	shudder [šʌrr̩]	muggy [mʌgi]
[ɔ]	auburn [ɔbr̩n]	bawdy [bɔri]	auger [ɔgr̩]
[ɑ]	lobby [lɑbi]	fodder [fɑrr̩]	groggy [grɑgi]
[ay]	fiber [faybr̩]	cider [sayrr̩]	tiger [tʰaygr̩]
[aw]	baobab [bawbab]	chowder [čʰawrr̩]	–
[ɔy]	foible [fɔybl̩]	broider [brɔyrr̩]	–
[yu]	cubit [kʰyubɪt]	feudal [fyurl̩]	bugle [byugl̩]

Familiar patterns reassert themselves here. The diphthong [aw] cannot occur before noncoronals (except for the borrowed *baobab*, which is, however, often pronounced [beəbab] or [beobab]). The sound [ɔy] is curiously absent before [g], but this may be due to the general statistical infrequency of [g], as we have seen repeatedly above.

The restriction against [aw] followed by a noncoronal could be formalized with an alignment constraint, but this treatment is countermanded by facts to be considered below. The restriction on [ɔy] followed by a noncoronal would seem to be clearly syllabic in nature, but again this is belied by further facts below.

The following chart shows which vowels can cooccur with a following intervocalic fricative.

Distribution of vowels relative to medial voiceless fricatives

Vowel	/f/	/θ/	/s/	/š/
[i]	prefect [pʰrifɛkt]	ether [iθr̩]	specie [spisi]	cliché [kʰliše]
[ɪ]	differ [dɪfr̩]	lithium [lɪθiə̃m]	lissome [lɪsm̩]	bishop [bɪšəp]
[e]	aphid [efəd]	pathos [pʰeθɑs]	caisson [kʰesã̩n]	glacier [glešr̩]
[ɛ]	heifer [hɛfr̩]	methane [mɛθẽn]	essay [ɛse]	pressure [pʰrɛšr̩]
[æ]	baffle [bæfl̩]	cathode [kʰæθod]	hassock [hæsək]	sachet [sæše]
[u]	tufa [tʰufə]	ruthenium [ruθĩniə̃m]	crusade [kʰrused]	minutia [mə̃nušə]
[ʊ]	–	–	pussy [pʰʊsi]	bushel [bʊšl̩]
[o]	trophy [tʰrofi]	–	loci [losay]	social [sošl̩]
[ʌ]	buffalo [bʌflo]	nothing? [nʌθĩŋ]	tussock [tʰʌsək]	usher [ʌšr̩]
[ɔ]	coffee [kʰɔfi]	author [ɔθr̩]	sausage [sɔsəʃ]	caution [kʰɔšn̩]
[ɑ]	prophet [pʰrɑfət]	apothecary [əpʰɑθəkeri]	posse [pʰɑsi]	–
[ay]	cipher [sayfr̩]	python [pʰayθã̩n]	biceps [baysɛps]	–
[aw]	dauphin [dawfn̩]	–	–	–
[ɔy]	–	–	moisten [mɔysn̩]	–
[yu]	euphony [yufn̩i]	euthanasia [yuθn̩ežə]	fusillade [fyusl̩ad]	fuchsia [fyušə]

Again, [ʊ] and the diphthongs [aw,ɔy] are more restricted, but the pattern with [ɔy] and [aw] is reversed. The diphthong [aw] occurs with at least one noncoronal [f] in *dauphin*, while [ɔy] only occurs with the coronal [s] in *moisten*. This reversal suggests that there is no general pattern regarding diphthongs and the coronal/noncoronal distinction intervocalically.

The voiced fricatives exhibit a slightly different pattern.

Distribution of vowels relative to medial voiced fricatives

Vowel	/v/	/ð/	/z/	/ž/
[i]	diva [divə]	either [iðr̩]	visa [vizə]	seizure [sižr̩]
[ɪ]	civet [sɪvət]	dither [dɪðr̩]	dizzy [dɪzi]	visual [vɪžuḷ]
[e]	navy [nevi]	–	razor [rezr̩]	aphasia [əfežə]
[ɛ]	bevy [bɛvi]	feather [fɛðr̩]	residue [rɛzədu]	measure [mɛžr̩]
[æ]	avid [ævɪd]	blather [blæðr̩]	azimuth [æzə̃məθ]	casual [kʰæžuḷ]
[u]	alluvium [əluviə̃m]	–	floozy [fluzi]	Hoosier [hužr̩]
[ʊ]	–	–	bosom [bʊzm̩]	–
[o]	clover [kʰlovr̩]	–	bozo [bozo]	ambrosia [æ̃mbrožə]
[ʌ]	coven [kʰʌvn̩]	brother [brʌðr̩]	buzzard [bʌzr̩d]	–
[ɔ]	grovel [grɔvḷ]	–	plausible [pʰlɔzəbḷ]	nausea [nɔžə]
[ɑ]	lava [lɑvə]	father [fɑðr̩]	blasé [blɑze]	–
[ay]	rival [rayvḷ]	either [ayðr̩]	geyser [gayzr̩]	–
[aw]	–	–	drowsy [drawzi]	–
[ɔy]	–	–	poison [pʰɔyzn̩]	–
[yu]	uvula [yuvyələ]	–	music [myuzɪk]	usual [yužuḷ]

Again, [ʊ] and the diphthongs [aw,ɔy] are more restricted, and, again, the voiced fricatives are more limited than the voiceless fricatives. However, here [aw] does not occur before the labial and does occur before the coronal, e.g. *drowsy*.

Nasals exhibit a similar pattern with one complication.

Distribution of vowels relative to medial nasals

Vowel	/m/	/n/	/ŋ/
[i]	femur [fĩmr̩]	arena [ərĩnə]	–
[ɪ]	glimmer [glĩmr̩]	cinema [sĩnə̃mə]	dinghy [dĩŋi]
[e]	famous [fẽməs]	mania [mẽniə]	–
[ɛ]	blemish [blẽmɪš]	enemy [ẽnəmi]	–
[æ]	amity [æ̃məɾi]	animal [æ̃nə̃ml̩]	clangor [kʰlæ̃ŋr̩]
[u]	rumor [rũmr̩]	tuna [tʰũnə]	–
[ʊ]	woman [wũmn̩]	–	–
[o]	nomad [nõmæd]	pony [pʰõni]	–
[ʌ]	hummock [hʌ̃mək]	bunny [bʌ̃ni]	–
[ɔ]	trauma [tʰrɔ̃mə]	tawny [tʰɔ̃ni]	–
[ɑ]	vomit [vɑ̃mət]	onyx [ɑ̃nəks]	–
[ay]	climate [kʰlãymət]	final [fãynl̩]	–
[aw]	–	–	–
[ɔy]	–	–	–
[yu]	acumen [əkʰyũmn̩]	eunuch [yũnək]	–

The diphthongs [aw,ɔy] and monophthong [ʊ] are relatively restricted, as in the previous cases.

However, the nasal [ŋ] disallows a preceding tense–lax contrast, just as it does in word-final position. This is expected on the analysis proposed so far. First, we have seen that the dorsal nasal cannot occur word-initially, and we concluded that it cannot occur syllable-initially. Second, we observed that word-final [ŋ] precludes a preceding tense–lax contrast. Hence, we conclude that syllable-final [ŋ] precludes a preceding tense–lax contrast. Since intervocalic [ŋ] can only be a syllable coda, it then follows that there should be no tense–lax contrast preceding intervocalic [ŋ] either.

The following chart shows the distribution of vowels and diphthongs before intervocalic liquids and affricates.

Distribution of vowels relative to medial liquids and affricates

Vowel	/l/	/r/	/č/	/ǰ/
[i]	velar	veral	feature	squeegee
	[vilr̩]	[virl̩]	[fičr̩]	[skwiǰi]
[ɪ]	billow	mirror	ritual	deciduous
	[bɪlo]	[mɪrr̩]	[rɪčul̩]	[dəsɪǰuəs]
[e]	sailor	fairy	nature	wager
	[selr̩]	[feri]	[nečr̩]	[weǰr̩]

Vowel	/l/	/r/	/č/	/ǰ/
[ɛ]	hello [hɛlo]	berry [bɛri]	catsup [kʰɛčʌp]	ledger [lɛǰr̩]
[æ]	callow [kʰælo]	marry [mæri]	statue [stæču]	badger [bæǰr̩]
[u]	coolie [kʰuli]	guru [guru]	suture [sučr̩]	jujube [ǰuǰubi]
[ʊ]	bully [bʊli]	jury [ǰʊri]/[ǰr̩i]	butcher [bʊčr̩]	–
[o]	folio [folio]	coral [kʰorl̩]	cloture [kʰločr̩]	logician [loǰɪšn̩]
[ʌ]	sully [sʌli]	curry [kʰʌri]/[kʰr̩i]	duchy [dʌči]	budget [bʌǰət]
[ɔ]	cholera [kʰɔlr̩ə]	aura [ɔrə]	–	fraudulent [frɔǰəlnt̩]
[ɑ]	dollar [dɑlr̩]	aria [ɑriə]	dacha [dɑčə]	logic [lɑǰɪk]
[ay]	asylum [əsayl̃m]	diary [dayri]	–	hygiene [hayǰĩn]
[aw]	–	dowry [dawri]	caoutchouc [kʰawčuk]	–
[ɔy]	doily [dɔyli]	–	–	–
[yu]	eulogy [yuləǰi]	fury [fyuri]	future [fyučr̩]	pugilism [pʰyuǰl̩ɪzm̩]

There appears to be no particular pattern with the liquids and affricates except for the familiar sporadic restrictions on [ɔy,aw,ay].

The general pattern with single intervocalic consonants is as follows. First, the diphthongs [aw,ɔy] are restricted, but not as systematically as in the monosyllabic words previously considered, showing that the restrictions there are syllable-based. The monophthong [ʊ] is also generally limited, though this is most plausibly related to the general rarity of [ʊ]. Third, voiced obstruents are also more restricted in their distribution, but this can also be traced to their infrequency, as can be seen from the following chart showing the absolute number of voiced and voiceless obstruents from a sample of 20,000 words.

Relative number of voiced and voiceless obstruents.

p	3857	2726	b
t	7731	3753	d
k	5591	1577	g
f	2139	1722	v
θ	459	137	ð
s	6361	1335	z
š	1610	116	ž
č	720	1123	ǰ

The only case where the voiced member of the pair is more frequent is [č,ǰ] and, in fact, [ǰ] does seem to enjoy a slightly freer pattern of occurrence than [č].

Finally, [ŋ] is generally quite limited. It might be thought that this shows that the restrictions on it are not syllable-based, but, as noted above, [ŋ] is precluded in onset position. The absence of various vowels before [ŋ] when it occurs intervocalically must then be traced to syllable-based concerns since [ŋ] cannot occur syllable-initially, and must be syllable-final, even when intervocalic.

Notice that this is *not* the case with the other consonants with which we saw similar restrictions in coda position: [ð,ž,r]. In the case of [r], we know that this consonant can occur syllable-initially, so the broader array of vowels that can occur before it when it occurs medially is surely a function of the fact that [r] is a possible onset in these positions.

The fricatives [ð,ž], however, are extremely limited in coda position, rarely occur as word onsets if ever, yet exhibit a free distribution of vowels when they occur intervocalically. The simplest explanation of this would have to be that these consonants are permitted as syllable onsets, but not as word onsets. We would then expect any vowel to be able to precede them in medial position, where they can be either syllable onsets or syllable codas.

Let us now turn to medial clusters. First, I present sC clusters.

Distribution of vowels relative to medial sC clusters

Vowel	/sp/	/st/	/sk/
[i]	–	eastern [istr̃n]	–
[ɪ]	whisper [wɪspr̩]	blister [blɪstr̩]	brisket [brɪskət]
[e]	–	tasty [tʰesti]	–
[ɛ]	vespers [vɛspr̩z]	festoon [fɛstũn]	escort [ɛskort]
[æ]	aspen [æspn̩]	castor [kʰæstr̩]	casket [kʰæskət]
[u]	–	acoustic [əkʰustɪk]	–

Vowel	/sp/	/st/	/sk/
[ʊ]	–	–	–
[o]	–	postern [pʰostr̩̃n]	–
[ʌ]	cuspid [kʰʌspɪd]	mustard [mʌstr̩d]	musket [mʌskət]
[ɔ]	auspice [ɔspɪs]	austere [ɔstir]	–
[ɑ]	prosper [pʰrɑspr̩]	pasta [pʰɑstə]	–
[ay]	–	feisty [faysti]	–
[aw]	–	ouster [awstr̩]	–
[ɔy]	–	oyster [ɔystr̩]	–
[yu]	–	Eustachian [yustešn̩]	–

Here an unexpected pattern shows up. First, there is the usual limited distribution for [ʊ]. There is, however, a striking absence of a tense–lax contrast before the s+noncoronal clusters (except for the sole example *auspice*) and the absence of the diphthongs [ay,aw,ɔy,yu] in the same environment. We would expect the full range of vowels to be possible here, since sC is a possible onset cluster. The following forms, repeated from Chapter 2, show that sC is a possible medial onset.

Medial sC onsets

tungsten [tʰʌ̃ŋstn̩]	hamster [hæ̃mstr̩]
obscure [əbskyr̩]	obstacle [ɑbstəkl̩]
seamstress [sĩmstrəs]	circumscribe [sr̩km̩skrayb]
subscribe [səbskrayb]	abstract [æbstrækt]

The following chart shows this pattern repeats itself with lC clusters.

Distribution of vowels relative to medial lC clusters

Vowel	/lp/	/lt/	/lk/
[i]	–	(fealty [filti])	–
[ɪ]	–	filter [fɪltr̩]	–
[e]	–	(frailty [frelti])	–
[ɛ]	–	sheltie [šɛlti]	–
[æ]	alpaca [ælpʰækə]	alto [ælto]	alcove [ælkʰov]
[u]	–	–	–

Vowel	/lp/	/lt/	/lk/
[ʊ]	–	–	–
[o]	–	poultice [pʰoltɪs]	polka [pʰolkə]
[ʌ]	pulpit [pʰʌlpət]	multiply [mʌltəpʰlay]	vulcanize [vʌlkn̩ayz]
[ɔ]	–	alter [ɔltr̩]	–
[ɑ]	–	–	volcano [vɑlkʰẽno]
[ay]	–	–	–
[aw]	–	–	–
[ɔy]	–	–	–
[yu]	–	–	–

The evidence for a tense–lax contrast before [lt] is more equivocal; the only evidence comes from morphologically complex forms like *fealty* and *frailty*. Also, [o] is again exceptional in (borrowed) *polka*.

The same pattern shows up with NC clusters.

Distribution of vowels relative to medial NC clusters

Vowel	/mp/	/nt/	/ŋk/
[i]	–	–	–
[ɪ]	whimper [wɪ̃mpr̩]	pinto [pʰɪ̃nto]	syncope [sɪ̃ŋkəpi]
[e]	–	dainty [dẽnti]	–
[ɛ]	temper [tʰɛ̃mpr̩]	dentist [dẽntɪst]	(flamenco [flɘmẽŋko]
[æ]	lampoon [læ̃mpʰũn]	bantam [bæ̃ntm̩]	anchor [æ̃ŋkr̩]
[u]	–	–	–
[ʊ]	–	(junta [hũntə])	–
[o]	–	–	–
[ʌ]	umpire [ʌ̃mpʰayr]	frontier [frʌ̃ntʰir]	hunker [hʌ̃ŋkr̩]
[ɔ]	–	jaunty [jɔ̃nti]	donkey [dɔ̃ŋki]

Vowel	/mp/	/nt/	/ŋk/
[ɑ]	pompous [pʰãmpəs]	contour [kʰãntʰur]	bronco [brãŋko]
[ay]	–	–	–
[aw]	–	bounty [bãwnti]	–
[ɔy]	–	–	–
[yu]	–	–	–

Again, a familiar pattern reasserts itself. The tense–lax contrast occurs before the coronal NC cluster, but not before the labial and dorsal NC clusters.

With stop-[s] clusters only lax vowels are allowed, regardless of the identity of the consonant.

Distribution of vowels relative to medial C + COR clusters

Vowel	/ps/	/ts/	/ks/
[i]	–	(pizza [pitsə])	–
[ɪ]	calypso [kʰəlɪpso]	(jujitsu [ǰuǰɪtsu])	elixir [əlɪksɾ̩]
[e]	–	–	–
[ɛ]	pepsin [pʰɛpsn̩]	jetsam [ǰɛtsm̩]	nexus [nɛksəs]
[æ]	capsize [kʰæpsayz]	patsy [pʰætsi]	taxi [tʰæksi]
[u]	–	–	–
[ʊ]	–	–	–
[o]	–	–	(folksy [foksi])
[ʌ]	–	–	tuxedo [tʰʌksiɾo]
[ɔ]	–	–	bauxite [bɔksayt]
[ɑ]	biopsy [bayɑpsi]	(matzo [mɑtsə])	toxin [tʰɑksn̩]
[ay]	–	–	–
[aw]	–	–	–
[ɔy]	–	–	–
[yu]	–	–	–

Here all three clusters are restricted to lax vowels except for borrowings like *pizza* and morphologically complex forms like *folksy*. The cluster [ks] shows a broader distribution in that it can occur with more back vowels.

The general pattern with medial clusters so far is somewhat surprising. It is as if clusters syllabify to the left to account for the distribution of vowel qualities. However, as we saw in Chapter 3, they must be able to syllabify to the right to account for the distribution of consonants.

So far we have only looked at medial clusters where at least one segment must affiliate to the left. Let us now consider a couple of cases where the medial consonants can both affiliate to the right.

Consider first obstruent-liquid clusters. Here, virtually all tense and lax vowels can occur, but once again, [aw,ɔy] cannot occur.

Vowels with a following medial
obstruent-liquid cluster

[i]	egret [igrət]
[ɪ]	citron [sɪtrə̃n]
[e]	apron [eprə̃n]
[ɛ]	metro [mɛtro]
[æ]	acrid [ækrəd]
[u]	rubric [rubrɪk]
[ʊ]	–
[o]	okra [okrɔ]
[ʌ]	buckram [bʌkrə̃m]
[ɑ]	goblin [gɑblə̃n]
[ɔ]	tawdry [tʰɔdri]
[yu]	hubris [hyubrəs]
[aw]	–
[ay]	cypress [sayprəs]
[ɔy]	–

The following chart shows that vowels are far more restricted with sN clusters. Here there are only the examples *isthmus* [ɪsməs], and *Christmas* [kʰrɪsməs].

Vowels with a following
medial sN cluster

[i]	–
[ɪ]	isthmus [ɪsməs]
[e]	–
[ɛ]	–
[æ]	–
[u]	–
[ʊ]	–
[o]	–
[ʌ]	–
[ɑ]	–

[ɔ]	–
[yu]	–
[aw]	–
[ay]	–
[ɔy]	–

We have reached something of a paradox. There are clear restrictions on the kinds of vowels that can precede a dorsal or labial consonant word-finally; the diphthongs [aw,ɔy] cannot occur in this position. In medial position, while there are a number of curious gaps, the general pattern is that any vowel can occur before a singleton dorsal or labial consonant. Together, these would seem to imply that the restriction against [aw,ɔy] word-finally is syllabic in nature.

On the other hand, we have seen that there are restrictions on vowels before medial two-consonant sC, lC, or NC clusters. Specifically, diphthongs and tense vowels cannot occur before medial sC, lC, or NC clusters if the rightmost member of the cluster is labial or dorsal. This would seem to imply that the restrictions against various vowels before clusters is linear in nature. For example, the word-final span [awk] is out because of syllable structure, but the word-final or medial span [awsk] is out because of a linear constraint.

The relevant facts are all summarized in the following chart. Contrasting cells are shaded.

Cluster facts summarized

		Lax	Tense	[ay]	[aw,ɔy]
Final	_(s)t]	✔	✔	✔	✔
	_sp/k]	✔	Ø	Ø	Ø
	_p/k]	✔	✔	✔	Ø
	_lt]	✔	✔	✔	Ø
	_lp/k]	✔	Ø	Ø	Ø
	_nt]	✔	✔	✔	✔
	_Np/k]	✔	Ø	Ø	Ø
Medial	_(s)tV	✔	✔	✔	✔
	_sp/kV	✔	auspice?	Ø	Ø
	_p/kV	✔	✔	✔	✔
	_ltV	✔	✔	Ø	Ø
	_lp/kV	✔	Ø	Ø	Ø
	_ntV	✔	✔	✔	✔
	_Np/kV	✔	Ø	Ø	Ø
	_Cr/lV	✔	✔	✔	boisterous?

There is another interpretation of these facts, however. Recall that the previous chapter ended with a certain amount of ambiguity regarding the affiliation of medial consonants. While sequences like V.hV and Vŋ.V are syllabified unambiguously, sequences like VkV are not. Nothing about the possible sequencing of consonants in English commits us to either V.kV or Vk.V for these cases.

With this in mind, the facts above can be made sense of by means of a rather simple proposal regarding medial VC_0V sequences. The fact that, for example, [aw,ɔy] are ruled out before word-final noncoronals, but not medial singleton noncoronals, can be understood if (i) the constraint is syllable-based, and ii) singleton consonants affiliate to the *right*: V.CV.

The fact that [aw,ɔy] are ruled out before both word-final and medial [sk] follows if (i) the constraint is also syllable-based, and (ii) medial sequences of more than one consonant are affiliated to the *left*: VCC.V. The following chart shows the equivalences this proposal entails for the word-final and medial sequences above.

Equivalences entailed

Word-final		Word-medial
Vt]	≠	V.tV
Vp/k]	≠	V.p/kV
Vst]	≈	Vst.V
Vsp/k]	≈	Vsp/k.V
Vlt]	≈	Vlt.V
Vlp/k]	≈	Vlp/k.V
Vnt]	≈	Vnt.V
VNp/k]	≈	VNp/k.V
?	≈/≠	VC.r/lV

This, in fact, is just what we observe in the previous chart. (This proposal leaves examples like *auspice* unexplained.)

To get this result, we need several constraints. First, I adopt the ONSET constraint, discussed in Chapters 2 and 3.

ONSET
Syllables must have onsets.

Second, I propose that ONSET is outranked by a constraint that has the effect of affiliating as many consonants to the left as possible, just in case there is more than one consonant. There are a number of ways this can be formalized, but I will adopt the following since it is as direct a formulation as possible.

MAX-CODA
Affiliate as many consonants to the left as possible when there are more than one.

The following tableaux show how this works for representative clusters. The abbreviation GOOD-CODA stands for the constraints developed in the preceding chapter that govern the well-formedness of coda sequences.

The constraints exemplified

/VstV/	GOOD-CODA	MAX-CODA	ONSET
V.stV		*!*	
Vs.tV		*!	
☞ Vst.V			*
/VtV/	GOOD-CODA	MAX-CODA	ONSET
☞ V.tV			
Vt.V			*!
/VtrV/	GOOD-CODA	MAX-CODA	ONSET
V.trV		**!	
☞ Vt.rV		*	
Vtr.V	*!		*

If this syllabification scheme is assumed, most of the restrictions observed for medial VC sequences are identical to the restrictions for word-final VC sequences; both are a consequence of syllable-based restrictions. These are treated in the following section.

Notice before we continue, however, that this proposal commits us to a different story for coronal consonants. In the previous chapter, I argued that coronal consonants at the edge of the word were unsyllabified. This was to account for the facts that (i) they could violate the sonority hierarchy, (ii) they could be appended beyond the normal upper bound on consonantal positions, and (iii) these extra coronal positions were only possible word-finally. We now see that medial coronal consonants also behave exceptionally. This will be taken up in the following section.

4.3. MORA-BASED RESTRICTIONS

In this section, I treat the restrictions observed above in terms of moras.

Recall from Chapter 2 that moras are associated with syllable peaks and codas as a measure of the weight of a syllable. In this section, I will argue that mora assignment is the appropriate vehicle to account for the majority of the restrictions on VC sequencing presented above. I will also use mora sequencing to account for the differing behavior of coronals in medial and final position.

The first generalization to be treated is that lax vowels cannot occur word-finally. This accounts for the fact that while words like *bee* [bi] and *bay* [be] are well-formed, hypothetical words like *[bɪ] and *[bɛ] are not. Both types of vowels can occur in closed syllables, e.g. *beet* [bit], *bait* [bet], *bit* [bɪt], and *bet* [bɛt].

> *Word-final lax vowels*
> Lax vowels cannot occur word-finally

The normal account of this sort of distribution is to maintain that words are subject to a minimum size restriction. Tense vowels and diphthongs satisfy that size requirement, but lax vowels do not. This is typically expressed in terms of moras. Words must be minimally bimoraic. Tense vowels and diphthongs are at least bimoraic, while lax vowels have only one mora. Coda consonants can also contribute a mora, bringing the mora count of a word like *bet* [bɛt] up to the requisite two.

> *Bimoraic minimum word constraint (MINWD)*
> Words must be at least two moras.

This constraint will have to be revised below.

A further refinement of this mora assignment scheme comes from the observation that the diphthongs [aw,ɔy] cannot occur in a syllable closed by a noncoronal. For example, while *bout* [bawt] and *noise* [nɔyz] are well-formed, *[bawk] and *[bɔyp] are not.

> *Heavy diphthong restriction*
> [aw,ɔy] do not occur before word-final noncoronals.

One way to capture this restriction would be as follows. Lax vowels have one mora, tense vowels and the diphthongs [ay,yu] have two moras, and the diphthongs [aw,ɔy] have three moras. Coronal consonants may bear a mora as a coda, but noncoronals must bear a mora when they occur as codas. Syllables are maximally trimoraic. This gives the following mora counts.

Calculated mora counts

Vowel	Consonant	Example	Count
lax	coronal	hat [hæt]	1 or 2
lax	noncoronal	lap [læp]	2
tense	coronal	heat [hit]	2~3
tense	noncoronal	leap [lip]	3
[ay,yu]	coronal	right [rayt]	2~3
[ay,yu]	noncoronal	ripe [rayp]	3
[aw,ɔy]	coronal	route [rawt]	3
[aw,ɔy]	noncoronal	*	4

Notice that a coronal consonant following a lax vowel must be moraic to make up the bimoraic minimum. (Hence the first case above must have precisely two moras.) Notice also that [aw] or [ɔy] cannot be followed by a noncoronal, since that would produce a four-mora count.

This array can be produced with the following constraints. First, the bimoraic minimum and the trimoraic maximum must both outrank faithfulness.

Trimoraic maximum (3μ)
Syllables can contain no more than three moras.

There must also be a constraint requiring noncoronal coda consonants to bear a mora and it must outrank M-Parse as well.

Noncoronal coda mora ($k/p\mu$)
Noncoronal codas must bear a mora.

The full ranking of these is given below.

Mora count and faithfulness rankings
$$\left.\begin{array}{c} k/p\mu \\ 3\mu \\ \text{MinWd} \end{array}\right\} \gg \text{M-Parse}$$

This system distinguishes three types of vowel and two types of consonant in terms of mora count. The facts of English, in fact, merit a three-way distinction among coda consonants as well. Recall that the singleton consonants [ž,ŋ] also restricted the preceding vowel. This is easily treated if we assume these consonants contribute two moras instead of one.

This accounts for [ŋ] directly. The pattern with [ž] was a little more complex, however; [ž] disallowed a preceding lax vowel and only allowed a preceding tense vowel. To capture this pattern of distribution, I propose that [ž] has two moras when it occurs as a coda consonant. Since syllables are maximally trimoraic, this predicts that it can only occur with lax vowels. The fact that the set of vowels that do occur with coda [ž] on the surface appear to be tense is attributed to a constraint requiring that vowels be tense (though short) before [ž].

Pre-[ž] tensing
Vowels are tense (short) before coda [ž]

One way to formalize this special category of tense yet short vowels would be to require that the first mora associated with coda [ž] be shared. This is shown below for *beige* [bež].

Mora sharing with [ž]

be ž

Ʌ/

μ μ μ

However it is formalized, the latter must of course be ranked with respect to faithfulness constraints (M-PARSE).

The pattern with [ð,r] was rather different. These consonants can only cooccur with a tense vowel or diphthong. (This is different from [ž], because [ž] could not occur with diphthongs.) The simplest treatment of this would be that [ð,r] contribute no mora to the syllable. In this way, they cannot occur with lax vowels, but can cooccur with any bimoraic or trimoraic vowel or diphthong. The consonants [ð,r] are different from the other coronals because other coronals may contribute a mora to a syllable containing a lax vowel if necessary. (There are other contexts where [r] does have to contribute a mora, as we will see below.)

The following chart summarizes the proposal so far with respect to intrinsic mora count for vowels and coda consonants of various types.

Intrinsic mora count

Lax vowels	μ
Tense vowels	$\mu\mu$
[ay,yu]	$\mu\mu$
[aw,ɔy]	$\mu\mu\mu$
Coronals	(μ)
Noncoronals	μ
[ž,ŋ]	$\mu\mu$
[ð,r]	$\varnothing$

A formal account of mora assignment can now be provided. First, we need a schema for assigning moras.

Mora assignment schema
$\{\emptyset,1,2,3\}\mu$/segment: Some number of moras are assigned to 'segment' when it occurs as a syllable peak or coda.

For example, $\emptyset\mu$/[r] says that coda [r] gets no moras, while 2μ/tense-vowels says that tense vowels receive two moras.

The mora assignment schema can be used to encode the requirements for morahood deduced above.

Mora requirements encoded with the
mora assignment schema

1μ/lax	1μ/coronals
2μ/tense	1μ/noncoronals
2μ/[ay,yu]	2μ/[ž,ŋ]
3μ/[aw,ɔy]	$\emptyset\mu$/[ð,r]

All of these, except 1μ/coronals, must be ranked above M-Parse. The constraint assigning one mora to coronals is violable. Hence it must be out-ranked by 3μ and outranked by M-Parse. In this way, coronal codas can be denied a mora to satisfy the three-mora maximum.

A few examples will suffice. Consider the tableaux for *fear* [fir], *feet* [fit], and *route* [rawt].

Tableau for fear

/fir/	2μ/tense	3μ/[aw]	$\emptyset\mu$/[r]	3μ	M-P	1μ/COR
☞ fi　r \n \\ \n μ μ						
fi　r \n \\ | \n μ μ μ			*!			

Tableau for feet

/fit/	2μ/tense	3μ/[aw]	Øμ/[r]	3μ	M-P	1μ/COR
fi t ∧ μμ						*!
☞ fi t ∧ | μμ μ						

Tableau for route

/rawt/	2μ/tense	3μ/[aw]	Øμ/[r]	3μ	M-P	1μ/COR
☞ raw t ∧\ μμμ						*
Ø					*!	
raw t || | μμ μ		*!				
raw t ∧\ | μμμμ				*!		

Let us now turn to the restrictions evident with complex codas. First, we observed that a final s-COR cluster can occur with even the heaviest diphthongs, e.g. *joust* [ǰawst], *joist* [ǰɔyst], while s-LAB and s-DORS codas are precluded even with tense vowels and light diphthongs [ay,yu].

This suggests that coronal consonants must provide a mora if followed by a moraic consonant. Hence, [st] clusters can provide between zero and two moras. This allows [st] to occur after any vowel or diphthong and provide a bimoraic minimum on one hand and not exceed the trimoraic maximum on the other. The [sp,sk] clusters, on the other hand, provide two moras. Hence they cannot occur after tense vowels or diphthongs.

Pre-mora mora assignment (PRE-MORA)
A consonant must be moraic if it precedes a moraic consonant.

I know of no language that violates this. It is therefore reasonable to suppose that this is not a constraint per se, but a part of GEN. Therefore remaining tableaux will not include candidates where a nonmoraic coda precedes a moraic coda.

Word-final lC clusters behave as monomoraic when the final consonant is a coronal, but as bimoraic when the final consonant is noncoronal. Thus monomoraic and bimoraic peaks can occur with l-COR, e.g. *kilt* [kʰɪlt], *field* [fild], *wild* [wayld], but only monomoraic peaks can cooccur with l-LAB or l-DORS, e.g. *bulb* [bʌlb], *bulk* [bʌlk].

The problem is that we would expect trimoraic diphthongs to be able to cooccur with l-COR clusters, since they can precede [l] alone, e.g. *foul* [fawl]. It would appear that [l] must contribute a mora when it is nonfinal in a coda. (These are allowed in heteromorphemic contexts, however, e.g. *fouls* [fawlz].) This can be captured with a small revision of the mora assignment constraints so as to allow sequences.

Moraic lateral
$1\mu/l/\_C$

This constraint must clearly be generalized to liquids to account for the absence of trimoraic diphthongs before [rt] clusters as well, e.g. *hour* [awr] vs. *[awrt], but *hours* [awrz].

Let us now turn to a superficially unfortunate consequence of the analysis presented so far; the generalization proposed above to account for the lateral will also suffice here. Word-final sequences of [ŋk] should, on the analysis presented so far, be trimoraic. The [k] is moraic because noncoronals are moraic and the [ŋ] is moraic because [ŋ] is subject to $2\mu/\eta$. The problem is that this predicts no vowel should be able to precede such a cluster, since any vowel would result in a syllable with at least four moras.

One way to treat this would be to have a constraint which outranks $2\mu/\eta$ that assigns a single mora to [ŋ] when it is preconsonantal.

Preconsonantal [ŋ]
$1\mu/\eta/\_C$

Another solution might be to limit in a general way the number of moras that can be contributed by the coda to two. This would allow any coda sequence generally allowed to cooccur with at least the lax vowels. Both accounts are compatible with the facts presented so far. A third possibility would be to assume that PRE-MORA operates in both directions. It forces a consonant that might otherwise contribute no mora to contribute a mora when preceding a moraic consonant, but also requires a consonant that might otherwise contribute two moras to contribute a single mora when preceding a moraic consonant. The last solution is the simplest and will be adopted here.

> *Pre-mora mora assignment (PRE-MORA revised)*
> A consonant must contribute precisely one mora if it precedes a moraic consonant.

The C+COR clusters behave as if they are bimoraic with respect to the distribution of preceding vowels if the first consonant is nonmoraic. For example, a word-final [ps] or [ks] sequence is incompatible with a tense vowel or diphthong, e.g. *lapse* [læps] vs. *[leps] and *box* [bɑks] vs. *[biks]. (Such spans are, of course, acceptable if heteromorphemic, e.g. *beaks* [biks] or *tapes* [tʰeps].) This creates a paradox, however. I have already argued that coronals are subject to low-ranked 1μ/coronals allowing them to contribute zero or one mora as a coda. (In a word like *pout* [pʰawt], the [t] contributes no mora; in a word like *bit* [bɪt], the [t] does contribute a mora.) In addition, we have seen how sC clusters where the second consonant is noncoronal contribute two moras, ruling out preceding tense vowels or diphthongs. However, on the basis of this system, clusters like [kt,ks,pt,ps] should be monomoraic; the final coronal need not contribute a mora, but the preceding noncoronal contributes one mora. This does not seem to be the case, since tense vowels and diphthongs are ruled out in this environment.

Therefore, coronal obstruents must contribute a mora in these clusters, but not in the following cases. First, coronals alone must have the option of not contributing a mora so as to allow trimoraic diphthongs to precede them, e.g. *pout* [pʰawt]. Second, coronals in NC clusters must not contribute a mora so as to allow tense vowels and diphthongs to precede them as well, e.g. *pounce* [pʰãwns]. Last, coronals in three-consonant C+COR codas must also not contribute a mora so as to allow a lax vowel to precede them, e.g. *text* [tʰɛkst].

This result can be achieved if it is proposed that a coronal must be moraic if it immediately follows a noncoronal consonant.

> *Post-mora mora assignment (prose version)*
> A coronal is moraic if it follows a noncoronal consonant.

Post-noncoronal mora

$$1\mu/C/\begin{Bmatrix}\text{LAB}\\\text{DORS}\end{Bmatrix} -$$

There are three situations where this will not apply: (i) singleton coronal consonants, as in *pout* [pʰawt], (ii) coronal NC clusters, as in *pounce* [pʰãwns], and (iii) the second member of a COR+COR sequence, as in *text* [tʰɛkst].

Notice that this approach commits us to affiliating these coronal consonants. On the assumption that moras are only assigned to syllabified segments, these coronal consonants must be affiliated. This, in turn, entails that the Sonority Hierarchy be relaxed to allow for obstruent+COR coda clusters.

There are, then, three possibilities for coronal consonants. They can be affiliated as moraic consonants. This occurs when required by MinWd, e.g. *bit* [bɪt]. Second, moraicity is required when the coronal occurs before a moraic consonant, e.g. *hasp* [hæsp]. Finally, as just argued, this also happens with [ps,ks] clusters, e.g. *ax* [æks]. Coronal consonants can also be affiliated as nonmoraic material. This is presumably the case for medial examples like *feisty* [faysti], but also for final cases like *beet* [bit]. Finally, coronal consonants can be unaffiliated entirely in word-final position, as in *text* [tɛkst].

The system proposed so far generalizes completely straightforwardly to word-medial cases on the assumptions regarding affiliation of medial consonants discussed above. Recall that a single consonant affiliates to the right and more than one consonant affiliates as much as possible to the left.

There is one additional constraint that must be mentioned. As noted above, lax vowels are disallowed prevocalically. This shows that *all* syllables must be at least bimoraic in English. Hence the MinWd constraint proposed above can be replaced with a more general constraint.

BIMORAICITY
All syllables must be bimoraic.

This constraint outranks both ONSET and MAX-CODA.

The following chart shows the contribution of codas to a preceding syllable in a variety of medial cases. The predictions made are exactly the right ones, as detailed above.

Medial affiliation and possible preceding vowels

Cluster	Coda moras	Lax	Tense/[ay,yu,ɾ]	[aw,ɔy]
Vst.V	(μ)	✔	✔	✔
Vsp/k.V	μμ	✔	Ø	Ø
V.p/kV	Ø	✔*	✔	✔

Cluster	Coda moras	Lax	Tense/[ay,yu,r̩]	[aw,ɔy]
V.tV	Ø	✔*	✔	✔
Vlt.V	μ	✔	✔	Ø
Vlp/k.V	μμ	✔	Ø	Ø
Vnt.V	(μ)	✔	✔	✔
VNp/k.V	μμ	✔	Ø	Ø
Vk/p.r/lV	μ	✔	✔	Ø
Vt.r/lV	(μ)	✔	✔	✔

The only cases where the predictions are not borne out are shaded. The first case is where tense vowels should not occur before an [sp,sk] cluster, but there is the one example *auspice* [ɔspəs]; the second case is where [ɔytr,awtr] should occur, but there is only *boisterous* [bɔystrəs]. These may be problems for the analysis or they may be statistical aberrations.

4.4. SYLLABIC CONSONANTS AND [r]

Let us now consider the distribution of syllabic consonants. We have seen that liquids and nasals can both occur in syllabic and nonsyllabic forms. Syllabic [r̩] is rather different from the other syllabic consonants in a number of respects, however. For example, it is the only one that can occur in monosyllabic words or stressed, e.g. *bird* [br̩d]. In monosyllabic words, [r̩] basically has the distribution of a tense vowel or diphthong.

First, it can occur word-finally in monosyllables. Other syllabic consonants are precluded in this position.

Syllabic [r̩] word-finally
in monosyllables

purr	[pʰr̩]
stir	[str̩]
fur	[fr̩]
blur	[blr̩]

(In some dialects, words like *bull* [bʊl] and *mull* [mʌl] are realized as [bl̩] and [ml̩].)

Second, it is precluded before the consonants and consonant clusters that disallow a tense–lax contrast. Among the singleton consonants, this includes [ž,ð,r,ŋ]. Syllabic [r̩] is disallowed before each of these.

Cooccurrence of [ɹ] with various coda consonants

	Tense	Lax	ay	aw	ɹ̩
p	leap [lip]	lip [lɪp]	ripe [rayp]	–	burp [bɹ̩p]
t	beet [bit]	bit [bɪt]	bite [bayt]	bout [bawt]	curt [kʰɹ̩t]
k	teak [tʰik]	tick [tʰɪk]	tike [tʰayk]	–	Turk [tʰɹ̩k]
b	grebe [grib]	rib [rɪb]	tribe [tʰrayb]	–	curb [kʰɹ̩b]
d	bead [bid]	bid [bɪd]	bide [bayd]	loud [lawd]	bird [bɹ̩d]
g	league [lig]	big [bɪg]	–	–	berg [bɹ̩g]
f	leaf [lif]	tiff [tʰɪf]	rife [rayf]	–	surf [sɹ̩f]
θ	wreath [riθ]	myth [mɪθ]	lithe [layθ]	mouth [mawθ]	mirth [mɹ̩θ]
s	lease [lis]	miss [mɪs]	rice [rays]	louse [laws]	purse [pʰɹ̩s]
š	leash [liš]	fish [fɪš]	–	–	–
v	leave [liv]	live [lɪv]	live [layv]	–	curve [kʰɹ̩v]
ð	seethe [sið]	–	writhe [rayð]	mouthe [mawð]	–
z	ease [iz]	fizz [fɪz]	rise [rayz]	house [hawz]	furze [fɹ̩z]
ž	liege [liž]	–	–	–	–
m	seem [sĩm]	rim [rɪ̃m]	rhyme [rãym]	–	firm [fɹ̩m]
n	teen [tʰĩn]	tin [tʰɪ̃n]	tine [tʰãyn]	town [tʰãwn]	turn [tʰɹ̩n]
ŋ	–	sing [sɪ̃ŋ]	–	–	–
l	seal [sil]	sill [sɪl]	rile [rayl]	cowl [kʰawl]	curl [kʰɹ̩l]
r	beer [bir]	–	fire [fayr]	flour [flawr]	–

It might be, though, that [r̩] should be able to occur before [r], since the latter is nonmoraic as a coda. This does not occur, however, and the absence of word-final *[r̩r] must be ascribed to something else, presumably the NoGEMINATES constraint above.

Syllabic [r̩] is also excluded before clusters that preclude tense vowels and diphthongs.

Cooccurrence of [r̩] with various coda clusters

	Tense	Lax	ay	aw	r̩
sp	–	hasp [hæsp]	–	–	–
st	beast [bist]	last [læst]	heist [hayst]	roust [rawst]	burst [br̩st]
sk	–	ask [æsk]	–	–	–
lp	–	help [hɛlp]	–	–	–
lt	bolt [bolt]	belt [bɛlt]	–	–	–
lk	–	milk [mɪlk]	–	–	–
mp	–	ramp [ræ̃mp]	–		–
nt	faint [fẽnt]	rant [ræ̃nt]	pint [pʰãynt]	count [kʰãwnt]	(burnt [br̩nt])
ŋk	–	rank [ræ̃ŋk]	–	–	–
ps	–	lapse [læps]	–	–	–
ts	–	blitz [blɪts̩]	–	–	–
ks	–	fix [fɪks]	–	–	–

As seen above, [o] is apparently the only tense vowel that can occur before [lt]. Also, *burnt* is the only example of [r̩nt].

There are then three relevant facts. First, [r̩] has the distribution of a tense vowel. Second, the tense–lax contrast is neutralized before coda [r]. (Only the low vowel [ɑ] and the mid back vowel [o] are allowed.) Looked at another way, [ɹ] contrasts with Vr word-finally and before coronals. Before noncoronals, there is only [ɹ].

Vr vs. [ɹ]

Word-final	Precoronal	Prenoncoronal
purr [pʰɻ]	pert [pʰɻt]	perk [pʰɻk]
fear [fir]	weird [wird]	–
pear [pʰer]	–	–
tour [tʰur]	–	–
four [for]	ford [ford]	fork [fork]
par [pʰɑr]	part [pʰɑrt]	park [pʰɑrk]

The third fact is the absence of syllable-final [ɻr].

This pattern makes perfect sense if we assume that an underlying nonlow lax vowel followed by a coda [r] is realized as [ɻ]. There is a contrast in word-final position because we expect both tense and lax vowels to occur in this position (before a single coronal). There is a contrast before an overt coronal consonant because we also expect tense and lax vowels to occur in this position (before two coronals). Finally, only [ɻ] occurs before noncoronals because in this context we only expect lax vowels, and by hypothesis a lax vowel followed by a coda [r] is realized as [ɻ].

This can be accounted for by positing a negative GA constraint against a lax vowel followed by a coda [r] and ranking this constraint higher than the faithfulness constraints, insuring the pronunciation of the vowel and preventing [r] from appearing as a nucleus.

Vr constraint (GA version)

$$*\begin{bmatrix} \text{vowel} \\ \text{nonlow} \\ \text{lax} \end{bmatrix} \begin{bmatrix} \text{coda} \\ \text{[r]} \end{bmatrix}$$

The last step in the analysis of [r] is the treatment of words like *port* [pʰort] and *pork* [pʰork], where a tense mid vowel shows up where we would expect either a syllabic [ɻ] or a low vowel followed by [r]. The proper analysis of these is suggested by the absence of *[pʰɔrt] or *[pʰɔrk]. It must be the case that [ɔr] sequences are realized as [or] on the surface. It is a trivial matter to formalize a constraint with this effect. It must also be the case that FAITH(Low) is relatively low-ranked.

*[ɔr] constraint (NGA version)

$$* \begin{bmatrix} \text{vowel} \\ \text{low} \\ \text{round} \end{bmatrix} \left\| \begin{bmatrix} \text{moraic} \\ \text{[r]} \end{bmatrix} \right.$$

Summarizing to this point, we have seen that [ɾ] in stressed syllables emerges as the pronunciation of any lax vowel followed by a coda [r].

4.5. SUMMARY

We have seen that there are a number of constraints on VC sequences. These constraints are quite similar word-medially and word-finally, but not the same. With a relatively simple characterization of what happens in the affiliation of medial consonant sequences, the two sets of facts can be reduced to one. The entire system can be reduced to to what segments are moraic and how many moras can occur in a syllable.

The analysis relies on several things. First, syllables are maximally trimoraic. In addition, vowels are subdivided into classes depending on how many moras they receive.

Vowel classes for mora assignment

Lax	μ
Tense/[ay,ɾ]	$\mu\mu$
[aw,ɔy]	$\mu\mu\mu$

Coda consonants also contribute a differing number of moras.

Intrinsic mora count

Coronals	(μ)
Noncoronals	μ
[ž,ŋ]	$\mu\mu$
[ð,r]	$\emptyset$

Finally, we posited several mora assignment principles that referred to neighboring segments.

Conditional mora assignment constraints
1μ/liquid/_C
PRE-MORA
1μ/C/$\begin{Bmatrix} \text{LAB} \\ \text{DORS} \end{Bmatrix}$ –

In conjunction, these constraints allowed for a simple characterization of possible VC sequences word-finally and word-medially. The only problem remaining is how to treat the CV restrictions noted above. This is taken up in Chapter 6.

4.6. FURTHER READING

The analysis presented in this chapter builds on moraic theory. Readers should look to Larry Hyman's important 1985 book or Bruce Hayes's 1989 paper. There is no clear elaboration of moraic theory in the context of OT.

5

Stress, Accent, and Feet

In this chapter, I will introduce stress and accent. I will propose that stress and accent should be treated in terms of a unit referred to as the metrical foot. Let us first consider what stress or accent is and then return to what the foot is.

5.1. WHAT IS STRESS?

The terms 'stress' and 'accent' can be used to refer to the same thing in English: syllables that are more prominent than their neighbors. Hence, a stressed or accented syllable is more prominent than an unstressed or unaccented syllable. From here on, I will use the term 'stress' exclusively to refer to syllable prominence.

Stress
A stressed syllable is more prominent than an unstressed syllable.

The term accent will be defined differently below (§5.5.2.1).

For example, a word like *happy* [hæpi] has stress on the first syllable and a word like *abound* [əbawnd] has stress on the second. Some words have more than one stress. For example, while *banana* [bənænə] and *bandanna* [bændænə] both have stress on the second syllable, *bandanna* has another stress on the first. Long words can have many stresses: *formaldehyde* [formældəhayd] has stress on the first, second, and fourth syllables and *Apalachicola* [æpəlæčəkʰolə] has stress on the first, third, and fifth syllables.

When a word has more than one stress, typically one stress is stronger than the others. This is termed the 'primary stress' and the others 'secondary stresses'. For example, in *bandanna*, the first stress is secondary and the second primary. In *formaldehyde*, the first syllable has secondary stress, the second has primary stress, and the fourth has secondary stress. In

Apalachicola, the fifth syllable has primary stress and the first and third have secondary stress.

Primary stresses are traditionally marked with an acute accent, ´, and secondary stresses with a grave accent, `. The examples cited above would then be transcribed as follows.

Primary and secondary stresses transcribed

happy [hǽpi]	abound [əbáwnd]
banana [bənǽnə]	bandanna [bæ̀ndǽnə]
formaldehyde [fòrmǽldəhàyd]	Apalachicola [æ̀pəlæ̀čəkʰólə]

Up to now stress has not been transcribed in examples, but from here on all stresses will be transcribed. For legibility, vowel nasalization will no longer be marked.

There is also a traditional vocabulary for describing what syllable of the word stress falls on, and I will make use of this. The 'ultima' refers to the last syllable of the word. The 'penult' refers to the second syllable from the right. The 'antepenult' is the third syllable from the right, and the 'preantepenult' (etc.) is the fourth syllable from the right.

Stress terms

Ultima	. . . ó
Penult	. . . óσ
Antepenult	. . . óσσ
Preantepenult	. . . óσσσ

There is another set of terms for referring to different stress patterns. 'Trochee' refers to a disyllabic pattern with stress on the first syllable. 'Iamb' refers to a disyllabic pattern with stress on the second syllable. 'Dactyl' refers to a trisyllabic pattern with stress on the first syllable. 'Anapest' refers to a trisyllabic pattern with stress on the last syllable. 'Amphibrach' refers to a trisyllabic pattern with stress in the middle. Finally, 'spondee' refers to a disyllabic pattern with stress on both syllables.

Word/foot types

Trochee	óσ
Iamb	σó
Dactyl	óσσ
Anapest	σσó
Amphibrach	σóσ
Spondee	óó

We can think of stress in terms either of production or of perception. In the production domain, it is generally thought that prominence is a function of greater duration, loudness, or pitch. Hence stressed syllables would be longer, louder, or higher in pitch than unstressed syllables. While this seems generally true, it is not an absolute, and the phonetic correlates of stress are quite complex.

5.2. WHAT IS A METRICAL FOOT?

Why should we believe that there is such a thing as stress? The main argument that stress is a linguistic category comes from the organizing function it has over utterances. There seem to be principles requiring and in turn governing the distribution of stress in words and phrases. Specifically, all autonomous words must be stressed somewhere. In addition, stresses recur at regular intervals.

To describe this requirement and these intervals, it has been proposed that there is a unit, termed the 'metrical foot', and that words are parsed into feet. Each foot includes one or two syllables. In addition, English is subject to the requirement that each stress occur on the left side of a foot. For example, a word like *Minnesota* [mìnəsórə] has two stresses and two feet. We can mark feet with square brackets: [Mìnne][sóta]. The foot structure for each of the words above is indicated below.

Footing indicated

[háppy]	a[bóund]
ba[nána]	[bàn][dánna]
[fòr][málde][hýde]	[Àpa][làchi][cóla]

Why should we believe this structure is part of what speakers know about English?

5.3. INTUITIVE EVIDENCE FOR THE FOOT

This can be answered in much the same way we answered the same question for the syllable. However, here the facts are somewhat different. It will turn out that while there was a predominance of 'extralinguistic' support for the syllable, there is far less extralinguistic support for the foot. On the other hand, there is more distributional evidence for the foot.

The first argument given for the syllable was that people can count them easily without any explicit training. This is far less clear with the foot. In fact, people seem to have little direct access to stresses and feet.

Another argument given for the syllable came from poetry. Here the argument for the foot is strong. Traditional English poetic meter very clearly regulates the distribution of stressed syllables. Moreover, the restrictions on the distribution of stresses are quite suggestive of foot structure. For example, it was noted in Chapter 2 that iambic pentameter has ten syllables per line. Iambic pentameter also restricts the distribution of stressed syllables, such that only even-numbered positions can be stressed. A canonical line of iambic pentameter can be schematized as follows. ($\acute{\sigma}$=stressed syllable, $\breve{\sigma}$= unstressed syllable.)

   Iambic pentameter schematized

$$\breve{\sigma}\left\{{\breve{\sigma} \atop \acute{\sigma}}\right\}z\breve{\sigma}\left\{{\breve{\sigma} \atop \acute{\sigma}}\right\}\breve{\sigma}\left\{{\breve{\sigma} \atop \acute{\sigma}}\right\}\breve{\sigma}\left\{{\breve{\sigma} \atop \acute{\sigma}}\right\}\breve{\sigma}\left\{{\breve{\sigma} \atop \acute{\sigma}}\right\}$$

The most common exception to this pattern allows a stress to occur in an odd-numbered position just in case a neighboring even-numbered position harbors a stressed syllable. The sonnet cited in Chapter 2 is repeated below with stresses marked. Exceptional cases are underlined.

   Iambic pentameter (Shakespeare's 18th Sonnet)

   Shall I compáre thee to a súmmer's dáy?
   Thou art more lóvely and more témperate:
   Róugh wínds do sháke the dárling búds of Máy,
   And súmmer's léase hath all too shórt a dáte:
   Sómetìme too hót the éye of héaven shínes,
   And óften is his góld compléxion dímm'd;
   And évery fáir from fáir sómetìme declínes,
   By chánce or náture's chánging cóurse untrímm'd;
   But thy etérnal súmmer shall not fáde
   Nor lóse posséssion of that fáir thou ówest;
   Nor shall Déath brág thou wánder'st in his sháde,
   When in etérnal línes to tíme thou gRówest:
       So lóng as mén can bréathe or éyes can sée,
       So lóng líves this and this gíves lífe to thee.

Another example cited in Chapter 2 is trochaic tetrameter, where each canonical line has eight syllables. Here it is only the odd-numbered positions that can bear stress. A line is schematized below.

Trochaic tetrameter schematized

$$\left\{\begin{matrix}\breve{\sigma}\\\acute{\sigma}\end{matrix}\right\}\breve{\sigma}\left\{\begin{matrix}\breve{\sigma}\\\acute{\sigma}\end{matrix}\right\}\breve{\sigma}\left\{\begin{matrix}\breve{\sigma}\\\acute{\sigma}\end{matrix}\right\}\breve{\sigma}\left\{\begin{matrix}\breve{\sigma}\\\acute{\sigma}\end{matrix}\right\}\breve{\sigma}$$

The stanza from *Hiawatha* (also cited in Chapter 2) is repeated below, with stresses marked and the same exceptional cases underlined.

Trochaic tetrameter (Longfellow's Hiawatha*)*

On the Móuntains of the Práirie,
On the gréat Réd Pípe-stóne Quárry,
Gítche Mánito, the míghty,
He the Máster of Life, descénding,
On the réd crágs of the quárry
Stóod eréct, and cálled the nátions,
Cálled the tríbes of mén togéther.

In fact, the regulation of stresses is a much more integral part of folk rhythms than the regulation of syllable count. Nursery rhymes in English are composed of lines that have four beats. Sometimes these beats are unfilled, though they are still part of the timing. On the other hand, the syllable count seems almost completely irrelevant.

A nursery rhyme

Híckory díckory dóck Ø
The móuse rán úp the clóck Ø
The clóck strúck óne, the móuse rán dówn
Híckory díckory dóck Ø

Other rhyming forms are based on the same fixed four-count. In the following example, positions where there is no stress per se, but where a beat is required and pronounced, are underlined.

A counting rhyme

Éenie méenie mínie mó [íni míni máyni mó]
Cátch a tíger by the tóe
If he hóllers, lét him gó
Éenie méenie mínie mó

While stresses are not easily counted on demand or consciously, they are used frequently and naturally in language games and art.

There was a popular song in the 1960s that taught the following rhyme to be played with different names. Here is how the Name Game is played with the name *Joey*.

Name Game: Joey

Joey, Joey bo boey [ǰói ǰói bo bói]
banana fana fo foey [bənǽnə fǽnə fo fói]
me my mo moey [mi may mo mói]
Joe-y [ǰói]

Interestingly, this game is still played today, thirty years later, by children who have never heard the original song. What is striking about this for our purposes is that there are prosodic restrictions on what kind of names the game can be played with.

Here are a few more examples to show how the game works more clearly.

Name Game: Steve

Steve, Steve bo beve [stív stív bo bív]
banana fana fo feve [bənǽnə fǽnə fo fív]
me my mo meve [mi may mo mív]
Ste-eve [stív]

Name Game: Anna

Anna, Anna bo banna [ǽnə ǽnə bo bǽnə]
banana fana fo fanna [bənǽnə fǽnə fo fǽnə]
me my mo manna [mi may mo mǽnə]
A-anna [ǽnə]

The game is played by taking the name and making different substitutions for the onset: [b,f,m].

However, the game cannot be played with all names. Monosyllabic names or disyllabic names with stress on the first syllable are possible.

Some possible Name Game names

Bób	Déb	Bóbby	Sálly
Tím	Káte	Stánley	Cáthy
Míke	Béth	Míchael	Nórma
Stán	Jóan	Jóseph	Írma

Disyllabic names with other stress configurations are either excluded outright or only possible if the name is altered in some way. For example, the name *Annette* [ənét] is either disallowed entirely or adapted to [nét], e.g. *nette nette bo bette* . . . Some excluded disyllabic names are given below.

Impossible disyllabic stress configurations

Hórtènce	Annétte	Dàniélle
Ómàr	Jeróme	Joàchím
Zsázsà	Michélle	Dìáne
Cónràd	Gerárd	Jòsé

(Some speakers do find names in the first column marginally acceptable.)

Longer names with any stress configuration are impossible in the Name Game. The following chart gives a number of possible stress configurations for trisyllabic names. All of these are dispreferred in the Name Game.

Impossible trisyllabic names

óŏŏ	Chrístopher [kʰrístəfr̩]
óòŏ	Búckmìnster [bʌ́kmìnstr̩]
óòŏ	Cónstantìne [kʰɑ́nstn̩tʰìn]
ŏóŏ	Cassándra [kʰəsǽndrə]
ŏóŏ	Dìána [dàyǽnə]
ŏóŏ	Achíllès [əkʰílìz]
òŏó	Bèrnadétte [br̩nədét]

(Some speakers find trisyllabic names like *Christopher* with initial stress marginally acceptable.)

The critical observation here is that the template for an acceptable name is a foot. Acceptable names must either be a (stressed) monosyllable or a disyllable with a stressed syllable followed by an unstressed syllable. These are the instantiations of a foot. This language game thus supports the idea that stress and the foot are not some sort of accidental confluence of acoustically prominent features, but part of the cognitive organization of language.

In Chapter 2, an extralinguistic argument for the syllable came from writing systems. There are, however, no writing systems built on the foot, and so no argument for the foot comes from this quarter.

5.4. DISTRIBUTIONAL EVIDENCE FOR THE FOOT

Let us now consider distributional arguments for stress and the foot.

5.4.1. **The vocative chant**

In considering whether the foot is a reasonable construct, we need to first consider whether stress per se is really in people's heads as opposed to being simply acoustic stuff, with no linguistic or psychological substance. A very dramatic argument comes from the vocative chant. (This argument is due originally to Mark Liberman.) The simplest characterization of the vocative chant is that it is the characteristic melody associated with calling a cat, dog, small child, or other loved one to eat: *oh Joooooeeeeeey*. There are three 'notes' associated with this melody. A low (L) note associated with *oh*, a high (H) note associated with the first syllable of *Joey*, and a mid (M) note associated with the final syllable of the name. This can be shown as follows.

The vocative chant: 'Oh Joey'

```
LHM
| ||
oǰói
```

In shorter names, the L tone goes away and the H and M tones squeeze onto a single syllable.

The vocative chant: 'Puck'

```
H M
 \/
pʰʌ́k
```

With longer names, the pattern is more interesting. Basically, the H tone aligns with the primary stress of the word. Any preceding syllable is pronounced on a low (L) tone. Following stressless syllables are pronounced on a mid (M) tone.

The following examples show how disyllabic names are pronounced. If the first syllable is stressed, it bears the H tone, the following syllable bears the M tone, and the L tone is absent. If the second syllable is stressed, then it bears the H and M tones and the initial syllable bears the L tone.

Vocative chant: 'Diane' and 'Joey'

```
L  H M   HM
|  \/    ||
dày  ǽn  ǰói
```

It does not matter whether the preceding syllable bears a secondary stress or not. A name like *Annette* [ənɛ́t] has a vocative chant form identical to that of *Diane* [dàyǽn].

Trisyllabic names are more complex. There are six possible stress configurations. (I leave out the stress properties preceding the main stress and mark such syllables with an 'x'.)

Possible stress configurations for trisyllabic names

100	Chrístopher [kʰrístəfr̩]	Pámela [pʰǽmlə]
102	Cónstantìne [kʰánstn̩tʰìn]	Ánnabèlle [ǽnəbèl]
120	Póindèxter [pʰɔ́yndèkstr̩]	Búllwìnkle [búlwìŋkl̩]
x10	Augústus [əgʌ́stəs]	Rebécca [rəbékə]
x12	Achilles [əkʰíliz]	
xx1	Dominíque [dàmn̩ík]	Bèrnadétte [br̩nədɛ́t]

The contrast between *Christopher*/*Constantine* and *Poindexter* provides evidence for the role of secondary stress. Basically, the M tone associates to the secondary stress or the right edge of the word if there is no secondary stress (or if the rightmost syllable bears secondary stress).

Vocative chant: 'Christopher', 'Constantine', and 'Buckminster'

The vocative chant thus provides evidence for stress as a linguistic construct and part of a speaker's knowledge of English.

Let us now consider distributional evidence for the foot. Three broad categories of evidence will be cited here: metrical licensing, expletive infixation, and syncope.

5.4.2. Metrical licensing

The argument from metrical licensing is difficult to provide because, in theoretical terms, PARSE-σ isn't nearly so highly ranked as PARSE (-SEGMENT). The PARSE-SEGMENT constraint is what forces segments to be syllabified, and it is rarely violated in English (except for some word-final coronal obstruents, as argued in Chapter 3). The PARSE-σ constraint is what forces syllables to be in feet; this constraint is occasionally violated.

Thus every well-formed sequence of sounds in English must be parsable into syllables. This was called Syllabic Licensing in Chapter 2 and is what rules out a potential word in English like *[bznɪk]. There is no way to group all these sounds together into a sequence of legal English syllables. On the other hand, a hypothetical word like [blɪk] is well-formed because these sounds can be grouped into a single well-formed syllable. PARSE (-SEGMENT) must be ranked high in English since it is never violated.

We have already seen evidence that not all syllables must be incorporated into feet. Recall that the feet of English are composed of a stressed syllable followed by an optional unstressed syllable. Hence a word like [hát] or [háppy] each consist of a single foot, and [Mìnne][sóta] and [Àpa][làchi] [cóla] comprise two and three feet respectively. However, there are a number of word types we have already considered that cannot be exhaustively parsed into feet of this sort, e.g. [Chrísto]pher or Re[bécca].

This distinction between fully footed names and partially footed names was critical in the treatment of the Name Game data above. Names that are partially footed, e.g. Re[bécca], or that have more than one foot, e.g. [Dì][ána], are equally ill-formed in the Name Game.

Be this as it may, cases of unfooted syllables are severely restricted, and an argument for feet can still be made from metrical licensing. In theoretical terms, I will argue that there is a constraint PARSE-σ, but it is not top-ranked.

PARSE-σ can be violated on the surface in English in only two circumstances. First, certain affixes don't need to be stressed. (This is treated in more detail in Chapter 8.) Second, a single syllable can be skipped between two feet, or between a foot and the edge of a word; two unfooted syllables in a row are therefore disallowed. This generalization is given below.

Adjacent unfooted syllables
Adjacent unfooted syllables are disallowed.

Let us focus in on this second restriction and consider the distribution of stresses in three-syllable words. The following chart shows all logically possible footings for words with three syllables. Each syllable is marked with a sigma, σ. Each stressed syllable is marked with an acute accent, and foot boundaries are marked with square brackets.

All possible footings of a three-syllable span

[óσ]σ	[óσ][ó]	σ[óσ]	[ó][óσ]
σσσ	*[ó]σσ	*σ[ó]σ	σσ[ó]
*[ó][ó]σ	*[ó]σ[ó]	σ[ó][ó]	[ó][ó][ó]

Let us assume first that the constraint hierarchy prefers a binary foot to a sequence of a monosyllabic foot followed by an unfooted syllable. Such cases are marked with asterisks above and removed from the revised inventory below.

All possible footings of a three-syllable span (reduced)

[όσ]σ	[όσ][ό]	σ[όσ]	[ό][όσ]
σσσ	σσ[ό]	σ[ό][ό]	[ό][ό][ό]

At this point I will not state the constraints, but the relevant generalization is given below.

Preference for binary feet
A binary foot is preferred to a sequence of a monosyllabic foot and an unfooted syllable. ([όσ] is better than [ό]σ.)

Notice how, by eliminating these sequences, we have not eliminated any surface stress configurations, just some redundant analyses. This proposal is confirmed below, in the discussion of Expletive Infixation in §5.4.3.

The restriction on adjacent unfooted syllables discussed above, however, restricts this inventory further and eliminates some possible stress patterns. The first chart below shows the patterns that are excluded when adjacent unfooted syllables are disallowed, and the second chart shows the patterns that remain.

Patterns eliminated

σσσ	σσ[ό]

Patterns remaining

[όσ]σ	[όσ][ό]	σ[όσ]
[ό][όσ]	σ[ό][ό]	[ό][ό][ό]

The prediction made by metrical licensing in conjunction with the ban on adjacent unfooted syllables is that only the second set of patterns is possible. None of the former patterns is possible among monomorphemic words. This is borne out in the examples below.

Predicted three-syllable patterns

[όσ]σ	alien [éliən]
[όσ][ό]	ánecdòte [ǽnəkdòt]
σ[όσ]	aróma [ərómə]
[ó][όσ]	bàndánna [bàndǽnə]
σ[ó][ó]	Monádnòck [mənǽdnàk]
[ó][ó][ó]	Tìmbùktú [tʰìmbʌktʰú]

Only two patterns are excluded, however, so this demonstration is not as dramatic as one might hope. More patterns are ruled out in longer spans, but other considerations prevent all predicted patterns from being instantiated. The following chart shows all possible four-syllable footings. Once again, each syllable is marked with a sigma. Each stressed syllable is marked with an acute accent and foot boundaries are marked with square brackets.

All possible footings of a four-syllable span

[όσ][όσ]	*[όσ][ό]σ	[όσ]σ[ό]	[όσ]σσ	σ[όσ]σ
[ό][όσ]σ	σ[όσ][ό]	[ό][όσ][ό]	σσ[όσ]	[ό][ό][όσ]
*[ό]σ[όσ]	σ[ό][όσ]	*[ό]σσσ	*[ό][ό]σσ	*[ό]σ[ό]σ
*[ό]σσ[ό]	*[ό][ό][ό]σ	*[ό][ό]σ[ό]	*[ό]σ[ό][ό]	[ό][ό][ό][ό]
σσσσ	*σ[ό]σσ	*σσ[ό]σ	σσσ[ό]	*σ[ό][ό]σ
*σ[ό]σ[ό]	σσ[ό][ό]	σ[ό][ό][ό]		

Eliminating monosyllabic feet followed by an unfooted syllable reduces this to the following set.

All possible footings of a four-syllable span (reduced)

[όσ][όσ]	[όσ]σ[ό]	[όσ]σσ	σ[όσ]σ	σ[ό][όσ]
[ό][όσ]σ	σ[όσ][ό]	[ό][όσ][ό]	σσ[όσ]	[ό][ό][όσ]
[ό][ό][ό][ό]	σσσσ	σσσ[ό]	σσ[ό][ό]	σ[ό][ό][ό]

The restriction on adjacent unfooted syllables restricts this inventory further and eliminates some possible stress patterns. The first chart below shows the patterns that are excluded when adjacent unfooted syllables are disallowed, and the second chart shows the patterns that remain.

Patterns eliminated

[όσ]σσ	σσ[όσ]	σσσσ	σσσ[ό]	σσ[ό][ό]

Patterns remaining

[όσ][όσ]	[όσ]σ[ό]	σ[όσ]σ	σ[ό][όσ]	[ό][όσ]σ
σ[όσ][ό]	[ό][όσ][ό]	[ό][ό][όσ]	[ό][ό][ό][ό]	σ[ό][ό][ό]

Unfortunately, however, not all of the latter patterns are possible among monomorphemic words either.

Predicted four-syllable patterns

[óσ][óσ]	Mìnnesóta	[óσ]σ[ó]	cátamaràn
σ[óσ]σ	América	σ[ó][óσ]	*
[ó][óσ]σ	càntánkerous	σ[óσ][ó]	arístocràt
[ó][óσ][ó]	Kàrbàssióun	[ó][ó][óσ]	ìnflùénza?
[ó][ó][ó][ó]	?	σ[ó][ó][ó]	*

The absence of some [ó][ó][ó][ó] may be a function of statistical factors. An explanation for the absence of the asterisked cases is proposed in Chapter 8. The force of the metrical licensing argument comes from the absence of the other patterns.

5.4.3. Expletive infixation

We have seen that there is an argument for metrical feet from metrical licensing, but that this argument is less compelling than the syllabic licensing argument. First, not all syllables must be footed. Second, not all the predicted stress patterns occur among monomorphemic words.

In this section I provide another argument, originally presented in an important paper by John McCarthy. It concerns the distribution of the expletive *fuckin'* (in some American dialects) or *bloody* (in some British and Australian dialects) when it occurs within words in some dialects, e.g. *fan-fuckin'-tastic*. We will see that the position of the expletive is a function of stress and foot structure. This process is termed expletive infixation.

(Some readers might be offended by this open use of obscene or offensive language. However, there are several compelling reasons for continuing with this example. First, the particular phenomenon is only exemplified with these words in English. While the general phenomenon occurs in a number of languages and makes use of no offensive speech in many of those languages, in English there is no choice. Second, the particular construction under discussion is remarkable in that it is a marker of particularly informal and slangy registers in certain dialects. Hence the example is particularly striking, in that it shows a sensitivity to prosodic structure that could not possibly be a consequence of any sort of explicit instruction. Moreover, it shows that informal speech or slang is no less capable of showing important linguistic facts.)

As noted above, not all dialects allow for expletive infixation. Therefore, if the reader is not a native speaker of English or not a native speaker of a dialect that allows for expletive infixation, the judgments cited will have to be trusted. However, the author is a native speaker of an infixing dialect, and it is generally the case that most speakers of English find these judgments plausible even if they do not themselves speak an infixing dialect. This fact—that the judgments make sense to most speakers of English even if they do not speak an infixing dialect—is surely indicative of the reality of the prosodic distinctions that underlie the locus of infixation.

Let us consider first the possibility of infixation in disyllabic words. If all words must have one primary stress, then it follows that there are four possible stress configurations for such words. The following chart gives these configurations, the associated foot patterns, and a few examples.

Possible stress patterns for disyllabic words

[ǒσ]	háppy [hǽpi], kítty [kʰíri], tíger [tʰáygr̩]
[ó][ò]	álpìne [ǽlpʰàyn], zígzàg [zígzæ̀g], thýròid [θáyrɔ̀yd]
σ[ó]	seréne [sr̩ín], syrínge [sr̩ínǰ], ravíne [rəvín]
[ò][ó]	prìstíne [pʰrìstín], sàrdíne [sàrdín], fròntiér [frʌntʰír]

Strikingly, expletive infixation is only possible with words of the final category. (In all following examples, the expletive will be abbreviated as f* in orthographic representation.)

Expletive infixation with disyllabic words

[ǒσ]	*tí-f*-ger [tʰáyfʌkŋgr̩]
[ó][ò]	*ál-f*-pìne [ǽlfʌkŋpʰàyn]
σ[ó]	*ra-f*-víne [rəfʌkŋvín]
[ò][ó]	sàr-f*-díne [sàrfʌkŋdín]

There are several possible ways of describing this pattern. One possibility is to claim that expletive infixation can only occur between two stressed syllables, where the first is a secondary and the second is a primary stress. Another possibility is to maintain that expletive infixation can only occur between two feet where the first marks secondary stress and the second primary stress. Trisyllabic forms will show us which is the correct characterization.

The following chart shows all possible trisyllabic stress patterns and gives the predicted footings and examples.

Possible trisyllabic stress patterns

[ǒσ]σ	Cánada [kʰǽnədə], ánimal [ǽnəml̩]
[ǒσ][ò]	ámpersànd [ǽmpr̩sæ̀nd], cárnivòre [kʰárnəvòr]
[ó][òσ]	cúcùmber [kʰyúkʌ̀mbr̩], trícỳcle [tʰráysɪ̀kl̩]
σ[ǒσ]	banána [bənǽnə], amóeba [əmíbə]

[ò][óσ]	bàndánna [bæ̀ndǽnə], fàntástic [fæ̀ntʰǽstɪk]
σ[ó][ò]	peróxìde [pʰɾáksàyd], eléctròn [əléktràn]
[ò][ó][ò]	bìchlórìde [bàykʰlórày d], mìscóndùct [mìskʰándʌkt]
[òσ][ó]	Tènnessée [tʰɛ̀nəsí], vìolín [vàyl̩ín]
σ[ò][ó]	alòngsíde [əlɔ̀ŋsáyd], appòintée [əpʰɔ̀yntʰí]
[ò][ò][ó]	Tìmbùktú [tʰìmbʌktʰú], chìmpànzée [čʰìmpʰǽnzí]

Expletive infixation is only possible in some of these cases.

Possible trisyllabic expletive sites

[óσ]σ	*Cánada
[óσ][ò]	ámpersànd [ǽmpr̩fʌ̀kn̩sæ̀nd]
[ó][òσ]	*cúcùmber
σ[óσ]	*banána
[ò][óσ]	bàndánna [bæ̀nfʌ̀kn̩dǽnə]
σ[ó][ò]	*peróxìde
[ò][ó][ò]	bìchlórìde [bàyfʌ̀kn̩kʰlórày d]
[òσ][ó]	Tènnessée [tʰɛ̀nəfʌ̀kn̩sí]
σ[ò][ó]	alòngsíde [əlɔ̀ŋfʌ̀kɪ̩sáyd]
[ò][ò][ó]	Tìmbùktú [tʰìmfʌ̀kn̩bʌ̀ktʰú] or [tʰìmbʌ̀kfʌ̀kn̩tʰú]

Several generalizations distinguish well-formed from ill-formed cases of infixation. First, expletive infixation can only apply if the primary stress occurs to the right (e.g. *cú-f*-cùmber*). Second, expletive infixation can only happen if there is a foot on either side (e.g. *ba-f*-nána*). Third, expletive infixation cannot interrupt a foot (e.g. *Tè-f*-nnessée*).

Because of *Tènne-f*-ssée*, the foot-based characterization must be adopted as opposed to the stress-based characterization. This also establishes that a monosyllabic foot cannot be followed by an unfooted syllable (as proposed above). In other words, the footing of *Tènnessée* must be [Tènne][ssée] as opposed to [Tè]nne[ssée]. If the latter footing were allowed, there would be no way to understand why infixation is blocked after the first syllable but not after the second syllable of such forms.

Notice also that words like *Tìmbùktú* exhibit two possible expletive infixation sites, since there are two locations that satisfy all restrictions. The possibility of *Tìm-f*-bùktú* shows that while the primary stress must follow the expletive, it need not immediately follow it.

This is all confirmed with quadrisyllabic words like *inflùénza*, where the expletive can be infixed in either position: *ìn-f*-flùénza* or *ìnflù-f*-énza*.

Other four-syllable patterns confirm the generalizations above, with one additional observation.

Infixation with four-syllable words

[óσ][óσ]	Mìnnesóta	[mìnəfʌkṇsóɾə]
[óσ]σ[ó]	àquamaríne	[æ̀kwəməfʌkṇrín] or
		[æ̀kwəfʌkṇmərín]
σ[óσ]σ	*América	
σ[ó][óσ]	elèctrícian	[əlèkfʌkṇtʰríšṇ]
[ó][óσ]σ	càntánkerous	[kʰæ̀nfʌkṇtʰǽŋkɾəs]
σ[óσ][ó]	*arístocràt	
[ó][óσ][ó]	mìsùnderstánd	[mìsfʌkṇʌndṛstǽnd] or
		[mìsʌndṛfʌkṇstǽnd]
[ó][ó][óσ]	ìnflùénza	[ìnfʌkṇflùénzə] or
		[ìnflùfʌkṇénzə]

The additional observation is that an unfooted syllable in between feet allows for two possible infixation sites, e.g. [àqua]-f*-ma[ríne] vs. [àqua]ma-f*-[ríne]. Recall that this kind of optionality does not occur with words like *Tennessee*, confirming again the fact that it is impossible for such words to surface with an unfooted second syllable. Longer words confirm this pattern. Words of the form [óσ]σ[ó] show the same pattern as words like *àquamaríne*.

Expletive infixation with words of the form [óσ]σ[óσ]

| àbracadábra | [æ̀brəfʌkṇkədǽbrə] or [æ̀brəkəfʌkṇdǽbrə] |
| Wìnnepesáukee | [wìnəfʌkṇpəsóki] or [wìnəpəfʌkṇsóki] |

Longer words with three feet and the primary stress on the right allow for multiple infixation sites just like *Tìmbùktú* or *ìnflùénza*.

Multiple infixation sites with longer words

phàntàsmagórical	[fæ̀nfʌkṇtʰæ̀zməgórəkḷ] or
	[fæ̀ntʰæ̀zməfʌkṇgórəkḷ]
hàmamèlidánthemum	[hæ̀məfʌkṇmèlədǽnθəməm] or
	[hæ̀məmèləfʌkṇdǽnθəməm]
Àpalàchicóla	[æ̀pəfʌkṇlæ̀čəkʰólə] or
	[æ̀pəlæ̀čəfʌkṇkʰólə]

Without positing the foot as part of the way people organize prosody unconsciously, it would be rather difficult to capture these patterns.

5.4.4. Syncope

Let us now consider a third distributional argument for the foot. (The facts here were discussed in a very early paper by Arnold Zwicky and in more recent work by Pat Pérez and myself. The relevance of these for the acquisition of prosody by children is explored in work by LouAnn Gerken, Allyson Carter and Andrea Massar.) There are words where a stressless vowel is occasionally unpronounced. The technical term for this is syncope. In casual speech a word like *géneral* [ǰénərəl]/[ǰénr̩l] can be pronounced [ǰénr̩l]. The following chart summarizes the environments where this can happen.

Environments for syncope

At the beginning of words:
    paráde [pʰəréd] or [pʰréd]
    Torónto [tʰəránto] or [tʰránto]
    Marína [mərínə] or [mrínə]
    Canádian [kʰənériən] or [kʰnériən]

Before a stressless syllable:
    ópera [ápr̩ə] or [áprə]
    géneral [ǰénr̩l] or [ǰénrl]
    chócolate [čʰákḷət] or [čʰáklət]

Before a stressless syllable before another stressed syllable:
    réspiratòry [résprətʰòri] or [résprətʰòri] or [réspr̩tʰòri]
    glòrificátion [glòrɪfɪkʰéšn̩] or [glòrfɪkʰéšn̩] or [glòrɪfkʰéšn̩]

The kinds of consonant that occur on each side are important, the character of the vowel matters, and the frequency or familiarity of the word plays a role. These are not the conditions I am interested in here. I will therefore only provide examples where the consonants on each side are appropriate, and will assume that the examples are sufficiently familiar and uttered at an appropriate rate. Making these assumptions will allow us to focus on the stress conditions.

What are the stress conditions on syncope? The vowel that exhibits syncope must be stressless. The vowel can be at the beginning of the word. It can also occur in the middle of a word before a string of one or more stressless syllables. Thus, a word like *opera* almost always becomes *opra*, a word like *general*, *genral*, a word like *chocolate*, *choclate*. In longer words, syncope is possible as well, and more options surface. For example, *respiratory* can surface as *respirtory* or *respritory*. Some comparisons are given below, with possible syncope sites marked with parentheses.

Comparisons

óp(e)ra [áprə]	òperátic [àpɹ̃ǽɾɪk]
gén(e)ral [ǰénr̩]	gènerálity [ǰènɾǽləɾi]
glórifỳ[glórəfày]	glòr(i)f(i)cátion [glòrfəkʰéšn̩]/[glòrɪfkʰéšn̩]
réspiràte [réspɹ̃èt]	résp(i)r(a)tòry [résprətʰòri]/[réspr̩tʰòri]

Thus the middle vowel of *opra* is easily elided, but in *operatic*, the vowel must remain: **opratic* is egregiously bad. In *general*, the vowel can syncopate, but not in *generality*. Notice especially that syncope is not a simple function of how long the word is.

Basically, vowels syncopate only when an optimal foot would result. For example, a word like *parade* has stress on the second syllable. This second syllable is a foot, and the first syllable is unfooted: pa[ráde]. That homeless syllable can syncopate and it improves footing, in the sense that more of the word is footed: licensing is enhanced, e.g. pa[ráde] → [práde]. In constraint-based terms, the pressure to foot syllables exceeds the pressure to pronounce some of them.

What about the second case, *opera*? *Opera* starts off with three syllables, so one syllable is left unfooted if no vowel is deleted: [ópe]ra. When the medial vowel syncopates, we end up with *opra*, which is now a lawful foot: [ópra].

In the third case, *respiratory*, there is a stress on [tòr] and a stress on [rés]. There are five syllables; each stressed syllable is grouped with the following syllable, e.g. [tòry] and [réspi]. Notice that if we delete one of the vowels in the middle, the word can be completely footed, either as [réspir][tòry] or [réspra][tòry].

The critical point is that in all three cases—*parade*, *opera*, and *respiratory*—deleting a vowel results in improved metrical licensing. This improved coverage can be seen when we consider the foot structures (square brackets) for the forms above. The structures here naturally assume that syncopated vowels are not counted.

Foot structures for syncopated words

[óp(e)ra]	[òpe][rátic]
[gén(e)ral]	[gène][ráli]ty
[glóri][fỳ]	[glòr(i)fi][cátion]
[réspi][ràte]	{[résp(i)ra][tòry]} / {[réspir(a)][tòry]}

Since the locus of syncope is only treatable in terms of feet, the facts here argue for feet as a part of what people know (unconsciously) about the structure of English.

5.4.5. Summary

I have outlined how the foot works and several arguments that it is a genuine part of how English speakers organize their language. The argument came from several sources. First, metrical licensing requires that words be (partially!) footed. Therefore the shape of feet (at least partially) determines the shape of words. A second argument came from the vocative chant. This showed that stresses are part of the linguistic system. It shows nothing about feet per se, though. A third argument came from expletive infixation. Where the expletive is placed can only be described using the foot. Finally, syncope provided a final argument for the foot and supporting evidence for metrical licensing. A vowel is deleted only if it improves licensing.

5.5. GENERAL THEORY OF THE FOOT

In this section I present a general theory of stress, focusing in on the foot. This section benefits from earlier discussions of metrical theory, especially by Bruce Hayes, Morris Halle and Jean-Roger Vergnaud, and a number of others. The OT account of stress presented here draws heavily on the work of Alan Prince and Paul Smolensky.

5.5.1. Basic constraints

There are several components to the theory of the foot. First, there must be constraints that require words be footed. Second, there must be constraints on the size and shape of the feet. Finally, there must be constraints on how those feet are aligned with words. The full apparatus of the theory will be presented as we go through the facts and present the analysis of English; but we will go through each of these here just to give the basic picture.

The first component of the theory is a constraint that requires that syllables be footed: PARSE-σ. This operates in conjunction with allowing GEN to add foot structure.

PARSE-σ
Syllables must be footed.

PARSE-σ then chooses a footed output over an unfooted output, as in the following tableau for *háppy*.

PARSE-σ exemplified with háppy

	/hæpi/	PARSE-σ
☞	[hǽpi]	
	hæpi	*!

The next step is to force the foot to be of a certain type. This is an extremely complex subject, but I will start with the simplest assumption and refine it as we go along. Let us assume that feet are composed of two syllables or one, and that the stress must be on the left if the foot has two syllables. Drawing on the literature of poetic meter, this foot is called a trochee.

TROCHEE (preliminary)
Feet are either monosyllabic or disyllabic. If the foot is disyllabic, then the head is on the left.

In conjunction with PARSE-σ, this constraint rules out additional candidates.

PARSE-σ exemplified with háppy

	/hæpi/	TROCHEE	PARSE-σ
☞	[hǽpi]		
	[hæpí]	*!	
	hæpi		*!
	[hǽ]pi		*!
	hæ[pí]		*!

It is not clear yet how this constraint should be ranked with respect to PARSE-σ. The full theory of stress allows for several other foot types as well, but I will not treat those, as they are unnecessary for the analysis of English.

5.5.2. Where do degenerate/monosyllabic feet come from?

In this section I treat the two main sources of monosyllabic feet: lexical accent and syllabic quantity.

The system developed thus far works satisfactorily with respect to [hǽ]pi, but not with *hæ[pí]. The problem is that the latter must be a possible footing with words like *propél* pʰrə[pʰɛ́l], *platoon* pʰlə[tʰún], *lacrosse* lə[kʰrɔ́s]. Another problem at this point is that we have not ruled out one additional candidate: *[hǽ][pí]. Again, while this needs to be ruled out as the footing for *háppy*, it cannot be ruled out generally, e.g. *aardvark* [árd][vàrk], *syntax* [sín][tʰæ̀ks]. There must therefore be some mechanism that allows different kinds of footing.

There are several options here. One possibility would be to maintain that the constraint set need only generate the set of possible stress configurations and is not responsible for finding the precise one that a word exhibits. On this view, PARSE-σ would have to be weakened in some way and the final tableau for /hæpi/ would look as follows.

A weaker theory exemplified with /hæpi/

	/hæpi/	TROCHEE	PARSE-σ
☞	[hǽpi]		
	[hæpí]	*!	
☞	[hǽ][pí]		
	hæpi		*!(?)
	[hǽ]pi		*!(?)
☞	hæ[pí]		

Three candidates would be selected because it is possible to find disyllabic words with all three of these patterns, e.g. *háppy*, *platóon*, and *áardvàrk*.

Another option would be to make the disyllabic foot optimal and allow degenerate feet to emerge only under pressure from higher-ranked constraints. On this view, PARSE-σ would remain as formulated, but some other constraint would have to be posited that would allow for words like *platóon* and *áardvàrk*.

I will provide extensive arguments below for choosing the second option. For now, it simply keeps the theory of stress developed here in line with the theory of the syllable proposed in Chapter 2.

5.5.2.1. *Accent*

So far, I have proposed that feet are disyllabic units (with a stress on the left in English). Under pressure from higher-ranked constraints, a monosyllabic foot is possible. This pressure can be lexical or phonological. Lexical pressure arises when stress must fall on a particular syllable in some word. This is typically captured by marking this syllable in some fashion in the input. Feet must then respect this marking, called 'accent'. Formally, accent will be denoted with a raised circle, °, e.g. /vanîlla/. We also need a constraint that will force accented syllables to bear stress.

> *FAITH(v̊)*
> Accented vowels must be stressed.

In turn, this constraint must be able to outrank the constraint which would otherwise force feet to be disyllabic.

> *Foot Binarity (FTBIN)*
> Feet must be disyllabic.

I will give just one example here to give a sense of the general idea. As will be argued in Chapter 7, the final syllable of a word like *áardvàrk* bears an accent. In conjunction with FAITH(v̊), accent allows us to select the correct candidate from some of the competitors (as shown in the following tableau).

Tableau for áardvàrk

	/ɑrdvǎrk/	FAITH(v̊)	FTBIN
☞	[árd][vàrk]		**
	[árdvr̩k]	*!	

How these constraints can interact is reviewed in §5.5.4 and in Chapters 7 and 8.

5.5.2.2. *Quantity*

Phonological pressure for monosyllabic feet also arises when stress must fall on a heavy, or polymoraic, syllable. In the latter case, it is commonly assumed that a constraint like the following plays a role in the system.

> *WEIGHT-TO-STRESS (WSP)*
> Stress heavy (polymoraic) syllables.

This was first proposed in an influential paper by Alan Prince. This constraint must also be able to outrank FTBIN. This constraint will be expanded into a constraint family in Chapter 7.

The word *platoon* [pʰlətʰún] provides an example of this. The WSP allows us to select among some of the candidates.

Tableau for platóon

	/plətun/	WSP	FTBIN
☞	plə[tún]		*
	[plǽtn̩]	*!	

There is another treatment of quantity that is quite prevalent in the literature. This involves requiring that feet be not just disyllabic, but bimoraic. We will see in the following chapter that such an approach simply will not work in English.

5.5.3. How feet are aligned with words

We must now consider how feet are aligned with words. The basic idea is that feet are aligned in a directional fashion. The Generalized Alignment (GA; Ch. 1) schema is usually used to force feet to appear closer to the left edge or the right edge of the span. For example, the following constraint will force a single foot to appear close to the right edge of the word. (The symbol Σ is used here and following to stand for a foot.)

RL (GA version)
ALIGN(Σ,R,Word,R); the right edges of all feet are aligned with the right edge of the word.

Such a constraint would adjudicate between the following two candidates for *banána*.

RL exemplified

	/bənænə/	RL
☞	bə[nǽnɔ]	
	[bə́næ]nə	*!

If footing is exhaustive, however, such a constraint governs the distribution of any monosyllabic feet; it forces them to appear to the right. Imagine, then, a form *pataka* in a language with a relatively low-ranked FTBIN requirement. The RL constraint would force the degenerate foot on the right.

Exhaustive footing with RL

	/pataka/	RL
☞	(páta)(ká)	*
	(pá)(táka)	**!

The mirror-image constraint, LR, would thus have the opposite effect. With only a single foot, the foot ends up on the left. With exhaustive footing, LR would force a degenerate foot on the left.

I will assume that all footing systems are edge-oriented in one of these ways, and that LR or RL thus plays a role in any such system. The other constraint would be either absent or too low-ranked to have an effect.

This constraint must be augmented with an additional constraint that prevents the final syllable from being footed. This can be stated readily with the negative GA formalism.

NONFINALITY

$$* \left. \begin{array}{c} \Sigma \\ \text{word} \end{array} \right|$$

If NONFINALITY outranks RL, it will force a foot on the third and second syllables from the right. These two constraints adjudicate between the following candidates for *América*.

NONFINALITY and RL exemplified with América

/əmɛrəkə/	NONFINALITY	RL
əmɛ[rə́kə]	*!	
☞ ə[mɛ́rə]kə		*
[ə́mɛ]rəkə		**!

Summarizing to this point, I have proposed the following constraints for stress: TROCHEE, PARSE-σ, WSP, FAITH(v̊), FTBIN, RL/LR, and NONFINALITY.

5.5.4. A typology

Let us now consider how these constraints can be ranked. If the (necessarily partial) theory of stress presented here is a reasonable one, then it should be the case that each distinct ranking corresponds to a real stress system in the world. Moreover, while the scope of the book does not permit us to test this here, it should be the case that all occurring stress systems are describable in terms of some ranking of these constraints.

For conceptual simplicity, let us group the constraints into two sets: Shape constraints and Assignment constraints. The TROCHEE constraint is in neither group, since its ranking is irrelevant with respect to the other constraints given. The PARSE-σ constraint is in both groups, since it affects both the shape of feet and when/where they are assigned.

Constraint sets
Shape constraints: PARSE-σ, FTBIN, FAITH(v̊), WSP
Assignment constraints: PARSE-σ, RL/LR, NONFINALITY

Let us consider the shape constraints first. FAITH(v̊) and WSP play the same role with respect to FTBIN. Therefore, I will consider only the WSP and assume that FAITH($\overset{\vee}{v}$) behaves the same way. Confining our attention to PARSE-σ, FTBIN, and WSP, there are, of course, six logically possible rankings of the three constraints (3!).

Logically possible rankings of shape constraints

PARSE-σ >> WSP >> FTBIN
PARSE-σ >> FTBIN >> WSP
WSP >> FTBIN >> PARSE-σ
WSP >> PARSE-σ >> FTBIN
FTBIN >> WSP >> PARSE-σ
FTBIN >> PARSE-σ >> WSP

The interaction of PARSE-σ and FTBIN is the easiest to treat first. If PARSE-σ outranks FTBIN, words are fully footed even if this results in monosyllabic feet. This is shown in the following tableau for a trisyllabic word. Notice that several candidates tie, since the alignment of feet is controlled by different constraints.

PARSE-σ >> FTBIN with a trisyllabic form

/$\sigma\sigma\sigma$/	PARSE-σ	FTBIN
$\sigma\sigma\sigma$	*!**	
[$\sigma\sigma$]σ	*!	
☞ [$\sigma\sigma$][σ]		*
σ[$\sigma\sigma$]	*!	
☞ [σ][$\sigma\sigma$]		*
[σ][σ][σ]		**!*

If the constraints are ranked the other way, degenerate feet are impossible and some syllable must surface unparsed in words with an odd number of syllables. This is shown in the following tableau.

FTBIN >> PARSE-σ with a trisyllabic form

/$\sigma\sigma\sigma$/	FTBIN	PARSE-σ
$\sigma\sigma\sigma$		**!*
☞ [$\sigma\sigma$]σ		*
[$\sigma\sigma$][σ]	*!	
☞ σ[$\sigma\sigma$]		*
[σ][$\sigma\sigma$]	*!	
[σ][σ][σ]	*!**	

Let us now consider the interaction of FTBIN with WSP. Here, the ranking of these constraints determines whether the pressure to stress heavy syllables can force degenerate feet. For purposes of this discussion, I will use H and L to stand in for heavy and light syllables respectively. Consider a disyllabic word with an initial heavy syllable: HL. In such cases, the ranking of these constraints is irrelevant because the heavy syllable will be stressed anyway by trochaic footing.

Ranking irrelevant with HL words

/HL/	FTBIN	WSP
☞ [HL]		
H[L]	*!	*

/HL/	WSP	FTBIN
☞ [HL]		
H[L]	*!	*

If the heavy syllable is final, LH, however, there is an interaction. If FTBIN outranks WSP, then the heavy syllable is unstressed. If they are ranked the other way, then the heavy syllable is stressed with a monosyllabic foot. This is shown in the following two tableaux.

Ranking matters with LH words

/LH/	FTBIN	WSP
☞ [LH]		*
L[H]	*!	

/LH/	WSP	FTBIN
[LH]	*!	
☞ L[H]		*

The interaction of these two constraints in trisyllabic words depends on the ranking of FTBIN. Let us consider first the case where FTBIN is top-ranked. In such a case, PARSE-σ is essentially irrelevant. Hence the relative ranking of PARSE-σ with WSP is irrelevant. WSP then controls where the foot gets built. The following tableau shows what happens if the initial syllable is heavy: HLL. The single binary foot is built over the first two syllables to satisfy WSP.

Ranking of WSP and PARSE-σ irrelevant with HLL

/HLL/	FtBin	WSP	Parse-σ
☞ [HL]L			*
H[LL]		*!	*
[H][LL]	*!		
[HL][L]	*!		

If the heavy syllable were in the middle, then the WSP would force the rightmost two syllables to be footed.

Ranking of WSP and PARSE-σ irrelevant with LHL

/LHL/	FtBin	WSP	Parse-σ
[LH]L		*!	*
☞ L[HL]			*
[L][HL]	*!		
[LH][L]	*!	*	

If the heavy syllable were on the right, then the WSP would be irrelevant, since no binary trochee could stress the final syllable.

Ranking of WSP and PARSE-σ irrelevant with LLH

/LLH/	FtBin	WSP	Parse-σ
☞ [LL]H		*	*
☞ L[LH]		*	*
[L][LH]	*!	*	
[LL][H]	*!	*	

With longer words, the ranking of PARSE-σ and WSP does matter when FtBin is top-ranked. First, as above, if the heavy syllable is in an odd-numbered syllable, WSP plays no role and its ranking with PARSE-σ is irrelevant.

Ranking irrelevant with a longer word

/LLHL/	FtBin	WSP	Parse-σ
☞ [LL][HL]			
[LL]HL		*!	**
L[LH]L		*!	**
LL[HL]			*!*
LLHL		*!	****
[L][LH][L]	*!*	*	

If the heavy syllable is in an even-numbered position, however, the ranking does matter. Ranking WSP above Parse-σ displaces the foot.

WSP >> Parse-σ with a longer word

/LHLL/	FtBin	WSP	Parse-σ
[LH][LL]		*!	
[LH]LL		*!	**
☞ L[HL]L			**
LH[LL]		*!	**
LHLL		*!	****
[L][HL][L]	*!*		

Ranking Parse-σ above WSP leaves the heavy syllable stressless.

Parse-σ >> WSP with a longer word

/LHLL/	FtBin	Parse-σ	WSP
☞ [LH][LL]			*
[LH]LL		*!*	*
L[HL]L		*!*	
LH[LL]		*!*	*
LHLL		*!***	*
[L][HL][L]	*!*		

Let us now consider the ranking of Parse-σ and WSP when FtBin is ranked at the bottom. Ranking FtBin at the bottom means that degenerate feet are allowed to satisfy either Parse-σ or WSP. With a disyllabic word with a heavy second syllable, the relative ranking of Parse-σ and WSP is irrelevant.

Ranking of Parse-σ and WSP irrelevant with bottom-ranked FtBin for LH

/LH/	Parse-σ	WSP	FtBin
[LH]		*!	
L[H]	*!		*
☞ [L][H]			**

With trisyllabic words, the ranking of Parse-σ and WSP is again irrelevant with bottom-ranked FtBin.

Ranking of Parse-σ and WSP with bottom-ranked FtBin with trisyllables

/HLL/	Parse-σ	WSP	FtBin
[HL]L	*!		
☞ [HL][L]			*
H[LL]	*!	*	
☞ [H][LL]			*
HLL	*!**	*	
[H][L][L]			**!*

Ranking of Parse-σ and WSP with bottom-ranked FtBin with trisyllables

/LHL/	Parse-σ	WSP	FtBin
[LH]L	*!	*	
[LH][L]		*!	*
L[HL]	*!		
☞ [L][HL]			*
LHL	*!**	*	
[L][H][L]			**!*

Ranking of PARSE-σ and WSP with bottom-ranked FTBIN with trisyllables

/LLH/	PARSE-σ	WSP	FTBIN
[LL]H	*!	*	
☞ [LL][H]			*
L[LH]	*!	*	
[L][LH]		*!	*
LLH	*!**		
[L][L][H]			**!*

With longer words, the relative ranking of PARSE-σ and WSP again does not matter with bottom-ranked FTBIN. If the heavy syllable falls in an odd-numbered position, regular binary footing prevails: e.g. [LL][HL]. With a heavy syllable in an even-numbered position, a more complex pattern results from either ranking of PARSE-σ and WSP.

WSP >> PARSE-σ with a longer word

/LHLL/	WSP	PARSE-σ	FTBIN
[LH][LL]	*!		
[LH]LL	*!	**	
L[HL]L		*!*	
LH[LL]	*!	**	
LHLL	*!	****	
☞ [L][HL][L]			**

PARSE-σ >> WSP with a longer word

/LHLL/	PARSE-σ	WSP	FTBIN
[LH][LL]		*!	
[LH]LL	*!*	*	
L[HL]L	*!*		
LH[LL]	*!*	*	
LHLL	*!***	*	
☞ [L][HL][L]			**

The final case to consider is where FTBIN is ranked between PARSE-σ and WSP. These patterns are very different. If PARSE-σ is top-ranked, all syllables are footed and degenerate feet only result in words with an odd number of syllables; syllable quantity only plays a role in such words. If WSP is top-ranked, quantity always plays a role.

Let us consider first a disyllabic word with a heavy second syllable. Top-ranked WSP forces a singleton degenerate foot on the heavy syllable.

WSP >> FtBin >> Parse-σ with LH words

/LH/	WSP	FtBin	Parse-σ
[LH]	*!		
☞ L[H]		*	*
[L][H]		**!	

Top-ranked PARSE-σ forces a binary foot which does not stress the heavy syllable.

PARSE-σ >> FtBin >> WSP with LH words

/LH/	PARSE-σ	FtBin	WSP
☞ [LH]			*
L[H]	*!	*	
[L][H]		*!*	

A similar pattern surfaces with trisyllabic words. With WSP at the top, heavy syllables must be stressed whereever they are, but binarity is only sacrificed as a last resort with LLH.

WSP >> FtBin >> Parse-σ with HLL

/HLL/	WSP	FtBin	Parse-σ
☞ [HL]L			*
H[LL]	*!		*
[HL][L]		*!	
[H][LL]		*!	
HLL	*!		***
[H][L][L]		*!**	

WSP >> FTBIN >> PARSE-σ with LHL

/LHL/	WSP	FTBIN	PARSE-σ
[LH]L	*!		*
☞ L[HL]			*
[LH][L]	*!	*	
[L][HL]		*!	
LHL	*!		***
[L][H][L]		*!**	

WSP >> FTBIN >> PARSE-σ with LLH

/LLH/	WSP	FTBIN	PARSE-σ
[LL]H	*!		*
L[LH]	*!		*
☞ [LL][H]		*	
[L][LH]	*!	*	
LLH	*!		***
[L][L][H]		**!*	

With PARSE-σ at the top, heavy syllables are only stressed if it does not interfere with PARSE-σ and FTBIN.

PARSE-σ >> FTBIN >> WSP with HLL

/HLL/	PARSE-σ	FTBIN	WSP
[HL]L	*!		
H[LL]	*!		*
☞ [HL][L]		*	
☞ [H][LL]		*	
HLL	*!**		*
[H][L][L]		**!*	

Parse-σ >> FtBin >> WSP with LHL

/LHL/	Parse-σ	FtBin	WSP
[LH]L	*!		*
L[HL]	*!		
[LH][L]		*	*!
☞ [L][HL]		*	
LHL	*!**		*
[L][H][L]		**!*	

Parse-σ >> FtBin >> WSP with LLH

/LLH/	Parse-σ	FtBin	WSP
[LL]H	*!		*
L[LH]	*!		*
☞ [LL][H]		*	
[L][LH]		*	*!
LLH	*!**		*
[L][L][H]		**!*	

Finally, the two rankings are also distinct for longer words with a heavy syllable in an even-numbered position.

WSP >> FtBin >> Parse-σ with LHLL

/LHLL/	WSP	FtBin	Parse-σ
[LH][LL]	*!		
☞ L[HL]L			**
L[H][LL]		*!	*
[L][H][LL]		*!*	
LHLL	*!		****

Parse-σ >> FtBin >> WSP with LHLL

/LHLL/	Parse-σ	FtBin	WSP
☞ [LH][LL]			*
L[HL]L	*!*		
L[H][LL]	*!	*	
[L][H][LL]		*!*	
LHLL	*!***		*

Let us now summarize the six different rankings for the six different word types we have considered. The following chart provides the six possible rankings as rows and the six word types as columns.

Patterns summarized

	LH	HLL	LHL	LLH	LLHL	LHLL
(a) Pσ>>FB>>WSP	[LH]	[HL][L] [H][LL]	[L][HL]	[LL][H]	[LL][HL]	[LH][LL]
(b) Pσ>>WSP>>FB	[L][H]	[HL][L] [H][LL]	[L][HL]	[LL][H]	[LL][HL]	[L][HL][L]
(c) WSP>>FB>>Pσ	**L[H]**	**[HL]L**	**L[HL]**	**[LL][H]**	**[LL][HL]**	**L[HL]L**
(d) WSP>>Pσ>>FB	[L][H]	[HL][L] [H][LL]	[L][HL]	[LL][H]	[LL][HL]	[L][HL][L]
(e) FB>>Pσ>>WSP	[LH]	[HL]L	L[HL]	[LL]H L[LH]	[LL][HL]	[LH][LL]
(f) FB>>WSP>>Pσ	[LH]	[HL]L	L[HL]	[LL]H L[LH]	[LL][HL]	L[HL]L

As noted above, patterns (b) and (d) are identical. All other patterns are distinct. We will see in Chapter 7 that English exhibits pattern (c) (bolded above).

Let us now consider the possibilities for the three assignment constraints: RL/LR (ALIGN-R/ALIGN-L), PARSE-σ, and NONFINALITY. As with the three shape constraints, there are six logically possible rankings. Since there is a choice of RL or LR, this results in twelve possible systems.

Logically possible rankings of Assignment constraints

RL/LR >> NONFINALITY >> PARSE-σ
NONFINALITY >> RL/LR >> PARSE-σ
RL/LR >> PARSE-σ >> NONFINALITY
PARSE-σ >> RL/LR >> NONFINALITY
PARSE-σ >> NONFINALITY >> RL/LR
NONFINALITY >> PARSE-σ >> RL/LR

As with the shape constraints, not all of these rankings are distinct. To distinguish these different cases, I will consider the tableaux for each for hypothetical three- and four-syllabled words: *pataka* and *patakasa*.

Let us consider first how the two rankings with bottom-ranked PARSE-σ fare with the three- and four-syllabled forms with RL. (There are many candidates for footing the four-syllabled case, so for practicality a number of less plausible candidates are excluded.) Regardless of the ranking of NONFINALITY and RL, footless forms are selected as optimal. Hence putting PARSE-σ at the bottom of the assignment hierarchy results in stressless forms.

RL >> NONFINALITY >> PARSE-σ: pataka

/pataka/	RL	NONFINALITY	PARSE-σ
☞ pataka			***
(pá)taka	*!*		**
pa(táka)		*!	*
(páta)ka	*!		*
(pá)(táka)	*!*	*	
(páta)(ká)	*!	*	
(pá)(tá)(ká)	*!**	*	

RL >> NONFINALITY >> PARSE-σ: patakasa

/patakasa/	RL	NONFINALITY	PARSE-σ
☞ patakasa			****
(páta)kasa	*!*		**
(páta)(ká)sa	*!**		*
(páta)(kása)	*!*	*	
pata(kása)		*!	**
pa(táka)sa	*!		**
(pá)(táka)sa	*!***		*
pa(táka)(sá)	*!	*	*
(pá)(táka)(sá)	*!***	*	

If RL is replaced with LR, the directionality constraint is no longer in conflict with NONFINALITY and a binary foot is built on the left edge in both cases.

LR >> *NONFINALITY* >> *PARSE-σ:* pataka

/pataka/	LR	NONFINALITY	PARSE-σ
pataka			**!*
(pá)taka			**!
pa(táka)	*!	*	*
☞ (páta)ka			*
(pá)(táka)	*!	*	
(páta)(ká)	*!*	*	
(pá)(tá)(ká)	*!**	*	

LR >> *NONFINALITY* >> *PARSE-σ:* patakasa

/patakasa/	LR	NONFINALITY	PARSE-σ
patakasa			***!*
☞ (páta)kasa			**
(páta)(ká)sa	*!*		*
(páta)(kása)	*!*	*	
pata(kása)	*!*	*	**
pa(táka)sa	*!		**
(pá)(táka)sa	*!		*
pa(táka)(sá)	*!***	*	*
(pá)(táka)(sá)	*!***	*	

Let us now consider the ranking: RL >> PARSE-σ >> NONFINALITY. Top-ranked RL rules out any foot not on the right edge. Putting PARSE-σ above NONFINALITY makes sure there is a foot as opposed to no foot (which would satisfy NONFINALITY).

RL >> *PARSE-σ* >> *NONFINALITY:* pataka

/pataka/	RL	PARSE-σ	NONFINALITY
pataka		**!*	
(pá)taka	*!*	**	
☞ pa(táka)		*	*
(páta)ka	*!	*	
(pá)(táka)	*!*		*
(páta)(ká)	*!		*
(pá)(tá)(ká)	*!**		*

RL >> *PARSE-σ* >> *NONFINALITY:* patakasa

/patakasa/	RL	PARSE-σ	NONFINALITY
patakasa		***!*	
(páta)kasa	*!*	**	
(páta)(ká)sa	*!**	*	
(páta)(kása)	*!*		*
☞ pata(kása)		**	*
pa(táka)sa	*!	**	
(pá)(táka)sa	*!***	*	
pa(táka)(sá)	*!	*	*
(pá)(táka)(sá)	*!***		*

If RL is replaced with LR, a different picture results, with a binary foot on the left edge.

LR >> *PARSE-σ* >> *NONFINALITY:* pataka

/pataka/	LR	PARSE-σ	NONFINALITY
pataka		**!*	
(pá)taka		**!	
pa(táka)	*!	*	*
☞ (páta)ka		*	
(pá)(táka)	*!		*
(páta)(ká)	*!*		*
(pá)(tá)(ká)	*!**		*

LR >> PARSE-σ >> NONFINALITY: patakasa

/patakasa/	LR	PARSE-σ	NONFINALITY
patakasa		***!*	
☞ (páta)kasa		**	
(páta)(ká)sa	*!*	*	
(páta)(kása)	*!*		*
pata(kása)	*!*	**	*
pa(táka)sa	*!	**	
(pá)(táka)sa	*!	*	
pa(táka)(sá)	*!***	*	*
(pá)(táka)(sá)	*!***		*

Third, top-ranked PARSE-σ results in fully footed words. With RL, if there are an odd number of syllables, there is a degenerate foot on the right. This holds regardless of the ranking of RL and NONFINALITY.

PARSE-σ >> RL >> NONFINALITY: pataka

/pataka/	PARSE-σ	RL	NONFINALITY
pataka	*!**		
(pá)taka	*!*	**	
pa(táka)	*!		*
(páta)ka	*!	*	
(pá)(táka)		**!	*
☞ (páta)(ká)		*	*
(pá)(tá)(ká)		**!*	*

PARSE-σ >> RL >> NONFINALITY: patakasa

/patakasa/	PARSE-σ	RL	NONFINALITY
patakasa	*!***		
(páta)kasa	*!*	**	
(páta)(ká)sa	*!	***	
☞ (páta)(kása)		**	*
pata(kása)	*!*		*
pa(táka)sa	*!*	*	
(pá)(táka)sa	*!	****	
pa(táka)(sá)	*!	*	*
(pá)(táka)(sá)		***!*	*

Replacing RL with LR puts the degenerate syllable with odd-syllabled words on the left.

PARSE-σ >> LR >> NONFINALITY: pataka

/pataka/	PARSE-σ	LR	NONFINALITY
pataka	*!**		
(pá)taka	*!*		
pa(táka)	*!	*	*
(páta)ka	*!		
☞ (pá)(táka)		*	*
(páta)(ká)		**!	*
(pá)(tá)(ká)		**!*	*

PARSE-σ >> LR >> NONFINALITY: patakasa

/patakasa/	PARSE-σ	LR	NONFINALITY
patakasa	*!***		
(páta)kasa	*!*		
(páta)(ká)sa	*!	**	
☞ (páta)(kása)		**	*
pata(kása)	*!*	**	*
pa(táka)sa	*!*	*	
(pá)(táka)sa	*!	*	
pa(táka)(sá)	*!	****	*
(pá)(táka)(sá)		***!*	*

The fourth case to consider is top-ranked NONFINALITY with bottom-ranked RL. This results in leaving the final syllable unfooted. If an odd number of syllables remain, the penult is a monosyllabic foot (as in the second tableau below).

NONFINALITY >> PARSE-σ >> RL: pataka

/pataka/	NONFINALITY	PARSE-σ	RL
pataka		**!*	
(pá)taka		**!	**
pa(táka)	*!	*	
☞ (páta)ka		*	*
(pá)(táka)	*!		**
(páta)(ká)	*!		*
(pá)(tá)(ká)	*!		***

NONFINALITY >> *PARSE-σ* >> *RL:* patakasa

/patakasa/	NONFINALITY	PARSE-σ	RL
patakasa		**!**	
(páta)kasa		**!	**
☞ (páta)(ká)sa		*	***
(páta)(kása)	*!		**
pata(kása)	*!	**	
pa(táka)sa		**!	*
(pá)(táka)sa		*	****!
pa(táka)(sá)	*!	*	*
(pá)(táka)(sá)	*!		****

This can be contrasted with bottom-ranked LR, which results in a final stressless syllable and the monosyllabic foot on the left, when an odd number of syllables remain.

NONFINALITY >> *PARSE-σ* >> *LR:* pataka

/pataka/	NONFINALITY	PARSE-σ	LR
pataka		**!*	
(pá)taka		**!	
pa(táka)	*!	*	*
☞ (páta)ka		*	
(pá)(táka)	*!		*
(páta)(ká)	*!		**
(pá)(tá)(ká)	*!		***

NONFINALITY >> PARSE-σ >> LR: patakasa

/patakasa/	NONFINALITY	PARSE-σ	LR
patakasa		**!**	
(páta)kasa		**!	
(páta)(ká)sa		*	**!
(páta)(kása)	*!		**
pata(kása)	*!	**	**
pa(táka)sa		**!	*
☞ (pá)(táka)sa		*	*
pa(táka)(sá)	*!	*	****
(pá)(táka)(sá)	*!		****

Let us summarize these eight patterns to see if they are distinct.

Eight directionality rankings compared

	Ranking	/pataka/	/patakasa/
(a)	{NONFINALITY,RL} >> PARSE-σ	pataka	patakasa
(b)	{NONFINALITY,LR} >> PARSE-σ	(páta)ka	(páta)kasa
(c)	RL >> PARSE-σ >> NONFINALITY	pa(táka)	pata(kása)
(d)	LR >> PARSE-σ >> NONFINALITY	(páta)ka	(páta)kasa
(e)	PARSE-σ >> {NONFINALITY,RL}	(páta)(ká)	(páta)(kása)
(f)	PARSE-σ >> {NONFINALITY,LR}	(pá)(táka)	(páta)(kása)
(g)	**NONFINALITY >> PARSE-σ >> RL**	**(páta)ka**	**(páta)(ká)sa**
(h)	NONFINALITY >> PARSE-σ >> LR	(páta)ka	(pá)(táka)sa

They are all distinct except for rankings (b) and (d). These two do diverge in the treatment of disyllabic forms, e.g. hypothetical *pata.*

NONFINALITY >> LR >> PARSE-σ: pata

/pata/	NONFINALITY	LR	PARSE-σ
pata			**!
(páta)	*!		
☞ (pá)ta			*
pa(tá)	*!	*	*
(pá)(tá)	*!	*	

LR >> *PARSE-σ* >> *NONFINALITY:* pata

/pata/	LR	PARSE-σ	NONFINALITY
pata		*!*	
☞ (páta)			*
(pá)ta		*!	
pa(tá)	*!	*	*
(pá)(tá)	*!	*	*

Therefore all eight rankings of the assignment constraints are distinct. We will see in Chapter 7 that English is an example of pattern (g) (bolded above).

The two constraint systems obviously interact. At the very least we can establish a total ranking, since both systems include the PARSE-σ constraint. It is not clear, however, whether the interactions, aside from PARSE-σ, result in different systems. This question is not explored here.

I have not provided a treatment of a number of factors that are involved in the analysis of English stress: kinds of syllable weight, lexical effects, and cyclicity. These different factors will be dealt with at the appropriate point in Chapters 7 and 8.

5.6. FURTHER READING

There is a huge literature on stress and accent. One of the best introductions to the phonetics of stress is Lehiste (1970).

The general theory of feet is introduced in several books by Hayes (1981) and a recent and different approach: Hayes (1995). For some discussion of the feet of English, see also Halle and Vergnaud (1977; 1987).

The following papers and books offer various sorts of external evidence about feet in English: Hammond (1990) offers a presentation of the Name Game. Liberman (1975) discusses the relevance of the vocative chant. The metrical licensing argument is discussed in Hammond (1997b). Expletive Infixation is discussed in McCarthy (1982) and Hammond (1991; 1997b). Syncope is discussed by Zwicky (1972), Pérez (1992), Massar (1996), and Hammond (1997b). Gerken (1996) motivates foot structure from child language acquisition. (See also Carter and Gerken, to appear, and Massar, 1996).

The theory of accent was first proposed in Halle and Vergnaud (1987), and developed in later work by Hammond (1989a; 1989b). The theory of quantity assumed here was first proposed by Prince (1990).

Recent versions of metrical theory are discussed in Prince and Smolensky (1993) and McCarthy and Prince (1993a).

6

Syllables and Stress

Let us now consider the facts of English stress. These will be treated in two broad sections: the effect of stress on syllabification (this chapter), the distribution of the rightmost stress (Chapter 7), and the distribution of other stresses (Chapter 8). Particular attention is paid in Chapters 7 and 8 to the effect of syllable structure on stress.

The analysis of these three chapters focuses on the distribution of stress in monomorphemic words. This is for three general reasons. First, we will see over the next three chapters that there is more than enough to occupy our attention in the analysis of monomorphemic forms. An analysis of polymorphemic forms will make much more sense in the context of the analysis of monomorphemic forms, and so it is reasonable to complete the latter before undertaking the former. A second reason to treat only monomorphemic forms here is the basic methodology adopted in previous chapters. A proper treatment of polymorphemic forms requires that we attend to alternations, and so far we have been able to focus entirely on distributional regularities. Finally, the facts concerning the stress of poly-morphemic forms are extremely murky and exception-ridden, while there are no exceptions to the facts presented over the next three chapters.

The analysis developed here entails a much more intimate relationship between syllabification and stress than in previous analyses of English. The content of this observation is that, on the analysis developed here, much more of the pattern of stress follows from concerns of syllabification than has previously been thought.

6.1. BASIC DISTRIBUTIONAL REGULARITIES

In this section I present the basic distribution of the rightmost stress in English words. These facts are presented here so that the role of stress with respect to syllables can be investigated. I defer to Chapters 7 and 8 the analysis of stress per se.

6.1.1. Where stresses go

First, the rightmost stress can occur on any of the last three syllables in nouns, adjectives, and verbs.

Final stress

Nouns	Adjectives	Verbs
bàyonét [bèənét]	pìcayúne [pʰìkəyún]	guàrantée [gæ̀rn̩tʰí]
kàngaróo [kʰæ̀ŋgɹú]	gràndióse [græ̀ndiós]	àcquiésce [æ̀kwiés]
Tènnessée [tʰènəsí]	dèbonáir [dèbənér]	negléct [nəglékt]
tàngeríne [tʰæ̀nǰɹín]	ròtúnd [ròtʰʌ́nd]	salúte [səlút]
mùscatél [mʌ̀skətʰél]	adróit [ədróyt]	vàmóose [væ̀mús]

Penultimate stress

Nouns	Adjectives	Verbs
asylum [əsáyləm]	intrepid [ìntʰrépəd]	finagle [fənégl̩]
cicada [səkérə]	exquisite [èkskwízət]	meander [miǽndɹ̩]
vanilla [vənílə]	happy [hǽpi]	imagine [əmǽǰn̩]
surrender [sɹéndɹ̩]	maudlin [mɔ́dlən]	deliver [dəlívɹ̩]
pajama [pʰəǰámə]	novel [návl̩]	demolish [dəmáləš]

Antepenultimate stress

Nouns	Adjectives	Verbs
zinnia [zíniə]	sinister [sínəstɹ̩]	massacre [mǽsəkɹ̩]
vitamin [váyəmn̩]	ornery [órnɹi]	remedy [rémǝri]
vertebra [vɹ́ɹəbrə]	mandarin [mǽndrən]	register [réǰəstɹ̩]
tragedy [tʰrǽǰəɾi]	halcyon [hǽlsiən]	jettison [ǰérəsn̩]
America [əmérəkə]	genuine [ǰényuən]	atrophy [ǽtrəfi]

Previous literature on English stress maintained that there was a clear difference between nouns and verbs with regard to the possibility of ante-penultimate stress. Statistical facts make this a rather difficult point to demonstrate. As the chart below shows, verbs are generally shorter than nouns and adjectives and antepenultimate stress is consequently much rarer among verbs.

Syllable count in nouns, adjectives, and verbs (sample = 20,000)

Syllables	Stress	Nouns	Adjectives	Verbs
1	σ́	3,028	638	2,240
2	σσ	3,652	1,294	2,072
2	σσ́	666	247	987
2	σ́σ̆	2,986	1,047	1,085
3	σσσ	2,074	666	378
3	σσσ́	188	64	151
3	σσ́σ̆	859	502	157
3	σ́σ̆σ̆	1,027	100	70

We will see below, however, that, aside from these numerical differences, antepenultimate stress with verbs shows up only under very restricted phonological circumstances.

Let us now consider the syllable structures associated with these different stress patterns. As already shown in the preceding chapter, monosyllabic content words must either contain a tense (=long) vowel or be closed by at least one consonant. In addition, this consonant must be capable of bearing a mora. Hence, monosyllabic words containing a lax vowel followed by [ð] or [r], which cannot be moraic, are also excluded. This is confirmed in the sample above.

In disyllabic words with stress on the second syllable, the same pattern occurs: the stressed second syllable of a disyllabic word either contains a tense vowel or is closed by at least one consonant.

Final closed syllables in disyllables with iambic stress

Nouns	Adjectives	Verbs
carafe [kʰərǽf]	enough [ənʌ́f]	abash [əbǽš]
cadet [kʰədɛ́t]	banal [bənǽl]	attack [ətʰǽk]
exam [ɪgzǽm]	kaput [kʰəpʰút]	chagrin [šəgrín]
hotel [hòtʰɛ́l]	pastel [pʰæ̀stɛ́l]	finesse [fənɛ́s]
shellac [šəlǽk]	quadrille [kʰwədríl]	harass [hərǽs]

Final syllables with tense vowels in disyllables with iambic stress

Nouns	Adjectives	Verbs
ado [ədú]	blasé [blàzé]	agree [əgrí]
fillet [fəlé]	okay [òké]	crochet [kʰròšé]
macaw [məkʰɔ́]	outré [ùtʰré]	eschew [èsčú]
shampoo [šæ̀mpʰú]	taboo [tʰæ̀bú]	puree [pyře]
goatee [gòtʰí]	risque [rìské]	saute [sɔ̀tʰé]

The stressed first syllable of a disyllabic word is not obviously subject to this requirement. It can contain a lax (= short) vowel in a syllable that might be open or closed. (As seen in preceding chapters, [ʊ] has a more restricted distribution.)

Initial light syllable in disyllabic words with trochaic stress

Nouns	Adjectives	Verbs
zíther [zíðɹ̩]	búsy [bízi]	bícker [bíkɹ̩]
véssel [vésl̩]	réady [réɾi]	héckle [hékl̩]
válley [væli]	tácky [tʰæki]	hárry [hæri]
súgar [šúgɹ̩]	–	–
yúcca [yʌ́kə]	útter [ʌ́ɾɹ̩]	núzzle [nʌ́zl̩]

In Chapter 4 I argued that all syllables are subject to a constraint requiring that they be minimally bimoraic: BIMORAICITY. If this is correct, superficially monomoraic first syllables can aquire a second mora from the following consonant. Therefore a word like *beckon* [bék.ņ] has a closed first syllable, while a word like *bacon* [bé.kņ] may have an open first syllable (marked with periods here).

6.1.2. Stressless final syllables

More striking are the restrictions on the content of a final stressless syllable. If the final syllable is open, only certain vowels and syllabic consonants are possible: [ə,i,o,u,ɹ̩,l̩,ņ,m̩]. No other vowel is possible in this position.

Final stressless open syllables

Nouns	Adjectives	Verbs
códa [kʰóɾə]	éxtra [ékstrə]	–
píty [pʰíɾi]	háppy [hæpi]	cópy [kʰápi]
wíndow [wíndo]	fállow [fælo]	hállow [hælo]
Hindu [híndu]	impromptu [ìmprámptu]	rescue [réskyu]
fáther [fáðɹ̩]	dápper [dæpɹ̩]	bóther [báðɹ̩]
bóttle [báɾl̩]	fíckle [fíkl̩]	hóbble [hábl̩]
bútton [bʌ́tņ]	súdden [sʌ́dņ]	bátten [bætņ]
bóttom [báɾm̩]	–	blóssom [blásm̩]

Although there are additional complications involving the identity of the preceding consonant, the analysis of §4.4 can be generalized to include other sonorants. (I leave this for future work.)

Complementary distribution of coda
sonorants and syllabic sonorants

[r]	[ər]	[r̩]
[l]	[əl]	[l̩]
[m]	[əm]	[m̩]
[n]	[ən]	[n̩]

I will therefore treat syllabic sonorants as closed, rather than open, stressless syllables. This leaves [ə,i,u,o] as the only vowels that can occur in a word-final open stressless syllable.

There are several facts to be accounted for here, given the analysis developed in Chapter 4. First, what is the distribution of [ə] generally? Second, why do the other tense vowels and diphthongs, [e,ɑ,ɔ,ay,aw,ɔy], not occur in this position? (It is impossible to have a word like *[álě] in English.)

If the final syllable is closed, there are also restrictions on what consonants and how many consonants can close it. The following chart shows the possibilities for trochaic nouns when only a single consonant closes the rightmost syllable.

What consonants can close the final syllable of a
disyllabic noun with trochaic stress?

[p]	dóllop [dáləp]	[b]	chérub [čʰɛ́rəb]
[t]	gámut [gǽmət]	[d]	bállad [bǽləd]
[k]	hámmock [hǽmək]	[g]	–
[č]	spínach [spínəč]	[ǰ]	cabbage [kʰǽbəǰ]
[f]	shériff [šɛ́rəf]	[v]	ólive [áləv]
[θ]	zénith [zínəθ]	[ð]	–
[s]	frácas [frǽkəs]	[z]	–
[š]	rúbbish [rʌ́bəš]	[ž]	–
[m]	≈ bottom [bárm̩]	[l]	≈ bottle [bárl̩]
[n]	≈ button [bʌ́tn̩]	[r]	≈ water [wɔ́rr̩]
[ŋ]	–		

The pattern is rather straightforward. Among the obstruents, only [g] and the voiced fricatives are excluded. This is most likely the same statistical skewing observed in Chapters 3 and 4. In addition, sonorant consonants are ruled out, but this is due to the complementary distribution of syllabic sonorants with schwa–sonorant sequences (see above). The absence of [ŋ] is rather surprising, but this is probably because there are virtually no clear cases of monomorphemic words ending in [ŋ]/[əŋ].

The following charts give the same facts for adjectives and verbs.

What consonant can close the final syllable of a
disyllabic adjective with trochaic stress?

[p]	–	[b]	–
[t]	rússet [rʌsət]	[d]	árid [ǽrəd]
[k]	–	[g]	–
[c]	–	[ɟ]	sávage [sǽvəǰ]
[f]	cáitiff? [kʰérəf]	[v]	–
[θ]	mammoth [mǽməθ]	[ð]	–
[s]	–	[z]	–
[š]	gárish [gǽrəš]	[ž]	–
[m]	–	[l]	≈ ample [ǽmpl̩]
[n]	≈ brazen [brézn̩]	[r]	≈ meagre [mígr̩]
[ŋ]	–		

Adjectives exhibit a rather striking regularity; only coronal consonants are possible word-finally in trochaic words. The only exception to this is the somewhat mysterious *caitiff* [kʰérəf]. Notice that this limitation to coronal consonants applies as well to the syllabic sonorants: [m̩]/[əm] is also ruled out. This confirms the proposal that the syllabic sonorants are in complementary distribution with sequences of schwa followed by a coda sonorant. The only exceptions to this pattern are *velum* [víləm] and *bosom* [búzəm], which are clearly derived from nouns.

Verbs are charted below.

What consonant can close the final syllable of a
disyllabic verb with trochaic stress?

[p]	gállop [gǽləp]	[b]	–
[t]	vísit [vízət]	[d]	–
[k]	frólic [frálək]	[g]	–
[č]	–	[ǰ]	fórage? [fórəǰ]
[f]	–	[v]	–
[θ]	–	[ð]	–
[s]	hárness [hárnəs]	[z]	–
[š]	fúrnish [fŕnəš]	[ž]	–
[m]	≈ [m̩]?	[l]	≈ amble [ǽmbl̩]
[n]	≈ batten [bǽtn̩]	[r]	≈ barter [bárrr̩]
[ŋ]	–		

Again, only coronal consonants are robustly attested and there are only two noncoronal examples: *frolic* [frálək] and *gallop* [gǽləp]. Among the syllabic sonorants, all noncoronal examples are also nouns, e.g. *fathom* [fǽðəm], *bottom* [bárm̩].

The following chart shows the possibilities for word-final clusters in the three classes.

Final clusters with disyllabic words with trochaic stress

	Nouns	Adjectives	Verbs
rl	–	–	–
rN	–	–	–
rC	–	–	–
lN	–	–	–
LC	–	–	–
r+COR	–	–	–
l+COR	túmult [tʰʌ́ml̩t]	–	–
N+COR	légend [léĵn̩d]	sílent [sáyln̩t]	bálance? [bǽln̩s]
C+COR	lúmmox [lʌ́məks]	hónest [ɑ́nəst]	hárvest? [hɑ́rvəst]

These are extremely striking in that only C+COR clusters are attested.

Notice that the verb examples *hárvest* and *bálance* are also both nouns. In fact, it turns out that all verbs that exhibit penultimate stress and end in more than one consonant are simultaneously nouns.

Verbs with penultimate stress
and a final consonant cluster

bálance	bállast	chállenge
dístance	fórest	gállant
gárland	gárment	hárvest
húsband	ínterest	pérfect
pígment	scávenge	sécond
sílence	témpest	tríumph
wárrant		

The simplest treatment of these would be to maintain that final clusters are impossible for verbs and that these words are examples of true nouns.

The same generalizations governing final syllables in words with penultimate stress reveal themselves in words with antepenultimate stress as well. Let us first consider the set of possible stressless open syllables in this position. The following chart is parallel to the corresponding one above for trochaic words and final open syllables.

Final stressless open syllables in words with antepenultimate stress

	Nouns	Adjectives	Verbs
[ə]	pléthora [pʰléθɾə]	sépia [sépiə]	–
[ɪ]	cómedy [kʰáməɾɪ]	órnery [órnɹɪ]	átrophy [ǽtɾəfɪ]
[o]	cúrio [kʰyɾio]	–	–
[u]	Kinkajou [kʰíŋkəǰu]	–	–
[ɹ̩]	sépulchre [sépḷkɹ̩]	sínister [sínəstɹ̩]	mássacre [mǽsəkɹ̩]
[l̩]	míracle [mírəkl̩]	–	–
[n̩]	skéleton [skélətn̩]	–	jéttison [ǰérəsn̩]
[m̩]	–	–	–

As has been noted above, [m̩] is ruled out by the general prohibition against coda noncoronals in final position with antepenultimate stress.

The following three charts show the set of possible word-final singleton consonants for nouns, adjectives, and verbs respectively with antepenultimate stress. The first chart gives the nouns.

What consonant can close the final syllable of a noun with antepenultimate stress?

[p]	–	[b]	–
[t]	víolet [váylət]	[d]	périod [pʰíriəd]
[k]	límerick [límɹɪk]	[g]	–
[č]	–	[ǰ]	–
[f]	–	[v]	–
[θ]	ázimuth [ǽzm̩əθ]	[ð]	–
[s]	ábacus [ǽbəkəs]	[z]	–
[š]	lícorice [líkɹɪš]	[ž]	–
[m]	–	[l]	≈ miracle [mírəkl̩]
[n]	≈ skeleton [skélətn̩]	[r]	≈ sepulchre [sépḷkɹ̩]
[ŋ]	–		

It is perhaps meaningful that there are no noncoronals except for the final dorsals of *límerick* and *máverick*. In addition, these are most commonly pronounced as disyllabic: [límrək]~[límɹ̀ɪk]~[límɹək]. It is not clear what to make of this, however. The bottom line is that there seem to be tighter restrictions on what can occupy the ultima of a dactylic noun than what can occupy the ultima of a trochaic noun, and that the restrictions on the final syllable of a noun with antepenultimate stress are analogous to the restrictions on the final syllable of a verb with penultimate stress.

The following chart gives adjectives.

What consonant can close the final syllable of an adjective with antepenultimate stress?

[p]	–	[b]	–
[t]	–	[d]	–
[k]	–	[g]	–
[č]	–	[ǰ]	–
[f]	–	[v]	–
[θ]	–	[ð]	–
[s]	–	[z]	–
[š]	–	[ž]	–
[m]	–	[l]	–
[n]	≈ halcyon [hǽlsin̩]?	[r]	≈ sinister [sínəstr̩]
[ŋ]	–		

Very strikingly, antepenultimate stress in adjectives only seems to be possible with some of the syllabic consonants in the previous chart.

This strange pattern holds for verbs as well.

What consonant can close the final syllable of a verb with antepenultimate stress?

[p]	–	[b]	–
[t]	–	[d]	–
[k]	–	[g]	–
[č]	–	[ǰ]	–
[f]	–	[v]	–
[θ]	–	[ð]	–
[s]	–	[z]	–
[š]	–	[ž]	–
[m]	–	[l]	–
[n]	≈ jettison [ǰérəsn̩]	[r]	≈ massacre [mǽsəkr̩]
[ŋ]	–		

As with the adjectives, only the syllabic consonants can close the final syllable of a dactylic verb.

As we would expect, there are no word-final clusters in adjectives and verbs with antepenultimate stress and only very limited clusters with antepenultimate nouns. The following chart gives a few examples.

Final clusters in nouns with antepenultimate stress

térmagant [tʰŕməgn̩t]	óbelisk [ábl̩ısk]	támarind [tʰǽmr̩ənd]
ásterisk [ǽstr̩ısk]	órient [óriənt]	

It is unclear what to make of *óbelisk* and *ásterisk*. Is the final syllable stressed in these words? Is *-isk* a suffix? Other than these examples, the final clusters are limited to coronal NC cases.

We have seen an asymmetry between the nouns and the other two categories. Nouns allow a fuller range of final syllable types. Specifically, verbs and adjectives do not allow vowels other than [i] as the final syllable when there is antepenultimate stress. Various syllabic consonants are allowed, however. The different patterns are summarized in the following chart, where ✔ indicates that a pattern is attested and Ø indicates that a pattern is absent.

Stressless final syllables

		N	A	V
Penult	[ə]	✔	✔	Ø
	[ə]+COR	✔	✔	✔
	[ə]+NONCOR	✔	Ø	Ø
	[ə]+C+COR	✔	✔	Ø
	[i,o,u]	✔	✔	✔
Antepenult	[ə]	✔	✔	Ø
	[ə]+COR	✔	Ø	Ø
	[ə]+NONCOR	Ø	Ø	Ø
	[ə]+COR+COR	✔	Ø	Ø
	[i]	✔	✔	✔
	[o,u]	✔	Ø	Ø

Let us try to make a little sense of these patterns at this point. First, the fact that the tense vowels [i,u,o] occur in these positions is treated in §6.2.2.

Second, the distinction between coronal and noncoronal consonants was made sense of in Chapter 4 by appealing to mora count; noncoronals necessarily contribute a mora, while coronals only optionally contribute a mora. If we make the same distinction here, we can say that penultimate stress in nouns is possible only if the word-final coda contributes no more than one mora. Adjectives can exhibit penultimate stress only if the word-final coda can be moraless. Finally, verbs can exhibit penultimate stress only if the final coda is exactly one consonant and contributes no mora.

What kind of final syllable can cooccur with penultimate stress?

Nouns	Adjectives	Verbs
VC_0	VC_0	$V(C)$
| |	|	|
$\mu(\mu)$	μ	μ

The restrictions basically step up a notch with antepenultimate stress. A noun can exhibit antepenultimate stress only if the coda contributes no mora. An adjective or verb can exhibit antepenultimate stress only if there is no coda.

What kind of final syllable can cooccur
with antepenultimate stress?

Nouns	Adjectives	Verbs
VC_0	V	V
|	|	|
μ	μ	μ

Why is only schwa possible in a word-final stressless closed syllable? It would be nice to relate this to mora count as well. The most attractive possibility is that schwa is moraless. This would make it possible to claim that only monomoraic and zero-moraic syllables can occur to the right of the rightmost stress. This would also require some revision of BIMORAICITY, since many syllables containing schwa would not satisfy it. These questions are taken up again in §6.2.

6.1.3. Stressless post-tonic penultimate syllables

Let us now consider the syllable types that can occur in penultimate position when there is antepenultimate stress. We will see that the penultimate syllable can only be heavy in nouns when the final syllable is [i] or contains a syllabic consonant. The following charts show all the closed penultimate syllables I was able to find for words that are plausibly monomorphemic.

Penult closed with a nasal in word with antepenultimate stress

búrgundy	[bŕgn̩di]	cálendar	[kʰǽln̩dr̩]
cárpenter	[kʰárpn̩tr̩]	cálumny	[kʰǽlm̩ni]
cólander	[kʰáln̩dr̩]	cýlinder	[síln̩dr]
dérringer	[dérn̩jr̩]	frómenty	[frómn̩ti]
frúmenty	[frúmn̩ti]	fúrmenty	[fŕmn̩ti]
lávender	[lǽvn̩dr̩]	hárbinger	[hárbn̩jr̩]
órgandy	[órgn̩di]	próvender	[pʰrávn̩dr̩]

Penult closed with a liquid in word with antepenultimate stress

báwarchi	[báwr̩či]	cávalry	[kʰǽvl̩ri]
fáculty	[fǽkl̩ti]	ópercle	[ɔ́pr̩kl̩]

Penult closed by another consonant in
a word with antepenultimate stress

cháracter	[kʰǽrəktr̩]

All of these involve a final syllabic consonant or [i].

Tense vowels are also restricted in penultimate position in words with antepenultimate stress. Specifically, only nonlow tense vowels are possible and only prevocalically.

Stressless nonlow tense prevocalic vowels in penultimate
position in words with antepenultimate stress

i		u	
alien	[éliən]	arduous	[árǰuəs]
mania	[méniə]	annual	[ǽnyul̩]
various	[vǽriəs]	genuine	[ǰényuən]

e		o	
Hebraism	[hébreɪzm̩]	heroin	[héroən]
archaism	[árkeɪzm̩]	benzoin	[bénzoən]
Judaism	[ǰudeɪzm̩]	jingoism	[ǰíŋgoɪzm̩]

These can be contrasted with the set of possible stressless tense vowels in the ultima. As we have seen above, in that position only [i,o,u] are possible. (The data are repeated below.) As with the cases above, these are only possible when there is no immediately following consonant.

[i,u,o] in stressless open ultimas

i		u		o	
country	[kʌ́ntri]	jujitsu	[ǰùǰítsu]	window	[wíndo]
happy	[hǽpi]	kinkajou	[kíŋkəǰu]	tomato	[təméɾo]
broccoli	[brákl̩i]	Kikuyu	[kəkúyu]	meadow	[méɾo]

Antepenultimate stress is possible if the penult contains schwa followed by a single (intervocalic) consonant. Examples are given in the following chart.

What consonant can follow the penult of a word with
antepenultimate stress?

[p]	canopy [kʰǽnəpi]	[b]	cannibal [kʰǽnəbl̩]
[t]	charlatan [šárlətn̩]	[d]	infidel [ínfədl̩]
[k]	abacus [ǽbəkəs]	[g]	asparagus [əspǽrəgəs]

[č]	–	[ǰ]	prodigy [pʰráɾəǰi]
[f]	paraffin [pǽrəfn̩]	[v]	carnival [kʰárnəvl̩]
[θ]	amethyst [ǽməθɪst]	[ð]	–
[s]	hyacinth [háyəsn̩θ]	[z]	courtesan [kʰórrəzn̩]
[š]	–	[ž]	–
[m]	abdomen [ǽbdəmn̩]	[l]	broccoli [brákli̩]
[n]	cabinet [kʰǽbn̩ət]	[r]	tamarind [tʰǽmrənd]
[ŋ]	–		

(As with the final cases treated in the previous section, syllabic sonorants replace stressless vowel+sonorant sequences.)

When the final vowel is not a syllabic sonorant or [i], then a schwa in penultimate position after a rightmost antepenultimate stress can be followed by two consonants only if those two consonants are a possible onset cluster.

Two-consonant sequences

algebra [ǽlǰəbrə]
cockatrice [kʰákətrɪs]
armistice [árməstɪs]
vertebra [vŕ̩əbrə]

Summarizing, the penultimate syllable of a word where the rightmost stress falls on the antepenult is restricted in the following ways. First, the penult can be clearly closed if the ultima contains a syllabic sonorant or [i]. In all other cases, the following conditions hold. First, the penult cannot contain a tense vowel unless it is nonlow and prevocalic. Second, the penult otherwise can only contain schwa and only when a single consonant, or a cluster that is a possible onset, follows.

6.2. THE ANALYSIS

Let us now summarize the patterns for the rightmost stress in morphologically simple words. First, all monomorphemic content words in English have a stress on one of the final three syllables. Second, a stressed ultima must be (at least) bimoraic. Third, with a noun, if the penult is stressed, the ultima can contain a syllabic consonant, [i,u,o], or a schwa followed by at most a single consonant (perhaps followed by a coronal obstruent). With an adjective, the ultima can only be closed by nonmoraic consonants. With a verb, the ultima cannot be closed. Fourth, if the antepenult is stressed, then the ultima can contain [i,o,u,ə], or a syllabic consonant. Adjectives and verbs with antepenultimate stress cannot have [o,u] in the ultima. In addition, the ultima can contain a schwa followed by a coronal or a coronal cluster only if the word is a noun. In addition, the penult of a word with antepenultimate stress can be closed if the final syllable contains [i,o] or a syllabic consonant.

6.2.1. Analysis of stress

Let us consider how these generalizations might be treated in a metrical theory. (The analysis here is preliminary, and is fleshed out more fully in Chapter 7.) First, the fact that all words have at least one stress tells us that PARSE-σ plays a role.

> *PARSE-σ*
> All syllables are footed.

Second, the fact that there is one stress in the final trisyllabic window tells us that there is a binary foot and that NONFINALITY plays a role.

> *NONFINALITY*
> The final syllable is not footed

> *FOOTBIN (preliminary)*
> Feet are binary.

These constraints must be ranked with respect to other constraints and other principles to allow stress to fall on *any* of the last three syllables. Determining what these other constraints are will clearly depend on how we account for the various syllable structure relationships and syntactic category restrictions noted above. Therefore, the analysis of stress per se will be continued in Chapter 7 after the facts of syllable structure are treated.

6.2.2. Analysis of vowel quality

In Chapter 4 I argued that there were three kinds of vowel in terms of mora count. Lax vowels have a single mora. Tense vowels and the diphthong [ay] have two moras. The diphthongs [aw,ɔy] have three moras. In this section I substantiate the hypothesis that schwa constitutes a fourth class and is moraless.

The facts for final syllables are summarized below. The four columns correspond to whether the final vowel is stressed and whether it is followed by a consonant. The five rows correspond to tense vowels, lax vowels, diphthongs, and schwa. The tense vowels have been divided into two groups because the tense vowels [i,u,o] have a broader distribution than [e,ɑ,ɔ]. If a vowel type occurs in a particular context, it is marked with a check. Otherwise, it is marked with a null.

The final syllable cases compared

	´#	ˇ#	´C#	ˇC#
i, u, o (tense)	✔	✔	✔	Ø
e, ɑ, ɔ (tense)	✔	Ø	✔	Ø
Diphthong	✔	Ø	✔	Ø
Lax	Ø	Ø	✔	Ø
Schwa	Ø	✔	Ø	✔

To treat this pattern, I propose that all schwas are derived and nonmoraic. The simplest way to do this is as follows. Any stressless preconsonantal vowel surfaces as schwa. At the end of a word, the high vowels and back mid vowels, [i,ɪ,u,ʊ,o,ʌ], surface as tense. The other vowels surface as schwa in word-final position. These proposals are summarized in the following chart.

Proposed vowel realizations

Vowels	Context	Surface form
Any vowel	_C	schwa
i ɪ u ʊ o ʌ	_#	bimoraic
Other vowels	_#	schwa

Let us now review the relevant constraints on the distribution of moras to see if this will work. First, I assume onset consonants cannot be moraic. This appears never to be violated and so I take this to be either part of GEN or top-ranked.

Nonmoraic Onsets (constraint or part of GEN?)
Onsets are not moraic.

In the tableaux that follow, violations of this will not be considered.

Second, I argued in Chapter 4 that there was a constraint family for assigning moras to peaks and codas.

Mora assignment schema
{Ø,1,2,3, . . .}μ/segment: Some number of moras are assigned to 'segment' when it occurs as a syllable peak or coda.

Third, with these constraints in place, I propose a constraint that denies a mora to a stressless preconsonantal vowel.

PRECONSONANTAL REDUCTION (PRE)
Stressless preconsonantal vowels are nonmoraic.

The PRE constraint must, of course, outrank BIMORAICITY.

BIMORAICITY
All syllables are at least bimoraic.

To insure reduction of appropriate final vowels, let us assume that there is a family of constraints, built on the mora assignment schema above, requiring final stressless syllables to be nonmoraic. These individual constraints are ranked from most sonorous vowel to least sonorous vowel, e.g. as below.

Stressless final syllables reject moras
Øμ/ǽ] >> Øμ/ĕ] >> Øμ/ǎ] >> . . . >> Øμ/ʌ̆] >> Øμ/ĭ] >> Øμ/ŏ]

That only [i,u,o] show up stressless can be achieved by inserting the BIMORAICITY constraint at the appropriate point of the hierarchy.

Positioning BIMORAICITY in the hierarchy
Øμ/ǽ] >> Øμ/ĕ] >> Øμ/ǎ] >> BIMORAIC >> Øμ/ʌ̆] >> Øμ/ĭ] >> Øμ/ŏ]

As in previous chapters, these kinds of hierarchy can be abbreviated (or encapsulated) as follows.

The same hierarchy abbreviated
Øμ/{ǽ,ĕ,ǎ}] >> BIMORAICITY >> Øμ/{ʌ̆, ĭ, ŏ}]

The constraints outranking BIMORAICITY will thus be free to enforce the reduction of those vowels; constraints ranked below BIMORAICITY will fail to do so.

Consider now PRECONSONANTAL REDUCTION (PRE). This constraint reflects the fact that preconsonantal vowels are shorter than prevocalic or final vowels and thus more susceptible to mora loss. As noted above, this constraint must also be ranked above the BIMORAICITY constraint.

Ranking of PRE

$$\left\{ \begin{matrix} \text{PRE} \\ \emptyset\mu/\{\breve{\text{æ}},\ \breve{\text{e}},\ \breve{\text{a}}\}] \end{matrix} \right\} \gg \text{BIMORAICITY} \gg \emptyset\mu/\{\breve{\text{Λ}},\ \breve{\text{I}},\ \breve{\text{o}}\}]$$

Let us consider how this system works for relevant cases. First, a final stressless /ĕ/ emerges reduced because of high-ranking Øμ/ĕ].

Reducing final /ĕ/

/ĕ/	Øμ/ĕ]	BIMORAICITY
μ	*!	*
μμ	*!	
☞ Ø		*

A final stressed /ĕ/, however, emerges as bimoraic because Øμ/ĕ] is irrelevant and BIMORAICITY carries the day.

Lengthening final /ĕ/

/ĕ/	Øμ/ĕ]	BIMORAICITY
μ		*!
☞ μμ		
Ø		*!

A final stressed /é/ would, of course, also surface as bimoraic (with no necessary intervention of BIMORAICITY). Hence final /é/ and /ĕ/ merge, but final /ĕ/ is distinct, surfacing as [ə].

A final stressless /ĭ/, however, emerges bimoraic as well because Øμ/ĭ] is ranked below BIMORAICITY.

Lengthening final /ĭ/

/ĭ/	BIMORAICITY	Øμ/ĭ]
μ	*!	*
☞ μμ		*
Ø	*!	

A final stressed /í/ will emerge bimoraic as well, because it will induce no violations of (irrelevant) Øμ/ĭ]. Hence final /í/, /í/, and /ĭ/ all surface as bimoraic.

Closed-syllable cases are as follows. A stressless /ĭC/ will surface as zero-moraic because of high-ranked PRE.

Reducing final /ɪ̆C/

/ɪ̆C/	PRE	BIMORAICITY
μ	*!	*
μμ	*!	
☞ Ø		*

Stressed /ɪ̆C/ emerges naturally as bimoraic, [ɪ́C], because of BIMORAICITY.

Lengthening /ɪ́C/

/ɪ́C/	PRE	BIMORAICITY
μ		*!
☞ μμ		
Ø		*!

The constraint-based analysis has several nice qualities. First, it provides a direct account of the role of sonority in reduction. The pressure for stressless vowels to reduce is encoded as a schema of constraints requiring reduction, ranked by sonority.

This explanatory argument is buttressed by an empirical one. The subset of constraints that appear above or below the BIMORAICITY constraint need not be expressible as a natural class: they are simply the most (or least) sonorous vowels. The OT analysis can thus include /ǎ/ as a reducing vowel, making the correct prediction that there is no word-final stressless [ǎ]. This is impossible for a rule-based analysis since the set [ɛ,æ,ɑ] is not a natural class.

Another desideratum of the OT approach is that it makes plausible typological predictions. The present constraint-based approach makes a strong typological claim, which can be expressed as a typological implication.

Reduction Generalization
If a vowel α exhibits reduction (zero-moraicity) in some language L, then any vowel β in L that is more sonorous than α must also exhibit reduction in L.

Testing this claim goes beyond the scope of this book, but the claim seems quite natural.

6.2.3. Vowel quality in medial syllables

In this section I argue that the distribution of vowel quality in medial syllables is readily accounted for by the analysis presented in the previous section, and that no substantive revision of the analysis is necessary.

Recall the distribution of stressless vowels. In preconsonantal position, there is only schwa.

Preconsonantal stressless vowels

Canada	[kǽnərə]	anecdote	[ǽnəkdòt]
America	[əmɛ́rəkə]	amethyst	[ǽməθìst]
conical	[kɑ́nəkl̩]	animal	[ǽnəml̩]

Prevocalically, there are only nonlow tense vowels.

Prevocalic stressless vowels

i		u	
alien	[éliən]	arduous	[árǰuəs]
mania	[méniə]	annual	[ǽnyul̩]
various	[vǽriəs]	genuine	[ǰɛ́nyuən]
e		o	
Hebraism	[hɛ́breɪzm̩]	heroin	[hɛ́roən]
archaism	[ɑ́rkeɪzm̩]	benzoin	[bɛ́nzoən]
Judaism	[ǰudeɪzm̩]	jingoism	[ǰíŋgoɪzm̩]

These facts follow straightforwardly from the analysis developed so far. Medial preconsonantal stressless vowels exhibit reduction because of PRE. Medial prevocalic stressless vowels emerge bimoraic because of BIMORAICITY.

The absence of tense low vowels in this environment follows from the NO-LOW constraint proposed in Chapter 4 above (and repeated below).

NO-LOW

$$*\begin{bmatrix} \text{V} \\ \text{low} \end{bmatrix} \Big| \mid \text{V}$$

This constraint must operate in conjunction with other constraints. Specifically, a constraint requiring underlying [+low] to surface must be ranked below the constraints requiring other features to surface. Additional evidence for NO-LOW comes from the distribution of medial stressed vowels.

In stressed position, the facts are a little more complex. As we saw in Chapter 4, preconsonantally, all full vowels are possible.

Medial stressed preconsonantal vowels

Tense		Lax		Diphthongs	
Rita	[rírə]	Minnie	[míni]	Ida	[áyrə]
Sadie	[séri]	Becky	[béki]	Howie	[háwi]
Rudy	[rúri]	Woodie	[wúri]	Boisie	[bɔ́yzi]
Mona	[mónə]	Buddy	[bʌ́ri]	Beula	[byúlə]
Augie	[ɔ́gi]	Hattie	[hǽri]		
		Tommy	[tʰámi]		

Prevocalically (in stressed position again), the available vowel qualities are more restricted. All the diphthongs and the nonlow tense vowels can occur stressed prevocalically, but the low tense vowels and the lax vowels cannot occur in this environment.

Medial stressed prevocalic vowels

Tense		Lax	Diphthongs	
idea	[àydíə]	–	bias	[báyəs]
gaiety	[géəri]	–	prowess	[práwəs]
bruin	[brúən]	–	sequoia	[səkóyə]
boa	[bóə]	–	skewer	[skyúṛ]
–		–		
–		–		

The absence of stressed prevocalic lax vowels follows from BIMORAICITY. A lax vowel that received stress in prevocalic position would fall under BIMORAICITY and emerge as a tense vowel. The absence of tense low vowels follows from NO-LOW.

The analysis presented in the previous section is thus confirmed by the data from the distribution of vowel quality in medial position.

I have, however, skipped over a problem concerning stressed lax vowels in preconsonantal position, e.g. in *Hattie* [hǽri]. How do such vowels escape becoming tense because of BIMORAICITY? In final position, a preconsonantal stressed lax vowel escapes the effects of BIMORAICITY because such a vowel is in a closed bimoraic syllable. Presumably, the same must be true of medial stressed lax vowels.

There are two cases to consider. First, there are stressed lax vowels in clearly closed syllables (column (a) below); then there are stressed lax vowels in syllables that could be open (column (b) below).

The problem for BIMORAICITY

(a)	Closed	(b)	Should be open
Mindy	[míndi]	Minnie	[míni]
Bentley	[béntli]	Betty	[béɾi]
–		Woodie	[wúɾi]
Bunky	[báŋki]	Buddy	[báɾi]
Mandy	[mǽndi]	Hattie	[hǽɾi]
Monty	[mánti]	Lottie	[láɾi]

The cases in column (a) escape the effects of BIMORAICITY because the stressed lax vowel is in a closed syllable. To account for the absence of vowel tensing in column (b), I propose that such syllables are in fact closed. That is, the bimoraic requirement is met not by lengthening/tensing an underlyingly lax vowel, but by bringing a following consonant into the syllable (even if it is followed by a vowel).

This can be brought about by positing a constraint that assigns violations to bimoraic vowels or diphthongs (and of course trimoraic vowels/diphthongs by extension). Such a requirement insures that the need for bimoraicity is met by making the following consonant moraic.

$*\mu\mu/V$
Avoid long vowels.

If underlying tense vowels are to be represented as bimoraic, this constraint must be outranked by a constraint requiring that underlying vocalic moras reach the surface unmolested.

Generalized Correspondence(μ, μ) [GC(μ,μ)]
Underlying moras map to surface moras.

Ranking of mora constraints
GC(μ,μ) >> $*\mu\mu/V$

It might be thought that GC(μ,μ) must also outrank the ONSET constraint, but this is not necessarily the case. If the moraic coda can simultaneously satisfy the ONSET requirement, via ambisyllabicity or gemination, no such ranking is required. Thus I propose that the requirement of BIMORAICITY is met by the following consonant in preconsonantal contexts, regardless of whether the following consonant is preconsonantal (*Mindy* [mín.di]) or prevocalic (*Minnie* [mín.i]).

Since bimoraic and trimoraic vowels are disallowed before many medial clusters, it must be the case that GC(μ,μ) is in turn outranked by the constraint that forces such clusters to affiliate to the left (Chapter 4).

Let us go through some relevant cases to see how the analysis works. A schematic form like /ɛ́CV/ (e.g. *Bennie*) takes the following consonant to satisfy the BIMORAICITY requirement.

/ɛ́CV/

/ɛ́CV/	BIMORAICITY	*μμ/V
ɛ́CV | μ	*!	
ɛ́CV ⟍ μ μ		*!
☞ ɛ́CV | | μ μ		

A form like /éCV/ (e.g. *Brady*) meets the BIMORAICITY requirement without change.

/éCV/

/éCV/	BIMORAICITY	GC(μ,μ)	*μμ/V
éCV | μ	*!	*	
☞ éCV ⟍ μ μ			*
éCV | | μ μ		*!	

A form like /ɛ́V/ (e.g. perhaps *Leia* [léə]) is forced to undergo tensing/lengthening, as no consonant is available to be moraic.

/ɛ́V/

/ɛ́V/	Bimoraicity	*$\mu\mu$/V
ɛ́V | μ	*!	
☞ éCV ⋀ μ μ		*

Casting this analysis in terms of OT thus provides for a natural treatment of the different ways bimoraicity is attained. The 'preference' for bimoraicity to be attained from a following consonant, rather than by lengthening the vowel, would be difficult to state in a traditional rule-based framework.

To summarize to this point, I have developed an analysis of vowel reduction in English on the basis of the distribution of quality and reduction in final syllables. When cast in terms of OT, the analysis has several arguments in its favor. First, it provides an account of the role of sonority in vowel reduction. Second, it allows for the expression of apparently unnatural but occurring classes in phonological generalizations. Third, it makes reasonable and testable typological claims. Fourth, it provides a natural treatment of the preference for Bimoraicity to be satisfied by a consonant rather than by vowel lengthening.

6.2.4. Expletive infixation again

The previous section left unresolved the question of whether a single intervocalic consonant after a lax vowel affiliates to the left or affiliates to both syllables. Can Onset and Bimoraicity be satisfied simultaneously with a single consonant?

In this section, I review some facts that support the claim that a single consonant can satisfy both constraints. Recall the process of Expletive Infixation from Chapter 5.

Expletive infixation again

typhoon	[tàyfún]	ty - fuckin' - phoon
fantastic	[fæntǽstɪk]	fan - fuckin' - tastic
Minnesota	[mìnəsórə]	Minne - fuckin' - sota
Tennessee	[tènəsí]	Tenne - fuckin' - see

Expletive Infixation behaves somewhat strangely, however, when it applies to disyllabic words where the first vowel is lax followed by a single consonant. Basically, Expletive Infixation seems to be blocked in such cases. The contrast between tense and lax first syllables is presented below. Number and type of intervocalic consonants are varied. In (a) are cases where the first syllable is necessarily closed, regardless of vowel quality. In such cases, Expletive Infixation can apply regardless of vowel quality. In (b) are cases with only a single intervocalic consonant. Here there is a strong contrast based on the vowel quality of the first syllable. If the first syllable contains a tense vowel, Expletive Infixation is grammatical; if the first vowel is lax however, Expletive Infixation is strongly disfavored. In (c), cases involving an intervocalic obstruent–liquid cluster are presented. Here, as in (b), Infixation is fine with a tense vowel. However, with a lax vowel, there are two possibilities. If the cluster is syllabified as an onset, Infixation is as likely as with the single intervocalic cases. For some speakers, however, it is marginally possible to split the cluster, in which case Infixation does become possible. Note, however, that there is no such cluster-splitting possibility with the tense vowels. In (d), s-obstruent clusters are presented. Here the facts are similar to those of (c). With tense vowels, Infixation is possible and the cluster is syllabified as an onset. With lax vowels, however, splitting the cluster seems to be preferred and Infixation is just fine.

Expletive infixation with disyllables

		Tense		Lax	
(a)	VC.CV	sardine [sàrdín]	sar-dine	mundane [mʌndén]	mun-dane
		gourmet [gùrmé]	gour-met	mankind [mænkʰáynd]	man-kind
(b)	VCV	typhoon [tʰàyfún]	ty-phoon	raccoon [rækʰún]	??ra(c)-coon
		motel [mòtʰél]	mo-tel	trapeze [tʰræpʰíz]	??tra(p)-peze
(c)	V.OLV	supreme [sùpʰrím]	su-preme	tableau [tʰæbló]	?tab-(b)leau, ??ta-bleau
		digress [dàygrés]	di-gress	doubloon [dʌblún]	?doub-(b)loon, ??dou-bloon
(d)	VsCV	respect [rìspékt]	re-spect	cascade [kʰæskéd]	cas-cade
		austere [òstír]	au-stere	Rasputin [ræspyútn̩]	Ras-putin

The critical fact about this chart is that, in certain cases, where the first syllable is lax and followed by a single consonant, Expletive Infixation is dispreferred (e.g. *ràccóon* and *tàbléau*). This fact can be used to support the present analysis.

With a single consonant or with an obstruent–liquid cluster, infixation after a lax vowel is dispreferred. Assuming that such clusters are simultaneously syllabified as codas and as onsets, this follows because Infixation would prevent the consonant from being simultaneously associated to two syllables. Infixation with a tense vowel in such contexts is, of course, no problem because the onset consonant of the second syllable is not affiliated with the first syllable.

If, on the other hand, this intervocalic consonant were affiliated solely with the first syllable, this would predict that Expletive Infixation should be fine with words like *raccoon*, and that the consonant should occur to the left of the expletive, e.g. *[ræðkfʌknún]. The contrast between *raccoon* and *typhoon* is shown below.

Raccoon vs. *typhoon*

rækun	tayfun
\/ ∖∖	\/∖ ∖∖
μμμμ	μμ μμ
∨ ∨	∨ ∨
σ σ	σ σ

Consider now the behavior of words with clusters. There are three cases to consider. First, there are clusters that are falling in sonority, e.g. *mundane*. Second, there are obstruent–approximant clusters, e.g. *tableau*. Finally, there are [s]–obstruent clusters, e.g. *cascade*.

Consider first the falling sonority case. These examples exhibit infixation easily between the two consonants. In Chapter 4 I argued that intervocalic clusters affiliate as much as possible to the left. We have now revised that so that the ONSET constraint can be satisfied by simultaneously syllabifying a consonant into two syllables. This entails the following syllable structure for a word like *mundane*.

Mundane

Clearly, the infix must be able to break the double association of the [d], just in case the first syllable ends up bimoraic and the second syllable ends up with an onset.

Contrast this with the obstruent–approximant case, e.g. *tableau*. If these words undergo infixation, the infix is positioned between the intervocalic consonants.

Tableau

tæblo

\ M

μ μμμ

V V

σ σ

The difference between this and the preceding case is that, while in *mundane* it is the coda affiliation that must be severed, in *tableau*, it is the onset affiliation that must be broken.

The final case, *cascade*, undergoes infixation as readily as *mundane*. As we would expect, these word types exhibit the same syllable structure.

Cuscade

kæsked

\ M l

μμ μμ

V V

σ σ

To summarize, I have considered some additional facts concerning Expletive Infixation in English. First, in disyllabic words where the first syllable is open and lax, Infixation is dispreferred. Second, in disyllabic words where the first syllable is open and lax, a following[s]–obstruent cluster (or any cluster exhibiting falling sonority) can be split. These facts can be explained on the analysis presented above. In both cases, the requirements of ONSET and BIMORAICITY must be met.

The analysis proposed would appear to predict that the medial consonant in words like *Minnie* should be long or geminate on the surface. However, there are several good reasons why we would not expect this consonant to be long phonetically, and several additional bits of evidence in support of the structure I have proposed.

First, Borowsky et al. (1984) argue that if a consonant is syllabified into two adjacent syllables, it must be treated as gemination. On their view, there is no such thing as ambisyllabicity. Any case of apparent ambisyllabicity must be treated as gemination, thus making the prediction that there will be no languages where ambisyllabicity could contrast with gemination. Their richer notion of gemination can be implemented phonetically in a variety of ways. They include the possibility that geminates may be realized without added length. Hence, phonological gemination need not be mirrored with phonetic length. If this is correct, then the structures posited here for English must be treated as gemination, which quite reasonably can be realized without added length.

Second, I have argued that gemination is restricted to intervocalic position after a lax vowel. Gemination is fully predictable phonologically; thus it bears no contrastive function. It is a truism of phonology that contrastive phonological properties are generally more salient phonetically than noncontrastive properties. Hence, general considerations of contrastiveness are consistent with no length difference.

Third, since geminates always follow lax vowels and tense vowels are never followed by geminates, there are a plethora of phonetic variables that allow words containing such sequences to be distinguished on the basis of the tense–lax distinction.

Finally, there is extensive psycholinguistic evidence that these consonants are syllabified differently from other intervocalic consonants. Psycholinguistic investigations of syllabification by Treiman and Danis (1988), Treiman and Zukowski (1990), and Hammond and Dupoux (1996) all show that an intervocalic consonant following a lax vowel tends to syllabify to the left. Similar investigation by Meador and Ohala (1993) shows that the relevant consonant is actually in both syllables.

Thus, theoretical considerations about available phonological structures, general considerations of contrast, and psycholinguistic considerations are all consistent with the position taken here.

Let us now put the whole analysis together. First, there is the BIMORAICITY constraint.

> *BIMORAICITY (repeated)*
> Syllables must be bimoraic.

This constraint interacts with the ONSET constraint.

> *ONSET (repeated)*
> Syllables must have onsets.

In addition, the ONSET constraint interacts with the MAX-CODA constraint.

MAX-CODA (repeated)
Affiliate as many consonants to the left as possible when there is more than one.

We must also figure in the NoCODA constraint.

NoCODA (repeated)
Syllables do not have codas.

In addition, we need a constraint to limit the occurrence of gemination (or ambisyllabicity).

NoGEMINATES
Consonants can occupy no more than one syllabic position.

The interactions between these are actually fairly simple. The BIMORAICITY constraint is never violated; hence it is not outranked by anything. Once we allow for the possibility of multiple affiliation, the ONSET constraint does not conflict with BIMORAICITY. Hence the former is not fixed in ranking with respect to the latter. MAX-CODA also does not conflict with ONSET; so again their ranking is free. NoCODA does not interact with ONSET, but does have to be ranked below BIMORAICITY and MAX-CODA, so that an intervocalic consonant can affiliate to the left when necessary. Finally, NoGEMINATES must be bottom-ranked so that violations can occur to satisfy the other constraints given. These generalizations are consistent with several rankings; here is one.

Ranking required

$$\left\{ \begin{matrix} \text{BIMORAICITY} \\ \text{MAX-CODA} \\ \text{ONSET} \end{matrix} \right\} \gg \text{NoCODA} \right\} \gg \text{NoGEMINATES}$$

Let us go through a few examples to show how this works. A word like *tacky* [tʰǽki], with a lax first vowel and a stressless second vowel, surfaces with the intervocalic consonant multiply affiliated. (For convenience in tableaux, multiply affiliated consonants will be represented as C.C, e.g. k.k.)

Tacky

/tæki/	BM	MC	O	NC	NG
tʰæ.ki	*!				
tʰæk.i			*!	*	
☞ tʰæk.ki				*	*

A word like *coda* [kʰóɾə], with a tense first vowel and a stressless second vowel, surfaces with the consonant fully in the second syllable.

Coda

	/kodə/	BM	MC	O	NC	NG
☞	kʰo.ɾə					
	kʰoɾ.ə			*!	*	
	kʰoɾ.ɾə				*!	*

A word like *mattress* [mǽtrəs], with a lax first vowel, a stressless second vowel, and a possible onset cluster, surfaces with the first consonant in the first syllable and the second consonant in the second syllable.

Mattress

	/mætrəs/	BM	MC	O	NC	NG
	mæ.trəs	*!	*			
☞	mæt.rəs				*	
	mæt.trəs				*	*!

A word like *cobra* [kʰóbrə], with a tense first vowel, a stressless second vowel, and a possible onset cluster, exhibits the same syllabification because of the contribution of relatively high-ranked MAX-CODA.

Cobra

	/kobrə/	BM	MC	O	NC	NG
	ko.brə		*!			
☞	kob.rə				*	
	kob.brə				*	*!

Finally, a word like *active* [ǽktɪv], with a lax first vowel, stressless second vowel, and impossible onset cluster, syllabifies the first consonant fully in the first syllable, with the second consonant in both.

Active

	/æktɪv/	BM	MC	O	NC	NG
	æk.tɪv		*!		*	
	ækt.ɪv			*!	*	
☞	ækt.tɪv				*	*

This analysis thus correctly formalizes the different syllabification cases we have seen.

6.2.5. [yu], [h], and aspiration

The analysis so far maintains that a single intervocalic consonant will affiliate to the right unless preceded by a lax vowel. A consonant cluster, however, will affiliate to the left. If the entire cluster cannot affiliate to the left, any remaining consonants affiliate to the right. So far, I have said nothing about schwa. In this section I cite several bits of evidence that suggest that an intervocalic consonant after schwa does not affiliate to the left: aspiration, [h], and [yu].

6.2.5.1. *Aspiration*

In §1.2 I presented the fact that the sounds [p,t,k,č] are pronounced in two different ways. Word-initially they are aspirated, while after a word-initial [s] they are unaspirated. The relevant figure is repeated below.

Allophonic variation of [p,t,č,k]

	Word-initial	After [s]
/p/	pin	spin
/t/	tin	stin(t)
/k/	kin	skin
/č/	chin	–

As we saw in Chapter 3, [č] cannot occur after [s] word-initially.

The generalization proposed in Chapter 1 was that the only sounds that exhibit aspiration are [p,t,k,č], the voiceless stops and affricates. In addition, aspiration only occurs word-initially. (This will be revised shortly in this section.)

Let us now consider the analysis that was proposed for these facts. First, there is a constraint requiring initial stops and affricates to be aspirated.

> *ASPIRATION constraint*
> Word-initial voiceless stops (and affricates) must be aspirated.

This constraint interacts with a variety of faithfulness constraints, and with a constraint excluding aspiration generally.

Some relevant faithfulness constraints
FAITH(ASPIRATION)
  The output is identical to the input with respect to aspiration.
FAITH(VOICING)
  The output is identical to the input with respect to voicing.
FAITH(POA)
  The output is identical to the input with respect to place of
  articulation.
FAITH(MOA)
  The output is identical to the input with respect to manner of
  articulation.
FAITH(VOWELS)
  The output is identical to the input with respect to the number of
  vowels.

NOASPIRATION constraint
Nothing is aspirated.

This system accurately accounts for the generalizations above. However,
it fails to treat the distribution of aspiration word-medially, e.g. *attack*
[ətʰǽk], *anticipate* [æntʰísəpʰèt]. The occurrence of medial aspiration shows
that the ASPIRATION constraint above cannot be right.

The facts are complex, however. It is not the case that all medial [p,t,k,č]
are aspirated, e.g. *pity* [pʰíri], *America* [əmɛ́rəkə]. Basically, two conditions
limit the distribution of aspiration: stress and adjacent consonants.

Let us review these data now. We will see that the facts suggest an
account of aspiration in terms of syllable structure, but where syllable structure is partially a function of stress. Four stress configurations for the sur-
rounding vowels will be considered: stressed–stressed, stressed–stressless,
stressless–stressed, and stressless–stressless. Seven different configurations
with respect to adjacent consonants will be considered as well: VCV,
VLCV, VNCV, VOCV, VCLV, VCwV, and VsCV. Crossed, this gives
twenty-eight different configurations to find four consonants.

First, let us consider cases where both adjacent vowels are stressed.

Stressed–stressed

	p	t	k	č
VCV	propane [pʰrópʰèn]	hotel [hòtʰέl]	acorn [ékʰòrn]	–
VLCV	alpine [ǽlpʰàyn]	yuletide [yúltʰàyd]	alcove [ǽlkʰòv]	–
VNCV	empire [émpʰàyr]	centaur [séntʰɔ̀r]	–	franchise [frǽnčʰàyz]
VOCV	–	nocturne [náktʰṛn]	–	–
VCLV	marplat [márpʰlàt]	quatrain [kʰwátʰrèn]	cyclone [sáykʰlòn]	–
VCwV	–	patois [pʰ` æ`tʰwá]	equine [íkʰwàyn]	–
VsCV	aspect [ǽspèkt]	costume [kʰástùm]	cascade [kʰæskéd]	–

Here the relevant consonant is always aspirated, except after [s].
The following chart gives the stressed–stressless cases.

Stressed–stressless

	p	t	k	č
VCV	happy [hǽpi]	pity [pʰíri]	picky [pʰíki]	butcher [búčṛ]
VLCV	scalpel [skǽlpḷ]	alter [ɔ́ltṛ]	falcon [fǽlkṇ]	vulture [vʌ́lčṛ]
VNCV	dimple [dímpḷ]	plenty [pʰlénti]	anchor [ǽŋkṛ]	penchant [pʰénčṇt]
VOCV	–	nectar [néktṛ]	napkin [nǽpkṇ]	–
VCLV	poplar [pʰáplṛ]	mattress [mǽtrəs]	okra [ókrə]	–
VCwV	–	–	sequin [síkwən]	–
VsCV	aspen [ǽspṇ]	mustard [mʌ́stṛd]	rascal [rǽskḷ]	bastion [bǽsčṇ]

Here the relevant consonants are all unaspirated.
The next chart gives the stressless–stressed examples.

Stressless–stressed

	p	t	k	č
VCV	appeal [əpʰíl]	attack [ətʰǽk]	cacao [kʰəkʰáw]	achieve [əčʰív]
VLCV	–	–	–	–
VNCV	–	until [ṇtʰíl]	–	–
VOCV	–	–	–	–
VCLV	applaud [əpʰlɔ́d]	attract [ətʰrǽkt]	accrue [əkʰrú]	–
VCwV	–	–	equip [əkʰwíp]	–
VsCV	–	astute [əstút]	mesquite [məskít]	

Here, all the relevant consonants are aspirated except after [s]. This case is thus just like the stressless–stressed case.

Finally, this chart gives the stressless–stressless cases.

Stressless–stressless

	p	t	k	č
VCV	canape [kʰǽnəpi]	abatis [ǽbəri]	silica [síləkə]	–
VLCV	–	–	–	neckerchief [nɛ́kṛčəf]
VNCV	–	–	–	–
VOCV	–	–	–	–
VCLV	discipline [dísəplən]	cockatrice [kʰákətrɪs]	–	–
VCwV	–	–	colloquy [kʰáləkwi]	–
VsCV	–	sacristan [sǽkrəstṇ]	–	–

Here again, nothing is aspirated.

The general pattern is summarized in the following chart. Aspiration is marked by Cʰ; lack of aspiration by C. Ø indicates that there are no examples of the relevant sort. The basic pattern is that a consonant after an [s] is always unaspirated; otherwise, medial consonants are aspirated when they precede a stressed syllable.

Aspiration patterns summarized

	v́_v́	v́_v̆	v̆_v́	v̆_v̆
VCV	Cʰ	C	Cʰ	C
VLCV	Cʰ	C	Ø	C
VNCV	Cʰ	C	Cʰ	Ø
VOCV	Cʰ	C	Ø	Ø
VCLV	Cʰ	C	Cʰ	C
VCwV	Cʰ	C	Cʰ	C
VsCV	C	C	C	C

The analysis of these facts should not make direct reference to stress. The problem with such an analysis is that while stress is relevant to the distribution of aspiration with medial consonants, it is irrelevant to the distribution of initial aspiration. A word-initial consonant is aspirated regardless of whether the following vowel is stressed.

Word-initial aspiration does not refer to stress

	Stressed	Stressless
[p]	party [pʰárri]	parade [pʰəréd]
[t]	topic [tʰápɪk]	tomorrow [tʰəmáro]
[č]	chortle [čʰórɾl̩]	cheroot [čʰr̩út]
[k]	copy [kʰápi]	career [kʰərír]

To account for the fact that stress only plays a role in medial position, Daniel Kahn (1976) originally proposed that aspiration is contingent on syllable structure, but syllable structure is contingent on stress. Specifically, he proposed that consonants affiliate to the right and the left when the following vowel is stressless. This is termed 'ambisyllabicity'.

Thus the [t] of *pity* and *vanity* would be ambisyllabic, while in *attack* it would affiliate only to the syllable to the right. Aspiration would only be applicable when the consonant was not ambisyllabic. On this view, the irrelevance of stress to word-initial consonants follows directly. Aspiration applies word-initially before a stressless vowel, e.g. *parade*, because the word-initial consonant can only affiliate to the right. Since there is no preceding syllable, it cannot be ambisyllabic.

Lisa Selkirk (1982) proposes an alternative to Kahn's where the consonant affiliates solely to the preceding syllable before a stressless vowel. The example *happy* is used below for both proposals.

Stress-based resyllabification

σ σ

Kahn: /\\|

hæpi

Selkirk: \\|/ |

σ σ

The problem with either of these proposals is that they would appear to be at odds with the syllabification scheme set up above to treat vowel quality. Recall first that an intervocalic consonant affiliates to the left only after a lax vowel. Second, complex clusters always affiliate to the left. This results in several apparent problems.

Consider first a word like *sneaky* [sníki], where the first vowel is stressed and tense but the second is stressless. Vowel-quality considerations suggest that such consonants affiliate to the right. The stress facts and aspiration evidence suggest that this consonant affiliates to the left (or to both syllables).

A pattern like *quatrain* [kʰwátʰrèn] evidences a second problematic case. Here, vowel-quality facts suggest that as much of the cluster affiliates to the left as possible, yet stress and aspiration would entail that the first consonant affiliates to the right.

The key to solving this paradox comes from the observation that the two kinds of evidence are really not at odds. The vowel-quality evidence bears on whether the consonant affiliates into the syllable to the left. If it does, then it can be moraic and can affect the set of possible preceding vowels. The aspiration evidence really concerns whether the consonant affiliates to the right; aspiration is only possible syllable-initially.

I propose, therefore, that while BIMORAICITY and MAX-CODA affect whether a consonant or cluster is affiliated to the syllable to the left, stress governs whether the consonant affiliates to the second syllable. The relevant constraint is NoOnset, and is given below.

NoOnset
A stressless syllable has no onset.

The constraint on aspiration needs to be revised so that aspiration is restricted to syllable-initial position.

ASPIRATION (revised)
Voiceless stops and affricates are aspirated syllable-initially.

NoOnset must, of course, be ranked above ASPIRATION so that the latter cannot be satisfied by resyllabifying an unaspirated consonant to the left.

Let us now consider the ranking of these constraints with respect to the others already motivated, after which we can consider tableaux for relevant examples. We have already seen that MAX-CODA, BIMORAICITY, and ONSET outrank NOGEMINATES.

Ranking already established

$$\left\{ \begin{array}{c} \text{MAX-CODA} \\ \text{BIMORAICITY} \\ \text{ONSET} \end{array} \right\} \gg \text{NOGEMINATES}$$

I also argued above that NOONSET must outrank ASPIRATION.

What remains is to merge the two rankings. Clearly, NOONSET must outrank ONSET, or it would have no effect. ASPIRATION clearly does not interact with any constraints in this set except NOONSET. Finally, while NOONSET is ranked above ONSET, its ranking with respect to MAX-CODA and BIMORAICITY cannot be determined. This results in a number of possible rankings, summarized in the following figure.

Merged ranking

$$\left\{ \begin{array}{c} \text{MAX-CODA} \\ \text{BIMORAICITY} \\ \text{NOONSET} \gg \text{ONSET} \end{array} \right\} \gg \left\{ \begin{array}{c} \text{ASPIRATION} \\ \text{NOGEMINATES} \end{array} \right\}$$

Let us now see how this system works. I have collapsed the critical cases into twenty-three examples as given in the chart below.

Aspiration patterns summarized

	v́_v́	v́_v̆	v̆_v́	v̆_v̆
VCV	C^h	C	C^h	C
Tense	motel	motor	–	–
Lax	raccoon	pity	–	–
Schwa	–	–	attack	vanity
V{L,N,O}CV	C^h	C	C^h	C
Tense	yuletide	fealty	–	–
Lax	alcove	bulky	–	–
Schwa	–	–	until	neckerchief
VC{L,G}V	C^h	C	C^h	C
Tense	macron	okra	–	–
Lax	patois	mattress	–	–
Schwa	–	–	attract	discipline

	v́_v́	v́_v̆	v̆_v́	v̆_v̆
VsCV	C	C	C	C
Tense	–	feisty	–	–
Lax	cascade	rascal	–	–
Schwa	–	–	mesquite	sacristan

The different cases are rather complex, so let us go through all twenty-three. We will see that the system proposed works in most cases, but needs some revision to handle all of them. (In all the following cases I will assume the position of stress is fixed; this is of course not the case, as we will see in the next chapter.)

The first cases are the VCV cases. The first case to consider is *motel*, where there is a single intervocalic consonant, the first vowel is tense, and both vowels are stressed. Here the consonant is aspirated and the consonant affiliates fully into the second syllable.

Motel

/mòtέl/	MC	B	NO	O	A	NG
mò.tέl					*!	
☞ mò.tʰέl						
mòt.έl				*!		
mòtʰ.έl				*!	*	
mòt.tέl						*!
mòt.tʰέl						*!

The second case is *motor*, where there is a single intervocalic consonant, the first vowel is tense, and the second vowel is stressless. Here the consonant is fully affiliated to the left and there is no aspiration.

Motor

/mótr̩/	MC	B	NO	O	A	NG
mó.tr̩			*!		*	
mó.tʰr̩			*!			
☞ mót.r̩				*		
mótʰ.r̩				*	*!	
mót.tr̩			*!		*	*
mót.tʰr̩			*!			*

The third case is *raccoon*, where there is a single intervocalic consonant, the first vowel is tense, and the second vowel is stressed. Here the consonant ends up affiliated to both syllables and aspirated.

Raccoon

/rὰekún/	MC	B	NO	O	A	NG
rὰe.kún		*!			*	
rὰe.kʰún		*!				
rὰek.ún				*!		
rὰekʰ.ún				*!	*	
rὰek.kún					*!	*
☞ rὰek.kʰún						*

The fourth case is *pity*, where there is a single intervocalic consonant, the first vowel is lax, and the second vowel is stressless. Here the consonant ends up affiliated to the first syllable and unaspirated.

Pity

/píti/	MC	B	NO	O	A	NG
pí.ti		*!	*		*	
pí.tʰi		*!	*			
☞ pít.i				*		
pítʰ.i				*	*!	
pít.ti			*!		*	*
pít.tʰi			*!			*

The fifth case is *attack*, with a single intervocalic consonant, the first vowel is schwa and the second vowel is stressed. (I will not represent it in the tableaux for space reasons, but schwa is subject to constraints like PRE which render BIMORAICITY irrelevant.) Here, the consonant is affiliated to the right and the consonant is aspirated.

Attack

/ətǽk/	MC	B	NO	O	A	NG
ə.tǽk					*!	
☞ ə.tʰǽk						
ət.ǽk				*!		
ətʰ.ǽk				*!	*	
ət.tǽk					*!	*
ət.tʰǽk						*!

The sixth case is *vanity*, where there is a single intervocalic consonant and both vowels are stressless. Here the consonant ends up affiliated to the first syllable and unaspirated.

Vanity

/vǽnəti/	MC	B	NO	O	A	NG
vǽnə.ti			*!		*	
vǽnə.tʰi			*!			
☞ vǽnət.i				*		
vǽnətʰ.i				*	*!	
vǽnət.ti			*!		*	*
vǽnət.tʰi			*!			*

Let us now turn to cases involving clusters. The first set includes cases where the first consonant must affiliate to the left because of sonority. The seventh example is *Yuletide* (monomorphemic for most speakers), where there are two consonants, the first must be affiliated to the left, the preceding vowel is tense, and the following vowel is stressed. The consonant ends up multiply affiliated and aspirated.

Yuletide

/yúltàyd/	MC	B	NO	O	A	NG
yúl.tàyd	*!				*	
yúl.tʰàyd	*!					
yúlt.àyd				*!		
yúltʰ.àyd				*!	*	
yúlt.tàyd					*!	*
☞ yúlt.tʰàyd						*

The eighth case is *fealty*, where there are two consonants, the first must be affiliated to the left, the preceding vowel is tense, and the following vowel is stressless. The consonant ends up fully affiliated to the left and unaspirated.

Fealty

/fílti/	MC	B	NO	O	A	NG
fíl.ti	*!		*		*	
fíl.tʰi	*!		*			
☞ fílt.i				*		
fíltʰ.i				*	*!	
fílt.ti			*!		*	*
fílt.tʰi			*!			*

The ninth case is *alcove*, where there are two consonants, the first must be affiliated to the left, the preceding vowel is lax, and the following vowel is stressed. The consonant ends up split and aspirated.

Alcove

/ǽlkòv/	MC	B	NO	O	A	NG
ǽl.kòv	*!				*	
ǽl.kʰòv	*!					
ǽlk.òv				*!		
ǽlkʰ.òv				*!	*	
ǽlk.kòv					*!	*
☞ ǽlk.kʰ.òv						*

The tenth case is *bulky*, where there are two consonants, the first must be affiliated to the left, the preceding vowel is lax, and the following vowel is stressless. Here the consonant ends up affiliated to the left and unaspirated.

Bulky

/bʌ́lki/	MC	B	NO	O	A	NG
bʌ́l.ki	*!		*		*	
bʌ́l.kʰi	*!		*			
☞ bʌ́lk.i				*		
bʌ́lkʰ.i				*	*!	
bʌ́lk.ki			*!		*	*
bʌ́lk.kʰi			*!			*

The eleventh case is *until*, where there are two consonants, the first must be affiliated to the left, the preceding vowel is lax, and the following vowel is stressed. Here the consonant ends up affiliated to both syllables and aspirated.

Until

/ʌntíl/	MC	B	NO	O	A	NG
ʌn.tíl	*!				*	
ʌn.tʰíl	*!					
ʌnt.íl				*!		
ʌntʰ.íl				*!	*	
ʌnt.tíl					*!	*
☞ ʌnt.tʰíl						*

The twelfth case is *neckerchief*, where there are two consonants (at some level), the first must be affiliated to the left, the preceding vowel is lax (at some level), and the following syllable is unstressed. (The relevant consonant here is [č].) This is the only example of this sort that I could find and it is rather unfortunate, since, as we have seen in Chapter 4, sequences of a lax vowel followed by a coda [r] are realized as [ɾ]. It is therefore unclear how to apply MAX-CODA to this word. The tableau below assumes that MAX-CODA does apply, but it turns out it does not matter because of other constraints. The consonant ends up affiliated to the left and unaspirated.

Neckerchief

/nékr̥čəf/	MC	B	NO	O	A	NG
nékr̥.čəf	*!		*		*	
nékr̥.čʰəf	*!		*			
☞ nékr̥č.əf				*		
nékr̥čʰ.əf				*	*!	
nékr̥č.čəf			*!		*	*
nékr̥č.čʰəf			*!			*

The next set of data involves words with consonant clusters that could in principle affiliate entirely to the second syllable. The thirteenth case is *macron*, with two intervocalic consonants, both could be affiliated to the right, the preceding vowel is tense, and the following vowel is stressed.

For this case to come out right, ONSET must be construed properly. Specifically, it is necessary to understand that onset requires as much material as possible to be put into an onset. On this interpretation, the intervocalic consonant ends up affiliated to both syllables and aspirated. (This, of course, would entail revising the ONSET Constraint. Another way to treat this would be to add a new constraint, call it MAX-ONSET, ranked right near ONSET.)

Macron

/mékràn/	MC	B	NO	O	A	NG
mék.ràn				*!		
mékʰ.ràn				*!	*	
mé.kràn	*!				*	
mé.kʰràn	*!					
mék.kràn					*!	*
☞ mék.kʰràn						*

The fourteenth case is *okra*, where there are two consonants, both could affiliate to the second syllable, the preceding vowel is tense, and the following vowel is stressless. Here the consonant is fully affiliated to the left and unaspirated.

Okra

/ókrə/	MC	B	NO	O	A	NG
☞ ók.rə			*	*		
ókʰ.rə			*	*	*!	
ó.krə	*!		**		*	
ó.kʰrə	*!		**			
ók.krə			**!		*	*
ók.kʰrə			**!			*

The fifteenth case is *patois*, where there are two consonants, both could affiliate to the second syllable, the preceding vowel is lax, and the following vowel is stressed. The consonant ends up affiliated to both syllables and aspirated.

Patois

/pʰǽtwà/	MC	B	NO	O	A	NG
pʰǽt.wà				*!		
pʰǽtʰ.wà				*!	*	
pʰǽ.twà	*!	*			*	
pʰǽ.tʰwà	*!	*				
pʰǽt.twà					*!	*
☞ pʰǽt.tʰwà						*

The sixteenth case is *mattress*, where there are two consonants, both could affiliate to the second syllable, the preceding vowel is lax, and the following vowel is stressless. The consonant affiliates fully to the first syllable and is unaspirated.

Mattress

/mǽtrəs/	MC	B	NO	O	A	NG
☞ mǽt.rəs			*	*		
mǽtʰ.rəs			*	*	*!	
mǽ.trəs	*!	*	**		*	
mǽ.tʰrəs	*!	*	**			
mǽt.trəs			**!		*	*
mǽt.tʰrəs			**!			*

The seventeenth case is *attract*, where there are two consonants, both could affiliate to the second syllable, the first vowel is schwa and the second vowel is stressed. With *attack* above, I assumed that BIMORAICITY was inapplicable to schwa. There is no evidence here for whether MAX-CODA applies to schwa. For simplicity, I will assume it does. Here the consonant ends up affiliated to both syllables and aspirated.

Attract

/ətrǽkt/	MC	B	NO	O	A	NG
ət.rǽkt				*!		
ətʰ.rǽkt				*!	*	
ə.trǽkt	*!				*	
ə.tʰrǽkt	*!					
ət.trǽkt					*!	*
☞ ət.tʰrǽkt						*

The eighteenth case is *discipline*, where the two consonants could both affiliate to the second syllable, the first vowel is schwa, and the second vowel is stressless. Here the consonant is affiliated to the left and unaspirated.

Discipline

/dísəplɪn/	MC	B	NO	O	A	NG
☞ dísəp.lɪn			*	*		
dísəpʰ.lɪn			*	*	*!	
dísə.plɪn	*!		**		*	
dísə.pʰlɪn	*!		**			
dísəp.plɪn			**!		*	*
dísəp.pʰlɪn			**!			*

The next few cases involve sC clusters. In all of these there are quite a few more options, since the entire cluster can in principle affiliate fully to the left or right. The nineteenth case is *feisty*, where the first vowel is a diphthong and the second vowel is stressless. Here the relevant consonant is fully affiliated to the left and unaspirated.

Feisty

/fáysti/	MC	B	NO	O	A	NG
☞ fáyst.i				**		
fáyst^h.i				**	*!	
fáy.sti	*!*		**			
fáy.st^{h}i	*!*		**		*	
fáys.ti	*!		*	*	*	
fáys.t^{h}i	*!		*	*		
fáys.sti	*!		**			*
fáys.st^{h}i	*!		**		*	*
fáyst.ti			*!	*	*	*
fáyst.t^{h}i			*!	*		*

The twentieth case is *cascade*, where the first vowel is lax and the second vowel is stresed. Here the consonant incorrectly ends up multiply affiliated and aspirated.

Cascade

/kǽskéd/	MC	B	NO	O	A	NG
kǽsk.éd				**!		
kǽsk^h.éd				**!	*	
kǽ.skéd	*!*	*				
kǽ.sk^{h}éd	*!*	*			*	
kǽs.kéd	*!			*	*	
kǽs.k^{h}éd	*!			*		
kǽs.skéd	*!					*
kǽs.sk^{h}éd	*!				*	*
kǽsk.kéd				*	*!	*
✗ kǽsk.k^{h}éd				*		*

This requires some revision, but the same move is required to treat another case below.

The twenty-first case is *rascal*, where the first vowel is lax and the second vowel is stressless. The consonant affiliates fully to the left and is unaspirated.

Rascal

/ræskl̩/	MC	B	NO	O	A	NG
☞ ræsk.l̩				**		
ræskʰ.l̩				**	*!	
ræ.skl̩	*!*	*	**			
ræ.skʰl̩	*!*	*	**		*	
ræs.kl̩	*!		*	*	*	
ræs.kʰl̩	*!		*	*		
ræs.skl̩	*!		**			*
ræs.skʰl̩	*!		**		*	*
ræsk.kl̩			*!	*	*	*
ræsk.kʰl̩			*!	*		*

The twenty-second case is *mesquite*, where the first vowel is schwa and the second vowel is stressed. The consonant is multiply affiliated and incorrectly aspirated.

Mesquite

/məskɪt/	MC	B	NO	O	A	NG
məsk.ít				**!		
məskʰ.ít				**!	*	
mə.skít	*!*					
mə.skʰít	*!*				*	
məs.kít	*!			*	*	
məs.kʰít	*!			*		
məs.skít	*!					*
məs.skʰít	*!				*	*
məsk.kít				*	*!	*
✗ məsk.kʰít				*		*

I return to this case below (along with *cascade*).

Finally, the twenty-third case is *sacristan*, where the first vowel is schwa and the second vowel is stressless. The consonant affiliates to the left and is unaspirated.

Sacristan

/sǽkrəstn̩/	MC	B	NO	O	A	NG
☞ sǽkrəst.n̩				**		
sǽkrəstʰ.n̩				**	*!	
sǽkrə.stn̩	*!*		**			
sǽkrə.stʰn̩	*!*		**		*	
sǽkrəs.tn̩	*!		*	*	*	
sǽkrəs.tʰn̩	*!		*	*		
sǽkrəs.stn̩	*!		**			*
sǽkrəs.stʰn̩	*!		**		*	*
sǽkrəst.tn̩			*!	*	*	*
sǽkrəst.tʰn̩			*!	*		*

The system presented is largely confirmed, except that it makes the wrong predictions about aspiration with words like *cascade* [kʰǽskéd]/ *[kʰǽskʰéd] and *mesquite* [məskít]/*[məskʰít]. The problem is that MAX-CODA outranks ONSET and steals away the [s] that would prevent aspiration of the following consonant. This was necessary to account for the fact that tense vowels do not occur before medial sp/sk sequences, e.g. *feisty* [fáysti], but *[fáyspi] and *[fáyski].

However, this was only really shown before a stressless vowel. It is not entirely clear whether tense vowels are ruled out before sC sequences before stressed vowels. The problem is that there are extremely few medial sp/sk clusters in words with a following stressed syllable. From a sample of 20,000 words, I was only able to glean the following four (all with lax vowels, of course).

sp/sk clusters in disyllabic words with two stresses

descant [déskæ̀nt]	escort [éskɔ̀rt]
esquire [éskwàyr]	mascot [mǽskὰt]

In words with trochaic stress, such clusters are more common. From the same sample, I found the following twenty-four words.

sp/sk clusters in words with trochaic stress

aspen [ǽspn̩]	aspic [ǽspək]
auspice [ɔ́spəs]	basket [bǽskət]
biscuit [bískət]	brisket [brískət]

buskin [bÁskn̩]   casket [kʰǽskət]
despot [déspət]   gasket [ɡǽskət]
gospel [ɡÁspl̩]   husky [hÁski]
jasper [ǰǽspr̩]   lascar [lǽskr̩]
musket [mÁskət]   osprey [ɔ́spri]
pesky [pʰéski]   prosper [pʰrÁspr̩]
rascal [rǽskl̩]   vesper [véspr̩]
viscous [vískəs]   whisker [wískr̩]
whisky [wíski]   whisper [wíspr̩]

Thus the absence of tense vowels preceding sp/sk in words with two stresses may be accidental.

If it is accidental, then a straightforward account of the lack of aspiration in examples like *cascade* and *mesquite* is possible: simply rank ONSET (and NOONSET) above MAX-CODA. Looking back through the tableaux above, this only makes a difference for *cascade* and *mesquite*. New tableaux exhibiting the revised ranking are given below.

Cascade again

/kǽskéd/	NO	O	MC	B	A	NG
kǽsk.éd		*!*				
kǽskʰ.éd		*!*			*ǀǫ	
kǽ.skéd			**!			
kǽ.skʰéd			**!		*	
kǽs.kéd		*!			*	
kǽs.kʰéd		*!				
☞ kǽs.skéd			*			*
kǽs.skʰéd			*		*!	*
kǽsk.kéd		*!			*	*
kǽsk.kʰéd		*!				*

Mesquite again

/məskít/	NO	O	MC	B	A	NG
məsk.ít		*!*				
məskʰ.ít		*!*			*	
mə.skít			**!			
mə.skʰít			**!		*	
məs.kít		*!	*		*	
məs.kʰít		*!	*			
☞ məs.skít			*			*
məs.skʰít			*		*!	*
məsk.kít		*!			*	*
məsk.kʰít		*!				*

With this revision, the distribution of aspiration is successfully accounted for. An interesting property of the analysis presented is that it treats ambisyllabicity/gemination in a completely different way from the standard analysis. Under the analysis presented, ambisyllabicity/gemination results in aspiration, whereas affiliation to the left results in nonaspiration (or flapping in the case of /t/).

6.2.5.2. *[h]*

In this section I consider some additional data that support the stress-conditioned syllabification proposal made in the previous section. As has been noted by numerous other scholars, the distribution of [h] is partially contingent on stress (see especially Borowsky 1986).

First, recall from Chapter 3 that because of the absence of [h] in word-final and preconsonantal position, we concluded that [h] is disallowed in coda position. This is enforced by relatively high-ranked *CODA/h. It turns out that [h] is also restricted in terms of stress. There are six cases to consider. (The first vowel can be stressed and tense, stressed and lax, or stressless; the second vowel can be stressed or stressless.)

Cases to consider for the distribution of [h]

1. tense-h-stressed
2. lax-h-stressed
3. tense-h-stressless
4. lax-h-stressless
5. stressless-stressed
6. stressless-stressless

Not all of these cases are instantiated. In fact the only cases that occur are where the second vowel is stressed and the first vowel is either tense or schwa.

Tense-h-stressed

jehu [ǰíhù]	mayhem [méhèm]
mohair [móhèr]	quahog [kʰwɔ́hɔ̀g]
wahoo [wáhù]	

Stressless-stressed

cahoot [kʰəhút]	mahout [məháwt]

This distribution follows directly from the analysis proposed in the previous section, plus the proposal from the previous section that BIMORAICITY can be satisfied by lengthening/tensing, if a consonant is not available. The relevant constraints to be added are *CODA/h and FAITH(μ). Tableaux for *mayhem* and *cahoot* are given below.

Mayhem

	/méhèm/	NO	*C/h	O	B	F(*M*)	NG
☞	mé.hèm						
	méh.èm		*!	*			
	méh.hèm		*!				*

Cahoot

	/kəhút/	NO	*C/h	O	B	F(μ)	NG
☞	kʰə.hút						
	kʰəh.út		*!	*			
	kʰəh.hút		*!				*

Consider, however, what happens if the preceding vowel is lax: hypothetical /mɛ́hèm/.

/mɛ́hèm/

	/mɛ́hèm/	NO	*C/h	O	B	F(μ)	NG
	mɛ́.hèm				*!		
☞	mɛ́.hèm					*	
	mɛ́h.èm		*!	*			
	mɛ́h.hèm		*!				*

A similar result obtains when the following vowel is stressless, regardless whether the preceding vowel is tense or lax: hypothetical /méhə/. Here the [h] can only be parsed as coda to the preceding syllable.

/méhə/

/méhə/	NO	*C/h	O	B	F(μ)	NG
mé.hə	*!					
☞ méh.ə		*	*			
méh.hə	*!	*				*

Since this does not happen, it must be assumed that the constraint against [h] as a coda *CODA/h outranks the constraint forcing [h] to be pronounced: FAITH[h].

The consonant [h], however, can only occur as a clear onset to a stressless syllable in word-initial position.

Word-initial [h] with a following stressless vowel	
historical [həstórək]]	habitual [həbíčuəl]
hello [həló]	hallucinate [həlúsn̩èt]
homogenize [həmáǰṇàyz]	

To accommodate this array of facts, it must be the case that a word-initial consonant must be pronounced regardless. There are many ways to enforce this. The most traditional is to make use of Generalized Alignment and require that the left edge of the word be aligned with the left edge of the prosodic word.

ALIGN-L
The left edge of the word is aligned with the left edge of the prosodic word.

The account offered can therefore relate the absence of pre-stressless [h] to the absence of post-lax [h]. Under previous accounts, the latter fact was not even noticed, let alone treated.

6.2.5.3. *[yu]*

There are additional facts that also support the analysis offered. Recall the distribution of the diphthong [yu]. In some dialects, it cannot occur after coronal consonants. However, in all dialects, it turns out that it can occur after a coronal sonorant when the preceding vowel is lax. Most examples are polymorphemic, but here are a few.

[Lax vowel]-sonorant-[yu] sequences

annual [ǽnyuəl]	attenuate [ətʰɛ́nyuèt]
continue [kʰɳtʰínyu]	deluge [dɛ́lyùǰ]
diminutive [dəmínyuɾɪv]	erudite [ɛ́ryudàyt]
evaluate [ivǽlyuèt]	extenuate [èkstɛ́nyuèt]
genuflect [ǰɛ́nyuflɛ̀kt]	genuine [ǰɛ́nyuən]
granule [grǽnyùl]	ingenuous [ìnǰɛ́nyuəs]
innuendo [ìnyuɛ́ndo]	insinuate [ìnsínyuèt]
manual [mǽnyuəl]	menu [mɛ́nyu]
milieu [mílyu]	minuet [mìnyuɛ́t]
prelude [pʰrɛ́lyud]	purlieu [pʰf̣lyu]
salutary [sǽlyutʰɛ̀ri]	sinew [sínyu]
sinuous [sínyuəs]	soluble [sályəbl̩]
strenuous [strɛ́nyuəs]	tenuous [tʰɛ́nyuəs]
value [vǽlyu]	venue [vɛ́nyu]
voluble [vályubl̩]	

In fact there are even several doublets where the preceding vowel can be tense or lax and the [y] is present or absent accordingly.

Doublets

deluge [dɛ́lùǰ]/[dɛ́lyùǰ]
prelude [pʰrílùd]/[pʰrélùd]/[pʰrɛ́lyùd]

The general pattern is also accommodated by the analysis proposed here. The [y] can only show up when the relevant consonant affiliates to the left. This only happens when the preceding vowel is lax. The mechanical steps are the following. First, there is a constraint against coronal-[y] sequences when the coronal is in onset position.

Constraint against onset coronal-[y] sequences

$$*\begin{bmatrix} \text{COR} \\ \text{onset} \end{bmatrix} [\text{y}]$$

Second, FAITH([y]) is outranked by this constraint.

Let us see how this works in the case of the doublets. The first tableau below shows how this works for the lax version of *deluge*.

/délyùĭ/

/délyùĭ/	NO	O	B	*[COR-O]-[y]	F([y])
☞ dél.yùĭ					
dél.ùĭ		*!			*
dé.lyùĭ			*!	*	
dé.lùĭ			*!		*
dél.lyùĭ				*!	
dél.lùĭ					*!

The same story does not quite work for the tense version.

/délyùĭ/

/délyùĭ/	NO	O	B	*[COR-O]-[y]	F(y)
✗ dél.yùĭ					
dél.ùĭ		*!			*
dé.lyùĭ				*!	
dé.lùĭ					*!
dél.lyùĭ				*!	
dél.lùĭ					*!

The problem here is that we need to rule out the first consonant syllabifying to the left.

We have, in fact, been assuming that [yu] is a diphthong, and therefore fully syllabified as a peak. On this view, the first candidate in the tableau above should incur a violation for the ONSET constraint. This would then result in the fourth or sixth candidate being optimal. If we factor in NOGEMINATES, then the fourth candidate wins easily. A revised tableau is given below.

/délyùĭ/

/délyùĭ/	NO	O	B	*[COR-O]-[y]	Ng	F(y)
dél.yùĭ		*!				
dél.ùĭ		*!				*
dé.lyùĭ				*!		
☞ dé.lùĭ						*
dél.lyùĭ				*!		
dél.lùĭ					*!	*

The key assumption is that Cy does not form a complex onset. Evidence for this comes from the language game Pig Latin, as described by Davis and Hammond (1995). The game is played by moving the first onset of a word to the end of the word and adding the vowel [e]. Here are a few examples.

Examples of Pig Latin

Word	English	Pig Latin
cat	[kʰǽt]	[ǽtkʰè]
Cathy	[kʰǽθi]	[ǽθikʰè]
brick	[brík]	[íkbrè]
spot	[spát]	[átspè]
splat	[splǽt]	[ǽtsplè]

Very strikingly, however, words beginning with consonant–glide sequences do not behave uniformly. If the glide is [w], then the consonant–glide sequence behaves just like the sequences above.

Word-initial Cw sequences and Pig Latin

Word	English	Pig Latin
queen	[kʰwín]	[ínkʰwè]
quality	[kʰwɔ́ləri]	[ɔ́lərikʰwè]
Gwen	[gwέn]	[έngwè]
guano	[gwáno]	[ánogwè]

If the word begins with a Cyu sequence, however, then there are a number of possibilities. Some speakers split the cluster leaving [yu] intact. Some speakers delete the [y]. A very small number of speakers do, in fact, split the diphthong.

Word-initial Cyu sequences and Pig Latin

Word	English	1	2	3
cute	[kʰyút]	[yútkʰè]	[útkʰè]	?[útkʰyè]
cupid	[kʰyúpəd]	[yúpədkʰè]	[úpədkʰè]	?[úpədkʰyè]
puce	[pʰyús]	[yúspʰè]	[úspʰè]	?[úspʰyè]

The key observation, however, is that most speakers treat [yu] as a diphthong rather than as contributing to a complex onset. This supports the analysis above.

To summarize, this section has offered an analysis of medial sonorant-[yu] sequences that fully supports the analysis of syllabification proposed above.

6.3. SUMMARY

I have argued that syllabification is affected by stress. The primary evidence for this came from aspiration. Basically, a voiceless stop or affricate is aspirated when it occurs word initially or medially before a stressed syllable. These environments can be treated in one move if we assume that syllabification is partially a function of stress. Specifically, stressless syllables reject onsets (formalized as NoOnset).

The NoOnset constraint interacts with the Bimoraicity constraint so that we find three possible configurations for an intervocalic stop. These are represented below. One possibility is for the consonant to be fully affiliated to the right (*accord*). The second possibility is for the consonant to be fully affiliated to the left (*tacky*). Finally, the consonant can be affiliated to both syllables (*raccoon*).

Three syllabic configurations for an intervocalic stop

accord	ə.kʰórd
tacky	tʰǽk.i
raccoon	ræ̀k.kʰún

Additional support for this scheme came from the distribution of [h] and [yu].

The system proposed establishes that syllable structure cannot be fixed without reference to stress. In the following chapter we will see that stress cannot be fixed without reference to syllable structure. This prima facie paradox is resolved with OT.

6.4. FURTHER READING

The following works discuss the relationship between stress and syllabification in English in various frameworks.

Chomsky and Halle (1968) is extremely important because it proposes an account of English that rejects the syllable! Kahn (1976) offers the first treatment of aspiration in terms of syllable structure and is the first to formalize the notion of ambisyllabicity. Selkirk (1982) revises this proposal, making the important observation that there was at that time no clear difference between saying that an intervocalic consonant was ambisyllabic and saying that it was a coda.

Borowsky (1986) offers a treatment of many of the facts of [h], [yu], and aspiration in a nonlinear framework. Pulgram (1970) was probably the first to argue that vowel quality affects syllabification. Kager (1990) and Hill and Zepeda (1992) have argued for moraless vowels in Dutch and Tohono O'odham respectively.

A number of my own papers explore the tension between syllabification conditioned by stress and syllabification conditioned by vowel quality, e.g. Hammond (1997a; 1997b) and Hammond and Dupoux (1996).

The Rightmost Stress

In this chapter I treat the regularities governing the distribution of the rightmost stress in monomorphemic words. I will start by reviewing the facts established regarding stress in the preceding chapter. Next, I go on to consider cases where different stress patterns are allowed, either because of lexical effects or because of syntactic category.

In the previous chapter I reviewed the facts concerning the rightmost stress in English nouns, verbs, and adjectives. This was necessary in order to revise the analysis of syllabification so that it would take account of stress. I also proposed a rudimentary analysis of stress there. However, several questions were left unanswered. First, how does the footing system respond to syllable weight? Second, how does the footing system treat lexical variation? Third, how does the system treat the difference between syntactic categories? I return to all of these after reviewing the results of the previous chapter.

7.1. REVIEW OF PREVIOUS RESULTS

In this section I review the facts concerning the distribution of the rightmost stress that were presented in Chapter 6. Many of these generalizations can be recast in light of the subsequent analysis in that chapter.

7.1.1. **Stressless final syllables**

If the final syllable is open, only certain vowels and syllabic consonants are possible: [ə,i,o,u,r̩,l̩,n̩,m̩]. No other vowel is possible in this position.

Final stressless open syllables

Nouns	Adjectives	Verbs
códa [kʰórə]	éxtra [ékstrə]	–
píty [pʰíri]	háppy [hǽpi]	cópy [kʰápi]
wíndow [wíndo]	fállow [fǽlo]	hállow [hǽlo]
Hindu [híndu]	impromptu [ìmprámptu]	rescue [réskyu]
fáther [fáðr̩]	dápper [dǽpr̩]	bóther [báðr̩]
bóttle [bárl̩]	fíckle [fíkl̩]	hóbble [hábl̩]
bútton [bʌ́tn̩]	súdden [sʌ́dn̩]	bátten [bǽtn̩]
bóttom [bárm̩]	–	blóssom [blásm̩]

The syllabic sonorants have two possible sources: an unsyllabified stray consonant in the input or an unidentifiable lax vowel followed by a sonorant. The vowels [i,u,o] could be input tense vowels [i,u,o], or input lax vowels [ɪ,ʊ,ʌ]. The schwa could be any of the other lax vowels. The simplest characterization of the occurring vowels is that any input lax vowel can occur in this position.

If the final syllable is closed, only schwa can occur in this position. There are also restrictions on what consonants and how many consonants can close this syllable. The following chart shows the possibilities for trochaic nouns when only a single consonant closes the rightmost syllable.

What consonant can close the final syllable of a disyllabic noun with trochaic stress?

[p]	dóllop [dáləp]		[b]	chérub [čʰérəb]	
[t]	gámut [gǽmət]		[d]	bállad [bǽləd]	
[k]	hámmock [hǽmək]		[g]	–	
[č]	spínach [spínəč]		[ǰ]	cabbage [kʰǽbəǰ]	
[f]	shériff [šérəf]		[v]	ólive [áləv]	
[θ]	zénith [zínəθ]		[ð]	–	
[s]	frácas [frǽkəs]		[z]	–	
[š]	rúbbish [rʌ́bəš]		[ž]	–	
[m]	≈ bottom [bárm̩]		[l]	≈ bottle [bátl̩]	
[n]	≈ button [bʌ́tn̩]		[r]	≈ water [wɔ́rr̩]	
[ŋ]	–				

The pattern is rather straightforward. Among the obstruents, only [g] and the voiced fricatives are excluded. This is most likely the same statistical skewing observed in Chapters 3 and 4. In addition, sonorant consonants are ruled out, but this is due to the complementary distribution of syllabic sonorants with schwa-sonorant sequences (see §4.4). The absence of [ŋ] is rather surprising, but this is because there are virtually no clear cases of monomorphemic words ending in [ŋ]/[əŋ].

The following charts give the same facts for adjectives and verbs.

What consonant can close the final syllable of a disyllabic adjective with trochaic stress?

[p]	–	[b]	–
[t]	rússet [rʌsət]	[d]	árid [ǽrəd]
[k]	–	[g]	–
[č]	–	[ǰ]	sávage [sǽvəǰ]
[f]	cáitiff? [kʰérəf]	[v]	–
[θ]	mammoth [mǽməθ]	[ð]	–
[s]	–	[z]	–
[š]	gárish [gǽrəš]	[ž]	–
[m]	–	[l]	≈ ample [ǽmpl̩]
[n]	≈ brazen [brézn̩]	[r]	≈ meager [mígr̩]
[ŋ]	–		

Adjectives exhibit striking near-regularity; only coronal consonants are possible word-finally in trochaic words. The only exception to this is the somewhat mysterious *caitiff* [kʰérəf]. Notice that this limitation to coronal consonants applies as well to the syllabic sonorants; [m̩] is also ruled out. This confirms the proposal above that the syllabic sonorants are in complementary distribution with sequences of schwa followed by a coda sonorant. The only exceptions to this pattern are *velum* [vílm̩] and *bosom* [búzm̩], which are clearly derived from nouns.

The simplest characterization of this difference between adjectives and nouns would be that only nonmoraic codas are possible in trochaic adjectives, while codas can be moraic in trochaic nouns.

Verbs are charted below.

What consonant can close the final syllable of a disyllabic verb with trochaic stress?

[p]	gállop [gǽləp]	[b]	–
[t]	vísit [vízət]	[d]	–
[k]	frólic [frálək]	[g]	–
[č]	–	[ǰ]	fórage? [fórəǰ]
[f]	–	[v]	–
[θ]	–	[ð]	–

[s]	hárness [hárnəs]	[z]	–
[š]	fúrnish [fŕ̩nəš]	[ž]	–
[m]	≈ [m̩]?	[l]	≈ amble [ǽmbl̩]
[n]	≈ batten [bǽtn̩]	[r]	≈ barter [bárr̩]
[ŋ]	–		

Again, only coronal consonants are robustly attested and there are only two noncoronal examples: *frolic* [frálək] and *gallop* [gǽləp]. Among the syllabic sonorants, all noncoronal examples are also nouns, e.g. *fathom* [fǽðm̩], *bottom* [bátm̩]. Thus verbs are like adjectives in that they generally only allow nonmoraic final codas with trochaic stress.

The following chart shows the possibilities for word-final clusters in the three classes.

Final clusters with disyllabic words with trochaic stress

	Nouns	Adjectives	Verbs
rl	–	–	–
rN	–	–	–
rC	–	–	–
lN	–	–	–
LC			
r+COR	–	–	–
l+COR	túmult [tʰʌ́mlt]	–	–
N+COR	légend [léǰn̩d]	sílent [sáylənt]	bálance? [bǽləns]
C+COR	lúmmox [lʌ́məks]	hónest [ánəst]	hárvest? [hárvəst]

These are striking in that only C+COR clusters are attested.

Notice that the verb examples *hárvest* and *bálance* are also both nouns. In fact, it turns out that all verbs that exhibit penultimate stress and end in more than one consonant are simultaneously nouns.

Verbs with penultimate stress and a final consonant cluster

bálance	bállast	chállenge
dístance	fórest	gállant
gárland	gárment	hárvest
húsband	ínterest	pérfect
pígment	scávenge	sécond
sílence	témpest	tríumph
wárrant		

The simplest treatment of these would be to maintain that final clusters are impossible for verbs and that these words are examples of true nouns.

The adjectival examples are also suspicious. From a sample of 20,000 words, only the following remotely plausible monomorphemic adjectives ending in two-consonant clusters could be found. These are broken up into three groups. First are the words ending in NC clusters.

Adjectives with penultimate stress and a NC cluster

absent	ancient	arrant	brilliant
cogent	couchant	current	extant
fecund	flagrant	fluent	fragrant
frequent	gallant	giant	infant
instant	jocund	lambent	piquant
plangent	pliant	poignant	pregnant
pungent	rampant	remnant	salient
second	silent	stagnant	tangent
trenchant	truant	urgent	vacant
vagrant	valiant	vibrant	

Second are the examples with final sC clusters.

Adjectives with penultimate stress and a final sC cluster

modest	honest	earnest

Finally, there are two remaining examples that I treat differently.

Remaining adjectives with penultimate stress and a final two-consonant cluster

orange	damask

It is surely no accident that there is a clear adjectival suffix [ənt,ənd], e.g. *vacate–vacant*, *divide–dividend*. I suggest that all the adjectival examples are actually polymorphemic. Many of them involve roots that do not otherwise occur, but these can be treated on a par with *cranberry morphs* like *huckle* in *huckleberry*. The second class of cases is similar. There is another adjectival suffix that marks the superlative, e.g. *big–biggest*. While the forms *modest*, *honest*, and *earnest* are clearly not superlative in interpretation, I suggest that speakers treat these too as polymorphemic.

The final class of cases, *damask* and *orange*, are also nouns and fall under the same rubric as the denominal verbs above. Therefore, monomorphemic adjectives with nonfinal stress cannot end in a consonant cluster.

The patterns presented so far can be summarized as follows. Trochaic verbs and adjectives allow only a single final consonant. Trochaic nouns allow one or two final consonants: [ət], [əp], [əst], or [əpt]. Complex clusters always terminate with a coronal.

Final codas in trochaic words

	ə	ət	ə{p,k}	əst	ə{p,k}t
Nouns	✔	✔	✔	✔	✔
Verbs	✔	✔	(✔)	Ø	Ø
Adjectives	✔	✔	(✔)	Ø	Ø

In the previous chapter, I diagrammed the acceptable final syllables of words with trochaic stress as follows.

What kind of final syllable can cooccur with penultimate stress?

Nouns	Adjectives	Verbs
VC_0	VC_0	$V(C)$
| |	|	|
$\mu(\mu)$	μ	μ

The results with final clusters in adjectives suggests this should be revised as follows.

Final syllables in words with penultimate stress (revised)

Nouns	Adjectives	Verbs
VC_0	$V(C)$	$V(C)$
| |	|	|
$\mu(\mu)$	μ	μ

As noted above, there are a few verbs and adjectives that end in moraic consonants, e.g. *caitiff* and *frolic*. I will assume these are unexceptional, and that adjectives and verbs can end in a single moraic consonant.

Final syllables in words with penultimate stress (revised again)

Nouns	Adjectives	Verbs
VC_0	$V(C)$	$V(C)$
| |	| |	| |
$\mu(\mu)$	$\mu\ (\mu)$	$\mu\ (\mu)$

Similar generalizations reveal themselves in words with antepenultimate stress as well. Let us first consider the set of possible stressless open syllables in this position. The following chart is parallel to the corresponding one above for trochaic words and final open syllables.

Final stressless open syllables with antepenultimate stress

	Nouns	Adjectives	Verbs
[ə]	pléthora [pʰléθɾə]	sépia [sépiə]	–
[i]	cómedy [kʰáməri]	órnery [órnɾi]	átrophy [ǽtrəfi]
[o]	cúrio [kʰyɾio]	–	–
[u]	Kínkajou [kʰíŋkəǰu]	–	–
[ɾ]	sépulchre [sépl̩kɾ]	sínister [sínəstɾ]	mássacre [mǽsəkɾ]
[l̩]	míracle [mírəkl̩]	–	–
[n̩]	skéleton [skélətn̩]	–	jéttison [ǰéɾəsn̩]
[m̩]	cardamom [kʰárrəməm]	–	–

The following three charts show the set of possible word-final singleton consonants for nouns, adjectives, and verbs respectively with antepenultimate stress. The first chart gives the nouns.

What consonant can close the final syllable of a noun with antepenultimate stress?

[p]	–	[b]	–
[t]	víolet [váyl̩ət]	[d]	périod [pʰíriəd]
[k]	límerick [límɾɪk]	[g]	–
[č]	–	[ǰ]	–
[f]	–	[v]	–
[θ]	ázimuth [ǽzm̩əθ]	[ð]	–
[s]	ábacus [ǽbəkəs]	[z]	–
[š]	lícorice [líkɾɪš]	[ž]	–
[m]	–	[l]	≈ miracle [mírəkl̩]
[n]	≈ skeleton [skélətn̩]	[r]	≈ sepulchre [sépl̩kɾ]
[ŋ]	–		

As noted in the previous chapter, there seem to be tighter restrictions on what can occupy the ultima of a dactylic noun than what can occupy the ultima of a trochaic noun, and that the restrictions on the final syllable of a noun with antepenultimate stress are analogous to the restrictions on the final syllable of a verb with penultimate stress. Final noncoronals are extremely rare in this position, with only a few examples like *limerick* [límṛɪk] or *maverick* [mǽvṛɪk].

The following chart gives adjectives.

What consonant can close the final syllable of an adjective with antepenultimate stress?

[p]	–	[b]	–
[t]	–	[d]	–
[k]	–	[g]	–
[č]	–	[ǰ]	–
[f]	–	[v]	–
[θ]	–	[ð]	–
[s]	–	[z]	–
[š]	–	[ž]	–
[m]	–	[l]	–
[n]	≈ halcyon [hǽlsiən]	[r]	≈ sinister [sínəstṛ]
[ŋ]	–		

Antepenultimate stress in adjectives is only possible with the syllabic consonants in the previous chart.

This strange pattern holds for verbs as well.

What consonant can close the final syllable of a verb with antepenultimate stress?

[p]	–	[b]	–
[t]	–	[d]	–
[k]	–	[g]	–
[č]	–	[ǰ]	–
[f]	–	[v]	–
[θ]	–	[ð]	–
[s]	–	[z]	–
[š]	–	[ž]	–
[m]	–	[l]	–
[n]	≈ jettison [ǰérəsṇ]	[r]	≈ massacre [mǽsəkṛ]
[ŋ]	–		

As with the adjectives, only the syllabic consonants can close the final syllable of a dactylic verb.

As we would expect, there are no word-final clusters in adjectives and verbs with antepenultimate stress, and only very limited clusters with antepenultimate nouns. The following chart gives a few examples.

Final clusters in nouns with antepenultimate stress

térmagant [tʰŕməgṇt]	óbelisk [ábḷɪsk]
támarind [tʰǽmṛənd]	ásterisk [ǽstṛɪsk]
órient [óriənt]	

It is unclear what to make of *óbelisk* and *ásterisk*. Is the final syllable stressed in these words? Is *-isk* a suffix? Other than these examples, the final clusters are limited to nasal + coronal.

A very striking fact about the nasal + coronal cases is that there is an independent suffix that ends in -[ṇt]/[ənt]. Some examples are given below.

The nominal suffix -ant

aberrant	accident	accountant	adjutant
agent	annuitant	adulterant	applicant
assistant	claimant	client	coefficient
coolant	covenant	currant	deodorant
desiccant	entrant	gradient	habitant
hydrant	immigrant	ingredient	inhalant
inpatient	litigant	lubricant	migrant
negotiant	officiant	pedant	penchant
pendant	pennant	postulant	president
proponent	protestant	quotient	reagent
recipient	servant	stimulant	student
tenant	vesicant	visitant	warrant

There are a number of nouns that end in -[ṇd]/[ənd], but this ending is far less clearly analyzable as a suffix. Some examples follow.

Words ending in -[ənd]

almond	brigand	diamond	errand
garland	gerund	legend	riband
second	thousand	viand	weasand

The general pattern for the final syllable of dactylic words is summarized below, if forms in -[əsk], -[ṇd], and -[ṇt] are treated as suffixed.

Final codas in dactylic words

	ə	ət	ə{p,k}	əCC
Nouns	✔	✔	(✔)	Ø
Verbs	Ø	Ø	Ø	Ø
Adjectives	✔	Ø	Ø	Ø

The following chart puts together the patterns observed with trochaic and dactylic words.

Stressless final syllables

		N	A	V
Penult	[ə]	✔	✔	Ø
	[ə]+COR	✔	✔	✔
	[ə]+NONCOR	✔	(✔)	(✔)
	[ə]+C+COR	✔	Ø	Ø
	[i,o,u]	✔	✔	✔
Antepenult	[ə]	✔	✔	Ø
	[ə]+COR	✔	Ø	Ø
	[ə]+NONCOR	Ø	Ø	Ø
	[ə]+COR+COR	✔	Ø	Ø
	[i]	✔	✔	✔
	[o,u]	Ø	Ø	Ø

(Notice that as a consequence of the hypotheses regarding morphological complexity, this chart is somewhat different from the one presented in the the previous chapter.)

7.1.2. Stressless post-tonic penultimate syllables

Let us now consider the syllable types that can occur in penultimate position when there is antepenultimate stress. We will see that the penultimate syllable can only be heavy in nouns when the final syllable is [i] or contains a syllabic consonant. The following charts show all the closed penultimate syllables I was able to find for words that are plausibly monomorphemic.

Penult closed with a nasal in word with antepenultimate stress

búrgundy [bŕgn̩di]	cálendar [kʰǽln̩dr̩]
cárpenter [kʰárpn̩tr̩]	cálumny [kʰǽləmni]
cólander [kʰáln̩dr̩]	cýlinder [síln̩dr̩]

dérringer [dérn̩jr̩]   frómenty [frómn̩ti]
frúmenty [frúmn̩ti]   fúrmenty [fŕ̩mn̩ti]
lávender [lǽvn̩dr̩]   hárbinger [hárbn̩jr̩]
órgandy [órgn̩di]   próvender [pʰrávn̩dr̩]

Penult closed with a liquid in word with antepenultimate stress

báwarchi [báwr̩či]   cávalry [kʰǽvl̩ri]
fáculty [fǽkl̩ti]   ópercle [ópr̩kl̩]

Penult closed by another consonant in
a word with antepenultimate stress

cháracter [kʰǽrəktr̩]

All of these involve a final syllabic consonant or [i]. These are most readily treated if we assume that the syllabic consonants are nonsyllabic in the input and that [i] in this position is also nonsyllabic in the input. This general approach needs to be fine-tuned to accommodate the fact that, while a heavy penult can be skipped in these circumstances, preantepenultimate stress is not possible.

Tense vowels are also restricted in penultimate position in words with antepenultimate stress. Specifically, only nonlow tense vowels are possible and only prevocalically.

Stressless nonlow tense prevocalic vowels in penultimate
position in words with antepenultimate stress

i		u	
alien	[élian]	arduous	[árǰuəs]
mania	[ménia]	annual	[ǽnyuəl]
various	[vǽriəs]	genuine	[ǰényuən]

e		o	
Hebraism	[hébreɪzm̩]	heroin	[héroən]
archaism	[árkeɪzm̩]	benzoin	[bénzoən]
Judaism	[ǰudeɪzm̩]	jingoism	[ǰíŋgoɪzm̩]

This pattern has been treated by supposing that BIMORAICITY forces vowel lengthening/tensing in this context. Hence the general absence of unequivocal underlying tense vowels in penult position can be maintained if we suppose that post-tonic prevocalic tense vowels are all underlyingly short/lax, and that any sensitivity to vowel quantity is with respect to input quantity and not output quantity.

These can be contrasted with the set of possible stressless tense vowels in the ultima. As we have seen above, in that position, only [i,o,u] are possible. (The data are repeated below.) As with the cases above, these are only possible when there is no immediately following consonant.

[i,u,o] in stressless open ultimas

i		u		o	
country	[kʰʌntri]	jujitsu	[ǰùǰítsu]	window	[wíndo]
happy	[hǽpi]	kinkajou	[kʰíŋkəǰu]	tomato	[tʰəmérro]
broccoli	[brákḷi]	Kikuyu	[kʰəkʰúyu]	meadow	[médo]

These are treated in the previous chapter by ranking the reduction constraints for these vowels below BIMORAICITY. As above, the general absence of unequivocal underlying tense vowels in this position can be maintained if we suppose that post-tonic word-final tense vowels are all underlyingly short/lax.

Antepenultimate stress is possible if the penult contains schwa followed by a single (intervocalic) consonant. Examples are given in the following chart.

What consonant can close the final syllable of a verb with antepenultimate stress?

[p]	canopy [kʰǽnəpi]	[b]	cannibal [kʰǽnəbḷ]
[t]	charlatan [šárlətn̩]	[d]	infidel [ínfədḷ]
[k]	abacus [ǽbəkəs]	[g]	asparagus [əspǽrəgəs]
[č]	–	[ǰ]	prodigy [pʰrárəǰi]
[f]	paraffin [pʰǽrəfn̩]	[v]	carnival [kʰárnəvḷ]
[θ]	amethyst [ǽməθɪst]	[ð]	–
[s]	hyacinth [háyəsn̩θ]	[z]	courtesan [kʰórrəzn̩]
[š]	–	[ž]	–
[m]	abdomen [ǽbdəmn̩]	[l]	broccoli [brákḷi]
[n]	cabinet [kʰǽbn̩ət]	[r]	tamarind [tʰǽmr̩ənd]
[ŋ]	–		

(As with the final cases treated in the previous section, syllabic sonorants sometimes replace stressless vowel + sonorant sequences.) These can, of course, all be treated as input lax/short vowels.

When the final vowel is not a syllabic sonorant or [i], then a schwa in penultimate position after a rightmost antepenultimate stress can be followed by two consonants only if those two consonants are a possible onset cluster.

Two-consonant sequences

algebra [ǽljȝbrȝ]
cockatrice [kʰákȝtrɪs]
armistice [ármȝstɪs]
vertebra [vɍ̩rȝbrȝ]

To summarize, the penultimate syllable of a word where the rightmost stress falls on the antepenult is restricted in the following ways. First, the penult can be clearly closed if the ultima contains a syllabic sonorant or [i]. These cases are treated by supposing that the relevant syllable is in fact the ultima in the input. In all other cases, the following conditions hold. First, the penult cannot contain a tense vowel unless it is nonlow and prevocalic. Second, the penult otherwise can only contain schwa and only when a single consonant follows or a cluster that is a possible onset. Both of these latter two cases can be grouped together by saying that antepenultimate stress is only possible if the penult is at most monomoraic.

7.2. THE BASIC ANALYSIS

The generalizations governing the rightmost stress in English are basically as follows. First, all content words in English have at least one stress on one of the final three syllables.

If the ultima is stressed, then it must be (at least) bimoraic, e.g. *kangaroo* [kʰæ̀ŋgɍ̩ú] or *molest* [mȝlést]. Otherwise, words with final stress are unrestricted.

If the penult is stressed (and the ultima unstressed), then the ultima cannot contain an underlying/input long vowel. In addition, the ultima cannot end in a consonant cluster where the rightmost consonant is not coronal. If the word is a verb or adjective, then the ultima cannot end in a cluster at all.

If the antepenult is stressed (and the penult and ultima unstressed), then the penult cannot contain a bimoraic syllable except under two circumstances. First, the penult may contain a [i,u,e,o] if it is prevocalic (not followed by a consonant), e.g. *alien* [éliȝn], *Bedouin* [béduȝn]. Second, the penult can be closed if the ultima contains [ɍ,i], e.g. *cylinder* [sílņdɍ], *burgundy* [bɍ̩gņdi]. If the antepenult is stressed and the word is a verb or adjective, then the ultima must be [ɍ,ņ], e.g. *jettison* [jɛ́rȝsņ], *sinister* [sínȝstɍ]. If the antepenult is stressed and the word is a noun, then the ultima cannot be closed by a cluster; words like *ásterisk* [ǽstɍɪsk] are treated as polymorphemic.

In the following sections, these generalizations will be treated. The facts and analysis are complex and will be spread out over several sections. In this section, the basic constraints needed are laid out and justified. In the following section, I treat (i) varying stress patterns, (ii) closed penultimate syllables in words with antepenultimate stress, and (iii) verbs and adjectives.

Let us consider now how these generalizations might be treated in a metrical theory. First, the fact that all words have at least one stress tells us that ROOTING plays a role.

ROOTING
All words are stressed.

This forces a word like *hat* to be stressed.

Stressing hat

/hæt/	ROOTING
☞ hǽt	
hæt	*!

Second, the fact that the rightmost stress may occur as far to the left as the antepenult tells us that feet are aligned with the right edge of the word.

ALIGN-R
All feet are aligned with the right edge of the word:
ALIGN(Σ,R,Wd,R).

It also shows that NONFINALITY plays a role.

NONFINALITY
The final syllable is not footed.

NONFINALITY must outrank ALIGN-R to allow for the possibility of antepenultimate stress. This is shown in the following two tableaux for *America*.

Why NONFINALITY *must outrank* ALIGN-R

America	NF	AR
☞ A[meri]ca		*
Ame[rica]	*!	

America	AR	NF
A[meri]ca	*!	
✗ Ame[rica]		*

ROOTING must outrank NONFINALITY so that monosyllabic words get stressed.

Why ROOTING must outrank NONFINALITY

/hat/	RT	NF
☞ [hát]		*
hat	*!	

/hat/	NF	RT
[hát]	*!	
✘ hat		*

This gives us the following partial ranking for the constraints proposed so far.

Partial ranking for constraints proposed so far
ROOTING >> NONFINALITY >> ALIGN-R

That stress can occur on the antepenult tells us that the feet are trochaic (i.e. that the stress occurs on the left side of the foot). This is clearly an instance of GA.

TROCHEE
The stress occurs on the left side of the foot.

The TROCHEE constraint insures that a word like *America* gets antepenultimate stress rather than penultimate stress.

TROCHEE exemplified

/America/	TROCHEE
☞ A[méri]ca	
A[merí]ca	*!

TROCHEE is never violated in English and so must be top-ranked. Since ROOTING is also never violated, we get the following ranking.

Partial ranking for constraints proposed so far
$\begin{Bmatrix} \text{ROOTING} \\ \text{TROCHEE} \end{Bmatrix}$ >> ... >> NONFINALITY >> ALIGN-R

TROCHEE must work in tandem with a constraint requiring binary feet.

FOOT BINARITY [FTBIN] (preliminary)
Feet are binary.

This allows for antepenultimate stress in words like *America*.

FTBIN exemplified

/America/	FTBIN
☞ A[méri]ca	
Ame[rí]ca	*!

Actually, FTBIN or NONFINALITY or TROCHEE must be violable to allow for penultimate stress in words like *vanilla* [vənílə] or final stress in a word like *bassinet* [bæsṇét]. It is unclear at this juncture precisely which constraint is violated here, and so this is left to the following section after syllable weight is treated. (The ranking above assumes that TROCHEE is never violated.)

7.3. THE ROLE OF SYLLABLE WEIGHT

Let us now turn to syllable structure restrictions. The generalizations are as follows. First, there are specific conditions under which the ultima must be stressed. With all syntactic categories, if the final syllable contains a long vowel, it is stressed (*balloon* [bḷún], *maroon* [mṛún], *agree* [əgrí]). With verbs, if the ultima is closed by two consonants, it is stressed (*molest* [mḷést]).

There are also specific conditions under which the penult must be stressed if the ultima is stressless. Consider first the case where the ultima is stressless and does not contain a syllabic sonorant or [i]. With nouns, stress must fall on the penult if it is heavy (*agenda* [əjéndə], *aroma* [ərómə]). With adjectives and verbs, the penult must be stressed regardless of its weight (*diminish* [dəmínəš]).

If the ultima contains a syllabic sonorant or [i], the facts concerning penult stress are a little different. With nouns, the penult may be skipped over if it is light or closed (*anarchy* [ǽnṛki]). With adjectives and verbs, antepenult stress is possible, but only if the penult is light (*sinister* [sínəstṛ], *jettison* [jɛrəsṇ]).

These facts would seem to suggest that the foot in English is the moraic trochee. The foot cannot be a syllabic trochee because the syllabic trochee is insensitive to syllable weight and, as just reviewed, stress in English is sensitive to syllable weight. The foot cannot be an iamb either. Iambic feet are right-headed feet where the head can be bimoraic or monomoraic, but the nonhead must be monomoraic. All the cases of weight sensitivity in English involve shifting stress to the right just in case some syllable on the right is heavy. The iambic foot does not have this effect. On the contrary, the weight restrictions on the iambic foot result in a shift to the left if a syllable to the left is heavy. If this argument is correct, we would need to revise the FTBIN constraint above as follows.

FTBIN (revised)
Feet are bimoraic.

There are several arguments against this move, however. These arguments cannot all be fully developed yet, but there are four: BIMORAICITY, NONFINALITY, secondary stress, and Expletive Infixation. The last two will be developed in Chapter 8. Let us consider the first two now.

First, there is already an independently motivated constraint requiring that syllables be bimoraic, BIMORAICITY, that does some of the work of moraic trochees. Consider a final stressed syllable in a word like *kangaroo* [kʰæ̀ŋgrú] or *cement* [səmɛ́nt]. A stressed syllable in this position must surface as bimoraic because of the BIMORAICITY constraint. This would also be required by moraic FTBIN. Hence, one of these constraints is redundant in this context. BIMORAICITY also forces lengthening in the final syllable of *pity* [pʰíri] or the second syllable of *alien* [éliən]. These latter effects cannot be obtained by moraic FTBIN, suggesting that it is moraic FTBIN that is redundant.

A second argument for BIMORAICITY over moraic FTBIN can be made based on NONFINALITY. There are weight restrictions on NONFINALITY which do not follow from the bimoraicity of the moraic trochee and must be independently specified. I turn to these now.

That stress can be attracted to a final syllable that is heavy shows that NONFINALITY is subject to syllable weight restrictions. There are at least two ways to formalize this. One possibility would be to parametrize NONFINALITY so that it only applies to syllables of certain types. One way to implement this would be a schema based on NONFINALITY and exhibiting some sort of universal ranking, for example as follows.

> *A possible universal ranking of parametrized NONFINALITY constraints*
> NONFINALITY(CV) >> NONFINALITY(CVC) >>
> NONFINALITY(CVV)

An alternative would be to suppose that there are constraints forcing syllables to get stress that can outrank NONFINALITY.

> *The Weight-to-Stress Principle*
> Heavy syllables must be stressed.

This could also be instantiated as a universally ranked series of parametrized constraints.

> *A possible universal ranking of parametrized WSP constraints*
> ... >> WSP(VV) >> ... >> WSP(VC) >> ...

The latter approach seems more general and is the usual tack taken in the literature (see e.g. Prince and Smolensky 1993). The latter approach also allows us to maintain the syllabic version of FTBIN. I will therefore assume that the Weight-to-Stress Principle, as applied to long vowels WSP(VV), outranks NONFINALITY.

Final long vowels attract stress
WSP(VV) >> NONFINALITY

A final closed syllable can be skipped over, which suggests that NONFINALITY outranks WSP(VC).

Final closed syllables do not attract stress
WSP(VV) >> NONFINALITY >> WSP(VC)

Let us look at a few cases to see how this works. Consider first the case of *América*. No ranking information can be derived in this case, since one candidate emerges with no violations of the relevant constraints.

Tableau for América

	/America/	TROCHEE	FTBIN	NONFINALITY
	Ame[ríca]			*!
	Ame[ricá]	*!		*
☞	A[méri]ca			
	A[merí]ca	*!		
	Ame[rí]ca		*!	*
	Ameri[cá]		*!	

Following is the tableau for *ánimal* [ǽnəml̩]. Since the final syllable is closed and skipped by NONFINALITY, this tableau shows how NONFINALITY must outrank WSP(VC).

Tableau for ánimal

	/animal/	TROCHEE	FTBIN	NONFINALITY	WSP(VC)
	a[nímal]			*!	*
	a[nimál]	*!		*	
☞	[áni]mal				*
	[aní]mal	*!			*
	a[ní]mal		*!	*	*
	ani[mál]		*!		

This can be contrasted with the tableau for *bassinet* [bæ̀sṇ́ét]. Here the wrong result is achieved, since NONFINALITY uniformly prevents a final short vowel in a closed syllable from getting footed. (This is necessary to allow antepenultimate stress in words like *ánimal*.) This is treated in §7.4.

Tableau for bassinet

/bassinet/	TROCH	FTBIN	NONFIN	WSP(VC)
ba[ssínet]		*!	*	*
ba[ssinét]	*!	*	*	
✗ [bássi]net				*
[bassí]net	*!			*
ba[ssí]net		*!		
bassi[nét]		*!	*	*

The following tableau shows how this system works for *agénda* [əǰéndə]. Here we see that WSP(VC) must outrank FTBIN.

Tableau for agénda

/agenda/	TROCH	NONFIN	WSP(VC)	FTBIN
a[génda]		*!		
a[gendá]	*!	*	*	
[ágen]da			*!	
[agén]da	*!			
☞ a[gén]da				*
agen[dá]		*!	*	*

The tableau for *aroma* [ərómə] shows that, as one would expect from transitivity of ranking, WSP(VV) outranks FTBIN.

Tableau for aróma

/aroma/	TROCH	WSP(VV)	NF	WSP(VC)	FTBIN
a[róma]			*!		
a[romá]	*!	*	*		
[áro]ma		*!			
[aró]ma	*!				
☞ a[ró]ma					*
aro[má]		*!	*		*

This system thus accounts for a number of the possible stress patterns exhibited with nouns and the role of syllable weight in attracting stress to heavy syllables and in forcing NONFINALITY to skip syllables containing long vowels.

We must now consider how to relate the WSP and BIMORAICITY. Specifically, why is WSP not satisfied with any syllable, since BIMORAICITY forces any stressed syllable to be bimoraic? Consider again the stress pattern of *America* [əmérəkə]. If stress were assigned to the penultimate syllable, it would become bimoraic (by covert gemination in this case), trivially satisfying WSP.

The key to the resolution of this problem is FTBIN. The FTBIN constraint will always prefer binary feet. Since BIMORAICITY can be satisfied by geminating either the [k] (if the penult is stressed) or the [r] (if the antepenult is stressed), FTBIN will militate for the antepenult to be stressed. This is shown in the following tableau. Here BIMORAICITY is tentatively ranked at the top, and only candidates where the stressed syllable is bimoraic are considered.

FTBIN salvages BIMORAICITY in America

/America/	BIMOR	TROCH	VV	NF	VC	FTBIN
Ame[ríc.a]				*!		
Ame[ricáa]		*!		*		
☞ A[mér.i]ca						
A[meríc]a		*!				
Ame[ríc]a						*!
Ameri[cáa]				*!		*

What remains is the following. First, this system must be generalized to account for the other patterns nouns can exhibit. Second, the system must be generalized to account for the verbal and adjectival stress patterns observed.

7.4. OTHER NOMINAL STRESS PATTERNS

How can a final syllable containing a short vowel get stressed at all, e.g. *bassinet* [bæ̀sņét], given that I have already argued that NONFINALITY outranks WSP(VC) in the system? We have already seen that a final long vowel is stressed because WSP(VV) outranks NONFINALITY. It cannot be the case that WSP(VC) outranks NONFINALITY, because if it did all final closed syllables would get stress, e.g. *[ænəmǽl].

A similar problem holds for words with penultimate stress. Words like *aróma* [ərómə], *agénda* [əǰéndə], and *América* [əmérəkə] all end up with the proper stress given WSP(VV)/WSP(VC) and a syllabic trochee that skips the final syllable (because of NONFINALITY). However, the system as outlined in the previous section fails to assign stress correctly in words like *vanílla* [vənílə]. The following tableau shows how *vanilla* is treated.

Tableau for vanílla

/vanilla/	TROCHEE	FTBIN	NONFINALITY
va[nílla]			*!
✗ [váni]lla			
va[ní]lla		*!	
[vaní]lla	*!		

There are, then, two cases where it looks like different stress patterns are possible: final closed syllables (*animal* vs. *bassinet*) and penultimate open(?) syllables (*America* [əmérəkə] vs. *vanilla* [vənílə]). The system as outlined so far disallows the patterns exemplified in *bassinet* or *vanilla*. Something extra must be said to allow for these other patterns.

Imagine that we did it the other way around. Rather than saying something extra for *bàssinét* and *vanílla*, we could treat them as normal and say something special for *ánimal* and *América*. This approach actually does not work.

Consider first the case of penultimate stressability. We could treat forms like *vanílla* as regular and forms like *América* as exceptional if we stipulate that feet are iambic, e.g. IAMB. Alternatively, we could treat *América* as regular if we stipulate that feet are trochaic, e.g. TROCHEE.

There is, however, extensive evidence that feet in English are trochaic. (I have already reviewed the evidence from language games, Expletive infixation, and syncope in Chapter 5.) I conclude that feet are trochaic, and that an account built on IAMB would fail. Therefore, forms like *vanílla* exceptionally attract stress to the penult.

The stressing of final closed syllables could also be handled differently. We could treat forms like *bàssinét* as regular and forms like *ánimal* as irregular, if we assume that WSP(VC) is ranked above NONFINALITY. However, parsimony suggests that forms like *bàssinét* be marked for exceptionally attracting stress to the ultima. In this way, we can treat both exceptional classes, *bàssinét* and *vanílla*, as some form of stress attraction.

How do we exceptionally assign stress in these words? There are at least four possibilities. First is parochial constraint ranking. That is, we could stipulate that certain classes of vocabulary are subject to different rankings (Tranel 1994). Another possibility would be to adopt constraints that are earmarked for certain classes of words: parochial constraints (Hammond 1994; Russell 1995; Pater 1995). Third, foot structure could be posited lexically (Inkelas 1994). Finally, we could adopt a theory of lexical accent, whereby certain elements are marked to attract stress (Halle and Vergnaud 1987; Hammond 1989*a*; 1989*b*).

Any of the above possibilities will work for present purposes. I will adopt the fourth because it is the least controversial. Accents will be notated with a raised circle.

Notating accent

| |
| bassinе̊t   vanîlla |

This representational move needs to be augmented with a constraint that forces accents to bear stress on the surface.

FAITH(v̊)
Accented elements are stressed.

This constraint is, of course, an instance of Generalized Correspondence (GC; Ch. 1). The tableau below shows how this works for words like *bàssinét*.

FAITH(v̊) exemplified

/ bassinе̊t/	FAITH(v̊)	NONFINALITY
(bassi)nе̊t	*!	
☞ (bassi)(nе̊t)		*

Notice that the constraint FAITH(v̊) must interact with BIMORAICITY so that vowels that are stressed via accent surface as bimoraic.

The analysis thus far treats forms like *bàssinét* and *vanílla* as instances of exceptional stress attraction. This is formalized with lexical accent and a constraint, FAITH(v̊). BIMORAICITY forces any final accented light syllable to surface as long.

One might wonder what would happen if an accent surfaced further to the left, outside the trisyllabic window. Would this result in a rightmost stress outside the window? This would only follow if only a single foot were built and/or the pressure exerted by ALIGN-R could be overridden by FAITH($\mathring{v}$). These issues are taken up in the next chapter.

On the basis of the description above, we might expect any final long vowel to attract stress. Yet forms like *cándy* and *mínnow* show this is not so. I have already argued that certain lax vowels surface as tense word-finally (*cándy*) and prevocalically (*álien*). Hence a form like *cándy* is not an exception to the Weight-to-Stress Principle (WSP; Ch. 5). Rather, it ends in a lax vowel underlyingly that, on a derivational analysis, tenses only after stress assignment. This shows that the WSP must be cast in terms of input vowel quantities, rather than output quantities. The WSP must thus be conceived of as a correspondence-theoretic constraint.

I have argued that exceptional stresses in English are assigned by exceptionally attracting stress to syllables that would otherwise surface stressless. This possibility is moderated by BIMORAICITY, which forces all stressed syllables (and some stressless ones) to be bimoraic.

7.5. FINAL SYLLABLES

Let us now return to final syllables with nouns. While in general antepenultimate stress is possible only when the penult is light, the penult can be closed just in case the ultima contains [i,r̩,l̩,n̩]. A related fact is that the final syllable of nouns with antepenultimate stress cannot be closed by more than one consonant, while the final syllable of a noun with penultimate stress can be closed by a C+COR cluster. These facts are all treated in this section.

7.5.1. **Final [i] and syllabic sonorants**

I propose that whatever it is that allows a closed ultima to be skipped to assign stress to a penult allows a closed penult to be skipped to assign stress to the antepenult. There are two parts to this story. First, there must be an account of how a closed ultima can be skipped. Second, there must be an account of how final [i,r̩,l̩,n̩] could be skipped.

First, recall that a closed ultima can be skipped because of the ranking of the WSP constraints and NONFINALITY.

Why a final heavy syllable can be skipped
WSP(VV) >> NONFINALITY >> WSP(VC)

A form like *canóe* [kʰənú] must stress the final syllable because of WSP(VV).

WSP(VV) >> NONFINALITY

/kʰənu/	WSP(VV)	NONFINALITY	WSP(VC)
☞ kʰə(nú)		*	
(kʰə́n)u	*!		

A form like *pánic* [pʰǽnɪk] surfaces with penultimate stress because NONFINALITY outranks WSP(VC).

NONFINALITY >> WSP(VC)

/pʰænɪk/	WSP(VV)	NONFINALITY	WSP(VC)
pʰæ(ník)		*!	
☞ (pʰǽn)ɪk			*

To account for the fact that forms ending in [i,ɾ,l,n] can have antepenultimate stress with a heavy penult, let us assume that these final syllables are phonologically nonsyllabic. (This proposal in a rule-based guise is due originally to Chomsky and Halle, 1968.) Specifically, the input representation for something like *cháracter* is /kærəktr/, with only two vowels. To make this representation work, we must assume that NONFINALITY and FTBIN only apply to vowels that are in the input. (This entails that both of these constraints are instances of Generalized Correspondence.)

The following tableau for *character* [kʰǽrəktɾ] shows how this works. The final [ɾ] must be invisible to both NONFINALITY and FTBIN.

Apparent success

/kærəktr/	WSP(VV)	NONFINALITY	WSP(VC)
kʰæ(rə́ktɾ)		*!	
☞ (kʰǽr)əktɾ			

Stress surfaces on the superficial antepenult because NONFINALITY applies to the input ultima (which is the output penult).

The problem with this account is that it predicts that monomorphemic words with final [i] or [ɾ] should be able to exhibit preantepenultimate stress. This is shown in the following tableau for a hypothetical form *ánaracter* [ǽnərəktɾ].

Incorrect preantepenultimate stress

/ænərəktr/	WP	NONFINALITY	μ/C
ænə(rə́ktr̩)		*!	
☞ (ǽnə)rəktr̩			

Monomorphemic forms of this sort never occur. Forms with this segmental shape consistently have penultimate stress.

Four-syllable cases with penultimate stress

gérrymànder [ǰérimǽndr̩]	vìgilánte [vìǰəlǽnti]
óleànder [óliǽndr̩]	sálamànder [sǽləmǽndr̩]

If the analysis proposed is correct, these forms show that, while a monosyllabic foot can be followed by a string like [əktr̩], a binary foot cannot.

There are two ways we might solve this. One possibility is to maintain that while a word-final syllabic sonorant is invisible to NONFINALITY, it is not invisible to footing. This would have the rather strange consequence of allowing discontinuous feet. The first and third syllables of *character* would be footed, while the second syllable would be skipped by NON-FINALITY.

Another solution would be to maintain that what renders these ill-formed is the string of three stressless syllables. I will term this the Lapse Generalization.

Lapse Generalization
Avoid three stressless syllables in a row.

The discussion of final clusters in nouns with antepenultimate stress and the discussion of verbal and adjectival stress in the next sections will provide an answer to this conundrum.

I have argued that final [r̩,n̩,l̩,i] are invisible to NONFINALITY. They may also be invisible to footing. Alternatively, some version of the Lapse Generalization must be in place.

7.5.2. Final clusters

We have seen that a final stressless syllable in a noun may not contain a long vowel or a final consonant cluster other than C+COR. We have also seen that the final syllable of a noun with antepenultimate stress may not be closed by a cluster of any sort. In this section I provide an analysis of these facts.

The absence of final clusters other than C+COR is surely a reflection of a moraic limit on final clusters. Recall that a final coronal does not necessarily contribute a mora to its syllable. This means that a C+COR final cluster does not need to contribute more than one mora. For example, the word *lummox* [lʌməks] ends in [ks]. While the [k] necessarily contributes a mora, the [s] does not.

Confirmation of this general approach comes from the absence of word-final consonants in nouns with nonfinal stress where the singleton consonant necessarily contributes more than one mora on its own. Recall from Chapter 4 that [ž,ŋ] contribute two moras each. Neither of these occur word-finally with monomorphemic nouns with nonfinal stress.

The sound [ž] does not occur word-finally in a stressless syllable under any conditions. The sound [ŋ] occurs word-finally in stressless syllables only if the word is polymorphemic or is plausibly analyzed as polymorphemic. First, there are words ending in the deverbal suffix *-ing*.

Nominalizing -ing

loathing	blueing	clothing
craving	cutting	daring
dealing	doing	dreaming
driving	fingering	flavoring
footing	forging	going
grating	hanging	hatching
hearing	hoarding	housing

Second, there is a suffix, *-ling*, which denotes diminutive or animal young.

Animal young -ling

yearling	underling	stripling
codling	darling	duckling
firstling	fledgling	foundling
gosling	grayling	hatchling
groundling	nestling	nursling
sapling	starling	starveling

Finally, there is a third category of remaining items, which are not obviously polymorphemic, but which may be best analyzed as *cranberry* morphemes, that is, as morphologically complex.

Other examples

morning	evening	shilling
sterling	farthing	herring
quisling	pudding	lightning
inning	inkling	bunting
cunning	awning	bushing

I conclude that the word-final coda of a stressless syllable can contribute no more than a single mora. To treat this fact, I propose that the WSP schema be expanded so that we can distinguish these different coda options.

The previous proposal was as follows.

Previous ranking of WSP constraints
WSP(VV) >> NONFINALITY >> WSP(VC)

To accomodate the C+COR and [ž,ŋ] facts, the WSP(VC) constraint must be split, with NONFINALITY interleaved. The basic idea is that the effect of the coda varies as a function of how many moras it contributes to the syllable.

New WSP constraints and rankings

$$\left\{ \begin{array}{l} \text{WSP(VV)} \\ \text{WSP(Coda>}\mu) \end{array} \right\} >> \text{NONFINALITY} >> \text{WSP(Coda<}\mu\mu)$$

Let us now see how this system works. The following example shows how NONFINALITY must outrank WSP(Coda<$\mu\mu$).

Tableau for panic

/pænɪk/	VV	>μ	NF	<$\mu\mu$
☞ [pǽn]ɪk				*
pə[ník]			*!	

The following example has a C+COR final coda and surfaces the same way.

Tableau for lummox

/lʌməks/	VV	>μ	NF	<$\mu\mu$
☞ [lʌ́m]əks				*
lə[mʌ́ks]			*!	

The following example contains a final long vowel and shows how WSP(VV) outranks NONFINALITY.

Tableau for typhoon

/tayfun/	VV	$>\mu$	NF	$<\mu\mu$
[táy]fn̩	*!			
☞ tay[fún]			*	*

Finally, the following case shows how WSP(Coda$>\mu$) must outrank NONFINALITY as well.

Tableau for alarm

/ælɑrm/	VV	$>\mu$	NF	$<\mu\mu$
[ǽl]r̩m		*!		
☞ ə[lɑ́rm]			*	*

Recall that in Chapter 4 I proposed a constraint that requires a coronal to be moraic after a moraic consonant (Post-Noncoronal Mora). The analysis proposed above requires that this be outranked by NONFINALITY.

The account provided thus treats the C+COR restriction with a straightforward extension of the WSP schema. Let us now turn to the restriction against final clusters when the antepenult is stressed.

The fact to be explained is that when a noun has penultimate stress, the ultima can have a complex C+COR coda, e.g. *edict* [írəkt], but when the antepenult is stressed, the ultima can be closed by no more than a single consonant, e.g. *animal* [ǽnəml̩]. This generalization can be violated when the noun is polymorphemic, e.g. *visitant* [vízətn̩t], or nearly so, e.g. *obelisk* [ábl̩ɪsk].

This cannot be a consequence of NONFINALITY, because NONFINALITY is invoked with words with penultimate stress as well, if the ultima is closed, e.g. *panic* [pʰǽnɪk]. This also cannot be a consequence of mora count since the clusters permitted in the word-final coda of a word with penultimate stress do not augment the mora count of a single-consonant coda.

I therefore posit the following constraint to treat this fact.

Final nominal cluster constraint
A syllable closed by two consonants cannot be unfooted when it occurs to the right of a stressless syllable.

This may be an instance of some more illuminating constraint family, but there is insufficient evidence on which to proceed at this at this point.

7.6. VERBS AND ADJECTIVES

Let us now turn to verbal and adjectival stress. Recall that verbs and adjectives exhibit final stress if the final syllable contains a long vowel or is closed by two consonants, penultimate stress if the final syllable does not contain a long vowel or two coda consonants, and antepenultimate stress if the final syllable is a syllabic sonorant and the penult is light.

Three things need to be done to treat these facts. First, there needs to be some way to restrict NONFINALITY to nouns. Second, there needs to be some way to allow for a final syllable closed by a single consonant when a verb or adjective exhibits penultimate stress. Third, there needs to be a way to allow antepenultimate stress just in case the ultima is a syllabic sonorant.

How then do we capture these restrictions? Previous accounts have had to posit independent mechanisms for these facts. Here, I will argue that a single parameter distinguishes nouns from verbs. To capture the general restriction against antepenultimate stress with adjectives and verbs, I propose that adjectives and verbs are followed by an invisible or catalectic syllable. From this assumption, both the distance from the right edge and the number of consonants necessary to close a syllable follow.

Burzio (1995) makes a proposal that is quite similar to the one here. However, his proposal is not made in terms of OT. In addition, the details of his proposal are not worked out, and so it is difficult to compare it with the current one in specific terms. Here, I first outline the catalexis proposal generally and then make a specific proposal to treat these facts in English.

7.6.1. Catalexis generally

Kiparsky (1991) proposes the mechanism of catalexis as a way of accounting for the following generalization: languages with trochaic feet (that count syllables) that permit final stress typically do not have a bisyllabic minimal word constraint.

> *The stress-minimality generalization*
> If a language has trochaic feet built over syllables and it allows for final stress, then it does not have a bisyllabic minimal word constraint.

This generalization can be seen by comparing Ono and Diyari. Both languages have trochaic stress, yet Ono (Phinnemore 1985) permits final stress and has no (bisyllabic) word minimum.

Ono

kúm	'palm bark'
déne	'my eye'
árilè	'I went'

Diyari (Austin 1981), on the other hand, has no final stresses and a bisyllabic word minimum.

Diyari

kána	'man'
pínadu	'old man'
wílapìna	'old woman'

The basic idea behind catalexis is that some languages allow for an invisible or catalectic syllable. Coupled with a strict disyllabicity requirement on feet, the option of catalexis will derive the two possibilities above. Ono allows for a catalectic syllable (marked with square brackets below); Diyari does not.

Ono

(kúm[σ])　(déne)　(ári)(lè[σ])

Diyari

*σ　(kána)　(pína)du　(wíla)(pìna)

The catalectic syllable in Ono allows for subminimal words (monosyllables) and final stress. The absence of catalectic syllables in Diyari, the requirement for every word to be stressed, and strict binarity work together to exclude monosyllabic words and stress on odd final syllables. The prediction is that there will be no (trochaic) language that has final stress and a bisyllabic minimal word, and no language that allows monosyllabic words but not final stress. (These predictions are extensively tested by Kager 1993.)

This proposal was made in pre-OT days, so if we find this general approach satisfactory, there will still be some work to do to recast it in constraint-based terms.

7.6.2. **Catalexis in English**

My proposal here is superficially quite simple. Verbs and adjectives, but not nouns, are marked with a catalectic suffix.

Catalexis in English (preliminary)
Verbs and adjectives are marked with a catalectic suffix.

This allows NONFINALITY to apply to all lexical categories.

NONFINALITY in English
All lexical categories are subject to NONFINALITY.

The intersection of these two principles with schematic lexical items in English is shown below. (Parentheses mark feet and square brackets mark catalexis.)

N	V	A
$(\sigma\,\sigma)\,\sigma$	$(\sigma\,\sigma)+[\sigma]$	$(\sigma\,\sigma)+[\sigma]$

Let us consider these three cases one by one. Nouns do not have the option of catalexis. Therefore the final syllable can be skipped by NONFINALITY, and antepenultimate stress is possible. Verbs do exhibit catalexis. Therefore a verb will have a catalectic suffix which is skipped by NONFINALITY: allowing only overt penultimate stress. An adjective has a catalectic suffix which is skipped by NONFINALITY: allowing only penultimate stress.

So far, the only reason for adopting the catalectic suffix proposal for English is that it allows us to generalize NONFINALITY. However, it does so only at the cost of introducing invisible/catalectic suffixes. There are, however, several additional arguments for the proposal.

The first argument is built on the difference between the number of consonants required to make a syllable heavy in the two conditions—with or without a following catalectic syllable. The contrast is shown below. Words exhibiting catalexis require two word-final consonants to close the (overt) word-final syllable. Words without catalexis require only a single coda consonant to close the penultimate syllable.

How many consonants make a syllable heavy?

	Catalexis	No catalexis
C	devélop[σ]	América
CC	adépt[σ]	agénda

This distinction follows from the catalectic-syllable proposal. Specifically, the catalectic syllable is subject to the usual principles of syllabification, including ONSET. If catalectic syllables are subject to ONSET, then the words above have the following syllabifications. (Syllable boundaries are marked with periods and nonmoraic coda affiliations are not indicated.)

Onset applies to catalectic syllables

develop	.də.vél.ə.pØ.	America	.ə.mér.ə.kə.
adept	.ə.dép.tØ.	agenda	.ə.jén.də.

If this is the syllabification, then it follows automatically that a superficially word-final syllable preceding a catalectic suffix is only going to count as heavy if there are at least two word-final consonants.

A second argument for the current proposal can be made on the basis of word-final syllabic sonorants. Recall that antepenultimate stress with verbs and adjectives is only possible if the word-final syllable contains a syllabic sonorant.

Dactylic verbs and adjectives with word-final syllabic sonorants

Verbs	Adjectives	
jettison [jɛ́rəsn̩]	sinister [sínəstr̩]	finicky [fínəki]
atrophy [ǽtrəfi]	alias [éliəs]	genuine [jényuən]
uppity [ʌ́pəri]	alien [éliṇ]	halcyon [hǽlsiən]
ornery [órnṛi]	feminine [fémənən]	mandarin [mǽndṛən]
pillory [pʰílṛi]	clarion [kʰlǽriən]	masculine [mǽskyələn]
remedy [réməri]		

We saw that, with nouns, a final syllabic sonorant alters the way heavy penults are treated but does not increase the final trisyllabic window. With verbs and adjectives, however, a final syllabic sonorant would superficially appear to increase the window (from two syllables to three). This follows automatically, however, from the catalexis proposal: the final catalectic syllable provides a home for the final sonorant (just as it provides a home for a word-final consonant). The trisyllabic window only seems to increase. In actual fact, the window is always trisyllabic and simply becomes overtly so when the final syllabic sonorant is seated in the catalectic syllable.

The third argument in favor of this proposal concerns the morphological structure of adjectives and verbs. (The general relationship between stress and morphology is discussed in Chapter 8, but the pertinent facts are relevant here.) It turns out that the superficial disyllabic stress window only applies to monomorphemic adjectives, and not suffixed adjectives. Suffixed adjectives can exhibit antepenultimate stress. (Certain suffixes can also result in stress further to the left.) The following table gives some examples.

Suffixed adjectives with antepenultimate stress

ous	amorous [ǽmṛəs], aqueous [ǽkwiəs], boisterous [bɔ́ystṛəs]
ant	arrogant [ǽrəgṇt], deviant [díviənt], aspirant [ǽspṛənt]
ent	ambient [ǽmbiənt], diffident [dífədənt], fraudulent [frɔ́j̧lənt]
al/ar	actual [ǽkčuəl], angular [ǽŋgyəlṛ], axial [ǽksiəl]
ful	wonderful [wʌ́ndṛf̧l], beautiful [byúrəf̧l], bountiful [báwntəf̧l]
tive	ablative [ǽblərɪv], additive [ǽrərɪv], cognitive [kʰǽgnərɪv]

This fact follows if we assume that the catalectic syllable is actually a suffix that attaches to otherwise unsuffixed verbs and adjectives (a common restriction among English affixes). The fact that suffixed adjectives can exhibit superficial antepenultimate stress follows from denying them a catalectic suffix and applying NONFINALITY to the overt suffixal syllable.

It is not clear whether the same restriction holds of verbs. Suffixed verbs do not allow for antepenultimate stress. However, all productive verbal suffixes appear to contain a long vowel, which always attracts stress regardless of whether the window is trisyllabic or disyllabic. Examples of the relevant verbal suffixes are given in the following three tables.

Sample verbs in -ize

acclimatize [əkʰláymətʰàyz]	advertise [ǽdvṛtʰàyz]
aggrandize [əgrǽndàyz]	agonize [ǽgṇàyz]
alkalinize [ǽlkələnàyz]	alkalize [ǽlķlàyz]
alphabetize [ǽlfəbətʰàyz]	americanize [əmérəkṇàyz]
amortize [ǽmṛtʰàyz]	novelize [návḷàyz]
organize [órgṇàyz]	ostracize [óstrəsàyz]
oxidize [áksədàyz]	particularize [pʰùrtʰíkələràyz]
pasteurize [pʰǽsčṛàyz]	

Sample verbs in -ify

justify [ǰʌ́stəfày]	magnify [mǽgnəfày]
modify [márəfày]	mollify [máləfày]
mortify [mórrəfày]	mummify [mʌ́məfày]
mystify [místəfày]	notify [nórəfày]
nullify [nʌ́ləfày]	amplify [ǽmpləfày]

beatify [biǽrəfày]   beautify [byúrəfày]
calcify [kʰǽlsəfày]   certify [sŕ̩rəfày]
citify [síɾəfày]   clarify [kʰlǽrəfày]
codify [kʰóɾəfày]   crucify [kʰrúsəfày]
dandify [dǽndəfày]   declassify [dìkʰlǽsəfày]
dehumidify [dìhyùmíɾəfaỳ]

Sample verbs in -ate

---

abbreviate [əbrívièt]   abdicate [ǽbdəkʰèt]
abnegate [ǽbnəgèt]   abominate [əbámn̩èt]
abrogate [ǽbrəgèt]   accelerate [æksélɾ̩èt]
accentuate [æksénčuèt]   acclimate [ǽkləmèt]
accommodate [əkʰámədèt]   accumulate [əkʰyúmyəlèt]
activate [ǽktəvèt]   actuate [ǽkčuèt]
adjudicate [əjúrəkʰèt]   adumbrate [ədʌ́mbrèt]
advocate [ǽdvəkʰèt]   estimate [éstəmèt]
evacuate [əvǽkyuèt]   evaluate [əvǽlyuèt]
evaporate [əvǽpɾèt]   eviscerate [əvísɾèt]
exacerbate [ɪgzǽsɾ̩bèt]   exaggerate [ɪgzǽɟɾ̩èt]
exasperate [ɪgzǽspɾèt]   excavate [ékskəvèt]
excogitate [èkskʰáɟətʰèt]   excommunicate [èkskəmyúnəkʰèt]
excoriate [èkskórièt]   exculpate [ékskl̩pʰèt]
execrate [éksəkʰrèt]

There are only two remotely plausible verbal suffixes that do not contain long vowels, *-esce* and *-ish*. The former always bears stress, presumably because of a lexical accent, which leaves only the latter as a possible example. This pseudo-suffix generally cooccurs with penultimate stress, but there is a single example, *impoverish* [ɪmpʰávɾɪš]/[ɪmpʰávrɪš]. The following tables contain complete lists of the relevant examples from a sample of 20,000 words.

All verbs in -esce

---

acquiesce [æ̀kwiés]   coalesce [kʰòlɛ́s]
convalesce [kʰɑ̀nvl̩és]   deliquesce [dèləkʰwés]
effervesce [èfɾ̩vés]   intumesce [ìntʰùmés]

All verbs in -ish

---

abolish [əbáləš]   accomplish [əkʰámpləš]
admonish [ədmánəš]   astonish [əstánəš]

demolish [dəmáləš]	diminish [dəmínəš]
establish [əstǽbləš]	extinguish [ɪkstíŋgwəš]
impoverish [ìmpʰávr̩əš]	refurbish [rìfŕ̩bəš]
relinquish [rəlíŋkwəš]	replenish [rəpʰlénəš]

Neither of these suffixes is productive in English. Thus it is reasonable to suppose that verbs, like adjectives, only undergo catalectic suffixation when otherwise unsuffixed. This entails that verbs will exhibit overt antepenultimate stress when suffixed (with a suffix containing no long vowel).

To summarize this section, verbs and adjectives can be treated with the same machinery proposed for nouns. The only difference is that unsuffixed verbs and adjectives undergo catalectic suffixation. This makes sense of four disparate sets of facts. First, this accounts for the fact that stress in verbs and adjectives seems to be generally limited to the final two syllables. Second, this proposal accounts for the fact that, while a single consonant is sufficient to make the penultimate syllable of a noun heavy, two consonants are required to make the final syllable of a verb or adjective heavy. Third, this proposal accounts for why a final syllabic sonorant extends the stress domain with verbs and adjectives, but does not extend the stress domain with nouns. Finally, this proposal accounts for the fact that the disyllabic stress window is only exhibited by unsuffixed adjectives (and theoretically unsuffixed verbs).

7.7. SUMMARY

This chapter has offered an account of the distribution of the rightmost stress in English. The central empirical issues addressed are as follows. First, in morphologically simple words, a stress must occur on at least one of the last three syllables. Second, there are restrictions on whether the rightmost stress can occur to the left of relatively heavy syllables. Third, within the trisyllabic window, stress is also a function of lexical factors, and certain exceptional cases must be simply marked. Finally, the stress pattern of nouns is different from that of verbs and adjectives.

The theoretical issues raised in this chapter are as follows. First, it was proposed that the sensitivity to quantity be described using a simple (syllabic) trochee and a parametrized Weight-to-Stress principle. Second, the difference between lexical classes was treated with catalexis. (Lexical exceptionality was treated with accent, but, as noted above, other treatments are possible.)

In the following chapter I turn to the distribution of stresses further to the left. We will see that the analysis proposed here extends directly to account for these additional facts.

7.8. FURTHER READING

The following works offer discussions of various metrical phenomena in English in various frameworks: Chomsky and Halle (1968), Ross (1970), Hayes (1981), Borowsky (1986), Kager (1989), Burzio (1995), Hammond (1984).

Catalexis is treated by Kiparsky (1991), Kager (1993), and Burzio (1995).

The theory of accent is discussed in Halle and Vergnaud (1987) and Hammond (1989a; 1989b). Alternatives to this theory are discussed by Inkelas (1994) and Hammond (1994).

The only treatments of English stress from an OT perspective are Pater (1995) and Hammond (1997b).

Other Stresses

In this chapter I treat the regularities governing the distribution of stresses further to the left. I will start by reviewing the relevant facts and then go on to provide an analysis. Finally, I will briefly consider the role of morphology in stress.

The general theoretical contribution of this chapter is to show that the mechanisms developed in the previous chapter extend only partially to describe the distribution of stresses further to the left. That system must be augmented in several ways to describe other stresses. Some of these extensions are natural and reasonable. However, we will see that some seem to radically alter some of the basic structure of OT.

8.1. NONRIGHTMOST STRESSES

Long monomorphemic words in English are quite rare. The majority of examples cited in this section are therefore borrowed words. In some languages, borrowed words exhibit rather different phonological patterns from those of native words, but this does not appear to be the case in the stress system of English. Rather, the distribution of stress revealed by borrowed words shows a single system, and one that is largely in conformity with the system developed in the previous chapter for the rightmost stress.

8.1.1. One pretonic syllable

With a single pretonic syllable, that syllable can be stressed or stressless. The following examples show that light syllables in that position may or may not be stressed.

Light stressless syllables in pretonic position

platóon [pʰlətʰún]	bonánza [bənǽnzə]	malária [məlériə]
gazélle [gəzél]	petúnia [pʰətʰúniə]	América [əmérəkə]

grenáde [grənéd]	tobóggan [tʰəbɔ́gn̩]	Napóleon [nəpʰóliən]
machíne [məšín]	spaghétti [spəgɛ́ri]	accórdion [əkʰórdiən]
canál [kənǽl]	penúmbra [pʰənʌ́mbrə]	chaméleon [kʰəmíliən]

Light stressed syllables in pretonic position

càfféine [kʰæ̀fín]	pàpríka [pʰæ̀pʰríkə]
plàteáu [pʰlæ̀tʰó]	màcrópsia [mæ̀krápsiə]
tràpéze [tʰræ̀pʰíz]	Gàstónia [gæ̀stóniə]
tàttóo [tʰæ̀tʰú]	bàdínerie [bæ̀dínṛi]
ràccóon [ræ̀kʰún]	pàróusia [pʰæ̀rúsiə]

For some reason, almost all the clear examples of stressed light syllables involve the vowel [æ]. There are also, however, a very few examples involving other vowels, i.e. *settee* [sɛ̀tʰí], *suttee* [sʌ̀tʰí].

Closed syllables in pretonic position can also surface stressed or stressless, though they are typically stressed.

Closed stressless syllables in pretonic position

confétti [kʰn̩fɛ́ri]	obsídian [əbsíriən]
cantáta [kʰn̩tʰárə]	gazpácho [gəspáčo]
Kentúcky [kʰn̩tʰʌ́ki]	samsára? [sm̩sárə]

Closed stressed syllables in pretonic position

bàmbóo [bæ̀mbú]	vòlcáno [vɔ̀lkʰéno]	wìstéria [wìstíriə]
càscáde [kʰæ̀skéd]	màrtíni [màrtʰíni]	ùmbílicus [ʌ̀mbíləkəs]
fròntíer [frʌ̀ntʰír]	bàndánna [bæ̀ndǽnə]	dìphthéria [dìpθíriə]
chàmpágne [šæ̀mpʰén]	vèndétta [vèndɛ́rə]	chàlcédony [kʰæ̀lsédni]
làmpóon [læ̀mpʰún]	scìntílla [sìntʰílə]	àrtíllery [àrtʰílṛi]

(It may be significant that there are no examples of stressless initial heavy syllables in disyllabic words, however.) Pretonic syllables containing long vowels are always stressed.

Long stressed syllables in pretonic position

tỳphóon [tʰàyfún]	ròtúnda [ròtʰʌ́ndə]	ùtópia [yùtʰópiə]
tòupée [tʰùpʰé]	mòsáic [mòzéɪk]	rhìnóceros [ràynásṛəs]
ròmánce [ròmǽns]	czàrína [zàrínə]	ràuwólfia [ràwúlfiə]

dècór [dèkʰór]	còyóte [kʰàyóɾi]	mỳópia [màyópiə]
pòmáde [pʰòméd]	ìdéa [àydíə]	Bòhémia [bòhímiə]

The pattern of stress here can be accommodated if degenerate feet are only forced in the case of long vowels. The analysis developed in the preceding chapter allows for differential sensitivity to different kinds of heavy syllables, though, as it stands, that analysis would appear to predict that both long vowels and closed syllables surface as stressed in this position. The relevant part of the hierarchy is repeated below.

Critical constraints and rankings from Chapter 7

$$\left\{ \begin{array}{l} \text{WSP(VV)} \\ \text{WSP(Coda>}\mu\text{)} \end{array} \right\} \gg \text{NONFINALITY} \gg \text{WSP(Coda<}\mu\mu\text{)} \gg \text{FTBIN}$$

Ranking WSP(VV) and WSP(Coda>μ) above NONFINALITY accounts for the fact that final long vowels are stressed, e.g. *kàngaróo* [kʰæ̀ŋgɹú], and that final syllables closed by a polymoraic coda are stressed, e.g. *alárm* [əlárm]. Ranking WSP(Coda<$\mu\mu$) below NONFINALITY allows for final syllables closed by at most a monomoraic coda to be skipped, e.g. *hélix* [híləks]. Recall that a coda like this can surface as monomoraic because NONFINALITY outranks the constraint that would supply a mora to the final [s]. Finally, ranking all three instances of WSP above FTBIN allows for a penultimate heavy syllable of any type to attract stress, e.g. *aróma* [ərómə], *agénda* [əjéndə]. However, this same ranking would force an initial degenerate foot incorrectly in words like *confétti* *[kʰànféɾi].

To account for the facts above, some revision is necessary. Before undertaking that revision, let us consider some additional facts.

8.1.2. Two pretonic syllables

In the case of two pretonic syllables, there are four logical possibilities for stress configurations (stressed, 2, stressless, 0) and nine possibilities for syllable weight combinations (light, V, closed, VC, long, VV). These are set out in the following table. When a particular type occurs, it is marked with a ✔; when a type does not occur, it is marked with a Ø.

Logical possibilities for stress patterns for two pretonic syllables

	V-V	V-VC	V-VV	VC-V	VC-VC	VC-VV	VV-V	VV-VC	VV-VV
001	Ø	Ø	Ø	Ø	Ø	Ø	Ø	Ø	Ø
201	✔	✔	Ø	✔	✔	Ø	✔	✔	Ø
021	Ø	Ø	Ø	Ø	Ø	Ø	Ø	Ø	Ø
221	Ø	✔	✔	Ø	✔	✔	Ø	✔	✔

Let us first go through the occurring patterns and then go back and consider the generalizations and how to account for them.

There is one overarching generalization: if there are two pretonic syllables, the first must be stressed. The immediate pretonic syllable must be stressed if it is long and cannot be stressed if it is light. Examples of all occurring types are given below.

Next, let us consider the syllable weight restrictions on the 201 pattern. This can occur quite freely. First, there are cases where both syllables are light.

Light syllable with secondary stress followed by a stressless light syllable

gàsolíne [gæ̀slín]	pànatéla [pʰæ̀nətʰélə]	nìckelódeon [nìklóriən]
clàrinét [kʰlæ̀rṇét]	pànacéa [pʰæ̀nəsíə]	hìppopótamus [hìpəpʰárəməs]
càvalíer [kʰæ̀vlír]	hàllelújah [hæ̀ləlúyə]	tèlestéria [tʰèləstíriə]
màgazíne [mæ̀gəzín]	gàllimáufry [gæ̀ləmɔ́fri]	Sènegámbia [sènəgǽmbiə]
mìnarét [mìnṛét]	bàrracúda [bæ̀rəkʰúrə]	Phìladélphia [fìlədélfiə]

There are also cases where the first syllable is light and the second stressless syllable closed.

Light syllable with secondary stress followed by a stressless closed syllable

pàlanquín? [pʰæ̀lŋkʰwín]	Èpictétus [èpəktʰírəs]	Èrichthónius [èrəkθóniəs]
Jàbalpúr [jæ̀blpʰúr]	Clèmentína [kʰlèmṇtʰínə]	àliptérion [æ̀ləptʰíriən]
rèmontóire [rèmṇtʰwár]	kìtambílla [kʰìrṃbílə]	Àlexándria [æ̀ləksǽndriə]
Jùbbulpóre [jʌ̀blpʰór]	Pìrandéllo [pʰìrṇdélo]	
	Nèfertíti [nèfṛtʰíri]	

Third, there are cases where the first syllable is long and the second light.

Long syllable with secondary stress followed by a stressless light syllable

sòuvenír [sùvṇír]	ùkuléle [yùkəléli]	Pòmeránia [pʰàmṛéniə]
Yùcatán [yùkətʰǽn]	Quàsimódo [kʰwàzimóro]	Pòsidónius [pʰàzədóniəs]
tòucanét [tʰùkṇét]	Òklahóma [òkləhómə]	òligúria [òləgúriə]
rèmoláde [rèmḷéd]	Òbadíah [òbədáyə]	Màuretánia [mɔ̀rətʰéniə]
Chàgatái [čʰàgətʰáy]	òcotíllo [òkətʰíyo]	còloquíntida [kʰàləkʰwíntərə]

Fourth, there are cases where the first syllable is long and the second is closed.

Long syllable with secondary stress followed by a stressless closed syllable

Pròvençál [pʰròvṇsál]	Ràwalpíndi [ràwḷpʰíndi]	còlumbárium [kàləmbǽriəm]
àmandíne [àmṇdín]	Cùpertíno [kʰùpṛtʰíno]	òpisthódomos [àpəsθárəməs]
bòugainvíllaea [bùgṇvíyə]		Clỳtemnéstra [kʰlàyrəmnéstrə]

Fifth, there are cases where the first syllable is closed and the second is light.

Closed syllable with secondary stress followed by a stressless light syllable

chàndelíer [šǽndḷír]	ènchiláda [ènčḷárə]	Sèxagésima [sèksəjésəmə]
màndolín [mǽndḷín]	càmpaníle [kʰǽmpəníli]	Thèsmophória [θèzməfóriə]
nègligé [nègləžé]	Ỳpsilánti [ìpsḷǽnti]	Scàndinávia [skǽndənéviə]
pàntalóon [pʰǽntəlún]	Tùscaróra [tʰʌ̀skərórə]	Màstigóphora [mǽstəgáfṛə]
èscadrílle [èskədríl]	Sùsquehánna [sʌ̀skwəhánə]	Àlfarábius [ǽlfərǽbiəs]

Finally, there are cases where the first two syllables are both closed.

Closed syllable with secondary stress followed by a stressless closed syllable

ìnvernéss	Kìnchinjúnga	Pènnsylvánia
[ìnvṛnés]	[kʰìnčn̥ǰóŋgə]	[pʰènsḷvéniə]
hàlberdíer	Hìspanióla	mỳxasthénia
[hǽlbṛdír]	[hìspənyólə]	[mìksəsθíniə]
gàspergóu	Gìlbertína	hèlminthíasis
[gǽspṛgú]	[gìlbṛtʰínə]	[hèlmn̥θáyəsɪs]
Èscondído	àxanthópsia	àspersórium
[èskn̥díro]	[ǽksn̥θápsiə]	[ǽspṛsóriəm]
Chàndarnágar		
[čʰǽndṛnǽgṛ]		

Now consider the 221 case. Here all possibilities occur except when the second pretonic syllable is light. First, there are cases with two closed syllables.

Closed syllable with secondary stress followed by a closed syllable with secondary stress

Tìmbùktú [tʰìmbʌktʰú]	Kìnchìnjúnga [kʰìnčʰìnǰóŋgə]
chìmpànzée [čḷìmpḷǽnzí]	Pànmùnjóm [pʰǽnmʊ̀nǰám]
Mìtnàgdím [mìtnàgdím]	Ìpsàmbúl [ìpsàmbúl]

Second, there are cases where a long syllable is followed by a closed syllable.

Long syllable with secondary stress followed by a closed syllable with secondary stress

Mòzàmbíque	Rùwènzóri	sỳnàxária [sàynǽksériə]
[mòzǽmbík]	[rùwènzóri]	
Zìguínchór	Àbùlféda	àcàlcúlia [èkʰǽlkúliə]
[zìgìnčʰór]	[èbùlférə]	
Màhèndrás	Còchìnchíne	
[màhèndrás]	[kʰòčʰìnčʰín]	

Third, there are cases with an initial light syllable followed by a closed syllable.

Light syllable with secondary stress followed by a
closed syllable with secondary stress

ànàmnésis [æ̀næ̀mnísɪs]	sỳnàxárium [sɪ̀næ̀ksériəm]
Ànàxárete [æ̀næ̀ksǽrəri]	ànàgnórisis [æ̀næ̀gnórəsɪs]
Ànáxíbia [æ̀næ̀ksíbiə]	

Fourth, there is one example of a closed syllable followed by a long syllable. (Since the [u] is pretonic, it could also be analyzed as a stressless vowel. If stressless, this would predict that Expletive Infixation between the first two syllables should be impossible. However, for some speakers, it is possible in this location, [ìnfʌknflùénzə], and so this form is cited as having two pretonic stresses.)

Closed syllable with secondary stress followed
by a long syllable with secondary stress

ìnflùénza [ìnflùénzə]

Fifth, there are examples of two long syllables.

Long syllable with secondary stress followed by a
long syllable with secondary stress

Zàhèdán [zàhìdán]	Zìùsúdra [zìùsúdrə]
Ràfàél [ràfàyél]	Tàmàulípas [tàmàwlípəs]
Cùyàpó [kùyàpó]	Sòlìména [sòlìménə]
gònyàuláx [gànyòlǽks]	Pùtùmáyo [pʰùtʰùmáyo]
Djìbòutí [jìbùtʰí]	Òkèechóbee [òkʰìčʰóbi]

Finally, there is a single example of a light syllable followed by a long syllable.

Light syllable with secondary stress followed
by a long syllable with secondary stress

àmàurósis [æ̀màwrósɪs]

Let us pick out the generalizations. The chart given above is repeated below.

Logical possibilities for stress patterns for two pretonic syllables (repeated)

	V-V	V-VC	V-VV	VC-V	VC-VC	VC-VV	VV-V	VV-VC	VV-VV
001	Ø	Ø	Ø	Ø	Ø	Ø	Ø	Ø	Ø
201	✔	✔	Ø	✔	✔	Ø	✔	✔	Ø
021	Ø	Ø	Ø	Ø	Ø	Ø	Ø	Ø	Ø
221	Ø	✔	✔	Ø	✔	✔	Ø	✔	✔

First, as already noted, there are no cases of 001 or 021. All the 201 patterns are attested except where the stressless syllable would contain a long vowel: X-VV. All the 221 patterns are attested except where the second stressed syllable would be light: X-V. The fact that the gaps can be described so simply argues that the patterns are not accidental.

The absence of 001 cases follows from the assumption that feet are trochaic—TROCHEE—and that syllables should be footed: PARSE-σ. Wherever PARSE-σ is in the ranking, a form with two unfooted pretonic syllables will always get an additional violation over a candidate where the same two syllables are footed. This is shown in the following tableau.

Ruling out 001 with PARSE-σ

	/$\sigma\sigma\sigma$. . ./	. . .	PARSE-σ	. . .
	. . .			
☞	[$\sigma\sigma$][σ. . .			
	$\sigma\sigma$[σ. . .		**!	
	. . .			

This, however, leads to an immediate paradox. The first syllable of a word with the rightmost stress on the second syllable need only be stressed if it is long, e.g. *amóunt* [əmáwnt], *cantáta* [kʰn̩tʰárə], but *typhóon* [tʰàyfún]. Or, put another way, a (necessarily monosyllabic) word with a single closed syllable must be stressed, but a single pretonic closed syllable need not be, e.g. *cantáta* [kʰn̩tʰárə] vs. *cán* [kʰǽn]. Basically, FTBIN is violated to build a single foot, but does not have to be violated to build a second one.

This can be treated if we separate the pressure for a syllable to be footed from the pressure to stress a word at all. The latter is sufficiently strong to force violation of FTBIN, but the former is not. The pressure to stress a syllable has already been formalized as PARSE-σ; the pressure to stress a word is formalized as ROOTING below.

ROOTING
Words must have a primary stress.

(This constraint occasionally goes by the name LxWᴅ≈PʀWᴅ, but we adopt the earlier nomenclature of Hammond, 1984.)

Rooting must dominate FᴛBɪɴ to force a single heavy syllable to be stressed. Bɪᴍᴏʀᴀɪᴄɪᴛʏ must be undominated to enforce the ban on mono-moraic words. Rooting is also undominated. To allow a closed pretonic syllable to surface as stressless, Pᴀʀsᴇ-σ must be dominated by FᴛBɪɴ.

Ranking
$$\left\{ \begin{matrix} \text{Bɪᴍᴏʀᴀɪᴄɪᴛʏ} \\ \text{Rooting} \end{matrix} \right\} >> \ldots >> \text{FᴛBɪɴ} >> \text{Pᴀʀsᴇ-}\sigma$$

Since pretonic closed syllables may be stressed, it must be the case that Fᴀɪᴛʜ(v̊) outranks FᴛBɪɴ. As we saw above, Fᴀɪᴛʜ(v̊) does not override the bimoraic minimum on stresses or words, so Fᴀɪᴛʜ(v̊) must be out-ranked by Bɪᴍᴏʀᴀɪᴄɪᴛʏ.

Revised ranking
$$\left\{ \begin{matrix} \text{Bɪᴍᴏʀᴀɪᴄɪᴛʏ} \\ \text{Rooting} \end{matrix} \right\} >> \ldots >> \text{Fᴀɪᴛʜ(v̊)} >> \text{FᴛBɪɴ} >> \text{Pᴀʀsᴇ-}\sigma$$

The absence of 021 cases is another matter. (For convenience, I will refer to this as the 'upbeat-secondary pattern', or USP.) The USP should occur if we allow accents to occur to the left of the rightmost stress (because Fᴀɪᴛʜ(v̊) outranks FᴛBɪɴ).

The excluded upbeat-secondary pattern (USP)
*ŏ[ŏ][ó . . .

Let us consider other patterns before formalizing any constraints to treat this regularity.

The third pattern above is the absence of stressless long vowels in the 201 and 021 patterns. Nothing needs to be said about this. Any long vowel in these positions would be stressed because of high-ranking WSP(VV).

Revised again
$$\left\{ \begin{matrix} \text{Bɪᴍᴏʀᴀɪᴄɪᴛʏ} \\ \text{Rooting} \\ \text{WSP(VV)} \end{matrix} \right\} >> \ldots >> \text{Fᴀɪᴛʜ(v̊)} >> \text{FᴛBɪɴ} >> \text{Pᴀʀsᴇ-}\sigma$$

The fourth case to treat is the absence of (immediately) pretonic light syllables in the 221 pattern. (For convenience, I will refer to this as the 'upbeat-light pattern', or ULP.) These cases are quite similar to the USP pattern above.

> *The excluded upbeat-light pattern (ULP)*
> *σ[ù][ó . . .

Both the ULP and USP involve a stressed second syllable immediately before the main stress (or rightmost stress). In the USP case, the preceding syllable must be unfooted. In the ULP case, any preceding syllable is apparently sufficient. Notice also that this latter case cannot be ruled out by BIMORAICITY because the bimoraic minimum could always be made up by including (or geminating) the following onset consonant.

Let us now consider longer pretonic spans. We will see that the ULP and USP cases generalize.

8.1.3. Three pretonic syllables

The following table shows the logical possibilities for stress and syllable weight with three pretonic syllables. There are eight possible stress configurations (stressed and stressless for each syllable) and twenty-seven possible syllable weight configurations (light, long, or closed for each syllable). Checkmarks show configurations that are instantiated.

Stress configurations for three pretonic syllables

	0001	2001	0201	0021	2201	2021	0221	2221
V-V-V		✔	✔		✔			
V-V-VC		✔				✔		
V-V-VV						✔		
V-VC-V		✔	✔					
V-VC-VC			✔			✔		
V-VC-VV								
V-VV-V			✔					
V-VV-VC								
V-VV-VV								
VC-V-V		✔			✔			
VC-V-VC								
VC-V-VV						✔		
VC-VC-V		✔			✔			
VC-VC-VC								
VC-VC-VV								
VC-VV-V								

	0001	2001	0201	0021	2201	2021	0221	2221
VC-VV-VC								
VC-VV-VV								
VV-V-V		✔			✔			
VV-V-VC						✔		
VV-V-VV						✔		
VV-VC-V								
VV-VC-VC								
VV-VC-VV						✔		
VV-VV-V					✔			
VV-VV-VC								
VV-VV-VV								

We will go through each of these and then come back and consider the generalizations that hold.

First, certain patterns do not occur at all: 0001, 0021, 2221, and 0221. The 2001 pattern is widely attested. It can occur with all light syllables.

2001 with light syllables

màrionétte [mæriənét]	càbriolét [kʰæbriəlé]
àbracadábra [æbrəkədæbrə]	còloratúra [kʰʌlɾətʰúrə]
mùlligatáwny [mʌləgətʰɔ́ni]	Càssiopéia [kʰæsiəpʰíə]
Ìphianéssa [ìfiənésə]	hèmianópsia [hèmiənápsiə]
Màchiavéllian? [mækiəvéliən]	

The 2001 pattern can also occur with an initial heavy syllable.

2001 with an initial heavy syllable

gàbionáde [gèbiənéd]	Àegialía [èǰiəlíə]
àntimacássar [æ̀ntəməkʰǽsɾ̩]	Àliacénsis [èliəsénsəs]
Bòadicéa [bòədəsíə]	Zèlienóple [zìliənópl̩]
Hèliogábalus [hìliəgǽbl̩əs]	Ìndianápolis [ìndiənǽpl̩əs]
Àdrianópolis [èdriənápl̩əs]	deùteranópia [dùrɾənópiə]

It can also occur with a single medial heavy syllable.

2001 with a medial heavy syllable

lègerdemáin [lèǰɾdəmén]	tàtterdemálion [tʰæ̀rɾdəmélian]

It can occur with a single third heavy syllable.

2001 with a third heavy syllable

Kìlimanjáro [kʰìləmɲǰáro]	Nèbuchadnézzar [nèbəkədnézr̩]

Finally, there is a single example of this pattern where the first two syllables are heavy.

2001 with initial and medial heavy syllables

Chàndernagór [čæ̀ndr̩nəgór]

The next pattern is 0201, where there are fewer examples. First, there are a few cases of three light syllables.

0201 with all light syllables

apèritíf [əpʰèrətʰíf]	Schehèrazáde [šəhèrəzád]
amànuénsis [əmæ̀nyuénsɪs]	Sefèriádes [səfèriáriz]
Mamàllapúram [məmæ̀ləpʰùrəm]	

There are also a number of cases where the second syllable is heavy.

0201 with a medial heavy syllable

Wazìrabád [wəzìrəbǽd]	Valènciénnes [vəlènsién]
kurìkatá [kʰərìkətʰá]	Sikànd(a)rabád [šəkʰɑ̀ndrəbǽd]
Belùchistán [bəlùkəstǽn]	Makhàchkalá [məhɑ̀čkəlá]
Tegùcigálpa [tʰəgùsəgálpə]	Risòrgiménto [rəsòrgəménto]
Protèsiláus [pʰrətʰìzəláws]	Quezàltenángo [kətsàltənáŋgo]
Polònnarúwa [pʰəlònnərúə]	Monòngahéla [mənɑ̀ŋgəhílə]
palùdaméntum [pʰəlùrəméntəm]	Magìndanáo [məgìndənáw]
Louìsiána [ləwìziǽnə]	estànciéro [əstæ̀nsiéro]
mitòkorómono [mətʰòkərómn̩o]	decàlcománia [dəkʰæ̀lkəméniə]

There is one example of a form with an initial heavy syllable (or plausibly so) and one example of a form with a medial and final heavy.

0201 with an initial heavy syllable

hespèrinós? [həspèrənós]

0201 with a medial and final heavy syllable

Tenòchtitlán [tʰənɑ̀ktɪtlán]

Turning now to the 2201 pattern, there are a number of cases where the first two syllables are heavy.

2201 with the first two syllables heavy

Dìyàrbekír	Tèzcàtlipóca
[dàyàrbəkír]	[tʰèzkʰæ̀tləpʰókə]
àyùntamiénto	àlcàptonúria
[àyʊ̀ntəmyénto]	[æ̀lkʰæ̀ptənúriə]
phàntàsmagória?	àlbùminúria
[fæ̀ntʰæ̀zməgóriə]	[æ̀lbyùmṇúriə]

There is also one case where all syllables are light, and a few cases where only the first syllable is heavy.

2201 with all light syllables

àffèttuóso [æ̀fèčuóso]

2201 with an initial heavy syllable

Èutỳchiánus [yùtʰìkiénəs]	àlfìlaría [æ̀lfìlṛíə]
àcciàccatúra [èčæ̀kətʰúrə]	

Finally, the last occurring case of three pretonic syllables is the 2021 case. First, there are examples of two light syllables followed by a heavy syllable.

2021 with a final heavy syllable

èlecàmpáne	Clàromòntánus
[èləkʰæ̀mpʰén]	[kʰlæ̀rəmɔ̀ntʰǽnəs]
Hàlicàrnássus	Hècatònchíres
[hæ̀ləkʰɑ̀rnǽsəs]	[hèkətʰɔ̀nkʰáyrìz]
Vlàdikàvkáz	kàrabùrán
[vlæ̀rəkʰɑ̀vkʰáz]	[kæ̀rəbùrán]
Pèrikèirómène	dàffodòwndílly
[pʰèrəkàyrómìn]	[dæ̀fədàwndíli]

Second, there are examples of two heavy syllables with an intervening light syllable.

2021 with an initial and final heavy syllable

Stèrlitàmák [stṛ̀lətʰɑ̀mák]	Shàhjahànpúr [šɑ̀jəhɑ̀npʰúr]
Hòlothùróidea [hɑ̀ləθùrɔ́yriə]	pòllakiúria [pʰɑ̀ləkʰɑ̀yúriə]
Buènavèntúra [bwènəvèntʰúrə]	

Finally, there are two examples of medial and final heavy syllables and a single example with all heavy syllables.

2021 with medial and final heavy syllable

Àlexàndrétta [æ̀ləksæ̀ndrɛ́ɾə]	Àlexàndrínus [æ̀ləksæ̀ndrínəs]

2021 with all heavy syllables

Àzerbàiján [æ̀zr̩bàyǰán]

Let us now put together the facts about three pretonic syllables and attempt to come up with an analysis that is compatible with what we have already said about two pretonic syllables.

First, the absence of 0001 and 0021 is easily accounted for because of PARSE-σ. There will always be a superior candidate with an extra foot over the first two or second two syllables.

Second, the absence of 0221 is surely an instance of the upbeat-secondary pattern above. The USP schema above is repeated, except that I have revised the second foot so that it can bear any stress, not just a primary.

The excluded upbeat-secondary pattern (revised)

$$*\breve{\sigma}[\grave{\sigma}][\left\{\begin{matrix}\grave{\sigma}\\\acute{\sigma}\end{matrix}\right\}\cdots$$

Third, the absence of the 2221 pattern would seem to follow from the excessive stress tendency (discussed in Chapter 5). It may be that this pattern is possible in principle.

The remaining patterns—2001, 0201, 2201, and 2021—are all instantiated with at least some syllable patterns. The chart above is repeated below with only these attested patterns included. As above, instantiated patterns are marked with ✔. In addition, excluded patterns involving a long vowel that would occur in stressless position are marked with -. Cases where a stressed noninitial monomoraic foot are excluded by the schema above are marked with %. The overwhelming majority of the remaining gaps are cases where a closed syllable would be stressless. These cases are marked with ? (if they are not already marked with - or %).

Legend for table below

✔	occurring pattern
-	absent because a long vowel would be stressless
%	absent because of *σ[μ̀][ó . . .
?	absent because a closed syllable would be stressless
✔ (shaded)	occurring, but should be absent because a closed syllable would be stressless

Remaining attested patterns

	2001	0201	2201	2021
V-V-V	✔	✔	✔	%
V-V-VC	✔	?	?	✔
V-V-VV	-	-	-	✔
V-VC-V	✔	✔		%
V-VC-VC	?	✔	?	✔
V-VC-VV	-	-	-	?
V-VV-V	-	✔		-,%
V-VV-VC	-	?	?	-
V-VV-VV	-	-	-	-
VC-V-V	✔	?	✔	%
VC-V-VC	?	?	?	
VC-V-VV	-	-	-	✔
VC-VC-V	✔ (shaded)	?	✔	%
VC-VC-VC	?	?	?	?
VC-VC-VV	-	-	-	?
VC-VV-V	-	?		-,%
VC-VV-VC	-	?	?	-
VC-VV-VV	-	-	-	-
VV-V-V	✔	-	✔	%
VV-V-VC	?	-	?	✔
VV-V-VV	-	-	-	✔
VV-VC-V	?	-		%
VV-VC-VC	?	-	?	?
VV-VC-VV	-	-	-	✔ (shaded)
VV-VV-V	-	-	✔	-,%
VV-VV-VC	-	-	?	-
VV-VV-VV	-	-	-	-

The remaining patterns are few, and it is predicted that they are just accidental gaps.

With one and two pretonic syllables, a closed syllable does not attract stress; with three pretonic stressless syllables, a closed syllable does seem to attract stress, though there are some attested cases where a closed syllable is stressless. (These cells are shaded above.) Let us look at this opposition a little more closely. Consider the 2001 pattern. The occurring and nonoccurring patterns are shown below. There is no clear generalization that separates the two columns.

Occurring and nonoccurring stressless
closed syllable patterns with 2001

Nonoccurring	Occurring
V-VC-VC	VC-VC-V
VC-V-VC	
VC-VC-VC	
VV-V-VC	
VV-VC-V	
VV-VC-VC	

This absence of a generalization is even clearer with the 2021 pattern.

Occurring and nonoccurring stressless
closed syllable patterns with 2021

Nonoccurring	Occurring
V-VC-VV	VV-VC-VV
VC-VC-VC	
VC-VC-VV	
VV-VC-VC	

The upshot is that the pattern uncovered with singleton and double pretonic syllables is confirmed: while long vowels appear to attract stress in pretonic position, closed syllables do not. There does appear to be some statistical skewing to this end, but the bottom line is that there are clear examples of stressless pretonic closed syllables that cannot be discounted. Hence, the cells marked with ? in the chart above need to be viewed as accidental rather than systematic gaps.

8.1.4. Four pretonic syllables

Let us now consider the case of four pretonic syllables. Again, these patterns are instantiated only by foreign borrowings. Moreover, as the pretonic spans get longer, the examples are sparser and the number of presumed accidental gaps increases. There is, of course, a necessary corresponding decrease in the confidence with which accidental gaps can be distinguished from systematic ones. As above, I will use the theory developed for simple words as a guide.

With four pretonic syllables, the 20201 pattern is attested quite broadly.

The 20201 pattern

Bhùtatàthatá [bùrətʰàrətʰá]	Hàleàkalá [hæ̀liàkəlá]
Kìchisàburó [kʰìčisàbɾó]	Ànaxàgoréan [æ̀nəksæ̀gɾíən]
Àntanànarívo [æ̀ntənànərívo]	àntoniniánus [æ̀ntənìniánəs]
Ànuràdhapúra [ànəràrəpʰúrə]	Àpalàchicóla [æ̀pəlæ̀čəkʰólə]
Ìchinòmiyá [ìčinòmiá]	ìminòuréa [ìminòəría]
ìpecàcuánha [ìpəkʰæ̀kuánə]	ítapètinínga [ìrəpʰὲrəníŋgə]
màlonỳluréa [mæ̀lənàyləría]	Tìruchìrapálli [tʰìruč̓ʰìrəpʰǽli]
Tùiàsosópo [tʰùiàsəsópo]	Vàlentíniánus [vǽlṇtʰìniánəs]
Àvalòkitésvara [æ̀vəlòkətʰésvɾə]	hàmamèlidánthemum
	[hæ̀məmὲlədǽnθəməm]

There are also a few cases of 02001.

The 02001 pattern

Serìngapatám [sɾìŋgəpətʰám]	Barràncaberméja [bɾùŋkəbɾméjə]
aficionádo [əfìsiənáɾo]	Asclèpiadéan [əsklὲpiədíən]
appàssionáto [əpʰàsiənáɾo]	corrègimiénto [kʰərὲjimiénto]

Finally, there is one example of 200201.

The 200201 pattern

Àreopàgitíca [æ̀riəpʰæ̀jətʰíkə]

These patterns are fully compatible with the generalizations and analysis already provided. It is perhaps striking that there are no adjecent stresses with these longer examples, but there are too few examples to make much out of this.

Moreover, a number of the transcriptions of these long items show unreduced but stressless vowels in positions they should not occur in. This suggests that these are really not native English words, and are given either a foreign pronunciation or a spelling pronunciation.

8.1.5. Analysis

Let us now summarize the generalizations above and provide an analysis of nonfinal stresses.

First, we have seen that any syllable can surface with stress or without except for long vowels, which only surface with stress. This is accounted for by presuming that WSP(VV) is highly ranked. (There is another way of treating this fact which I return to below.)

Second, we have seen that a single pretonic (light or closed) syllable can surface stressed or stressless. This is treated by assuming that ROOTING is distinct from PARSE-σ, and that FTBIN is ranked between them, with ROOTING and BIMORAICITY top-ranked.

Partial ranking

$$\left\{ \begin{array}{c} \text{BIMORAICITY} \\ \text{ROOTING} \end{array} \right\} \gg \text{FTBIN} \gg \text{PARSE-}\sigma$$

Third, we have seen that it is impossible to have two unfooted syllables in a row. This is true both word-initially and medially. This generalization is responsible for the absence of all the following patterns.

Patterns ruled out

001	0001	00001
	0021	00021
		00201
		00221
		20001

This restriction emerges naturally from the presence of PARSE-σ in the system. Any candidate with two unfooted syllables in a row will always get violations of this constraint where the alternative candidate with a foot built over the same two syllables will not.

There are three remaining problems. First, there is the upbeat-secondary pattern (USP). Second, there is the upbeat-light pattern (ULP). The third problem is that while closed syllables seem to attract stress when in the domain of the rightmost foot, they do not when further to the left. I will provide an analysis of each of these in turn.

The upbeat-secondary pattern is repeated below.

The upbeat-secondary pattern (USP) (repeated)

$$*\breve{\sigma}[\grave{\sigma}][\begin{Bmatrix}\acute{\sigma}\\\acute{\sigma}\end{Bmatrix} \dots$$

The USP rules out a secondary stress when (i) it is immediately followed by a stressed syllable, and (ii) it is preceded by an unfooted syllable. This rules out the following patterns. (Foot structure is indicated with square brackets since it is relevant.)

Patterns ruled out by the USP schema

0[2][1	00[2][1*	000[2][1*
	0[2][2][1	00[2][2][1*
		0[2][2][2][1
		0[2][20][1
		([20]0[2][1)

(The patterns marked with asterisks are already ruled out by PARSE-σ and FTBIN. The last pattern is marked with parentheses because it is the only case of a medial instantiation of this pattern, and such long pretonic spans are quite rare.)

Relaxing any of the conditions given above results in a grammatical form. For example, if there is no following stress, a secondary stress in a degenerate foot following an unfooted syllable is attested. Such forms are only possible when the secondary stress is word-final, so the following chart cites relevant forms from §8.2 below.

Final degenerate foot with secondary stress where the preceding syllable is unfooted

[10]0[2]	
catamaran [kǽrəməræ̀n]	budgerigar [bʌ́ǰr̩əgɑ̀r]
espionage [ɛ́spiənɑ̀ž]	gobbledegook [gɑ́bl̩digùk]
hullabaloo [hʌ́ləbl̩ù]	rigmarole [rɪ́gəmr̩òl]
toreador [tóriədòr]	

If the secondary stress is replaced with a primary stress in either final or prestress position, the resulting form is grammatical. The following examples are of a word-final degenerate primary stress preceded by an unfooted syllable.

Attested patterns where the degenerate foot is final

0[1]	[20]0[1]
amóunt [əmáwnt]	màrionétte [mæ̀riənét]
políce [pʰəlís]	lègerdemáin [lɛ̀jɻdəmén]
cajóle [kʰəj́ól]	àvoirdupóis [æ̀vɻdəpɔ́yz]

Following are examples where the degenerate primary stress is immediately followed by another stress.

Allowed 012 patterns

apostate [əpástèt]	bolivar [bəlívàr]
gesundheit [gəzúntàyt]	impromptu [ɪmprámptù]?
apartheid [əpártàyt]	Monadnock [mənǽdnàk]

Finally, if the preceding syllable is footed, then a pretonic secondary stress is acceptable.

With an immediately preceding foot

[20][2][1	[2][2][1
Halicarnassus [hæ̀ləkʰàrnǽsəs]	Timbuktu [tʰìmbʌ̀ktʰú]
arbitrageur [àrbətràžɻ̀]	chimpanzee [čʰìmpʰænzí]
chromakalim [kʰròmək̀àlím]	bourgeoisie [bùržwàzí]
	raconteur [ræ̀kʰànt̀ʰɻ]

I will argue that formalizing the USP forces us to relax one of the very basic assumptions of OT. Let us look at the USP a little more closely and see why this is the case. I will first attempt several orthodox treatments of the USP. The shortcomings of these analyses will provide the basis of the argument for a more radical treatment.

The key part of the USP is that all of the excluded patterns can be paired with a candidate where a binary foot is built and the preceding syllable footed. This is shown in the following figure where all the patterns ruled out and given above are paired with such a candidate.

Patterns ruled out by the first schema with superior pairs

0[2][1	[20][1
00[2][1*	0[20][1
000[2][1*	00[20][1 *
0[2][2][1	[20][2][1
00[2][2][1*	0[20][2][1

```
0[2][2][2][1        [20][2][2][1
0[2][20][1          [20][20][1
([20]0[2][1)        [20][20][1
```

The import of this observation is that the USP effect could be achieved if we could find a constraint that would select the forms in the right over the forms in the left. This constraint would have to outrank a number of other constraints.

First, the relevant constraint would have to outrank WSP. This is because the excluded patterns are ruled out regardless of the weight of the syllable making up the degenerate foot.

Second, the relevant constraint would also have to outrank FAITH($\overset{\circ}{v}$). This is because the excluded patterns are ruled out regardless of whether the relevant syllable is accented.

> *Constraints that would have to be outranked*
> FAITH($\overset{\circ}{v}$)
> WSP

There are two broad approaches we can take to this. One would be to parametrize FTBIN so that it can be specific to feet that (i) are medial or peripheral, and (ii) bear secondary stress or primary stress. This approach ultimately does not work, but I illustrate the basic idea now.

First, there is a parametrized FTBIN constraint.

> *Parametrized FTBIN*
>
> $$\text{FTBIN}\left(\left\{\begin{array}{c} \text{medial} \\ \text{peripheral} \end{array}\right\}, \left\{\begin{array}{c} \text{1ary} \\ \text{2ndary} \end{array}\right\}\right)$$

There would then be four versions of FTBIN. Three would be ranked where the old FTBIN constraint was ranked, but one would be ranked above FAITH($\overset{\circ}{v}$) and WSP.

> *Proposed ranking*
>
> $$\text{FTBIN(medial,2ndary)} \gg \left\{\begin{array}{c} \text{FAITH}(\overset{\circ}{v}) \\ \text{WSP} \end{array}\right\} \gg \left\{\begin{array}{c} \text{FTBIN(medial,1ary)} \\ \text{FTBIN(peripheral)} \end{array}\right\}$$

Let us now do some examples and see how this proposal fails. First consider the case of an initial stressless syllable, e.g. *amount* [əmáwnt].

Tableau for amóunt

/əmawnt/	FB(M,2)	F-V	WSP	FB(ETC.)
[ə][máwnt]				*!
☞ ə[máwnt]				

The following tableau shows how an initial accent case fares, e.g. *raccoon* [rǽkʰún].

Tableau for ràccóon

/rǽkun/	FB(M,2)	F-V	WSP	FB(ETC.)
☞ [rǽ][kún]				*
rə[kún]		*!		

The next tableau shows how a word with multiple accents fares, e.g. *Timbùktú* [tʰimbʌktʰú]. Notice that the incorrect output results.

Tableau for Tìmbùktú

/tǐmbʌ̊ktu/	FB(M,2)	F-V	WSP	FB(ETC.)
[tìm][bʌk][tú]	*!			**
təm[bʌk][tú]	*!	*		*
✗ [tìmbək][tú]		*		*

The problem here is that binarity is enforced even though the preceding syllable would otherwise be footed.

An incorrect output also results with a form like *Hàlicàrnássus* [hæləkʰὰrnǽsəs], where a medial degenerate foot is permitted, because the preceding syllable is footed.

Tableau for Hàlicàrnássus

/hæləkɑ̊rnæsəs/	FB(M,2)	F-V	WSP	FB(ETC.)
[hæ̀lə][kὰr][nǽsəs]	*!			
✗ [hæ̀][lìkr̩][nǽsəs]		*		*

These incorrect results in the case of examples like *Tìmbùktú* and *Hàlicàrnássus* come about because foot binarity in medial contexts can be satisfied by violating other constraints, e.g. FAITH(v̊) or FTBIN(peripheral). This consequence might be avoided if, instead of parametrizing

FtBin, we parametrize Parse-σ. This approach will also fail, but, like the parametrized FtBin proposal, its failure is instructive.

The basic idea is that an unparsed syllable generates a violation that varies in significance depending on what kind of foot follows the violation. As above, there are two parameters: peripherality and primary/secondary.

Proposed parametrization of Parse-σ

$$*\sigma[(\left\{\begin{array}{c}\text{medial}\\\text{peripheral}\end{array}\right\},\left\{\begin{array}{c}\text{1ary}\\\text{2ndary}\end{array}\right\})$$

As with the previous approach, the version of the constraint relevant to medial feet with secondary stress would be ranked highest.

Required ranking

$$*\sigma[(\text{medial,2ndary}) \gg \left\{\begin{array}{c}\text{Faith}(\mathring{v})\\\text{WSP}\\\text{FtBin}\end{array}\right\} \gg \left\{\begin{array}{c}*\sigma[(\text{medial,1ary})\\*\sigma[(\text{peripheral})\end{array}\right\}$$

In order to derive forms like *agénda* or *vanílla*, *σ[(medial,1ary) must be outranked by WSP and Faith(v̊). To derive forms like *cátamaràn*, *σ[(peripheral) must be outranked by WSP and Faith(v̊). To rule out the upbeat-secondary pattern, *σ[(medial,2ndary) must outrank WSP and Faith(v̊).

Let us now consider the same examples to show how this works. First, is the new tableau for *amóunt*.

Tableau for amóunt

	/əmawnt/	*σ[(M,2)	F-V	WSP	FB	*σ[(ETC.)
	[ə][máwnt]				**!	
☞	ə[máwnt]				*	*

The next case to consider is *ràccóon*.

Tableau for ràccóon

	/ræ̊kun/	*σ[(M,2)	F-V	WSP	FB	*σ[(ETC.)
☞	[ræ̀][kún]				**	
	rə[kún]		*!		*	*

Third is the tableau for *Tìmbùktú*. Recall that the parametrized FtBin approach failed to derived the correct form here. Notice that the parametrized Parse-σ approach does derive the correct form. This is because, while the correct form made for a violation of FtBin(medial,2ndary), the correct form does not make for a violation of $*\sigma[$(medial,2ndary).

Tableau for Tìmbùktú

/tìmb**å**ktu/	$*\sigma[$(M,2)	F-V	WSP	FB	$*\sigma[$(ETC.)
☞ [tìm][b**ʌ**k][tú]				***	
təm[b**ʌ**k][tú]	*!	*		**	
[tìmbək][tú]		*!		*	

Last is the tableau for *Hàlicàrnássus*. Here again the preceding proposal resulted in the wrong form, because the correct form produced a violation of FtBin(medial,2ndary). Under the new proposal, the correct form does not produce a violation of $*\sigma[$(medial,2ndary).

Tableau for Hàlicàrnássus

/hælək**å**rnæsəs/	$*\sigma[$(M,2)	F-V	WSP	FB	$*\sigma[$(ETC.)
☞ [hæ̀lə][kàr][næ̌səs]				*	
[hæ̀][lìkr̩][næ̌səs]		*!		*	

The parametrized Parse-σ proposal thus accounts for the upbeat-secondary pattern.

The right question to ask at this stage is whether this proposal is ad hoc. I suggest that it is. Basically, this approach simply stipulates that a gap is disallowed just in case a degenerate foot with secondary stress that could include the relevant syllable is in precisely the right place. The 'conditional' nature of this restriction damns the proposal.

Let us try a different tactic. The key insight is that the USP is a consequence of too many violations of too many constraints. This proposal stems from the observation that the components of the USP all seem to be dispreferred structures. I list these below and then motivate each.

Components of the USP

1. An unparsed syllable
2. A degenerate foot
3. A foot not on the right edge of the word
4. A stress clash
5. Secondary stress

The first three components of the USP are clearly connected to Parse-σ, FtBin, and Align-R. The fourth component of the USP can be connected to a familiar constraint on stress systems: *CLASH. This constraint is not treated in this book, but is responsible for the following alternations involving the distribution of primary stress in phrases.

Examples of phrasal clash resolution

bàmbóo	bámbòo cúrtain
pròpáne	própàne stóve
Tènnessée	Ténnessèe áir
Tìmbùktú	Tímbùktù Tím

The last component of the USP is only hypothesis: primary stresses are preferred to secondary stresses. This is given below.

*SECONDARY (*2)
Secondary stresses are dispreferred.

The excluded structure would thus seem to violate PARSE-σ, FTBIN, ALIGN-R, *CLASH, and *2. Violations of any one of these constraints is not sufficient alone. Together, however, these violations are sufficient to rule out the USP.

One way to implement this would be to make use of the Local Conjunction mechanism proposed by Smolensky (1993). This device allows any two constraints to be composed and ranked independently from the singleton constraints. Assuming this operation is recursive, this would allow us to rank a superconstraint composed from component constraints. The superconstraint we can call the upbeat-secondary constraint and the components would be as follows.

Upbeat-secondary constraint (USC)
PARSE-σ & FTBIN & *CLASH & ALIGN-R & *2

Such a device allows us a formalism to describe the USP, but we should not lose track of the key insight. It looks as though, while individual violations are insufficient to overpower FAITH($\mathring{v}$) and the WSP, the collected violations of these otherwise outranked constraints is sufficient to overpower FAITH($\mathring{v}$). A number of scholars have adopted and argued for Local Conjunction, but the bottom line is that a theory incorporating this device effectively gives up on strict ranking of constraints.

Let us now turn to the second schema, the ULP (repeated below). What is excluded is a nonperipheral foot where (i) BIMORAICITY is satisfied with gemination, and (ii) there is an immediately following foot.

The upbeat-light pattern (repeated)

*σ[ù][ó . . .

This rules out the configurations in the first column below, but allows those in the second column.

Disallowed and allowed configurations

. . . 0[cv][1 . . .	but	[cv][1 . . .
. . . [2][cv][1 . . .		[cv][2 . . .
. . . [20][cv][1 . . .		

The following chart gives examples of the permitted (peripheral) cases.

Permitted peripheral configurations

[cv][1 . . .	[cv][2 . . .
tattoo [tʰæ̀tʰú]	satyre [sǽtʰàyr]
ballet [bæ̀lé]	atoll [ǽtʰɔ̀l]
baboon [bæ̀bún]	asset [ǽsèt]
chalet [šæ̀lé]	jacquard [jǽkʰàrd]
trapeze [tʰræ̀pʰíz]	rabbi [rǽbày]

This is clearly similar to the USP. Again, a monosyllabic foot is ruled out. There are several differences, however. First, this foot is only ruled out if BIMORAICITY is only satisfied by violating NoGEMINATES. Second, this constraint does not care whether the preceding syllable is footed or not, as long as a syllable is there. Third, this constraint does not care whether the 'monomoraic' foot would bear primary or secondary stress.

The simplest treatment of this is to parametrize NoGEMINATES so that it can distinguish peripheral and medial feet. While NoGEMINATES (peripheral) is fairly low-ranked, NoGEMINATES(medial) is sufficiently high-ranked to make the USP follow.

Proposed parametrization and ranking

NoGEMINATES(medial) >> . . . >> NoGEMINATES(peripheral)

The empirical content of this proposal is that geminates are only allowed in the first syllable of an English word. This is a reasonable proposal, as it is quite common for syllable weight of various sorts to be restricted to some peripheral syllable.

Let us now turn to the final point that needs to be dealt with. We have already seen that closed syllables attract stress in penultimate position (in nouns). This is shown by the absence of forms like *ágenda [ǽjn̩də]. We already saw that a heavy syllable in ultima position in a noun does not necessarily attract stress. This followed from the ranking of NONFINALITY above WSP(Coda<$\mu\mu$) and below WSP(VV). The fact that a heavy penult (of a noun) attracts stress whether it is long or closed (agénda or aróma) follows from ranking FTBIN below all WSP constraints.

The question now is why a closed syllable to the left of the rightmost stress does not attract stress (cantata [kʰn̩tʰárə]), while a long vowel does (typhoon [tʰàyfún]). The key insight is that only a closed syllable in the domain of the final foot must be stressed. With a noun, this means that a closed penult must be stressed, e.g. agénda [əjɛ́ndə]. With a verb or adjective, this means the final overt syllable must be stressed if it is closed (once the final consonant is factored out as the onset of the catalectic suffix, e.g. evíct [əvíkt]). Another way of looking at this is that while a long vowel must be stressed anywhere, a closed syllable must only be stressed when it would otherwise occur as the right member of the rightmost binary foot.

This suggests two revisions to the WSP(VC) constraints. First, the WSP(VC) should refer specifically to membership in a foot.

WSP(VC) preliminary revisions
*[σ $C_0VC_{<\mu\mu}$]   *[σ $C_0VC_{>\mu}$]

This allows a closed syllable to occur stressless outside the domain of the foot, either skipped via NONFINALITY, e.g. animal [ǽnəml̩], or unfooted to the left of a foot, e.g. cantata [kʰn̩tʰárə]. To capture the fact that only the rightmost foot is subject to this constraint, the revised WSP(VC) constraints must specify that the relevant foot is at the right edge of the prosodic word. (I use curly braces to denote the prosodic word in the formalism below.)

WSP(VC) final revisions
*[σ $C_0VC_{<\mu\mu}$] $\}_{pw}$ *[σ $C_0VC_{>\mu}$] $\}_{pw}$

This revision allows a closed syllable to occur in the nonhead branch of a nonprimary foot, e.g. ánecdòte [ǽnəkdòt]. This revision would apply to both versions of the WSP(VC) constraint: WSP(Coda<$\mu\mu$) and WSP(Coda>μ). WSP(VV) is more general, ruling out a stressless long vowel whether footed or not. Thus a final long vowel or initial long vowel must be stressed.

Let us summarize the system for nonfinal stress assignment. First, PARSE-σ is applicable, but subordinate to FTBIN. FTBIN, in turn, is subordinate to FAITH($\hat{v}$). WSP(VV), the revised WSP(VC), NOGEMINATES (medial), and USC are unviolated. Finally, PARSE-σ outranks ALIGN-

RIGHT, allowing for multiple feet. The full ranking needed is given below.

Constraints and ranking needed for nonfinal footing

$$\left\{\begin{array}{c} \text{NG(med)} \\ \text{USC} \\ \text{WSP(VV)} \\ \text{WSP(VC)} \end{array}\right\} \gg \text{FAITH}(\overset{\circ}{v}) \gg \text{FTBIN} \gg \text{PARSE-}\sigma \gg \text{ALIGN-R}$$

Let us now consider some examples to see how this system works. The following tableau shows how a closed pretonic syllable can surface stressless, e.g. in *cantáta*. (For convenience, in the following tableaux, WSP represents all the WSP constraints.)

Tableau for cantáta

	/kVntaata/	WSP	USC	NG	F($\overset{\circ}{v}$)	FTBIN	PARSE-σ
☞	kVn[taa]ta					*	**
	[kVn][taa]ta					**!	*
	[kVntaa]ta	*!					*

Forms with a single pretonic closed syllable that are stressed must be accented. FAITH($\overset{\circ}{v}$) thus outranks FTBIN. The following tableau shows how this works for a word like *tàmpíco* [tʰæmpʰíko].

Tableau for tàmpíco

	/tæ̊ mpiiko/	WSP	USC	NG	F($\overset{\circ}{v}$)	FTBIN	PARSE-σ
	tæ̊ m[pii]ko				*!	*	**
☞	[tæ̊ m][pii]ko					**	*
	[tæ̊ mpii]ko	*!					*

Only the rightmost closed syllable (pace NONFINALITY) attracts stress; the others can only tolerate it (via accent and FAITH($\overset{\circ}{v}$)).

Let us now consider the case of two pretonic syllables. There are twelve logical possibilities involving closed syllables and light syllables. Only six of these are instantiated.

Two pretonic syllables with only light and closed syllables

	20	22	02
V-V	gàsolíne	–	–
V-VC	pàlanquín	ànàmnésis	–
VC-V	màndolín	–	–
VC-VC	gàspergóu	chìmpànzée	–

The cases in the first column are straightforward. Parse-σ forces the two pretonic syllables to be stressed. FtBin militates for a disyllabic foot. The words in the second column arise from an accent on the first and second syllables, resulting in foot structures as follows.

Foot structures for words in the second column

[àn][àm][né]sis   [chìm][pàn][zée]

The following tableau shows how this works for *chìmpànzée*.

Tableau for chìmpànzée

/čǐmpǽnzii/	WSP	USC	NG	F(v̊)	FtBin	Parse-σ
☞ [čìm][pæ̀n][zíi]					***	
čìm[pæ̀n][zíi]		*!		*	**	*
čm̩pṇ[zíi]				*!*	*	**
[čìmpṇ][zíi]				*!	*	
[čìm]pən[zíi]				*!	**	*

The other imaginable distributions of accent both result in one of the patterns already given. First, an accent on the first syllable is irrelevant as this is the normal position of stress for such words. Accent on a light second syllable would never surface because of the USC and NoGeminates (medial) constraints above. This is shown in the following tableau.

Hypothetical accent on a light second syllable

/cvcv̊[1/	WSP	USC	NG	F(v̊)	FtBin	Parse-σ
☞ [cv̀cv][1				*		
[cv̀][cv̀][1			*!		**	
cvcv[1				*		*!*
cv[cv̀][1		*!	*		*	*
[cv̀]cv[1				*	*!	*

If the second syllable were closed, then we would end up with the *chìmpànzée* pattern.

Hypothetical accent on a closed second syllable

/cvcv̊c[1/	WSP	USC	NG	F(v̊)	FtBin	Parse-σ
[cv̀cvc][1				*!		
☞ [cv̀][cv̀c][1					**	
cvcvc[1				*!		**
cv[cv̀c][1		*!			*	*
[cv̀]cvc[1				*!	*	*

Let us consider the case of three pretonic syllables. Here there are more logical possibilities, all diagrammed below.

Logically possible combinations of closed and light syllables in pretonic spans of three syllables

	200	202	220	020
V-V-V	àbracadábra	–	àffèttuóso	apèritíf
V-V-VC	Kìlimanjáro	èlecàmpáne	–	–
V-VC-V	lègerdemáin	–	–	Monòngahéla
V-VC-VC	–	Àlexàndrétta	–	Tenòchtitlán
VC-V-V	Ìndianápolis	–	àlfìlaría	–
VC-V-VC	–	–	–	–
VC-VC-V	Chàndernagór	–	Tèzcàtlipóca	–
VC-VC-VC	–	–	–	–

The default stress pattern with three pretonic short syllables is that the second syllable should get stress.

The default stress pattern
σ[ò σ][ó . . .

This is shown in the following tableau.

Tableau for apèritíf

/aperitif/	WSP	USC	NG	F(v̊)	FB	P-σ	A-R
☞ ə[pèrə][tíf]					*	*	*
[æ̀pɾ]ə[tíf]					*	*	**!
[æ̀][pèrə][tíf]					**!		****
əpɾə[tíf]					*	**!*	
[æ̀pɾ][æ̀][tíf]			*!		**		***

Most of the other configurations are a consequence of lexical accents. For example, accent on the second of three light syllables would result in the same shape as *apèritíf*. An accent on the third syllable would never be realized because of NoGeminates(medial).

Going through all accentual configurations would take quite a while, so let us just go through each of the occurring cases. A form like *àbracadábra* results from an initial accent.

Tableau for àbracadábra

/ǻbracadabra/	WSP	USC	NG	F(v̊)	FB	P-σ	A-R
ə[brǽkə][dǽbrə]				*!		*	**
☞ [ǽbrə]kə[dǽbrə]						*	***
[ǽ][brǽkə][dǽbrə]					*!		******
[ǽbrə][kǽ][dǽbrə]			*!		*		*****

A form like *àffèttuóso* has accent on the first two syllables.

Tableau for àffèttuóso

/ǽfěčuoso /	WSP	USC	NG	F(v̊)	FB	P-σ	A-R
ə[fèču][óso]				*!		*	**
[ǽfə]ču[óso]				*!		*	***
☞ [ǽ][fèču][óso]					*		******
[ǽfə][čù][óso]				*!	*		*****

If the third syllable is heavy, initial secondary stress is a consequence of initial accent. This is shown in the following tableau for *Kìlimanjáro*.

Tableau for Kìlimanjáro

/kǐlɪmænǰɑro/	WSP	USC	NG	F(v̊)	FB	P-σ	A-R
kə[lìmn̥][ǰáro]				*!		*	**
☞ [kìlə]mn̥[ǰáro]						*	***
[kì][lìmn̥][ǰáro]					*!		******
[kìlə][mǽn][ǰáro]					*!		*****

The rightmost syllable can surface stressed if it is accented, e.g. *èlecàmpáne*.

Tableau for èlecàmpáne

/ɛlɛkǽmpen/	WSP	USC	NG	F(v̊)	FB	P-σ	A-R
ə[lèkm̩][pén]				*!	*	*	*
[èlə]km̩[pén]				*!	*	*	**
ələ[kæ̀m][pén]		*!			**	**	*
[è][lèkm̩][pén]				*!	**		****
☞ [èlə][kæ̀m][pén]					**		***

No other patterns should be possible for this weight configuration.

If the second syllable is closed, we expect only two patterns. With no accent, we get stress on the second syllable, e.g. in *Monòngahéla*.

Tableau for Monòngahéla

/manaŋgahila/	WSP	USC	NG	F(v̊)	FB	P-σ	A-R
☞ mə[nàŋgə][hílə]						*	**
[mànəŋ]gə[hílə]						*	***!
[mà][nàŋgə][hílə]					*!		******
[mànəŋ][gà][hílə]			*!		*		*****

It is also possible for the first syllable to surface with stress if accented; this is exemplified with forms like *lègerdemáin* [lèj̊rdəmén].

Tableau for lègerdemáin

/lɛ̊j̊rdəmen/	WSP	USC	NG	F(v̊)	FB	P-σ	A-R
lə[j̊rdə][mén]				*!	*		*
☞ [lèj̊r]də[mén]					*		**
[lè][j̊rdə][mén]					*!		****
[lèj̊r][dè][mén]			*!		*		***

Let us now consider cases where the rightmost two syllables are heavy. A word like *Àlexàndrétta* has accent on the third syllable.

Tableau for Àlexàndrétta

/ælɛksǽndrɛtə/	WSP	USC	NG	F(v̊)	FB	P-σ	A-R
æleksæn[drétə]				*!		***	
[ǽ]ləksn̩[drétə]				*!	*	**	****
[ǽ][lèksn̩][drétə]				*!	*		******
ə[lèksn̩][drétə]				*!		*	**
ə[lèk]sn̩[drétə]				*!	*	*	***
ələk[sæn][drétə]		*!			*	**	**
☞ [ǽlək][sæn][drétə]					*		*****
[ǽlək]sn̩[drétə]				*!		*	***
[ǽ][lèk]sn̩[drétə]				*!	**	*	*******
[ǽ]lək[sæn][drétə]		*!			**	*	******
ə[lèk][sæn][drétə]		*!			**	*	*****
[ǽ][lèk][sæn][drétə]					***!		*********

No accent results in a different pattern, exemplified by *Tenòchtitlán*.

Tableau for Tenòchtitlán

/tɛnɑktɪtlɑn/	WSP	USC	NG	F(v̊)	FB	P-σ	A-R
☞ tə[nàktət][lán]					*		*
[tɛ̀][nàktət][lán]					*!		****
[tɛ̀nək][tìt][lán]					*!		***
[tɛ̀nək]tət[lán]						*	**!

Turning now to cases with an initial closed syllable, accent on the first syllable results in first syllable stress, e.g. *Ìndianápolis* [ìndiənǽpl̩əs].

Tableau for Ìndianápolis

/ɪ̀ndɪənæpələs/	WSP	USC	NG	F(v̊)	FB	P-σ	A-R
n̩[dìən][ǽpl̩]əs				*!		**	****
[ìn][dìən][ǽpl̩]əs					*!	*	********
[ìndi][ǽ][nǽpl̩]əs			*!		*	*	********
☞ [ìndi]ən[ǽpl̩]əs						**	*****

Accent on the first two syllables puts stress on both those syllables, e.g. as in *àlfilaría* [æ̀lfìlr̩íə].

Tableau for àlfilaría

/ǽlfīləriə/	WSP	USC	NG	F($\overset{\circ}{v}$)	FB	P-σ	A-R
☞ [ǽl][fīlə][rí]ə					*	*	******
əl[fīlə][rí]ə				*!	**	***
[ǽfə]lə[rí]ə				*!	**	****
[ǽfə][lù][rí]ə			*!	*	*	*	******

We would also expect to find initial stressless syllables in this class, but there are no examples of this sort.

Finally, there are cases where the first two syllables are closed. If the first syllable is accented, it gets stressed, e.g. *Chàndernagór* [čʰǽndṛnəgór].

Tableau for Chàndernagór

/čǽndṛnəgʊɪ/	WSP	USC	NG	F($\overset{\circ}{v}$)	FB	P-σ	A-R
☞ [čǽndṛ]nə[gór]					*	*	**
[čǽndṛ][nǽ][gór]			*!		**	***
čṇ[dṛnə][gór]				*!	*	*	*
[čǽn][dṛnə][gór]				**!	**	****

If the first two syllables are accented, then both are stressed, e.g. *Tèzcàtlipóca* [tʰèzkʰǽtləpʰókə].

Tableau for Tèzcàtlipóca

/tèskǽtlɪpokə/	WSP	USC	NG	F($\overset{\circ}{v}$)	FB	P-σ	A-R
[tèskət]lə[pó]kə				*!	*	****
[tèskət][lì][pó]kə			*!	*	*	******
təs[kǽtlə][pó]kə				*!	*	***
☞ [tès][kǽtlə][pó]kə					*	*******

Examples involving four or more pretonic syllables behave the same way.

To summarize, I have proposed that nonfinal stresses are assigned in much the same way as final stresses. Several constraints must be revised and several added. The NOGEMINATES constraint was revised to recognize a difference in the acceptability of gemination medially and peripherally. Second, the WSP(VC) constraints were revised to recognize the fact that closed syllables only attract stress in the rightmost foot. Finally, the USC constraint was proposed. This constraint accounts for the absence of the upbeat-secondary pattern, but was only formalizable by making use of the Local Conjunction mechanism.

8.2. LONG VOWELS

I have argued that long vowels attract stress in any context (except the USP/USC case) via the WSP(VV) constraint. However, the facts both in this chapter and in the preceding one are actually amenable to a simpler analysis. Since an unstressed long or short vowel will reduce to the same targets, it is possible to argue that long vowels do not attract stress at all. If a long vowel happens to get stressed, it will surface as long. If a long vowel happens not to get stressed, it will surface as reduced.

The problem with this view is that it goes against the typological norm. It has been known for a long time that the general case is that if the closed syllables of a language attract stress, then the long vowels will also attract stress (Hayes 1981). Therefore, the analysis proposed above and in Chapter 7 stands, since it is in conformity with the general theory of quantity sensitivity.

8.3. NONFINAL PRIMARY STRESS

In this section, I briefly consider cases of nonfinal primary stresses. Since the goal of this book is a treatment of syllable and foot structure, higher-order effects like this are really irrelevant. This section will merely sketch out the facts and lay out the generalizations.

In all the examples above, the rightmost stress was also the main stress of the word. This is not always the case. The main stress can sometimes be the second stress from the right. The basic generalization seems to be that when the rightmost stress is not primary, it must necessarily be a degenerate foot.

Two other facts emerge from the review below. First, in contrast to earlier work, there appears to be no pattern to the content of the skipped stress. Second, nouns, verbs, and adjectives all exhibit the shift, but only nouns do so robustly.

The following chart shows that two-syllable nouns with all possible vowels in the final syllable can exhibit a nonrightmost primary stress.

Every possible final vowel for two-syllable nouns with nonrightmost primary stress

aesthete [ǽsθìt]	banshee [bǽnšì]	benzene [bénzìn]
hygiene [háyǰìn]	praline [pʰrélìn]	essay [ésè]
decade [dékèd]	chilblane [čʰílblèn]	mandrake [mǽndrèk]
membrane [mémbrèn]	cashew [kʰǽšù]	cuckoo [kʰúkʰù]
hoodoo [húdù]	fichu [fíšù]	etude [étʰùd]
alcove [ǽlkʰòv]	aerobe [éròb]	charcoal [čʰárkʰòl]
cosmos [kʰázmòs]	encore [áŋkʰòr]	argon [árgàn]
crouton [kʰrútʰàn]	crayon [kʰréàn]	icon [áykʰàn]
jacquard [ǰǽkʰàrd]	asphalt [ǽsfɔlt]	centaur [séntʰɔr]
gewgaw [gúgɔ]	kobold [kʰóbɔld]	quahog [kʰwɔ́hɔg]
argyle [árgàyl]	bovine [bóvàyn]	endive [éndàyv]
esquire [éskwàyr]	magpie [mǽgpʰày]	landau [lǽndàw]
luau [lúàw]	powwow [pʰáwwàw]	decoy [díkʰɔy]
hautboy [óbɔy]	accent [ǽksènt]	afghan [ǽfgæn]
asset [ǽsèt]	ambush [ǽmbừš]	capstan [kʰǽpstæn]
apex [épʰèks]	anthrax [ǽnθræks]	biceps [báysèps]
cognac [kʰɔ́nyæk]	cossack [kʰásæk]	

The following charts show that two-syllable words of all categories can exhibit a nonrightmost primary stress as well. The following chart gives verbs and adjectives that exhibit nonrightmost stress.

Two-syllable verbs and adjectives with nonrightmost primary stress

blaspheme [blǽsfìm]	rampage [rǽmpʰèǰ]	parlay [pʰárlè]
assay [ǽsè]	issue [íšù]	mildew [míldù]
creole [kʰríòl]	ersatz [érzàts]	ribald [ríbɔld]

The following chart shows longer words with a nonrightmost primary on the penultimate syllable.

Longer words with penultimate nonrightmost primary stress

aristide [ərístìd]	mahathir [məháθìr]
andante [àndántʰè]	apartheid [əpʰártʰèt]
aqazadeh [ǽkəzádè]	aspartame [əspártʰèm]
infante [ìnfántʰè]	bolivares [bòləvárèz]

alarcon? [əlárkʰàn]   yamatake [yàmətʰákʰè]

chihuahua [čʰɪwáwà]   liaison [liézàn]

mlotok [məlátʰàk]   vorontsov [vr̩ántsàv]

jinrikisha [jìnríkšɔ̀]   italtel [ɪtʰǽltʰèl]

adamantine [æ̀rəmǽntʰìn]

Words with antepenultimate nonrightmost primary stress are quite frequent. The following chart gives examples of trisyllabic nouns of this type.

Trisyllabic nouns with antepenultimate nonrightmost stress

kerosine [kʰérəsìn]	limousine [líməzìn]
guillotine [gílətʰìn]	mezzanine [mézənìn]
parrakeet [pʰǽrəkʰìt]	barricade [bǽrəkʰèd]
carapace [kʰǽrəpʰès]	caraway [kʰǽrəwè]
chatelaine [šǽr̩lèn]	hurricane [hárəkʰèn]
nincompoop [nínkm̩pʰùp]	albacore [ǽlbəkʰòr]
anecdote [ǽnəkdòt]	artichoke [árrəčʰòk]
creosote [kʰríəsòt]	catacomb [kʰǽrəkʰòm]
amazon [ǽməzàn]	lancelot [lǽnsl̩àt]
apricot [éprəkʰàt]	marathon [mǽrəθàn]
ocelot [ásl̩àt]	panama [pʰǽnəmɔ̀]
albatross [ǽlbətʰrɔ̀s]	alcohol [ǽlkəhɔ̀l]
mackinaw [mǽkn̩ɔ̀]	tomahawk [tʰáməhɔ̀k]
alibi [ǽləbày]	appetite [ǽpətʰàyt]
argentine [árjn̩tʰàyn]	calomine [kʰǽləmàyn]
lullaby [lʌ́ləbày]	sauerkraut [sáwr̩kràwt]
corduroy [kʰórdərɔ̀y]	acrobat [ǽkrəbæ̀t]
alphabet [ǽlfəbèt]	amaranth [ǽmr̩æ̀nθ]
marmoset [márməsèt]	palimpsest [pʰǽlm̩psèst]
almanac [ɔ́lmn̩æ̀k]	artefact [árrəfæ̀kt]
bailiwick [béliwìk]	boomerang [búmr̩æ̀ŋ]

There are also some examples of this latter sort with verbs and adjectives.

Trisyllabic adjectives and verbs with antepenultimate
nonrightmost primary stress

ricochet [ríkəšè]	rendezvous! [rándèvù]
caterwaul [kʰǽrr̩wɔ̀l]	pettifog [pʰérifɔ̀g]
benefit [bénəfìt]	flabbergast [flǽbr̩gæ̀st]
gallivant [gǽləvæ̀nt]	vagabond [vǽgəbànd]

aquiline [ǽkwəlàyn]   argentine [árǰṇtʰàyn]
difficult [dífəkʰʌlt]   manifest [mǽnəfèst]
taciturn [tʰǽsətʰṛ̩n]

Some examples of longer forms with antepenultimate nonrightmost primary stress are given below.

Longer words with antepenultimate nonrightmost primary stress

anopheles [ənáfḷìz]	antipodes [ǽntʰípədìz]
Piscataway [pʰəskǽrəwè]	conquistador [kʰəŋkʰístədòr]
amiprilose [əmíprəlòs]?	Arapaho [ərǽpəhò]
chiapparone [čʰiǽpṛòn]	camelopard [kʰəmélə pʰàrd]
Saskatchewan [səskǽčuàn]	Baryshnikov [bəríšnəkʰɔ̀v]
Kalashnikov [kʰəlášnəkʰɔ̀v]	Beregovoy [bərégəvɔ̀y]
videlicet [vədélɔsèt]	Afghanistan [ə̀fgǽnəstæ̀n]
anafranil? [ənǽfrənìl]	Uzbekistan [ùzbékəstæ̀n]
orangutan [ərǽŋətʰæ̀ŋ]	prolegomenon [pʰràləgámənàn]

There are also some examples of words with preantepenultimate nonrightmost main stress. These examples show that the distribution of nonrightmost primary stress is different from the distribution of rightmost primary stress (which is limited to the three-syllable window on the right).

Preantepenultimate nonrightmost primary stress

cyanazine? [sáyənəzìn]	mangiapane? [mǽnǰiəpʰèn]
gobbledegook [gábḷdigùk]	hullabaloo [hʌ́ləbəlù]
toreador [tʰóriədòr]	catamaran [kʰǽrəməræ̀n]

Finally, there are a few examples of words where the following secondary stress appears to be nonfinal. All of these involve a word-final syllabic sonorant or [i]. The first examples below exhibit antepenultimate main stress.

Antepenultimate main stress with a penultimate secondary stress

badminton [bǽdmìntṇ]	boondoggle [búndàgḷ]
carbuncle [kʰárbʌ̀ŋkḷ]	cucumber [kʰyúkʰʌ̀mbṛ]
peduncle [pʰírʌ̀ŋkḷ]	pinochle [pʰínʌ̀kḷ]
saltpetre [sɔ́ltpʰìrṛ̩]	hierarchy [háyràrki]

The following examples exhibit preantepenultimate main stress.

Preantepenultimate main stress with penultimate secondary stress

caterpillar [kʰǽɾɾpʰìlɾ]	cauliflower [kʰʌ́liflàwɾ]
dandelion [dǽndəlàyən]	haberdasher [hǽbɾdæ̀šɾ]
hootenanny [hútn̩æ̀ni]	kindergarten [kʰíndɾgàrtn̩]
lederhosen [léɾɾhòzn̩]	mollycoddle [málikʰàdl̩]
oleander [óliæ̀ndɾ]	periwinkle [pʰέriwìŋkl̩]
piccalilli [pʰíkəlìli]	pickaninny [pʰíkənìni]
ragamuffin [rǽgəmʌ̀fn̩]	tabernacle [tʰǽbɾnæ̀kl̩]

To summarize, the main stress of an English word is sometimes not the rightmost stress. There are two clear generalizations. First, main stress is never separated from the right edge of the word by more than one secondary stress (but *rendezvous*?). Second, the secondary stress that falls to the right is always either the final syllable or the penult (only if the final syllable is a syllabic sonorant).

8.4. MORPHEMES AND FEET

In this and the previous chapter, I have outlined the general picture of stress in English entirely on the basis of monomorphemic words. In this section we will briefly consider polymorphemic words. First, I will argue that there is a class of affixes which require a small modification of the theory. Specifically, these affixes are outside the domain of stress assignment. Second, I treat superficial violations of the USC that occur with polymorphemic words.

8.4.1. **Neutral suffixes**

We have seen that monomorphemic words in English always have a stress on at least one of the last three syllables. This is not true of polymorphemic words. I refer to this phenomenon as 'extrafenestral stress'. Some examples follow below.

Some examples of extrafenestral stress

abominable [əbámn̩əbl̩]	accompaniment [əkʰʌ́mpn̩imənt]
accuracy [ǽkyərəsi]	actually [ǽkčuəli]
aerialist [ériəlɪst]	associative [əsósiəɾɪv]
charactery [kʰǽɾəktɾi]	disinterested [dəsíntɾəstəd]
mutableness [myúrəbl̩nəs]	spirituous [spíɾəčuəs]

The examples above all involve preantepenultimate stress, but there are a few examples with a rightmost stress even further to the left.

Extreme extrafenestral stress

alienable [éliənəb̩l]	habitableness [hǽbərəb̩lnəs]
variableness [vériəb̩lnəs]	spiritualism [spírəčuəlɪzm̩]

There are several striking facts about such words. First, they are limited to words that end in certain affixes. For example, words ending in -*able* make up a sizeable percentage of these words. Here are just a few examples.

Extrafenestral stress with -able

abominable [əbámṇəb̩l]	alienable [éliənəb̩l]
amiable [émiəb̩l]	attributable [ətʰríbyurəb̩l]
comfortable [kʰʌ́mfr̩rəb̩l]	communicable [kʰomyúnəkəh̩l]
dutiable [dúriəb̩l]	eligible [ɛ́ləǰəb̩l]
favorable [févrəb̩l]	habitable [hǽbərəb̩l]
heritable [hɛ́rərəh̩l]	immeasurable [ɪmmɛ́žrəb̩l]
impenetrable [ɪmpʰɛ́nətrəb̩l]	imperishable [ɪmpʰɛ́rɪšəb̩l]
incalculable [ɪŋkʰǽlkyələb̩l]	incomparable [ɪŋkʰámprəb̩l]
inconsiderable [ɪ̀ŋkṇsírrəb̩l]	indubitable [ɪndúbərəb̩l]
inestimable [ɪnɛ́stəmɔb̩l]	inevitable [ɪnɛ́vərəb̩l]
inoperable [ɪnáprəb̩l]	insufferable [ɪnsʌ́frəb̩l]
insuperable [ɪnsúprəb̩l]	inviolable [ɪnváyələb̩l]
irrecoverable [ɪrəkʰʌ́vrəb̩l]	irrefragable [ɪrəfrǽǰəb̩l]
malleable [mǽliəb̩l]	measurable [mɛ́žrəb̩l]
medicable [mɛ́rəkəb̩l]	enviable [énviəb̩l]
negligible [nɛ́gləǰəb̩l]	operable [áprəb̩l]
palatable [pǽlərəb̩l]	pleasurable [pʰlɛ́žrəb̩l]
predicable [pʰrɛ́rəkəb̩l]	preferable [pʰrɛ́frəb̩l]
seasonable [sízn̩əb̩l]	tolerable [tʰálr̩əb̩l]
unalienable [ʌnéliənəb̩l]	vulnerable [vʌ́lnr̩əb̩l]
venerable [vénr̩əb̩l]	violable [váyələb̩l]

A second fact about these words is that a heavy syllable can be skipped over in the assignment of stress outside the window. The following chart shows a few examples where a heavy nonfinal syllable has been skipped over to assign extrafenestral stress.

Skipped heavy syllables with neutral suffixes

belligerency [bəlíǰṛənsi]	charactery [kʰǽrəktṛi]
comfortable [kʰʌ́m̩fṛrəbl̩]	constituency [kʰənstíčuənsi]
exigency [égzəǰṇsi]	expediency [ɪkspíriənsi]
mutableness [myúrəbl̩nəs]	occupancy [ákyəpṇsi]
similarly [síməlṛli]	singularly [síŋgyəlṛli]
variableness [vǽriəbl̩nəs]	

The following chart shows a list of all the stressless suffixes that permit extrafenestral stress.

Affixes that permit extrafenestral stress

Suffix	Example
-y	charactery [kʰǽrəktṛi]
-able	variable [vǽriəbl̩]
-ism	barbarism [bárbṛɪzm̩]
- $\begin{Bmatrix} u \\ i \end{Bmatrix}$ al	spiritual [spírəčuəl]
-ness	appropriateness [əpʰrópriətnəs]
-ment	accompaniment [əkʰʌ́mpṇimənt]
-ly	similarly [síməlṛli]
-ed	interested [íntṛəstəd]
-ing	jettisoning [ǰérəsṇɪŋ]
-ist	alienist [éliənɪst]
-ative	associative [əsósiərɪv]
-s	audiences [óriənsəz]
-er	discipliner [dísəplɪnṛ]
-man	infantryman [ím̩fṇtrimṇ]
-son	Cinnaminson [sínəmṇsṇ]

The examples above all involve preantepenultimate stress. Most of the same suffixes permit a closed syllable to be skipped over to assign stress to an antepenultimate syllable.

Affixes that permit a skipped heavy syllable

Suffix	Example
-y	allergy [ǽlṛǰi], galaxy [gǽləksi], agency [éǰṇsi]
-able	N/A

-ism	obscurantism [ʌbskyf̩əntɪzm̩], synergism [sínr̩ǰɪzm̩]
-al	interval [íntr̩vl̩]
-ness	fixedness [fíksədnəs], wilderness [wíldr̩nəs], rancidness [rǽnsədnəs]
-ment	blandishment [blǽndɪšmn̩t], devilment [dévl̩mn̩t], government [gʌ́vr̩mn̩t]
-ly	fixedly [fíksədli], instantly [ínstn̩tli], inwardly [ínwr̩dli]
-ed	properticd [pʰrápr̩rid]
-ist	allergist [ǽlr̩ǰɪst], columnist [káləmnɪst], liturgist [lír̩ǰɪst], monarchist [mánr̩kɪst]
-ative	N/A
-es	helixes [híləksəz]
-er	harbinger [hárbɪnǰr̩], messenger [mésnǰr̩], passenger [pʰǽsnǰr̩]
-man	alderman [ɔ́ldr̩mn̩], fisherman [fíšr̩mn̩], motorman [mór̩mn̩]
-son	Cinnaminson [sínəmn̩sn̩]
-ton	Washington [wɔ́šɪŋtn̩], simpleton [símpl̩tn̩], singleton [síŋgl̩tn̩]

There is another potential source of evidence for neutral affixation. A number of affixes do not affect the stress pattern of the base. There are three groups of these depending on whether the affix is stressless or bears secondary or primary stress.

Following are examples of each of these. The first examples below are stressless affixes that do not affect the stress of the base.

Stressless neutral affixes

-ist	abolition [æ̀bl̩íšn̩]	abolitionist [æ̀bl̩íšn̩ɪst]
-ly	absolute [æ̀bsl̩út]	absolutely [æ̀bsl̩útli]
-ance	accept [æ̀ksépt]	acceptance [æ̀kséptn̩s]
-ence	occur [əkʰf̩]	occurrence [əkʰf̩əns]
-ant	account [əkʰáwnt]	accountant [əkʰáwntn̩t]
-ent	inhere [ìnhír]	inherent [ìnhírn̩t]
-er	accuse [əkʰyúz]	accuser [əkʰyúzr̩]
-age	acre [ékr̩]	acreage [ékr̩əǰ]
-al	addition [ədíšn̩]	additional [ədíšn̩əl]
-ive	adopt [ədápt]	adoptive [ədáptɪv]
-ment	advise [ədváyz]	advisement [ədváyzmn̩t]
-less	age [éǰ]	ageless [éǰləs]

-y	air [ér]	airy [éri]
-able	alien [éliən]	alienable [éliənəbl̩]
-ish	amateur [ǽməč̣r̩]	amateurish [ǽməč̣r̩š]
-ism	amateur [ǽməč̣r̩]	amateurism [ǽməč̣r̩ɪzm̩]
-ed	assure [əṣ̌f̣]	assured [əṣ̌f̣d]
-en	awake [əwék]	awaken [əwékn̩]
-s	cabinet [kʰǽbn̩ət]	cabinets [kʰǽbn̩əts]
-ous	danger [dénǰr̩]	dangerous [dénǰrəs]
-ure	forfeit [fórfət]	forfeiture [fórfəč̣r̩]
-dom	free [frí]	freedom [fríɾm̩]
-ness	green [grín]	greenness [grínnəs]
-ace	grim [grím]	grimace [gríməs]
-ian	guard [gárd]	guardian [gárdiən]
-ward	land [lǽnd]	landward [lǽndwr̩d]
-or	resist [rəzíst]	resistor [rəzístr̩]
-t	restrain [rəstrén]	restraint [rəstrént]
-ton	single [síŋgl̩]	singleton [síŋgl̩tn̩]

The second set below are affixes that bear a secondary stress and do not affect the stress of the base.

Neutral affixes with secondary stress

-ate	amalgam [əmǽlgəm]	amalgamate [əmǽlgəmèt]
-ite	anchor [ǽŋkr̩]	anchorite [ǽŋkr̩àyt]
-ine	brilliant [brílyənt]	brilliantine [brílyəntìn]
-hood	false [fɔ́ls]	falsehood [fɔ́lshùd]
-ize	federal [fériəl]	federalize [férr̩əlàyz]
-itude	inept [ɪnépt]	ineptitude [ɪnéptətʰùd]
-ful	master [mǽstr̩]	masterful [mǽstr̩fùl]
-eme	phone [fón]	phoneme [fónìm]
-ship	town [tʰáwn]	township [tʰáwnšìp]

Finally, the affixes below bear primary stress and do not affect the stress of the base (except by demoting a primary in the base to secondary).

Neutral affixes with primary stress

-ette	kitchen [kʰíčn̩]	kitchenette [kʰìčn̩ét]
-ee	employ [èmpʰlɔ́y]	employee [èmpʰlɔ̀yí]
-ée	divorce [dəvórs]	divorcée [dəvòrsé]
-eer	auction [ɔ́kšn̩]	auctioneer [ɔ̀kšn̩ír]

-ade	block [blák]	blockade [blàkéd]
-ine	nectar [néktr̩]	nectarine [nèktr̩ín]
-esque	picture [pʰíkčr̩]	picturesque [pʰìkčr̩ésk]

In general, I have stayed away from alternation evidence like that above, and I will therefore not make much of the relationships above.

Summarizing, there is a set of affixes that allow the rightmost stress to occur outside the three-syllable window, and that allow a heavy syllable to be skipped over by the rightmost foot. The simplest treatment of these is to suppose that these affixes are not included in the prosodic word. Specifically, there is a top-ranked constraint that penalizes a candidate that includes one of these affixes in the prosodic word.

NEUTRALITY
Certain affixes cannot be in the prosodic word.

More could be said on this point, but that would require a treatment outside the scope of this book.

8.4.2. Cyclic suffixes

In this section I consider cyclic affixation in English. It turns out that there is no distributional evidence for cyclic affixation. Hence, since the focus of this book is distributional regularities, no analysis of cyclicity will be attempted.

The key idea behind cyclicity in a derivational approach to stress is that stress is assigned to some part of the word before affixation. Stress is then reapplied after affixation.

Evidence for this double assignment of stress comes from words with extra stresses. The words *compensation* [kʰàmpn̩séšn̩] and *condensation* [kʰàndènséšn̩] form a classic opposition. The second syllable of the first word, [pn̩], is stressless, while the second syllable of the second word, [dèn], is not. The generalization is that in certain contexts a syllable that would otherwise be stressless surfaces as stressed just in case the corresponding syllable in a more basic form is also stressed. Hence, [dèn] in *condensation* is stressed because the same syllable is stressed in *condense* [kʰn̩déns]. There is no basic form *compense* [kʰm̩pʰéns] from which *compensation* might be derived. *Compensation* is most likely derived from *compensate* [kʰámpn̩sèt], with a stressless second syllable.

The derivational analysis of cyclicity is to first assign stress to the morphological base, e.g. *condense* and *forest*, and then reassign stress to the morphologically complex form. The extra stress in the morphologically complex forms arises from preserving some of the stress properties assigned in the first pass of the stress rules.

The problem with cyclicity is twofold. First, as pointed out by Halle and Kenstowicz (1991), a number of examples do not work as expected. For example, *ostentation* [ɔ̀stènt^héšn̩] has no derivational source, yet is stressed as if it did. On the other hand, *transformation* [t^hrænsfr̩méšn̩] does have a derivational source, *transform* [t^hrænsfórm], yet is stressed as if it did not.

A second problem with cyclicity is that it is only marked by extra stresses, for which we already have a formal device. That is, there is no particular reason why we cannot mark cases like *ostentation* and, by extension, *condensation*, with a diacritic accent on their second syllable.

Such a move enables us to treat cases of cyclicity without making the false prediction that all words with morphological bases should exhibit extra stresses.

The only problem for this view are the polymorphemic words that violate the USC above. Recall that a secondary stress could not occur after an unfooted syllable if it immediately precedes a stress. This was treated by making use of the mechanism of Local Conjunction.

> *Upbeat-secondary constraint (USC)*
> PARSE-σ & FtBin & *Clash & Align-R & *2

While this constraint is unviolated with monomorphemic words, it is violated with polymorphemic examples. Here are a few cases.

Polymorphemic words violating the USC

appointee [əp^hɔ̀ynt^hí]	appoint [əp^hɔ́ynt]
departmental [dəp^hùrtméntl̩]	department [dəp^hártmn̩t]
electrician [əlèktríšn̩]	electric [əléktrɪk]
electricity [əlèktrísəɾi]	electric [əléktrɪk]
electrolysis [əlèkt^hráləsɪs]	electric [əléktrɪk]
electronic [əlèkt^hránɪk]	electron [əléktràn]
remonstration [rəmànstréšn̩]	remonstrate [rəmánstrèt]

The upshot of these forms is that while there is no general cyclicity effect, it is only polymorphemic forms that can violate the USC. Put another way, an accent in a monomorphemic form is not stressed in defiance of the USC, but an accent in a polymorphemic form is.

Similar effects have been observed in a number of languages by a number of people, e.g. Kenstowicz (1996), Fitzgerald (1997), and Fountain (1997). The English case is interesting because there is no clear general cyclicity effect. Rather, cyclicity is manifested only in the violation of the USC. The generalization can be expressed as follows: an accent can be stressed in defiance of the USC only if this results in placing a stress on the same syllable as the base form.

This too can be expressed with Local Conjunction. First, there is the USC, which in general outranks FAITH($\overset{\circ}{v}$). Then there is a constraint, proposed by Kenstowicz (1996), which requires that morphologically derived forms mirror the stress of their underived counterparts.

BASE-IDENTITY (BE)
The stress of a derived form mirrors that of its base.

As we have already seen, a form like *transformation* [tʰrænsfr̩mésn̩] shows that cyclicity and BE are not general in English. Therefore, the USC outranks BE. However, the existence of words like *electrician* [əlèktʰɹíšn̩] shows that the local conjunction of FAITH($\overset{\circ}{v}$) and BE does outrank the USC. These ranking assumptions are given below.

Required rankings

$$[\text{FAITH}(\overset{\circ}{v}) \text{ \& BE}] \gg \text{USC} \gg \begin{Bmatrix} \text{FAITH}(v) \\ \text{BE} \end{Bmatrix}$$

Ranking the locally conjoined constraint above the USC allows forms like *electrician* to surface appropriately. Ranking FAITH($\overset{\circ}{v}$) below the USC prevents lexical accent from generally overruling the USC. Ranking BE low allows forms like *transformation* to be stressed acyclically.

8.5. SUMMARY

I have provided a treatment of nonrightmost stresses in English. This has necessitated revisions of the WSP constraints so as to distinguish unfooted from footed heavy syllables and to distinguish final from nonfinal feet. In addition, to capture the upbeat-secondary pattern, we were forced to turn to the mechanism of Local Conjunction. To allow violations of the USP with morphologically complex forms, we were again forced to turn to Local Conjunction.

Adopting Local Conjunction is a very powerful move, and it would be nice to restrict its use in some way. I can only note that it is perhaps significant that it was in the treatment of morphologically complex forms that

Local Conjunction was necessary.

This chapter also discussed, but did not provide an analysis of, nonfinal primary stresses.

8.6. FURTHER READING

Hayes (1981), Halle and Vergnaud (1987), Kager (1989), Hammond (1989*a*), and Halle and Kenstowicz (1991) offer useful discussions of secondary stresses in English in pre-OT frameworks. The only OT-based discussion of some of these phenomena is Pater (1995).

9

Afterword

9.1. SOME REMAINING ISSUES

I would like to very briefly consider some issues raised and not raised in the preceding chapters. First, I summarize the empirical and theoretical results of the preceding chapters.

9.2. SUMMARY

Chapter 1 presented the basic consonantal and vocalic inventories of English. In addition, it presented a basic descriptive vocabulary for sounds and outlined the essentials of Optimality Theory. Most importantly, it outlined several of the constraint schemata that would recur throughout the book: FAITH, General Alignment, and Generalized Correspondence.

Chapter 2 introduced the syllable and outlined the basics of an OT account of the syllable. The syllable was first defined and then motivated on the basis of a variety of linguistic and extralinguistic evidence. A detailed argument was given for the syllable from the distribution of consonants in clusters word-medially. Finally, a general theory of the syllable was provided in terms of OT. This theory drew on several constraint schemata: *PEAK/X, *ONSET/X, *CODA/X, and a preliminary mora assignment schema.

Chapter 3 offered a detailed discussion of the clustering possibilities of English consonants. It was shown that the syllable must be invoked to account for some of these clustering possibilities, but that linear (negative) general alignment constraints are also necessary. The facts of this chapter compelled us to posit the sonority hierarchy and formalize it in terms of syntactically combined constraints and derived ranking. Syntactically combined constraints also offered a treatment of sC clusters. This chapter did not treat morphologically complex forms.

Chapter 4 presented a discussion of the restrictions holding between vowels and adjacent consonants. As in the preceding chapter, some of these can be handled sequentially and some require reference to syllabic structure. The ones referring to syllabic structure refer to mora count. There are general constraints requiring that syllables have between two and three moras. Vowels and diphthongs can have between one and three moras, and coda consonants can have between zero and two moras. (In Chapter 6 it is proposed that schwa has no mora.)

Chapter 5 introduced and defined stress and the metrical foot. Extensive linguistic and extralinguistic support was adduced from poetry, language games, intonation, metrical licensing, expletive infixation, and syncope. The basic theory of stress was then presented along with an extensive discussion of the typological predictions of that theory.

Chapter 6 treated the relationship between stress and syllabification. First, the distribution of stress is clearly a partial function of syllable structure. Paradoxically, for a rule-based analysis, syllable structure is also a function of stress! This is readily treated in terms of OT. Another issue treated in the chapter is the complex relationship between stress, vowel quality, and syllabification. The analysis offered is the first to unify all three of these domains. The analysis depends critically on the following assumptions: (i) schwa is zero-moraic, and (ii) there is covert gemination in English. Specific analysis of the distribution of [h] and [yu] in terms of stress are also offered.

Chapter 7 analyzed the distribution of the rightmost stress in English. The constraints required are essentially just those introduced in the previous chapter. However, the analysis motivates a more generous understanding of the definition of a morpheme. First, forms like *honest* are treated as polymorphemic in this new sense. Second, verbs are argued to exhibit an invisible catalectic suffix (when otherwise unsuffixed).

Finally, in Chapter 8 I treated the nonrightmost stresses of a word. There are two general problems here. First, one has to account for the differential sensitivity to syllable weight in nonrightmost vs. rightmost position. Second, one has to treat the various upbeat restrictions. Most of these can be treated with simple extensions of the framework already proposed, but one of the upbeat patterns seems to require constraint conjunction, a mechanism otherwise unnecessary in the phonology of English.

9.3. STATISTICS AND FREQUENCY

The generalizations discussed in this book have been corroborated by detailed searches of several computer databases. Are such generalizations legitimate? One might think that generalizations made over such corpora are potentially false.

First, the generalizations presented here, while based on various data-bases, are all supported by intuitions of grammaticality. Thus, since most previous discussions of English syllabification and stress have been based solely on intuitions, the present array of facts can only be seen as a step forward in terms of empirical confidence.

Second, one might think that generalizations proposed on the basis of lexical searches are susceptible to statistical reanalysis. It may be that some particular pattern is absent, not because the pattern is ruled out by the gram-mar, but because the particular combination of segments is otherwise so rare as to be simply absent accidentally. (This point is made most clearly by Pierrehumbert 1994.)

For example, I have argued that word-final voiced velar obstruents are quite rare. Therefore the absence of various vowel-[g] sequences should not be taken as a fact to be accounted for in terms of moras, but as a fact about the infrequency of [g] in coda position generally.

There are then two questions. First, is there a difference between gaps in the lexicon that seem to be traceable to statistical factors, e.g. *[ʊg], and gaps that are not, e.g. *[awg]? Second, if we accept that it is reasonable to suppose such a distinction, what patterns are assigned to which category?

These are extremely important questions that cannot be answered defini-tively here. The tactic adopted in this book is twofold. First, if there are good reasons to believe that some restriction is statistical in nature, then it has been assigned to the accidental category. The absence of word-final [ʊg] sequences has been treated as statistical because [ʊ] and word-final [g] are separately quite rare.

A second criterion employed is that a gap has been treated as system-atic/phonological if it otherwise makes sense phonologically. The absence of [awg] sequences makes sense phonologically, and so has been treated as a systematic gap.

These criteria simply beg the question, however, of whether the grammar really makes any such distinction. It may very well be the case that native speakers treat restrictions that emerge from statistical concerns identically with restrictions that emerge from phonological concerns.

Some evidence that intuitions of grammaticality are partially a function of statistical concerns comes from the Rhythm Rule in English. (The facts to be cited here are summarized from Hammond, to appear.) The Rhythm Rule phenomenon refers to the shift of stress that occurs in phrases like *thírtèen mén*. Modifiers like *thìrtéen* exhibit retracted stress in certain phrasal contexts, essentially when the following word begins with a stressed syllable. Interestingly, however, subjects' judgments of the well-formedness of this shift of stress is a function of the statistical frequency of the modifier. Specifically, high-frequency modifiers like *àntíque* undergo the shift more readily than infrequent modifiers like *àrcáne*.

The key fact is that frequency plays a role in the judgments. If this is the case, it suggests that phonologists should pay closer heed to issues of phonological and lexical frequency.

9.4. RUSSIAN

This book has treated distributional regularities separately from generalizations based on alternations. This was done for several reasons. First, the data sources make this a particularly easy way to begin. Second, I have argued that OT lends itself to this tactic. Third, this has resulted in a full plate of facts in any case.

Readers familiar with the classic generative phonology literature may note that this would seem to fly in the face of a classic argument for generative phonology over its predecessor, American Structuralist, or taxonomic, phonology. The argument is due to Halle (1959) and is based on data from Russian. In this section, I review the argument and show how the current theory avoids this objection.

Russian exhibits an asymmetrical consonant inventory. The sounds [tʲ,dʲ,č] are fully contrastive elements of the language.

Contrastive elements

dača	'cottage'
dʲadʲa	'uncle'
tʲɔtʲa	'aunt'

Preconsonantally, things change. Before a voiced obstruent, voiceless obstruents are impossible. Halle cites the following paradigms.

Voicing alternations

datʲ 'to give'	datʲ lʲi 'to give?'	dadʲ bɨ 'would give'
žeč 'to bake'	žeč lʲi 'to bake?'	žeǰ bɨ 'would bake'

Notice how the contrastive element /tʲ/ shows up as [dʲ] before the conditional particle [bɨ]; the contrastive element /č/ shows up as [ǰ]. Notice that only the former neutralizes a contrast, while the latter does not.

Under the theory Halle characterizes as taxonomic phonology, the generalization that there is a uniform process of voicing assimilation could not be captured. This is because that theory maintains that neutralizing generalizations are distinct from non-neutralizing generalizations and are expressed at different structural levels. On this view, there would be three levels of representation.

Three levels of representation

Surface	Non-neutralizing	Neutralizing
datʲ lʲi	datʲ lʲi	datʲ lʲi
dadʲ bɨ	dadʲ bɨ	datʲ bɨ
žeč lʲi	žeč lʲi	žeč lʲi
žeǰ bɨ	žeč bɨ	žeč bɨ

The surface level of representation would correspond to our output representation. The intermediate level would undo the effects of non-neutralizing instances of voicing assimilation, resulting in /žečbɨ/, but /dadʲbɨ/. The deepest level would undo neutralizing instances of voicing assimilation, resulting in //datʲbɨ//.

Since voicing assimilation must appear on each level, the fact that the process is the same at both levels is missed on the taxonomic phonological view.

Is the approach I have proposed subject to the same problem? No. These facts are straightforwardly treated on the distributional OT approach developed here. The analysis goes as follows (see Chapter 1 for similar treatments). First, there is a constraint ruling out voiceless obstruents before voiced obstruents.

Constraint against voicing conflicts (*GC)

$$*\begin{bmatrix} \text{obst} \\ \text{voiceless} \end{bmatrix}\begin{bmatrix} \text{obst} \\ \text{voiced} \end{bmatrix}$$

This constraint must be ranked above FAITH(voiceless), but below faithfulness with respect to obstruency and voicedness.

Ranking

$$\begin{Bmatrix} \text{FAITH(obst)} \\ \text{FAITH(voiced)} \end{Bmatrix} \gg *\text{GC} \gg \text{FAITH(voiceless)}$$

These constraints with this ranking will insure that a sequence /tʲb/ surfaces as [dʲb]. Voiceless consonants in other contexts will surface unmolested.

What remains is to account for the fact that [ǰ] is only permitted before a voiced obstruent. The segment is otherwise ruled out in the inventory of Russian. First, there must be a general constraint against [ǰ].

Constraint against [ǰ] (*[ǰ])

$$\ast \begin{bmatrix} \text{voiced} \\ \text{palatoalveolar} \\ \text{affricate} \end{bmatrix}$$

This constraint must be outranked by *GC so as to allow [ǰ] just in case the following consonant is a voiced obstruent. The following ranking does this.

Ranking (revised)

$$\left\{ \begin{matrix} \text{FAITH(obst)} \\ \text{FAITH(voiced)} \end{matrix} \right\} \gg \ast\text{GC} \gg \left\{ \begin{matrix} \text{FAITH(voiceless)} \\ \ast[\text{ǰ}] \end{matrix} \right\}$$

The ranking predicts that any potential input /ǰ/ not preceding a voiced obstruent would surface as e.g. [ž] (which is, in fact, in the Russian consonant inventory).

The general approach proposed here (distributional OT), where OT is applied to distributional regularities, independent of whatever alternations may exist, is thus unproblematic when confronted with this classic piece of Russian data.

9.5. REMAINING EMPIRICAL ISSUES

The facts and analysis here are necessarily incomplete. In this section, I review some of what has *not* been treated.

First, a number of segmental generalizations in English have not been treated, e.g. palatalization and spirantization. The main reason for this gap is that (i) these rules can only be motivated with alternations, and (ii) they are rife with exceptions.

Second, the Vowel Shift has not been treated, along with a number of generalizations that affect vowels, e.g. Trisyllabic Shortening and Closed Syllable Shortening. These have not been treated for the same reasons.

Third, prosodic alternations have not been explored, e.g. the Rhythm Rule, Sonorant Destressing, and Nanni's Rule.

9.6. REMAINING THEORETICAL ISSUES

Finally, let us briefly consider the theoretical proposals made, with an eye to further evidence for or against them. I will divide these into two classes: proposals that are relatively independent of OT and proposals which are clearly specific to OT. In the former class, four main ones can be considered.

First, this whole project is an exemplification of what I have termed Distributional OT. The basic idea is that OT lends itself best to an account of distributional regularities, rather than alternations. The latter are of course worthy of phonological attention, but the present approach leaves open the question of what the best treatment of phonological alternations should be.

Second, I proposed in Chapter 4 that the mora count of English syllables was constrained to be between two and three moras (though schwa violates this, of course, as established in Chapter 6). In addition, I argued that vowels and coda consonants could vary in the number of moras they contributed. Vowels and diphthongs contribute between zero and three moras. Coda consonants contribute between zero and two moras. These proposals were motivated on the basis of a careful consideration of the clustering possibilities of consonants and the cooccurrence possibilities of vowels and following consonants.

However, this proposal clearly has wider implications. For example, we might expect these to have consequences in other domains contingent on mora count, e.g. stress, prosodic morphology, and poetry. Unfortunately, most of these other domains are not relevant for English. English has minimal prosodic morphology, and none that seems to care about mora count. We have also seen that stress in English is dependent on the WSP schema, rather than directly on mora count *per se*. English poetry is uniformly insensitive to moraic structure (though see Kiparsky 1989 for an extremely interesting exception).

A third general proposal that has come out of this work is that syllabification and stress are far more intertwined than previously thought. The standard pre-OT analysis of English prosody had it that first syllable structure was assigned, then metrical structure, and then there were adjustments of syllable structure as a consequence of the stress pattern. This analysis has a number of shortcomings. First, it necessitates several passes of syllabification. Second, it implies a degree of autonomy between syllable structure and stress that is not the case. We have seen that these two domains must be investigated together in English. The strongest position that we could maintain here would be that stress and syllable structure are always intertwined, and that parametric variation in syllable structure cannot occur without corresponding variation in metrical structure. This obviously requires serious typological investigation.

A fourth major proposal with far-reaching implications is the enriched notion of morpheme developed in the discussion of stress. Recall, for example, that adjectives like *hónest* are treated as polymorphemic. The basic idea is that the stress system treats classical examples like *cranberry* as the norm. Any potential morpheme with the right phonological and syntactic distribution is treated as a separate morpheme. Hence, since *-est* is a suffix that occurs in adjectives, the word *hónest* is polymorphemic. This proposal has consequences for any domain of phonology that cares about morphological structure, as well as for the theory of morphology generally.

This work has also made a number of proposals of a general sort that are specific to Optimality Theory.

The first proposal of this sort is the extensive use of schemata. The basic idea here is that the universal and finite constraint set must be expanded so as to allow parametric constraints. Such parametric constraints go some way towards developing a substantive theory of what constraints can be.

Notice that parametric constraints, or schemata, leave open the question of whether the constraint set is universal or finite. If the parameters are finite, then the constraint set *can* still be finite. If unwanted constraints can always be rendered irrelevant by ranking them low enough, then the constraint set *can* be universal.

Another proposal developed in the context of OT was derived ranking of syntactically combined constraints. This proposal was made to deal with the role of sonority in consonant clusters. The basic idea was to let constraint ranking do as much of the work as possible.

Finally, it was argued that some facts of stress seem to require Local Conjunction, the binding together of two or more other constraints into a new superconstraint. This is an extremely powerful device, however, and merits serious further attention.

9.7. FURTHER READING

Hammond (to appear) offers a nice discussion of the relevance of statistical frequency in an OT-based analysis of English rhythm. Berkley (1994), Pierrehumbert (1994), and Coleman and Pierrehumbert (1997) offer a nice discussion of the relevance of statistics to database generalizations. The earliest discussions of the role of frequency in phonology are to be found in Fidelholtz (1975) and Hooper (1976).

See Hyman (1990) for a general proposal to treat the relationship between metrical structure and syllable structure.

See Halle (1959) for a full discussion of Taxonomic Phonology and the Russian voicing assimilation facts cited above.

Chomsky and Halle (1968) offer a classic treatment of most of the segmental rules not treated here.

Hammond (1984) and Hayes (1984) offer pre-OT treatments of the English Rhythm Rule.

REFERENCES

(Papers available through the Rutgers Optimality Archive on the Web are marked [ROA]. The URL is http://ruccs.rutgers.edu/roa.html.)

ARCHANGELI, D., and LANGENDOEN, D. T. (eds.) (1997), *Optimality Theory* (Oxford, Blackwell).

AUSTIN, P. (1981), *A Grammar of Diyari, South Australia* (Cambridge, Cambridge University Press).

BERKLEY, D. M. (1994), 'The OCP and gradient data', *Studies in the Linguistic Sciences* 24: 59–72.

BLOOMFIELD, L. (1933), *Language* (New York, Holt).

BOROWSKY, T. (1986), 'Topics in the Lexical Phonology of English' (doctoral dissertation, University of Massachusetts).

—— ITÔ, J., and MESTER, R.-A. (1984), 'The formal representation of ambisyllabicity: evidence from Danish', *NELS* 14: 34–48.

BURZIO, L. (1995), *Principles of English Stress* (Cambridge, Cambridge University Press).

CARTER, A. (1996), 'An acoustic analysis of weak syllable omissions: evidence for adult prosodic representations in young children's speech' (MS, University of Arizona).

—— and GERKEN, L. (to appear) 'Evidence for adult prosodic representations in weak syllable omissions of young children', *Proceedings of the Stanford Child Language Research Forum* 29.

CHOMSKY, N. (1957), *Syntactic Structures* (The Hague, Mouton).

—— (1986), *Knowledge of Language* (New York, Praeger).

—— and HALLE, M. (1968), *The Sound Pattern of English* (New York: Harper and Row).

CLEMENTS, G. N., and KEYSER, S. J. (1983), *CV Phonology: A Generative Theory of the Syllable* (Cambridge, MIT Press).

COLEMAN, J., and PIERREHUMBERT, J. (1997), 'Stochastic phonological grammars and acceptability' (MS, Northwestern University).

DAVIS, S. (1991), 'Coronals and the phonotactics of nonadjacent consonants in English', in C. Paradis and J.-F. Prunet (eds.), *The Special Status of Coronals* (Orlando, Fla., Academic Press), 49–60.

—— and HAMMOND, M. (1995), 'Onglides in American English', *Phonology* 12: 159–82.

FIDELHOLTZ, J. (1975), 'Word frequency and vowel reduction in English', *Chicago Linguistic Society* 11: 200–13.

FITZGERALD, C. (1997), 'O'odham Rhythms' (doctoral dissertation, University of Arizona). [ROA]

FOUNTAIN, A. (1996), 'Against subsyllabic constituency in Western Apache: evidence from the syllabification of /n/', presented at the Linguistic Society of America annual meeting.

FOUNTAIN, A. (1997), 'Output–output correspondence in Navaho', paper presented at Southwest OT Conference, University of California at Los Angeles.

GERKEN, L. A. (1996), 'Prosodic structure in young children's language production', *Language* 72: 683–712.

HALLE, M. (1959), *The Sound Pattern of Russian* (The Hague, Mouton).

—— and KENSTOWICZ, M. (1991), 'The free element condition and cyclic versus noncyclic stress', *Linguistic Inquiry* 22: 457–501.

—— and VERGNAUD, J.-R. (1977), 'Metrical phonology: a fragment of a draft' (MS, Massachusetts Institute of Technology).

—— —— (1987), *An Essay on Stress* (Cambridge, Mass., MIT Press).

HAMMOND, M. (1984), 'A Modular Theory of Rhythm and Destressing' (doctoral dissertation, University of California at Los Angeles; distributed by IULC, 1984–8; New York, Garland, 1988).

—— (1989*a*), 'Cyclic secondary stresses in English', *West Coast Conference on Formal Linguistics* 8.

—— (1989*b*), 'Lexical stresses in Macedonian and Polish', *Phonology* 6: 19–38.

—— (1990), 'The "name game" and onset simplification', *Phonology* 7: 159–62.

—— (1991), 'Poetic meter and the arboreal grid', *Language* 67: 240–59.

—— (1994), 'There is no lexicon!' (MS, University of Arizona). [ROA]

—— (1997*a*), 'Vowel quantity and syllabification in English', *Language* 73: 1–17.

—— (1997*b*), 'Optimality theory and prosody', in Archangeli and Langendoen (1997: 33–58).

—— (to appear), 'The embarrassment of lexical frequency', in M. Darnell et al. (eds.), *Functionalism and Formalism in Linguistics* (Amsterdam, John Benjamins).

—— and DUPOUX, E. (1996), 'Psychophonology', in J. Durand and B. Laks (eds.), *Current Trends in Phonology: Models and Methods* i (Salford, University of Salford).

HAYES, B. (1981), 'A Metrical Theory of Stress' (doctoral dissertation, MIT; revised version distributed by IULC and published by Garland, New York).

—— (1984), 'The phonology of rhythm in English', *Linguistic Inquiry* 15: 33–74.

—— (1989), 'Compensatory lengthening in moraic phonology', *Linguistic Inquiry* 20: 253–306.

—— (1995), *Metrical Stress Theory* (Chicago, University of Chicago Press).

HILL, J., and ZEPEDA, O. (1992), 'Derived words in Tohono O'odham', *International Journal of American Linguistics* 58: 355–404.

HOOPER, J. (1972), 'The syllable in phonological theory', *Language* 48: 525–40.

—— (1976), 'Word frequency in lexical diffusion and the source of morphophonological change', in W. Christie (ed.), *Current Progress in Historical Linguistics* (Amsterdam, North-Holland), 96–105.

HYMAN, L. M. (1985), *A Theory of Phonological Weight* (Cinnaminson, NJ: Foris).

—— (1990), 'Nonexhaustive syllabification: evidence from Nigeria and Cameroon', in M. Ziolkowsky, M. Noske, and K. Deaton, (eds.), *CLS 26: Parasession on the Syllable in Phonetics and Phonology*, 175–96.

INKELAS, S. (1994), 'Exceptional stress-attracting suffixes in Turkish: representations vs. the grammar', Workshop on Prosodic Morphology, Utrecht. [ROA]

ITÔ, J. (1989), 'A prosodic theory of epinthesis', *Natural Language and Linguistic Theory* 7: 217–60.

KAGER, R. W. J. (1989), 'A Metrical Theory of Stress and Destressing in English and Dutch' (doctoral dissertation, University of Utrecht).

—— (1990), 'Dutch schwa in moraic phonology', *CLS* 26: 241–56.

—— (1995), 'Consequences of catalexis', in H.van der Hulst and J. van de Weijer (eds.), *Leiden in Last* (*Leyden in Trouble*), 269–98.

KAHN, D. (1976), 'Syllable-Based Generalizations in English Phonology' (doctoral dissertation, Massachusetts Institute of Technology; distributed by IULC).

KENSTOWICZ, M. (1996), 'Base identity and uniform exponence: alternatives to cyclicity', in J. Durand and B. Laks (eds.), *Current Trends in Phonology: Models and Methods* (Salford, University of Salford Publications). [ROA]

KIPARSKY, P. (1989), 'Sprung rhythm', in P. Kiparsky and G. Youmans (eds.), *Rhythm and Meter* (San Diego, Calif., Academic Press), 305–40.

—— (1991), 'Catalexis' (MS, Stanford University).

LADEFOGED, P. (1975), *A Course in Phonetics* (New York, Harcourt Brace Jovanovich).

—— and HALLE, M. (1988), 'Some major features of the International Phonetic Alphabet', *Language* 64: 577–82.

LAMONTAGNE, G. (1993), 'Syllabification and Consonant Cooccurrence Conditions' (doctoral dissertation, University of Massachusetts).

LEHISTE, I. (1970), *Suprasegmentals* (Cambridge, Mass., MIT Press).

LIBERMAN, M. (1975), 'The Intonational System of English', (doctoral dissertation, Massachusetts Institute of Technology).

LIGHTFOOT, D. (1982), *The Language Lottery: Toward a Biology of Grammars* (Cambridge, Mass., MIT Press).

MCCARTHY, J. (1982), 'Prosodic structure and expletive infixation', *Language* 58: 574–90.

—— and PRINCE, A. (1993a), 'Constraint interaction and prosodic morphology' (MS, University of Massachusetts and Brandeis University).

—— —— (1993b), 'Generalized alignment', *Yearbook of Morphology*, 79–153.

—— —— (1995), 'Faithfulness and reduplicative identity', in J. Beckman, L. Dickey, and S. Urbanczyk (eds.), *University of Massachusetts Occasional Papers in Linguistics* 18: Papers in Optimality Theory 249–384.

MASSAR, A. (1996), 'Syllable omission and the prosodic structure of two-year-olds' (MS, University of Arizona).

MEADOR, D., and OHALA, D. (1993), 'The status of ambisyllabicity in English', presented at the Linguistic Society of America.

OHALA, D. (1996), 'Cluster Reduction and Constraints in Acquisition' (doctoral dissertation, University of Arizona).

PATER, J. (1995), 'On the nonuniformity of weight-to-stress and stress preservation effects in English' (MS, McGill University). [ROA]

PÉREZ, P. (1992), 'Gradient sonority and harmonic foot repair in English syncope', *Coyote Papers* 8: 118–42.

PHINNEMORE, T. R. (1985), 'Ono phonology and morphophonemics', *Papers in New Guinea Linguistics* 22: 173–214.

PIERREHUMBERT, J. (1994), 'Syllable structure and word structure: a study of triconsonantal clusters in English', in P. Keating (ed.), *Phonological Structure and Phonetic Form* (Cambridge, Cambridge University Press), 168–88.

POSTAL, P. M. (1968), *Aspects of Phonological Theory* (New York, Harper and Row).

PRINCE, A. (1990), 'Quantitative consequences of rhythmic organization', *CLS* 26: 355–98.

—— and SMOLENSKY, P. (1993), 'Optimality Theory' (MS, Brandeis University and University of Colorado).

PULGRAM, E. (1970), *Syllable, Word, Nexus, Cursus* (The Hague, Mouton).

ROSS, J. R. (1972), 'A reanalysis of English word stress (part I)', in M. Brame (ed.), *Contributions to Generative Phonology* (Austin, University of Texas Press).

RUSSELL, K. (1995), 'Morphemes and candidates' (MS, University of Manitoba). [ROA]

SAGEY, E. (1990), *The Representation of Features and Relations in Nonlinear Phonology* (New York, Garland).

SAPIR, E. (1921), *Language* (New York, Harcourt, Brace).

SELKIRK, E. (1982), 'The syllable', in H. van der Hulst and N. Smith (eds.), *The Structure of Phonological Representations (Part II)* (Cinnaminson, NJ, Foris), 337–84.

SMOLENSKY, P. (1993), 'Harmony, markedness and phonological activity', Rutgers Optimality Workshop-1. [ROA]

STERIADE, D. (1982), 'Greek Prosodies and the Nature of Syllabification' (doctoral dissertation, Massachusetts Institute of Technology).

TRANEL, B. (1994), 'French liaison and elision revisited: a unified account within Optimality Theory' (MS, University of California at Irvine). [ROA]

TREIMAN, R., and DANIS, C. (1988), 'Syllabification of intervocalic consonants', *Memory and Language* 27: 87–104.

—— and ZUKOWSKI, A. (1990), 'Toward an understanding of English syllabification', *Journal of Memory and Language* 29: 66–85.

Wells, J. C. (1992), *Accents of English* (Cambridge, Cambridge University Press).

ZWICKY, A. (1972), 'Note on a phonological hierarchy in English', in R. Stockwell and R. Macaulay (eds.), *Linguistic Change and Generative Theory: Essays from the University of California at Los Angeles Conference on Historical Linguistics in the Perspective of Transformational Theory* (Indiana University Linguistics Club), 275–301.

SUBJECT INDEX

WORD INDEX

flamenco 129
flat 11, 52
flavor 52
flavoring 273
fledgling 79, 273
float 109
floozy 124
flotsam 75
flour 144
fluent 252
fodder 122
foible 122
foist 115
folds 66
folio 126
folksy 130
font 59, 117
food 110
footing 273
forage 197, 250
forced 67
ford 146
forest 198, 251, 327
forfeit 326
forfeiture 326
forged 67
forging 273
fork 62, 86, 146
forked 67
forks 67
form 62, 86
formaldehyde 149, 150,
    151
formed 67
forms 67
forth 62
foul 140
fouls 140
foundling 273
fount 117
fountain 72
four 146
fourth 70
fracas 53, 196, 249
fracture 82
fragrant 252
frailty 128, 129
franchise 223
frankfurter 81
fraudulent 126, 280
fray 11, 53
free 326
freedom 326
freeze 112
frequent 252
fresh 110
frill 53
Fritz 63

frolic 197, 198, 250, 251,
    253
fromenty 202, 258
frontier 129, 162, 285
frumenty 202, 258
fuchsia 123
fuel 52, 114
fugue 110
fulcrum 81
fume 113
fumigate 52
fur 143
furmenty 202, 258
furnish 197, 251
furniture 82
fury 126
furze 144
fuse 112
fusillade 123
future 126

gabionade 294
gaiety 211
galaxy 324
gallant 198, 251, 252
gallimaufry 287
gallivant 320
gallop 197, 198, 250, 251
gamut 196, 249
garage 112
garbed 67
garish 197, 250
garland 198, 251, 256
garlic 35, 79
garment 198, 251
gasket 239
gasoline 287, 311
gaspergou 289, 311
Gastonia 285
gawky 121
gazelle 284
gazpacho 285
general 165, 166
generality 166
generative 50
genre 34, 48, 50
genuflect 243
genuine 193, 203, 210, 243,
    258, 279
Gerard 155
gerrymander 272
gerund 256
gesundheit 303
gewgaw 319
geyser 77, 124
giant 252
gigantic 72
Gilbertina 289

gill 9
gin 2, 7, 9, 33
giraffes 63
give 34
glacier 123
glamour 52
glare 52
glimmer 125
glimpse 64
glimpsed 65
glorification 165, 166
glow 85
glue 52
gnarl 62, 86, 94
gnarled 67
gnarls 67
gnat 7, 9, 33
goatee 194
gobbledegook 302, 321
goblin 131
going 273
golfed 66
gonyaulax 290
gorge 62
gorged 67
gorp 62
gosling 273
gospel 239
gouge 114
gourmet 215
government 325
grabbed 63
gradient 256
gradual 53
grandiose 193
granule 243
grapnel 78
grass 53
grating 273
gray 53
grayling 273
grebe 110, 144
green 326
greenness 326
grenade 285
grim 326
grimace 326
grizzly 79
groggy 122
groundling 273
grovel 124
grow 85
guano 53, 245
guarantee 193
guard 326
guardian 326
gubernatorial 52
guillotine 320

gules 52
gulfs 66
gulp 61, 85
gulped 66
gulps 66
gumption 81
gun 2, 7, 33
guppy 121
guru 126
Gwen 53, 56, 245

haberdasher 322
habitable 323
habitableness 323
habitant 256
habitual 242
had 3, 10, 106
hafnium 79
halberdier 289
halcyon 193, 200, 255, 279
Haleakala 300
Halicarnassus 296, 303, 305, 307
hall 114
hallelujah 287
hallow 195, 249
hallucinate 242
halter 35
ham 113
hamamelidanthemum 164, 300
hammock 196, 249
Hampton 84
hams 60
hamster 81, 128
hand 59
hanged 59
hanger 49
hanging 273
happy 38, 40, 70, 149, 150, 151, 158, 162, 168, 169, 193, 195, 203, 223, 225, 249, 259
harass 194
harbinger 202, 258, 325
harbor 35, 72
hard 62
hark 117
harm 62
harms 67
harness 197, 251
harp 62, 117
harped 67
harpsichord 81
harry 195
harsh 62
harvest 198, 251
has 112

hasp 60, 73, 115, 142, 145
hasps 65
hassock 123
hat 31, 44, 45, 136, 158, 261
hatching 273
hatchling 273
Hattie 211, 212
haughty 121
haul 114
hautboy 319
hawed 3, 10, 106
hayed 3
head 3, 10, 106
health 61
hearing 273
heart 117
hearth 62
hearths 67
heat 136
Hebraism 203, 210, 258
Hecatonchires 296
heckle 195
heed 3, 10, 106
hefty 73
heifer 123
heist 115, 145
Heliogabalus 294
helix 286
helixes 325
hello 126, 242
helm 61, 94
helminthiasis 289
help 11, 61, 86, 116, 145
helped 66
helps 66
hem 113
hemianopsia 294
hemlock 79
hemp 117
hen 113
hens 60
heritable 323
heroin 203, 210, 258
herring 274
hesperinos 295
hex 118
heyed 10, 106
hid 3, 10, 106
hierarchy 321
Hindu 195, 249
hint 9
hippopotamus 287
Hispaniola 289
historical 242
hit 9
hoarding 273
hoax 118
hobble 195, 249

hockey 121
hod 3, 10, 106
hodgepodge 35, 72
hoed 3, 10, 106
Holothuroidea 296
homogenize 242
honest 198, 251, 252, 338
honesty 31, 32
honk 117
hood 3, 10, 106, 110
hoodoo 122, 319
hoof 111
hook 109
Hoosier 124
hootenanny 322
Hortence 155
hot 2, 7, 34
hotel 194, 223
hour 114, 140
hours 140
house 144
housing 273
Howie 211
hubris 131
huckleberry 252
hud 10, 106
HUD 3
hue 2
hugs 63
hulk 11
hull 114
hullabaloo 302, 321
hum 113
humdinger 72
hummock 125
Humpty Dumpty 84
hunk 117
hunker 129
hurricane 320
husband 72, 73, 198, 251
husk 73
husky 239
hyacinth 204, 259
hydrant 256
hygiene 77, 126, 319

Ichinomiya 300
ichthyology 75
icon 35, 121, 319
Ida 211
idea 211, 286
idol 72
igloo 79
ilk 61
ilks 66
imagine 193
iminourea 300
immeasurable 323